CRIME
DICTIONARY

CRIME DICTIONARY

Revised and Expanded Edition

Ralph De Sola

Facts On File Publications
New York, New York • Oxford, England

CRIME DICTIONARY: Revised and Expanded Edition

copyright © 1982, 1988 by Ralph De Sola

Library of Congress Cataloging-in-Publication Data

De Sola, Ralph, 1908-
  Crime dictionary.

  1. Crime and criminals—Dictionaries. I. Title.
HV6025.D43 1988   364′.03′21   87-20133
ISBN 0-8160-1872-3

British CIP data available on request

Printed in the United States of America

10 9 8 7 6 5 4 3 2 1

Dedicated to the men and women in law enforcement
who risk their lives and their reputations
in defense of law-abiding citizens.

". . . for the land is full of bloody crimes
and the city is full of violence."

Ezekiel 7:23

CONTENTS

PREFACE

Readers may wonder why this book contains so many abbreviations unless they recall that between 10 and 20 percent of most modern communications include abbreviations, as well as acronyms, contractions, initialisms, signs and symbols referring to organizations, places and things. For more complete coverage anyone may refer to the *Abbreviations Dictionary*, now in its sixth edition, and also compiled by this author.

Definitions relating to alcoholic and narcotic addiction loom large, and were supplied in the main by the Drug Enforcement Administration of the United States Department of Justice. Some were rewritten and simplified from the many appearing in medical books and journals.

Blood brotherhoods and crime syndicates flourish almost worldwide. They, too, have their own terminology, and every attempt was made to include multilingual terms of interest to general readers as well as law-enforcement officers.

Criminal slang entries resulted from many interviews and a widespread reading of contemporary periodicals.

Historical and literary allusions are found in these pages as appropriate.

Medical and psychiatric expressions relative to criminals and their problems are explained as simply as possible.

Nicknames and shortcuts are characteristic of underground and underworld speech, and they, too, are included, along with many popular colloquialisms.

Penal institutions are often identified by their geographical place-names; these names find a place in this *Crime Dictionary*.

Terrorist groups are included because no matter how political their motives may be, it is apparent that their acts are criminal.

Underground argot and underworld jargon reflect all phases of clandestine and illicit activity.

Weaponry is included for obvious reasons.

Multilingual equivalents of common words having to do with crime, in particular with alcohol and drug abuse, are included in the section on foreign terms, because often the mere knowledge of a foreign word unlocks most interesting conversations with people we meet from other lands. Many expressions from many languages are included. The eleven most often found in this compilation include Chinese, Dano-Norwegian, Dutch, French, German, Italian, Japanese, Latin, Portuguese, Russian and Spanish. Dialects include Calo or Mexican-American, Puerto Rican Spanish and Yiddish.

Crime has been defined many times by great authors. Their works, too, have been included, in the section entitled "Selected Sources."

Perceptive readers realize that the morbid interest in crime and the lascivious taste for illicit sex have been exploited by many who fail to reveal the other side of the seemingly glittering coin, payable in addiction, affliction, disease and death.

Vice is anything but nice for its victims, although its exploiters garner great profits until they are detected, arrested, indicted, tried, convicted and imprisoned.

Finally, a contribution attesting to the popularity of criminology from the pen of a 10-year-old neighbor named Matt. His succinct, and unedited, account follows:

"The Story of Detetive Homes. Arourd 60 years ago there was a man named Homes. He was the best detetive in the whrold."

ACKNOWLEDGMENTS

The author, the publisher and all who refer to the *Crime Dictionary* must thank many law-enforcement officers who provided essential reference material and in some cases took time to read the text and make constructive comments. Security prevents us from thanking them by name except for a few, such as Lieut. Richard B. Snider of the San Diego Police Department, who provided a tour of the crime-cluttered Mexican border, and the staff of the Senate Subcommittee to Investigate the Administration of the Internal Security Act and Other Security Laws. Students at San Diego Evening College volunteered terms drawn from all parts of the world and from all walks of life, but they, too, have reasons for remaining anonymous.

Librarians everywhere were most helpful. Outstanding assistance was rendered by Lucy Celia Donck, Jeanne C. Newhouse and Angela Patterson, as well as by Keith Anderson, who is also a firearms expert. Other executive and reference librarians who assisted include Patricia Allely, Michael J. Archuleta, Barbara Barth, Girard Billard, Elizabeth Byrne, Lettie Ford, David Gault, Dorothy Grimm, Matt Katka, Anna Martinez, Mildred Nevin, James Newbold, Margaret E. Queen, Evelyn Roy, Lynn Slomowitz, John Vanderby.

Friendly and talented neighbors assisted: Richard W. Amero—metropolitan planner, Jerome J. Barstow—insurance executive and former law-enforcement officer, Charles Breyer—journalist and world traveler, Jack E. Lindquist—ethical leader, Daniel W. Russell—firefighter and urban reformer, Michael S. Sideman—attorney and public defender, Dean A. Stahl—book lover and journalist, Kari Sherkin—teacher and traveler and my little wife Dorothy, who patiently stood by and assisted in many ways. All deserve our gratitude.

David C. Anderson, editor of Criminal Justice Publications, was most helpful, as was Robert A. Farrar, physician's assistant at the Metropolitan Correction Center in San Diego. Let us not overlook the publisher, as well as others involved in the production and distribution of the *Crime Dictionary*.

Finally, thanks to Laura Gulotta, who suggested I contact Edward W. Knappman, vice president of Facts On File Publications, and his staff.

A NOTE ON SOURCES

Men and women from all walks of life contributed information compiled in *Crime Dictionary*; many did so without knowing it. Hence they spoke with the greatest candor, as did a call girl who gave me a glossary of call-girl talk in exchange for help in writing the story of her life.

Names of individual contributors appear in the various editions of the *Abbreviations Dictionary* and in *Worldwide What & Where*—my geographic glossary and traveler's guide. Some were shipmates or shore friends, whereas others were students in my English classes. Many, for one reason or another, asked to remain unnamed.

Contributors came from or lived in places as diverse as Algeria and Argentina, Australia and Austria, Belgium and Bolivia, Brazil and Bulgaria, Canada and Chile, China and Colombia, Costa Rica and Cuba, Cyprus and Czechoslovakia, Denmark and the Dominican Republic, Ecuador and England, France and Germany, Greece and Guatemala, Guinea and Guyana, Haiti and Hong Kong, India and Indonesia, Ireland and Italy, Jamaica and Japan, Mexico and Morocco, Nicaragua and Norway, Peru and the Philippines, Poland and Portugal, Samoa and Scotland, Singapore and South Africa, Spain and Sweden, Switzerland and Syria, Tahiti and Tonga, Trinidad and Turkey, Uganda and Uruguay, the United States and the USSR, Venezuela and Vietnam, Yemen and Yugoslavia.

Many of the best and most interesting books about crime and related topics are included in the section on selected sources. Periodicals of the greatest aid included the *Los Angeles Times*, the *New York Times*, *The Times* of London, *Time* Magazine, the *Manchester Guardian*, the *San Diego Union* and its *Evening Tribune*, the *San Francisco Chronicle*, the *New Yorker*—a gift from John and Fay Silverstein—and many clippings sent by two other old friends, K.G. and Betty Brown.

Ralph De Sola
San Diego

CRIME DICTIONARY

A

A: alcohol; amphetamines

AA: Alcoholics Anonymous

AAAC: American Association for the Advancement of Criminology

AAC: American Academy of Criminalistics; American Association of Criminology

AACFO: American Association of Correctional Facility Officers (q.v.)

AACP: American Association of Correctional Psychologists (q.v.)

AACPT: American Association of Correctional Personnel Training

AAEOCJ: American Association of Ex-Offenders in Criminal Justice

AAFS: American Academy of Forensic Sciences

AAIAN: Association for the Advancement of Instruction about Alcohol and Narcotics

AALA: Afro-American Liberation Army (q.v.)

AALAPSO: Afro-Asian-Latin American People's Solidarity Organization (q.v.)

AALE: Associate of Arts in Law Enforcement

AALL: American Association of Law Libraries

AAMC: American Association of Medico-Legal Consultants

AAMHPC: American Association of Mental Health Professionals in Corrections

A&ES: Arson and Explosion Squad

a&r: assault and robbery

A-A P: Afro-American police in the United States

AAPL: Afro-American Patrolmen's League (q.v.); All-American Policemen's League

AAPLE: American Academy for Professional Law Enforcement (q.v.)

AAPP: American Association of Police Polygraphists (q.v.)

AAPRA: All-African People's Revolutionary Army (q.v.)

AAPRP: All African People's Revolutionary Party (q.v.)

AARC: Association for the Advancement of Released Convicts

AASI: American Association for Scientific Interrogation

AASP: American Association for Social Psychiatry

AAWA: American Automatic Weapons Association

AAWS: American Association of Wardens and Superintendents (q.v.)

ab: abortion (both legal and illegal abortions are so nicknamed); abscess (which can be produced by injections with unsterile hypodermic needles; abscesses are thus often observed on the limbs of drug addicts)

abactor: legalism referring to a cattle thief or a horse thief

ABAJ: American Bar Association Journal

abasia: inability to walk due to hysteria or to incoordination brought about by the abuse of alcohol or other drugs

abbott: nembutal sleeping tablet (nicknamed for its producer, Abbott Laboratories)

ABC: Aberrant Behavior Center

abc (ABC): alarms by carrier (q.v.)

abduct: kidnap

Abe: five-dollar bill, bearing the portrait of Abraham Lincoln

Abe's cabe: slang for a five-dollar bill

ABLE: Action for Better Law Enforcement; Advocates for Better Law Enforcement; Advocates for Border Law Enforcement

abnormal criminal: psychopath or psychotic whose mental illness creates in him or her the potential for criminal behavior

A-bomb: heroin and marijuana cigarette; opium and hashish cigarette

ABs: Autonome Brigaden (French—Autonomous Brigades) anarchist terrorists

abscond: to depart from a geographical area or jurisdiction prescribed by one's parole or probation without authorization; to absent oneself intentionally or conceal oneself unlawfully to avoid a legal procedure such as appearing in court; as defined by Ambrose Bierce in the *Devil's Dictionary*, to move in a mysterious way with the property of another

abstinence: habitual avoidance of alcoholic drinks and addictive drugs

abstinence syndrome: symptoms resulting from withdrawal from alcohol or other drugs

Abu Ammar: Yasir Arafat's pseudonym

abuse: to attack physically or with words; to maltreat or misuse; wrongful use of alcohol, other drugs, sex, etc.

abusive dosage: amount of a drug needed to produce the actions and effects desired by the user; so-called because this amount is usually toxic (see also **lethal dosage, maximal dosage, minimal dosage** and **toxic dosage**)

abusive language: defamatory, harsh or scurrilous language

AC: Appeal Cases

ACA: American Correctional Association (q.v.); Anti-Corruption Agency (Singapore); Association of Correctional Administrators

Academy of Criminal Justice Sciences: organization whose goal is to foster excellence in education and research concerning criminal justice; founded in 1963, it publishes the *Journal of Criminal Justice*

▷ *ACA Directory: American Correctional Association Directory* of Juvenile and Adult Correctional Departments, Institutions, Agencies, and Paroling Authorities in the United States and Canada; published yearly by the American Correctional Association (q.v.)

ACA Directory of Juvenile and Adult Correctional Departments, Institutions, Agencies, and Paroling Authorities: issued annually by the American Correctional Association

ACAN: Action Committee Against Narcotics

ACAP: American Council on Alcohol Problems

Acapulco gold: high-grade golden-brown marijuana grown around Acapulco, Mexico

ACC: Assistant Chief Constable

ACCA: American Correctional Chaplains Association

▷ **accelerant:** gasoline or another highly flammable substance used by arsonists to speed up fires they have set (see also **accelerator**)

accelerator: fire starter used by arsonists and others; commonly used accelerators include coal oil, kerosene, gasoline or petrol, jet fuel and naphtha (see also **accelerant**)

accessory: anyone encouraging or inciting another (or others) to commit a felony is called an accessory before the fact; anyone concealing the fact of a crime or aiding the escape of its perpetrator (or perpetrators) is called an accessory after the fact

accidentally on purpose: planned to look like a real accident: *just as he stepped off the curb he was kiilled by a passing car, accidentally on purpose*

acco collar: accommodation collar (arrest made to meet an arbitrary quota)

accommodation house: British euphemism for a whorehouse

accomplice: anyone participating in a crime or advising and encouraging the commission of a crime

account executive: euphemism for a pimp procuring high-priced whores

accusatorial system: criminal law administered on the assumption that justice and truth can best be obtained by contest between the accused and the accuser

ace: excellent person; generous male; marijuana cigarette; one-dollar bill

ace of spades: underworld nickname for a widow

ACEP: American College of Emergency Physicians

ACF: Anti-Crime Foundation

ACFSA: American Correctional Food Service Association

ACGLA: Alcoholism Council of Greater Los Angeles

ACHSA: American Correctional Health Services Association

aci (ACI): adult correctional institution

acid: l-acetyl-d-lysergic acid diethylamide, better known as LSD-25 (q.v.)

acid freak: frequent user of LSD; person whose behavior is freakish as a result of using LSD

acid funk: LSD-induced depression

acid head: user of hallucinogenic drugs, such as lyssergic acid diethylamide—LSD

Acid King: ex-Harvard professor Dr. Timothy Leary, whose writings encouraged many of his young followers and readers to experiment with LSD; more recently he has had sober second thoughts about the use of LSD and other drugs

acid lab: illegal laboratory producing LSD and/or other hallucinogenic drugs

acid pads: places where drugs are taken

acid trip: hallucinatory experience derived from taking lysergic acid diethylamide—LSD

ACJ: Arlington County Jail (in Virginia, near Washington, D.C.)

A.C.J.: Associate in Criminal Justice

ACJA: American Criminal Justice Association (q.v.)

ACJA-LAE: American Criminal Justice Association-Lambda Alpha Epsilon

ACJC: Assembly Criminal Justice Committee

ACJHSIS: Arkansas Criminal Justice/Highway Safety Information System

ACJS: Academy of Criminal Justice Sciences (q.v.)

ack: accidentally killed (police jargon)

ACLR: American Criminal Law Review

ACLU: American Civil Liberties Union

aconite: poisonous alkaloidal depressant, also known as monkshood or wolfsbane, used in ancient times in China, Gaul and India as an arrow poison

ACOP: Association of Chief Officers of Police (in England and Wales)

ACP: Academy for Contemporary (Criminal) Problems; Association of Correctional Psychologists; automatic Colt pistol (designation of a cartridge of a stated caliber for use in arms chambered for one of several cartridges developed by Colt)

ACPC: American College of Probate Counsel

ACPO: Association of Chief Police Officers

▷ **acquisitive vandalism:** legal term for damage to property accompanying the looting of automatic vending machines, parking meters, telephone coin boxes, etc.; of metal from buildings and public places (see also **junk**); and of ornamental plants and shrubs

acquittal: judgment of a court, based on the verdict either of a judicial officer or of a jury, that a defendant is not guilty of the offense(s) for which he or she was tried

ACR: American Criminal Review

ACRIM: Association for Correctional Research and Informational Management

ACSI-MATIC: Assistant Chief of Staff—Intelligence (automatic processing system for large-scale intelligence information used by the CIA)

action: a piece of the action (a bit of the business); also refers to sexual intercourse

▷ **active crowd:** police term for an angered and excited mob

activist: anyone—whether centrist, left-wing or right-wing—who is actively engaged in political affairs

activity: sexual activity

ACTL: American College of Trial Lawyers

ACTO: Advisory Council on the Treatment of Offenders

acts of God: occurrences beyond human control, such as blizzards, earthquakes, electrical storms, floods, violent winds, volcanic eruptions, etc.; most insurance policies do not protect the insured from acts of God; under such circumstances

looting is often widespread.

ACU: Abused Child Unit of the Los Angeles Police Department

ADA: Assistant District Attorney

Adam: nickname of methylene—dioxy-methamphetamine

ADAMHA: Alcohol, Drug Abuse, and Mental Health Administration

Adamsite: mob-control gas that causes nausea and severe vomiting

ADAPCP: Alcohol and Drug Abuse Prevention and Control Program

ADAPT: Alcohol and Drug Abuse Prevention Team

ADCO: Alcohol and Drug Control Office(r)

add.: average daily dose (medical term)

Add-Can: Addicts-Canada

addict: victim of addiction (q.v.)

addicted infants: narcotic addiction in infants born to morphine-dependent mothers has been known for more than a century; today addicted infants are on the increase as overall narcotic addiction is also on the increase; drug-addicted infants suffer tremors, vomiting, high-pierced crying, restlessness, frantic fist sucking, sleeplessness, sweating, fever and generalized convulsions—just like their drug-addicted mothers

addiction: state of chronic or periodic intoxication caused by repeated consumption of alcohol or another drug; addiction involves an overpowering need to take the drug and thus to obtain it by any means whatsoever; the level of consumption usually increases as time goes on; physiological as well as psychic (psychological) dependence, once established, has harmful effects on both the addict and society

Addiction Research and Treatment Corp.: drug treatment program based in Brooklyn, N.Y.

addictive drugs: physiologically or psychologically addictive drugs include alcohol, amphetamines, barbiturates, opiates (heroin, morphine, opium) and tranquilizers

Adirondack: Camp Adirondack (minimum-security prison in the Adirondack Mountains near Lake Placid, N.Y.)

▷ **ADIT:** Alien Documentation, Identification and Telecommunications (computer system utilized by the Immigration and Naturalization Service)

adjudicated: determined a delinquent, status offender or dependent in criminal or juvenile proceedings

adjudication: see **criminal adjudication** and **juvenile adjudication**

adjudicatory hearing: fact-finding process wherein a court determines whether or not there is sufficient evidence to sustain allegations made in a petition

adjustment center: segregated section of any prison used for the protection of inmates who refuse to be intimidated by prison gangs and cannot defend themselves adequately

ADL: Anti-Defamation League (B'nai B'rith)

▷ **administrative segregation:** (penological jargon) solitary confinement

admiralty law: maritime law (q.v.)

▽ **ADPRIN:** Automatic Data-Processing Intelligence Network (operated by the U.S. Bureau of Customs to foil smugglers)

— **Adrian:** Girls Training School at Adrian, Mich. (holding many female juvenile delinquents)

ADT: American District Telegraph Security Systems (q.v.)

adult book: advertising euphemism for a pornographic publication—refers not only to books, but also to magazines and posters

adult business district: neighborhood zoned for use by such enterprises as pornographic bookstores and movie theaters, striptease cocktail bars, etc.

adult entertainment center: euphemism for an area catering to the sex trade through cocktail bars, massage parlors, pornographic shows and shops, X-rated motion pictures and the like; Boston's "combat zone" gives visitors the illusion that the city has legitimized alcoholism, prostitution and trafficking in dangerous drugs; mobsters admit that such areas are highly profitable for the underworld

adult fiction: advertising euphemism used to describe pornographic novels

adultery: voluntary sexual intercourse between a married man and a woman who is not his wife or between a married woman and a man who is not her husband

adw (ADW): assault with a deadly weapon (abbreviation appears both ways but small letters are preferable, as ADW also stands for "Air Defense Warning")

AELE: Americans for Effective Law Enforcement

A-E S: Arson-Explosion Squad (of the New York City Police Department)

affd per cur: affirmed by the court

AFI: Air Force Intelligence (including the National Reconnaissance Office); Association of Federal Investigators

AFIO: Association of Former Intelligence Officers (q.v.)

AFIS: Automated Fingerprint Identification System

AF of P: American Federation of Police (q.v.)

AFP: Air Force Police; American Federation of Police (q.v.)

African black: African-grown marijuana

▷ **African dominoes:** dice

Afro-American Liberation Army: black terrorist group active on campuses and in urban neighborhoods, including many ghettos

Afro-American Patrolmen's League: organization seeking to improve relationship between black citizens and police departments; publishes *Black Watch* weekly and *National Black Police Association News* quarterly

Afro-Asian-Latin American People's Solidarity Organization: Cuban overseas underground

after-hour clubs: unlicensed and often unsafe places selling liquor after legal closing hours while pretending to be neighborhood social centers

AG(s): Attorney General(s)

Agaña: Adult Correctional Facility and Community Correction Center in Agaña, Guam

agent in place: espionage agent having legal access to material ranging in classification from confidential to top secret

agent of influence: espionage agent in high places, where he or she can help formulate policies favorable to his or her backers as well as giving them valuable information

aggravated assault: serious bodily injury brought about unlawfully and intentionally, with or without a deadly weapon; unlawful, intentional attempt at, or threat of, serious bodily injury or death with a deadly weapon

aggression: behavior characterized by physical or verbal attack or both

aggressive patrol: police-patrol technique of stopping and questioning suspicious-seeming characters

aggro: aggression

agricrime: agricultural crime (theft of crops and/or equipment)

A-head: acid head (q.v.)

AHS: American Home Security

AI: Adult Institutions

AI: Amnesty International (q.v.)

AIB: Assassination Information Bureau (q.v.)

AI Car: (traffic) accident investigation unit

▷ **aida (AIDA):** automatic intruder-detector alarm

AIDP: *Association Internationale de Droit*

Pénal (French—International Association of Penal Law)

AIDRB: Army Investigational Drug Review Board

AIDS: Automated Identification Division System (of the FBI)

aikido: Japanese art of self-defense utilizing not only holds and locks, but also the opponent's momentum (to the opponent's disadvantage)

AIM: American Indian Movement (militant underground force)

AINL: Association of Immigration and Nationality Lawyers

AIO: Air Intelligence Organization

A-I-P: heroin derived from opium grown in Afghanistan, Iran and Pakistan and usually transported via Turkey to Europe, Canada and the United States

▷ **air bear:** police-manned helicopter

▷ **air dance:** execution by hanging (also called the air jig, the air polka, the air rhumba, etc.)

air gun: weapon that uses compressed air or gas to launch a bullet or other projectile

Air Gunn Museum: see **Daisy International Air Gun Museum**

air injec: air injection (death brought about by injecting air into a vein)

air interdiction: anti-smuggling program of the U.S. Customs Service along the Mexican border

air mail: garbage tossed from windows

Air Opium: nickname of a private "airline" manned by pilots of fortune who fly opium out of Laos to other parts of the world and, more often, to rendezvousing ships, which pick up watertight bags thrown from the planes into the Gulf of Siam

air piracy: airplane hijacking(s)

air pirate: airplane hijacker

AISA: Association Internationale pour la Securité Aérienne (French—International Air Security Association)

AJ: Americans for Justice (q.v.)

AJCA: Association of Juvenile Compact Administrators

AJI: American Justice Institute

AJIS: Automated Juvenile Justice System Technique (of storing criminal data for instant retrieval)

AJS: American Journal of Sociology

aka: also known as

AKA: Associated Klans of America

AK-47: Russian assault rifle

Alabama State Training School: school for female delinquents at East Lake, near Birmingham

ALAL: Association of Legal Aid Lawyers

Alameda: Alameda County Prison and Rehabilitation Center, near San Francisco

alarms by carrier: panic-button device alerting fire stations or police headquarters; such a system uses high frequencies, which are carried on the ordinary telephone system in the United Kingdom

Al-Assifa: Syrian terrorist group

Albany: city and site for prison in California, Georgia, Indiana, Kentucky, Missouri, New York, Oregon and Texas

Albion: Albion State Institution and Western Correctional Facility at Albion, N.Y.

Albuquerque: Girls Welfare Home at Albuquerque, N.M.

alc: alcohol; approximate lethal concentration (of a drug or poison)

Alcatraz: (Spanish—Albatross) island in San Francisco Bay, formerly the maximum-security penitentiary of the United States; the National Park Service conducts tours through the old cell blocks

alcoholic: person whose drinking habits prevent him or her from leading a useful life and often interfere with the lives of associates and family members as well as friends and neighbors; an alcoholic can be a burden to all those with whom he or she comes into contact during the destructive course of this costly habit, which is often connected with crime; after years of working with millions of alcoholics, Alcoholics Anonymous has concluded that an alcoholic is a person who can never again drink safely

alcoholism: the compulsive abuse of alcohol by the alcoholic, who not only has difficulty holding a job, maintaining a family or pursuing educational plans, but often injures other people, including family members and society in general, while under the influence of alcohol

alcoholomania: abnormal craving for alcoholic intoxicants

Alcohol, Tobacco & Firearms: bureau of the U.S. Treasury Department charged with the collection of specific taxes on alcohol and tobacco as well as the enforcement of laws concerning firearms and explosives

alcohometer: see **drunkometer**

Alderson: Federal Correctional Institution at Alderson, W. Va. (for women serving lengthy sentences)

ALECS: Automated Law-Enforcement Communications System

ALEOA: American Law Enforcement Officers Association (q.v.)

ALERT II: Automatic Law Enforcement Response Time (computerized file on criminals kept by the Kansas City, Mo. police)

Alexander: Arkansas Training School for Girls at Alexander; $10 bill

ALF: Arab Liberation Front (q.v.)

Al Fatah: Palestinian terrorist organization led by Yasir Arafat

algolagnic: person who derives pleasure from inflicting or suffering pain (a sadist or masochist)

ALI: American Law Institute

alias: any nickname different from a person's legal name used for an official purpose, such as cashing a check or obtaining a driver's license

alibi: (Latin—elsewhere) legal defense alleging that an accused person could not have committed the crime in question because he or she was somewhere other than at the scene of the crime when the crime was committed

Alibi Ike: nickname for anyone who always has an excuse or whose defense is that he could not have committed the crime with which he is charged because he was somewhere else at the time

Alice B. Toklas: marijuana-filled brownie (named for Gertrude Stein's companion whose cookbook contains a recipe for a fudge that includes cannabis among its ingredients)

alien: foreign-born non-citizen, traveler or vagrant

alienation: social phenomenon marked by anomie, despair, loneliness, loss of values as well as beliefs, pessimism and a sense of meaninglessness and rootlessness

alienist: specialist in mental diseases who appears in court to testify about the mental state of a criminal or a suspect either at the time of the hearing or when the crime was committed

alkie(s): alcoholic(s)

All-African People's Revolutionary Army: a communist organization

All African People's Revolutionary Party: an organization headquartered in Washington, D.C. that has charged the CIA and FBI with murdering such African and Afro-American leaders as King and Lumumba; its posters, which demand smashing the CIA and the FBI, have been seen on many campuses where blacks are enrolled

Allenwood: Federal Prison Camp at Allenwood, Pa.

▷ **alley:** corridor between rows of cells in a jail or prison

alley cat: streetwalker

alley rat: a thief

all-night money: standard price for sexual services rendered by prostitutes willling to stay with their customers all night

▷ **Alpha 66:** organization dedicated to the destruction of the communist government in Cuba

Alston Wilkes Society: organization that aids families of inmates in South Carolina prisons as well as inmates who are being paroled and released

▷ **alteration of a gaming device:** a serious crime in Nevada, where there are hundreds of roulette wheels and slot machines

amapola: blood-red Mexican poppy from which opium and derivative opiates are extracted

ambidexter: attorney or juror who takes bribes from both parties involved in a lawsuit or other litigation

ambulance chaser: corrupt lawyer on the lookout for victims of accidents, barroom brawls and street fights where the institution of a lawsuit for costs and damages may be feasible

‑ **Amenia:** Amenia Center for Girls at Amenia, N.Y.

American Academy for Professional Law Enforcement: organization created by the merger of the Academy of Police Science and the Law Enforcement Association

American Association of Correctional Facility Officers: publisher of *The Corrections Officer* newsletter

American Association of Correctional Psychologists: publisher of the *Journal of Criminal Justice and Behavior*

American Association of Police Polygraphists: organization which recognizes outstanding contributors to polygraphy; publishes *Journal* quarterly

American Association of Wardens and Superintendents: organization founded in 1870 as the Wardens Association of America; publishes *The Grapevine* bimonthly

American Correctional Association: organization that publishes *Corrections Today* and books about correctional problems

American Criminal Justice Association: organization that makes annual key award recognizing outstanding attainment in criminal justice; formerly Lambda Alpha Epsilon

American District Telegraph Security Systems: organization founded in 1874 to provide alarms and crime detection devices for commercial, industrial and residential properties

American Federation of Police: 50,000-member organization; formerly United States Federation of Police; publishes *Police Times Magazine* weekly

American Law Enforcement Officers Association: 55,000-member organization; publishes *Police Times* monthly

American Nazi Party: group of adherents to Hitler's anti-black, anti-Semitic racial doctrines (see also **National Socialist White People's Party**)

American Polygraph Association: organization created by the merger of the Academy of Scientific Interrogation, the American Academy of Polygraph Examiners and the National Board of Polygraph Examiners

American Society of Criminology: organization formerly known as the Society for the Advancement of Criminology; publishes *Criminology* quarterly

American tweezers: burglar tools; jimmies

America's Devil's Island: post-Civil-War nickname for the military prison at Fort Jefferson on the Dry Tortugas about 65 miles (105 kilometers) west of Key West in the Gulf of Mexico

AMI: Associated Marine Institutes (q.v.)

- **Amistad:** Amistad Reservoir on the Rio Grande near Ciudad Acuña, Mexico and Del Rio, Texas; this lake-filled international recreation area offers many opportunities for such clandestine activities as the illegal entry of aliens and narcotics

Am J Corr: American Journal of Correction
Am L: American Lawyer

Amnesty International: organization concerned with the release of political prisoners worldwide on a country-by-country basis

▵ **amotivational syndrome:** general lack of any motivation and loss of personal will, rendering the victim highly prone to suggestions and manipulation by other people; sometimes evidenced in chronic drug users

amped: high on amphetamines or other stimulants

amphetamines: central nervous system stimulants producing, among other effects, anxiety, irritability, rapid heartbeat and restlessness

amphets: amphetamines

amps: ampules

Am Soc Soc: American Sociological Society

amt (or AMT): amphetamines

anarchism: revolutionary doctrine insisting that all government is undesirable and unnecessary; in its stead anarchists advocate free association and voluntary cooperation of groups and individuals replacing the state; anarchists are anti-capitalist and anti-communist

anarcho-syndicalism: revolutionary doctrine stating that the final control of society must be in the hands of the trade unions; adherents' main weapon is the general strike

anascha: resinous hashish grown in the Moslem areas of the southern USSR

Anchorage: the McLaughlin Youth Center at Anchorage, Alaska

Andersonville: Confederate prisoner-of-war camp near a town of the same name in south-central Georgia where nearly 14,000 Union prisoners lost their lives due to overcrowded conditions and lack of good food

anfo (ANFO): ammonium nitrate plus fuel oil (a blasting agent)

angel dust: the animal tranquilizer phencyclidine, called pcp or PCP, originally used by drug pushers as a substitute for tetrahydrocannabinol (THC), the active ingredient in marijuana, but now sold on its own; pcp can cause amnesia, coma, and, in the event of overdose, death

▷ **angler:** pickpocket

Angleton: maximum-security prison at Angleton, Texas, south of Houston

Anglo: Anglo-American—person of Anglo-Saxon (as opposed to Latin or Latin-American) origin; also applied to Americans, Britons and Canadians, traditionally viewed with some distrust by many Latins and Latin Americans

- **Angola:** Louisana State Penitentiary at Angola on the Mississippi River in West Feliciana Parish; reputedly its prison administration is one of the most severe in the country

animal crackers: LSD-impregnated animal crackers

▷ **animal theft:** stealing cattle, horses, poultry, rare birds, wildlife specimens and other animals

ankle: ankle holster

ankles: ankle shackles

▷ **ankle shackles:** shackles similar to handcuffs, but heavier, that are locked around the ankles

A-N-L: Anti-Nazi League

- **Annandale:** New Jersey State Reformatory, northwest of Raritan

anomie: absence of any well-defined sense of right and wrong

anomy: absence of regard or respect for law; lawlessness

ANP: American Nazi Party (q.v.)

Antabuse: trade name for tetraethylthiuram disulfide, used in treating alcoholism; another drug, Temposil (citrated calcium carbamide), is, however, considered safer, as it is weaker

Anteroom of Auschwitz: nickname of the Dutch transit camp established by the Nazis in World War II (see **Lager Westerbork**)

anthropophagy: cannibalism

antidepressants: antidepressant drugs prescribed to lessen severe depression; some brand names are Elavil, Marplan, Nardil, Parnate and Tofranil

anti-penetration glazing: windows built to resist blowtorches, gunfire, and sledgehammers

anti-Semitism: antipathy to or hatred of Jews

antisocial offender(s): convict(s); criminal(s)

antisocial personality: sociopathic character disorder marked by moral deviation and often by extensive involvement in crime

anti-terrorist hot line: see **red telephone**

ao (AO): arresting officer

aob: alcohol on breath

ap (AP): aiming point; armor-piercing (bullet)

APA: Adult Parole Authority; American Polygraph Association (q.v.); American Protective Association; American Psychiatric Association; American Psychological Association; Anti-Papal Association; Association for the Prevention of Addiction; Association of Paroling Authorities; American Prison Association; Automobile Protection Agency

APAP: American People for American Prisoners (in overseas prisons)

apartment girls: call girls who operate in and out of their own apartments

APB: all-points bulletin (police radio-car call)

APCO: Associated Public Safety Communications Officer

APFF: American Police and Fire Foundation

APFO: Association on Programs for Female Offenders

api: armor-piercing incendiary (bullet)

AP-LS: American Psychology-Law Society

APPA: American Penal Press Association

APPA: American Probation and Parole Association

apparatus: fire-fighting equipment such as hook and ladder vehicles, hose wagons, pumpers, etc.

appeal: a request by either the defense or the prosecution that a case be removed from a lower court to a higher court so that a completed trial can be reviewed by the higher court

appearance: act of coming into a court and submitting to its authority

appear citation: written order issued by a law-enforcement officer directing an alleged offender to appear at a specific court at a specific time to answer a criminal charge

appellant: person initiating an appeal

APPLE: Association of Public and Private Labor Employees (q.v.)

apprehend the perpetrator: police term meaning to arrest a criminal

APS: Alternative Press Syndicate (originally the Underground Press Syndicate—UPS)

apw: anti-personnel weapon

ar (AR): armed robbery

Arab Liberation Front: Palestinian terrorists active in Israel and surrounding countries

arbitrary deprivation of life: killing

ARC: Addicts Rehabilitation Center; Alcoholic Rehabilitation Center

ARCI: Addiction Research Center Inventory

ARD: Accelerated Rehabilitative Disposition

ARI: Alcoholic Rehabilitation, Inc. (in Arlington County, Va., near Washington, D.C.)

ARIO: Association of Retired Intelligence Officers

Arisaka: Japanese rifle named for its designer, Col. Nariake Arisaka

ARJIS: Automated Regional Justice Information System (q.v.)

Arkansas toothpick: hunting knife

Armagh: prisoner's place-name nickname for H M Prison at Armagh in Northern Ireland and the penal facility for female offenders

armed propaganda: terrorist euphemism referring to such deeds of violence as assassinations, bombings, clubbings, the destruction of airports, banks or railroad yards, etc.

armed robbery: act of taking or attempting to take property in the immediate possession of another by using or threatening to use a deadly or dangerous weapon

Armstrong: famous English firm of ordnance makers headed by Sir W.G. Armstrong; the name has long been synonymous with firearms

army disease: addiction to morphine among soldiers given the drug for medical reasons

▷ **arr (ARR):** arrest(ed)

arraignment: stage in the judicial process when the defendant is read the charges, informed of her or his rights and required to enter a formal plea regarding the charges

arrest: to take a person into custody by authority of law in order to charge her or him with a criminal offense

arrest warrant: document issued by a judicial officer directing a law-enforcement officer to arrest a person accused of an offense

arsab: arsonist sabotage; arsonist saboteur

arsenal: collection or stockpile of weapons

arson: intentional destruction by explosive or fire of the property of another, of public property or of one's own property with intent to defraud

arson—first degree: burning of dwellings

arson—fourth degree: an attempt to burn buildings or property

arsonist: criminal who maliciously sets fires

arson ring: two or more persons engaged in setting fires, intending to profit by defrauding insurance companies

arson—second degree: burning of buildings, etc., other than dwellings

arson—third degree: burning of property other than buildings

ARSU: Alcohol Rehabilitation Services Unit (Navy Regional Medical Center in Long Beach, Calif.)

ARTC: Addiction Research and Treatment Center; Addiction Research and Treatment Corp. (q.v.)

artillery: drug-injecting equipment; drug laboratory equipment

artist: see **police artist**

Art Squad: police department group investigating art thefts and swindles

Aryan Brotherhood: neo-Nazi white-supremacist underground gang engaged in contract killing

AS: auto squad (of a police department)

▷ **ASAC:** Assistant Special Agent in Charge (pronounced *ay-sack* in the FBI)

ASAPs: Alcohol Safety Action Projects (for apprehending, detecting and diagnosing alcohol-dependent drivers requiring education and rehabilitation)

ASC: American Society of Criminology (q.v.)

ASCA: Association of State Correctional Administrators (q.v.)

ASCLD: American Society of Crime Laboratory Directors

→ **Ashland:** Federal Youth Center at Ashland, Ky.

ASIL: American Society of International Law

Asinara: Italian penal colony, prison and prison farm on Asinara Island off the northwest coast of Sardinia in the Gulf of Asinara

ASJJA: Association of State Juvenile Justice Administrators

ASL: Anti-Saloon League

ASMH: Association for Social and Moral Hygiene

asocial: asocial prisoner, often a habitual criminal or sex offender

ASP: American Schutzhund Products (guard dog and police dog outfitters carrying everything from choke-chain collars to vaccines, located in Manhattan Beach, Calif.; Arizona State Prison; Association of Seattle Prostitutes

ASPCA: American Society for the Prevention of Cruelty to Animals

ASPCC: American Society for the Prevention of Cruelty to Children

asphyxiation: death due to lack of oxygen, often caused by breathing a lethal gas; execution carried out in a gas chamber; suicide committed by breathing a lethal gas, such as the exhaust of an automobile

aspirin smoke: cigarette tobacco laced with crushed aspirin

▷ **asport:** to carry off; to take away feloniously; to transport stolen goods

assassin: murderer; person who, with premeditation, sets out to kill a prominent person such as a head of state

Assassination Act: see **Congressional Assassination**

Assassination Information Bureau: organization set up to investigate the assassinations of Pres. John F. Kennedy, his brother Sen. Robert F. Kennedy and the Rev. Martin Luther King Jr., the attempted assassination of Gov. George Wallace, etc.

assassin's special: .22-caliber automatic fitted with a silencer, a favorite weapon of Mafia killers

assassrep: assassination report

assault: attempting or threatening to inflict injury upon another

assault and battery: an attempt or a threat to strike a person is called an assault, whereas actually striking someone is called battery

assault rifle: one-man machine gun such as the Soviet AK-47 or the U.S. M-16

assaults: assault dogs; assault guards; assault squads

assault with a deadly weapon: unlawfully and intentionally inflicting or attempting or threatening to inflict injury or death with a deadly weapon

Associated Marine Institutes: Florida's federation of correctional programs for young offenders

association: sexual contact with a prostitute

Association of Former Intelligence Officers: national organization demanding that a federal law prohibiting the identification of American intelligence operatives be instituted

Association of Public and Private Labor Employees: union, thought to be controlled by New York mafiosi, active in organizing Atlantic City's private detective and guard services

Association of State Correctional Administrators: publisher of *Correctional Memo* quarterly

ASSPHR: Anti-Slavery Society for the Protection of Human Rights

Astra: Spanish-design 25-caliber semiautomatic pocket pistol

ASU: Administrative Systems Unit

asylum: ancient practice of some churches and, more recently, governments, of granting refuge or sanctuary to criminals fleeing from law-enforcement officers; short form for insane asylum

ataraxics: ataraxic tranquilizer drugs

Atascadero: institution for the criminally insane and mentally-disordered sex offenders at Atascadero, Calif., north of Santa Barbara, near San Luis Obispo

ATC: Alcohol Treatment Center

ATF: (U.S. Bureau of) Alcohol, Tobacco & Firearms (q.v.)

Atlanta: Atlanta Youth Development Center in Atlanta, Ga., which holds female juvenile delinquents up to the age of 17; U.S. penitentiary at Atlanta, Ga., a maximum security prison

Atlantic Avenue: Brooklyn House of Detention for Men at 275 Atlantic Ave. in Brooklyn, N.Y.

Atmore: Fountain Correctional Center at Atmore, Ala.

ATPE: Association of Teachers in Penal Establishments

attaché-casing: handling bribes of money so large the paper money must be carried in attaché cases; small-scale suitcasing

attack dog: canine trained to attack burglars, muggers, etc.

attack-survival: appellation attached to the model-18 Randall attack-survival knife whose hollow handle holds antibiotics, fish hooks and fish line, pep pills for escape and evasion, waterproof matches, water-purification tablets, etc.; its handle is wound with rawhide thong for use in fastening the knife to a pole so that it can be used as a spear

Attica: Attica Correctional Facility (for males) at Attica, N.Y.

Attica Rebellion: four-day revolt in 1971 of 1,200 inmates of the Attica Correctional Facility in Attica, N.Y., where prisoners held 38 guards hostage; during an assault on the prison staged by more than 1,000 police and state troopers, nine hostages and 28 inmates were killed

attitude arrest: arrest made by a law-enforcement officer because he or she does not like the attitude of the person arrested

ATU: Anti-Terrorist Unit (of a police department)

A-2: U.S. Air Force Intelligence

Auburn: Auburn Correctional Facility, a maximum-security institution formerly named Auburn Prison, in Auburn, N.Y.

Auburn System: see **silent system**

audio wall probe: miniature microphone, also known as a limpet or a limpet bug, used by law-enforcement agents and by spies who wish to listen to the conversations of others without being detected

aunt emma: morphine

AUSA: Assistant United States Attorney

authoritarian: diplomatic doubletalk describing an anti-communist totalitarian regime that denies human rights to its people and persecutes dissidents

autocompress: automobile metal compression device for smashing junk vehicles into a square mass of metal for the smelter; gangsters sometimes lock their victims in the trunks of junked vehicles about to be smashed

automag: automatic-loading magnum (handgun)

Automated Regional Justice Information System: fully computerized system aiding police in the apprehension and detection of criminals (known to many by its acronym—ARJIS)

auto pimps: pimps who supply girls to men who drive into outdoor drive-in theaters alone seeking sexual companionship for a price

autopsy: examination of a corpse made to determine the cause of death

auto-repair fraud: highly-profitable illegal enterprise flourishing wherever there are automotive vehicles

Auto Squad: police department group responsible for identifying abandoned vehicles, returning stolen vehicles to their rightful owners and investigating vehicles confiscated during arrests

AUTOSTATIS: Automatic Statewide Theft Inquiry System (California)

AV: Avtomat Kalashnikov (Russian—Kalashnikov automatic) Soviet assault rifle

ava: automatic voice alarm

▷ **aversion therapy:** treatment by punishment involving the association of some unpleasantness with undesirable behavior; electric shock and nausea-producing drugs are but two of several successful means of altering the behavior of alcoholic and narcotic addicts, child molesters, compulsive eaters, gamblers and smokers

awa: native Hawaiian root sometimes chewed for its narcotic effect; absent without authority

AWAIC: Abused Women's Aid in Crisis

AWARE: Addiction Workers Alerted to Rehabilitation and Education

away: imprisoned

awol (AWOL): absent without leave (or permission)

AWS: Alston Wilkes Society (q.v.)

axle grease: slang for bribe

B

B: unit of marijuana measurement consisting of just enough to fill a small matchbox

Baader-Meinhof gang: German terrorist gang named after two of its members; also known as the Red Army Faction

Babi Yar: concentration camp outside Kiev where more than seventy thousand Jews and several hundred thousand Russian troops were killed by Nazi forces during World War II

baby: intimate way of addressing a man or a woman; marijuana (pushers of hard drugs sometimes use this term to indicate that marijuana is used only by babies)

baby battering: descriptive British term for child abuse

baby bear: police trainee; rookie patrolman or patrol woman

baby pro: prostitute between 12 and 16 years of age

babysitter: bodyguard; experienced drug user who guides another through his or her first drug experience

back-alley: red-light district

back-alley butcher: abortionist

back-gate exit: dying in prison (and being carried out the back gate)

Back Home: convicts' nickname for the Tombs Prison in downtown New York City

backlog: pending cases that exceed the capacity of a court and which may not as a result be acted upon until the court has acted upon older cases

back time: unserved portion of a prison sentence any parole violator must serve once he or she is apprehended

backups: high-intensity backup lights installed in the armor-plated autos driven by some executives; they may be flicked on to blind terrorists pursuers

backwards: tranquilizers

bad bag: oversize shopping bag used by shoplifters, who also refer to it as a booster bag

bad bundle: heroin diluted or exposed to dampness and hence sold for less than usual

baddie: bad guy; incorrigible criminal

badger game: blackmail that involves framing the victim by catching him in the act of intercourse with a female posing as the wife of the extortionist

badhouse: bawdyhouse

bad rap: long prison sentence

bad scene: unpleasant drug experience; in general, any unpleasant experience or situation

bad secrets: secrets relating to bureaucratic ineptitude or official misconduct (the Watergate and Koreagate cover-ups are recent examples of bad secrets)

bad trip: anxiety-filled reaction to such drugs as LSD and marijuana

Baffin Correctional Centre: prison in Frobisher Bay, Northwest Territories

BAFS: British Academy of Forensic Sciences

bag: small glassine bag filled with heroin or another drug

bag job: burglary; illegal break-in (sometimes made by law-enforcement agencies in need of otherwise unobtainable evidence)

baglady: woman charged by a numbers racket with collecting or paying off bets

bagman: racketeer designated to collect bets, bribes or so-called loans or to pay off other racketeers or venal politicians; anyone holding or receiving money during the course of an illegal transaction; peddler of dangerous drugs

bail: money or other security deposited with a court by a defendant to secure release from custody while awaiting trial; bail is intended to guarantee that the defendant will appear for trial; the amount of money or security posted will be forfeited if the defendant fails to appear

bail bond: document obligating the person signing it to pay the amount of bail set by the court if the defendant does not appear for trial

Baird House: residence of the Quaker Committee on Social Rehabilitation at 135 Christopher St. in New York City

bait-and-switch: technique of advertising a big bargain and, when a customer tries to buy it, offering him or her a similar product that is supposed to be better and is almost invariably more expensive than what he or she came for, which, the seller will claim, has proven faulty or has been sold out

bait money: money in a bank teller's drawer set to trigger a robbery alarm if it is removed

Bakirkoy: hospital for the criminally insane in Istanbul, Turkey

bale: one pound of hashish or marijuana (both are usually sold by the kilogram—2.2 pounds)

balisong: another name for the batangas knife (q.v.)

Balkan route: route by which heroin made from opium grown in Afghanistan, Iran and Pakistan, along with Turkish opium products, is smuggled through Turkey and the Balkans to western Europe

Ballester-Molina: 45-caliber Argentine semi-automatic pistol

ballistics: the science of firearms and the study of the motion of projectiles, such as bullets

ballistophobia: unusually strong fear of bullets

balloon: balloon used for carrying or storing heroin

balloon room: place or room where marijuana is smoked; rendezvous of marijuana smokers and drug pushers

BALSA: Black American Law Students Association

bam: barbiturate + amphetamine (depressant-stimulant mixture)

bambalacha: marijuana

BAMM: Black Afro Militant Movement (q.v.)

bammies: poor-quality marijuana

banana peelers: youngsters who dry and smoke banana peelings in imitation of their elders who smoke hashish or marijuana

Bananas: popular mispronunciation of the name of an old-time racketeer and Mafia family head—Joe Bonanno

bandbox: county workhouse

b & e: breaking and entering

bandit: marauding robber who lives by terrorizing others

Banditos: motorbike gang active in the Pacific Northwest and especially in the states of Oregon and Washington

b & w: bread and water (diet often imposed on prisoners in solitary confinement or on traditionally unruly prisoners)

bane: kill with poison

bang: bombing; explosion; injection of a narcotic drug; sniff of cocaine

Bangalore torpedo: dynamite-filled length of pipe detonated by a blasting cap or a fuse

bang 'em up: automobile smash-up

banging: under the influence of drugs

Bangkok connection: exportation of narcotics to the United States and Canada from southeast Asia through the port of Bangkok

banishment: removal to another country or to some far place belonging to the land of the person banished; prisoners, such as Napoleon, who was first exiled to Elba in the Mediterranean between his native Corsica and the west coast of Italy and later banished to Saint Helena Island in the South Atlantic Ocean, find exile preferable to banishment as it is usually closer to home

banji: hashish plant grown in Arabia, Iran and other Middle Eastern countries

bank bandits: barbiturate pills; sedatives

banker: casino or gambling house owner or operator who may become involved in crime by using gangsters to protect him from other gangsters or to help collect gambling debts; financier of a drug-importing ring—the one least likely ever to be arrested or jailed

Banning: Banning Rehabilitation Center (California)

baptized: watered (liquor)

bar: marijuana compressed into a solid block and held together with honey or dried sugar

BAR: Browning automatic rifle (see **Browning**)

barb: barbiturate

barbecue stool: electric chair

barbidex: barbiturate and amphetamine mixture

barbiturates: central nervous system depressants such as amobarbital (Amytal), Luminal (phenobarbital), Nembutal (pentobarbital), Seconal (secobarbital), Tuinal (amobarbital and secobarbital); slang names include blue devils, downs, goof balls, peanuts, rainbows, red devils, spacers, yellow jackets, et al.; effects are somewhat similar to those of alcohol; protracted use affects blood pressure and pulse and may eventually bring on convulsions

BARC: Bay Area Research Collective (q.v.)

barfly: drunken person; individual who frequents bars and is usually under the influence of alcohol

Barlinnie: Glasgow, Scotland's prison and its Young Offenders Institution

barracoon: improvised prison; place of temporary confinement

barratry: illegal act by the captain or crew of a ship such as casting her away, deserting her, diverting her from her proper course with intent to put her in peril or selling her or any of her safety devices, such as fire extinguishers, lifeboats, etc.

barrel fever: delirium tremens

barrelhouse: whorehouse

Barrio Boyle: crime-ridden, predominantly Mexican-American district near downtown Los Angeles, Calif., also known as Boyle Heights

Bartholomew Fair: nickname of the solitary-confinement section of London's Fleet Prison in Elizabethan times

Bartons Mills: medium-security prison near Perth in Western Australia

Bastille: (French—small fortress)—La Bastille, the infamous prison of Paris, was destroyed by French revolutionaries on July 14, 1789—a day celebrated ever since by Frenchmen everywhere; long a synonym for prison and especially one holding political prisoners

Bastille by the Bay: inmates' nickname for San Quentin Prison on San Francisco Bay

bastinado: stick used for thrashing or whipping; blow delivered with a stick; blow on the soles of the feet with a stick or switch

Bastrop: Federal Youth Center at Bastrop, Texas (for inmates under 21 years of age)

bat: prostitute

batangas: balisong switch-handled knife developed in Batangas Province in the Philippines and consisting of two half handles pivoting on the blade and locking either when closed or opened; experts consider it superior to any gravity type or spring-loaded switchblade

BATF: Bureau of Alcohol, Tobacco & Firearms (see **Alcohol, Tobacco & Firearms**)

baton: nightstick; policeman's club

Baton Rouge: Louisiana's Juvenile Reception and Diagnostic Center for delinquent and neglected male and female juveniles at Baton Rouge

batted out: arrested

battering: domestic violence

battering ram: tool used to batter down doors or breach walls

battery: striking a person (see also **assault and battery**)

battery girls: girls and women kept under the influence of narcotics while performing sexual services for a number of men who may live in a barracks, a boarding house or aboard a ship

Baumes Law: New York State statute requiring that life imprisonment be. imposed upon anyone convicted four times of felonies

Baumettes: France's great cobblestone-walled prison in Marseilles

Bay Area Research Collective: Berkeley, Calif. publisher of the *Dragon*—a bimonthly dealing with the underground in the United States

bayonet: dagger designed to be fitted to the muzzle end of a rifle

B-bombs: benzedrine inhalers

BCC: Board of Crime Control (Montana)

BCC: Bureau of Charities and Corrections (South Dakota)

BCI: Bureau of Criminal Identification (former name of the Identification Section of the New York City Police Department)

BCI: Bureau of Correctional Institutions (Iowa)

bcp: blanket crime (insurance) policy

BC Pen: British Columbia Penitentiary in New Westminster adjacent to Vancouver

BCPU: Border Crime Prevention Unit (operating along the Mexican border of San Diego)

B.C.S.: Bachelor of Criminal Science

BCS: Bureau of Criminal Statistics

BCTF: Border Crime Task Force (active on the Mexican border from California to Texas)

B-D: Becton-Dickinson (hypodermic syringe)

BDAC: Bureau of Drug Abuse Control

BDC: Bomb Data Center (FBI)

b-d squad: bomb-disposal squad

BDU: bomb disposal unit (q.v.)

bd unit: bomb disposal unit (q.v.)

Beaconsfield: Marian Hall for delinquent English-Catholic juvenile offenders at Beaconsfield, Quebec

beagle: detective; investigator

bean bag: birdshot-filled or sand-filled bag shot from a shotgun to control mobs while causing only minor injuries

bear bait: speeding vehicle

bear bite: traffic ticket given for speeding

bear den: police station

bear in the air: police-manned helicopter

bears wall to wall: (an area) patrolled by many police

bear trap: radar trap set to detect speeding vehicles

beast: LSD-25

beat: tired out; to cheat; to rob; to steal

BEAT: Breaking, Entering, and Auto Theft (computerized file on criminals kept by the police of Lowell, Mass.)

beat the box: outsmart a lie-detector test

beat the gong: smoke opium

beat the rap: to be acquitted; to be freed from prosecution

Beaune-la-Rolande: site of a French concentration camp just southeast of Pithiviers

Bedak: Bureau of Drug Abuse Control officer

bedbugs: fellow addicts

Bedford Hills: Bedford Hills Correctional Facility at Bedford Hills, N.Y.

bed house: a brothel where each girl is supposed to have her own bed and her own bedroom; a whorehouse

Bedlam: nickname of Saint Mary of Bethlehem, the celebrated lunatic asylum of old London, where many of the inmates were criminally insane

bedpain: police-academy mnemonic for recalling items to be reported in one type of burglary—break, enter, dwelling, person, armed, (with) intent (to kill), (at) night

beef: any criminal charge

Beersheba: Israel's largest prison located between Jerusalem and the Negev desert; built during British Mandate days as a police fortress and prison

behavioral control unit: solitary-confinement prison cell or dungeon

beheading: capital punishment long popular in many "civilized" countries such as Britain and France, where the guillotine was invented

behind the iron door: in jail

behind the iron house: in jail

beinsa: Burmese narcotic plant whose botanical name is *Mitragyna speciosa*

belduque: narrow-sheath knife popular in Mexico and along the Mexican border

Belfast Welfare Unit 14: euphemism for Her Majesty's Prison Camp outside Belfast, Northern Ireland

belladonna: (Italian—beautiful lady) psychotomimetic drug extracted from the leaves and roots of this poisonous perennial plant, also called deadly nightshade; known since ancient times for its ability to enlarge the pupils of the eyes and to produce hallucinogenic effects

Belle Isle: prisoner-of-war camp in the James River near Richmond, Virginia; many Federals died there due to prolonged exposure and lack of food in the Confederate prison camp

Bellevue: Bellevue Hospital Prison Ward at First Avenue and 30th Streeet in New York City

belly habit: taking drugs orally

belong: to be addicted to a drug

Belsen: Nazi concentration camp near Hannover, Germany

belt: restraining belt fitted with a steel ring through which handcuffs may be locked; the belt buckle is adjusted behind the prisoner's back to prevent the prisoner from unbuckling it

belted: under the influence of drugs

Belzec: German extermination camp in this Polish village on the railway line running through Lublin province during World War II; it was known as Beltzec to the Poles and Belzhets to the Russians

bench warrant: document issued by a judicial officer directing that a person who has failed to obey an order or notice to appear be brought before the court; court order to capture a criminal who has escaped detention, jumped bail or violated parole or probation

Benjy: a $100 bill, which bears the portrait of Benjamin Franklin

benny: benzedrine (amphetamine) pill, producing alertness followed by depression

bent: intoxicated

benz: benzedrine; benzine

benzedrine: an amphetamine

Bergen-Belsen: Nazi concentration camp near Celle in Lower Saxony, Germany

Berhala Island: prisoner-of-war camp run by the Japanese in North Borneo during World War II

Bernadelli: palm-size Italian .22 automatic, also called a vest-pocket gun

Bernalillo: Bernalillo County Detention Home in Albuquerque, N.M.

Bernice: slang name for cocaine

bernies flake: cocaine

bertillonage: identification of criminals or others based upon measurements of certain unchanging parts of the skeleton

BET: Biker Enforcement Team (of law-enforcement investigators studying the criminal world of motorcycle gangs such as Hell's Angels)

betsy: handgun

Betty's Place: St. Elizabeth's Hospital in Washington, D.C. where Ezra Pound was held during most of World War II

Bexar: Bexar County Jail in San Antonio, Texas

bg: background

BGA: Better Government Association

BHD: Bronx House of Detention

Bialoleka: Polish prison camp southeast of Bialystok

Bialystok: Nazi concentration camp northeast of Treblinka in Poland

Bianchi(s): Bianchi leather products (B-lites [q.v.], holsters, etc.)

bid (BID): brought in dead

BId: Bureau of Identification

Big A: underworld nickname of the Federal Penitentiary in Atlanta, Ga.

bigamy: having more than one husband or wife at the same time

big bags: $10 bags of heroin

big bench: Supreme Court of the United States

big bloke: cocaine

big boy: nickname for heroin

big bull: police chief

big chief: mescal buttons of the peyote cactus; mescaline derived from peyote buttons

big con: fraudulent business deals, real estate and stock swindles, securing money under false pretenses from people of wealth, are all termed big con(fidence) crimes

big D: LSD-25

big day: visiting day in a prison

big demo: big demonstration, or unrest

big enchilada: chief; head of a gang

big fence: see **master fence**

big gate(s): prison(s)

big H: big house (any penitentiary)

Big House up the River: Sing Sing Prison at Ossining, N.Y.

big J: big John (policeman)

big juice: racketeer enjoying police protection

big man: drug "wholesaler" who supplies neighborhood pushers

big O: opium

big pasture: penitentiary

big sheet: a long criminal record

big supplier: see **big man**

bike mama: see **motorcycle mama**

biker: motorcycle gang(ster)

bilbo: leg shackle consisting of an iron bar fitted with adjustable fetters

Bilibid: great maximum-security Philippine prison built in Spanish times at Muntinlupa in Rizal Province close to Manila

bilk: defraud

Billeshave: youth home for delinquent boys on the western edge of Denmark's island of Funen

billy: policeman's baton or club

bindle: small packet of any drug

bing: solitary confinement

bingle: drug pusher; narcotics peddler

bingler: seller of narcotics

bingo: to inject drugs

biphet: biphetamine (drug stimulant)

BIR: Bureau of Intelligence and Research (of the U.S. Department of State)

bird: aircraft assisting Coast Guard cutter(s) searching for and rescuing distressed seamen or apprehending smugglers

birdcage: prison cell

birdie powder: heroin and morphine mixture

bird in the air: police-manned helicopter

birdseed: insufficient sum of money; petty cash

bird's eye: tiny packet of narcotics

birdwood: marijuana

Birkena: (German—birch grove)—concentration camp built next to Auschwitz and also built by the Nazis near Oswiecim, Poland

Birmingham: prison in Birmingham, Ala., and prisons in smaller Birminghams in Iowa, Michigan and Saskatchewan

biscuit: gun; revolver; worldy woman

Biscuit Factory: nickname of old Reading Gaol in Berkshire, England where it adjoined Huntley & Palmer's biscuit factory

Bismarck: North Dakota Penitentiary at Bismarck

BISSI: Burns International Security Services Inc. (q.v.)

bit: time served in prison; a 10-year bit is 10 years of incarceration

bitch kitty: bad-tempered or disagreeable girl

biz stuff: drug-injecting equipment (sometimes shortened to "biz")

BJA: Bureau of Justice Assistance

BJC: Bureau of Juvenile Correction (Delaware)

BKA Bundeskriminalam: (German—Federal Criminal Ministry) contains computerized files of criminal histories maintained at its center in Wiesbaden

Bklyn HTF: Brooklyn Homicide Task Force (of the New York City Police Department)

bl: bank larceny

BLA: Black Liberation Army (q.v.)

BLA: British Legal Association

black: blackmail; opium

black act: lock picking in the dark

Black Afro Militant Movement: terrorists who have claimed credit for several bombings and acts of violence

black-and-white: black and white highway patrol, police or sheriff's office automobile

black-and-white stripes: old-fashioned convict colors that have adorned many prisoners' uniforms

black-bag job: burglary; illegal entry

black beauty: a biphetamine stimulant in the form of a tablet with a black bottom and a white top

blackbird: kidnap and enslave or sell into slavery; person or ship engaged in the slave trade

black book: prison's register of inmates

black box: device for bypassing the telephone company's switching system so that calls can be made to anywhere else in the U.S. without charge by, or knowledge of, the telephone company; technical device used in gathering intelligence, which may range from a telephone wiretapping apparatus to an aerial satellite

black broadcasting: transmissions allegedly broadcast by political groups (imaginary or real)

black camp: prison largely populated by blacks

Black December: Pakistani terrorists active in the United Kingdom, mainly in and around London

Black Flower of Society: Nathaniel Hawthorne's nickname for any jail, penitentiary, prison, or other place of imprisonment

Black Guerrilla Family: Maoist-oriented underground group associated with the SLA and involved in kidnappings and killings in California and elsewhere

black gungi: marijuana grown in India

black gunion: gummy marijuana

Black Hole: the Black Hole of Calcutta, a small underground prison cell within Calcutta's Fort William where, during the Indian Mutiny of 1756, some 146 Europeans were imprisoned; the following morning only 23 were still alive; the term is thus applied to any particularly dreaded penal institution or prison cell

black intelligence: information obtained by espionage conducted by an agent or agents working with some undercover or underground source

blackjack: to coerce or frighten by threats or by gangster or hoodlum tactics; weapon consisting of a leather-enclosed bulbous metal rod attached to a springy handle; blackjack blows range in impact from stunning to skull cracking

Black June: Baghdad, Iraq-based Palestinian terrorists active throughout the Middle East; their bombings of buildings and crowded streets and killings of high officials are part of their plot to topple conservative Arab regimes in these countries

Black Liberation Army: militant black group formerly active in many U.S. cities

blacklist: list of persons to be denied employment or to be punished in some other manner; to put on a blacklist

black lock: solitary confinement

blackmail: use of threats to extract favors or money from persons who have something to conceal or to lose

black maria: prison van

black market: marketplace where otherwise unobtainable goods are sold or where money is exchanged for less than the legally-established price or rate

black money: funds not reported to tax collectors, usually because they were gained by gambling or illegal operations

black operator: secret agent

blackout: censorship; extinguishment of all light; suppression of information

Black P: Black P Stone Nation (Chicago's Woodlawn district gang, also known as the Blackstone Rangers or the Moorish Americans; members are reportedly still active inside prisons, where they deal in heroin)

Black Panthers: militant black party formerly active in the United States and overseas

black peter: Australian slang—solitary-confinement prison cell

black pills: opium pellets

black powder: ammunition propellant often made up of 15 parts of charcoal to 75 parts of saltpeter and 10 parts of sulfur

black propaganda: disinformation consisting of lies combined with some distortions, half-truths and even bits of the whole truth

black Russian: very dark and very potent variety of hashish

Black September Organization: Arab terrorists active in the Middle East that have claimed responsibility for many bombings

blackstuff: opium

black tar: nickname of a deadly Mexican-made heroin also called *Mexican mud* or *Tootsie Roll*

blackthorn: bludgeon, club or knob-handled walking stick made from the hard root and stem of the blackthorn shrub of Ireland; often used as a weapon

Blackwell's Island: earlier name of Welfare Island (now Roosevelt Island) in New York City's East River, which long held public correctional and medical institutions

blade: dagger, knife or razor-blade; person skilled in the use of daggers, knives, razors and other sharp-edged weapons

blank: non-narcotic white powder sold to gullible drug users

blast: drug producing a strong effect

blast a joint: smoke marijuana

blast a stick: smoke marijuana

blasted: intoxicated by alcohol or another drug

blast party: marijuana-smoking party

blind: blind drunk; excessively intoxicated

blindfold act: execution by hanging or shooting (so called because the victim is usually blindfolded)

blind tiger: cheap or low-grade whiskey

B-lite: baton-flashlight combination (manufactured by Bianchi)

blaxploitation: exploitation of black people

BLD: Burglary Larceny Division (of the New York City Police Department, with such subunits as the Auto Squad, Forgery Squad, Missing Persons Unit, Property Recovery Unit, Safe and Loft Unit)

bleach: bribe; bribe money

bleed: bring to the brink of ruin; impoverish

Blitz: one of a number of German shepherd dogs trained to assist law-enforcement officers in detecting marijuana; the dogs actually smell out the weed concealed in baggage as well as in various vehicles

blitzed: completely under the influence of narcotics

blockbusters: barbiturates

blond hash: golden-brown hashish

Blonde Beast of Belsen: nickname of wardress Irma Grese, given in memory of her many cruelties to prisoners in the concentration camp run by the Nazis at Belsen

blood box: ambulance

blood bread: blood money (money made by selling one's blood in order to buy drugs)

blood feud: vendetta marked by prolonged hostility

bloodguilt: guilt due to bloodshed or murder

bloodhound: large hound dog whose keen sense of smell fits it for the task of tracking criminals as well as missing persons; unlike the German police dog, the bloodhound does not attack and bite the person it is tracking

blood money: material retribution paid for injury, loss of life or loss of property; restitution

bloodworm: particularly parasitic and ruthless pimp

blow: discover or reveal the identity of an espionage or law-enforcement agent; smoke marijuana

blow a stick: smoke a marijuana cigarette

blowback: exposure of espionage activity due to an unsuccessful attempt to recruit a secret agent

blow charlie: sniff cocaine

blowgun: hollow tube used for blowing arrows or poisoned darts; a primitive weapon still used by natives in parts of tropical Southeast Asia and South America and adopted by some underground groups seeking inexpensive and silent weapons

blow hay: smoke marijuana

blow horse: sniff heroin

blown away: narcotically-induced euphoria; reaction to an unbelievable revelation

blown out: high on drugs

blow one's mind: astonish (as an unusual drug-induced experience might)

blowout: drunken spree; wild party

blow out: to die

blow snow: inhale cocaine

blow the lid off: expose a criminal racket or a political scandal

blow the whistle: expose criminal activity; notify law-enforcement authorities

bludgeon: short leather-enclosed stick with a weighted end; bludgeon blows are similar to blackjack blows and range in impact from stunning to skull cracking

blue: amytal (barbiturate)

blue acid: pale-blue liquid LSD-25

blue angels: amytal (barbiturate)

bluebirds: capsules of sodium amytal

blue box: electronic device allowing users to dial toll-free exchanges and then keep the like open while dialing another number once the original conversation is completed; used by people wishing to avoid paying for long-distance telephone calls

blue boy: policeman

blue bullet: blue-tipped bullet color-coded so that users will know it is used for incendiary purposes

blue devils: amobarbital capsules

Blue Fox: code name of anti-Soviet espionage group determined to undermine communist control behind the Iron Curtain

blue heaven: amytal capsule

blue law: law prohibiting dancing, drinking or working on Sunday

blue lib: nationwide movement of law-enforcement officers to support civil lawsuits against people who beat them up, libel them or slander them

blue mornings: blue morning-glory seeds prized for their hallucinogenic effect

blue movie: pornographic film

blue pellets: hydrogen-cyanide pellets marketed under the trade name of Zyklon-B and used by the Nazis in their gas chambers; as the blue pellets were poured into ceiling openings of the murder chambers they turned into deadly gas

blue ruin: low-grade gin

blue tip: incendiary bullet identified in the United States by its blue-painted tip

blue velvet: codeine and elixir terpin hydrate combination taken as a sedative

bly: British burglar's oxy-acetylene blow torch (for opening safes and vaults)

Blythe: Blythe Branch of the Riverside County Jail in California

B-Ms: Baader-Meinhoff gang (q.v.)

BND: *Bundesnachrichtendienst* (German—Federal Intelligence Service)

BNDD: Bureau of Narcotics and Dangerous Drugs (U.S. Department of Justice)

BNI: Black Nation of Islam

'bo: hobo (vagrant)

board: board of control; board of governors; board of supervisors; parole board; etc.

board(ed): blindfold(ed)

Bobbies: nickname for the blue-coated metropolitan police of London whose organization was founded in 1829 by British Home Sec. Sir Robert Peel

bobo bush: marijuana

B o C: Bureau of Correction (Pennsylvania); Bureau of Corrections (Virgin Islands)

BOCCI: Bureau of Organized Crime and Criminal Intelligence (State of California)

body bag: heavy-duty bag, usually made of zippered rubber or rubberized cloth, that is large enough to hold a corpse

body-cavity search: anal or vaginal search for contraband such as diamonds or narcotics

body drug: physically addictive drug such as heroin

body shake: search down to the skin and into the body

body snatch: to steal a corpse from a grave, a hospital, a morgue, or some other place; body snatchers are sometimes called resurrectionists—a term that originated in the 18th century, when medical students sometimes had to hire people to get them dissection material for their anatomical studies

body snatchers: grave robbers such as the ones described by Robert Louis Stevenson in his novel *The Body Snatcher*, so unforgettably portrayed by Boris Karloff; more recently, a nickname given undertakers

B of I: Bureau of Investigation (q.v.)

Bofors: Swedish ammunition and armament maker

B of P: Bureau of Prisons (U.S. Department of Justice)

B of R: Bureau of Rehabilitation (in Washington, D.C.)

bogue: Afro-Americanism referring to drug-withdrawal sickness

boiled owl: intoxicated person

boilermaker's delight: low-grade whiskey

boilerplate: legal language characterized by excessive verbiage

Boise: Idaho State Penitentiary at Boise

bol: be on the lookout (police alert)

Bolivar: Bolivar County Jail in Cleveland, Miss.; its name is evenly accented—*Bol-i-var*

bolo: bolo bayonet made to fit the Krag rifle; heavy-blade bolo knife of original Philippine design, a favorite weapon of many insurgents and others

bolo: be on the lookout (for a criminal at large)

bol-148 (also BOL-148): d-2-bromolysergic acid tartrate (LSD-type hallucinogen)

Bolshoi Dom: (Russian—Big House)—prison

bolt cutter: heavy-duty hardware tool used to cut bolts, chain-link fencing, handcuffs, steel bars, etc.

bombs: explosive devices designed to destroy people and property; eggs (prison argot); highly potent hashish or marijuana; king-size hashish or marijuana cigarette; lethal dose of any drug

bomb disposal unit: trained team of experts in the disposal of unexploded bombs

bombed: overcome by alcohol or narcotics; thoroughly intoxicated (also ''bombed out'')

bomber: very thick marijuana-filled cigarette

bombidos: injectable benzedrine

bomb sniffers: dogs trained to use their keen sense of smell to detect the presence of plastic bombs in aircraft, airport lockers and other hiding places; bomb sniffers can also be trained to detect hidden narcotics; a number of law-enforcement agencies buy, train and use such dogs

bomb squad: specially-equipped and trained metropolitan police squad handing bombs and often removing bombs set to destroy people and property

Bompo: Frank Bompensiero—mob boss in San Diego, Calif. for many years until his murder by the Mafia in February 1977, when it was discovered that he had provided the FBI with information about organized crime for more than a decade during his retirement

bomrep: bombing report

bone box: hearse

boneyard: cemetery; graveyard

Boniato: Cuban prison in Oriente Province

boo: marijuana

booby hatch: insane asylum

booby trap: device or scheme for apprehending, injuring or killing a person or a wild beast

boodler: grafter

boogie: derogatory term for a black person; drug-buying trip to Colombia, Jamaica, Mexico, or nearby Caribbean or Central American smuggler's markets; syphilis; syphilis in its secondary stage, when eruptions occur in the mucous membrane and skin of its victims

book bomb: explosive plastic bomb concealed in a book and detonated by anyone who opens its cover

bookie: bookmaker—person who receives money for gambling and pays off to the winner(s); many bookies also determine the odds wagered

booking: stage in the criminal justice process when the suspect arrested is formally logged by the police or other law-enforcement agency as well as being fingerprinted and photographed

boost: shoplift; steal

booster bloomers: pocket-fitted undergarments used by shoplifters to secrete stolen merchandise

booster boxes: boxes that appear to be carefully wrapped packages but that actually have a hinged fast-access side; used to conceal shoplifted merchandise

booster pants: oversize pants with deep pockets used to hold shoplifted merchandise

boosting: boosting the amounts of suppliers' invoices and often splitting the boosts with the suppliers

boot: boot knife designed to be carried or concealed in the top of a boot

boot and shoe: down-and-out alcoholic and/or drug addict

boot and shoot: drug addict who steals to get money to pay for drugs needed to sustain his or her habit

boot knife: long-bladed knife designed to be concealed in the top of a boot

bootlegger's turn: evasive action used by criminals escaping from law-enforcement officers; involves locking the emergency brake and then turning the steering wheel 90 degrees, then quickly releasing the brake and accelerating the car in the opposite direction

bootlegging: illegal distribution or manufacture of alcohol, alcoholic products, ammunition, drugs, explosives, firearms, tobacco, weapons or other highly taxed or illegal goods

booze babies: infants born to alcoholic mothers who drank during pregnancy

booze blind: drunk

B o P: United States Bureau of Prisons

BoPat: Border Patrol

Bordentown: Youth Correctional Institution (at Bordentown, N.J.)

Border Country: the U.S.-Mexican border, extending for 1,952 miles or 3,141 kilometers from Brownsville, Texas, opposite Matamoros, Tamaulipas, to San Diego, Calif., opposite Tijuana, Baja California Norte

borstal: British name for a juvenile reformatory

Borstal Prison: in Kent, England where the first juvenile-delinquent reformatory was established in 1902 for boys 16 to 21, made famous by the book of Brendan Behan entitled *Borstal Boy*

Boss of Bosses: Lucky Luciano (Salvatore Lucania) whose mobsters controlled many political bosses throughout the United States as well as other places, such as pre-Castro Cuba

Bossi: Bureau of Special Services (New York City Police Department)

bot (BOT): balance of time to be served by anyone violating parole and returned to prison

bottle baby: alcoholic addict

bottle dealer: drug pusher selling 1,000-capsule or 1,000-tablet quantities

bounce: write a bad check

bouncer: bar employee hired to keep order and, when necessary, bounce or eject unprofitable or unruly customers; bad check

bouncing powder: cocaine

bounty hunter: person specializing in tracking down bail jumpers; well rewarded by bail bondsmen and law-enforcement agencies

Bourgoin: maximum-security prison near Lyons, France

bov's: burned-out veins useless for injection

Bowery: The Bowery, an avenue in New York City, traditionally occupied by many alcoholics

bowie: heavy-blade sharp-point hunting knife of type used by American frontiersman Jim Bowie, who died defending the Alamo

box: prison cell (also "boxcar")

boxcar(s): prison cell(s)

boxed: black boxed (submitted to a lie-detector test); slang for intoxicated

boxed up: (New Zealand slang) imprisoned; jailed; locked up

box(es): prison cell(s)

boxer: very intelligent breed of guard or police dog of the bulldog type

boy: heroin

Boys Ranch: Group Home for Boys at Agana, Guam (juvenile correctional facility)

boys uptown: political bosses and other un-apprehended criminals too smart to go to prison

bp: black pimp

BP: Board of Parole

b-p cartridge: barricade-penetrating cartridge

bpe: black powder express (cartridge)

BPP: Black Panther Party

bprf: bulletproof (article of clothing, vehicle, etc.)

BPS: British Police Service

BPT: Board of Prison Terms

bpv: bullet-proof vest

br: bread (money)

bracelets: handcuffs

brain: hit on the head

brain picker: clever pocket picker

brains: leader of a well-organized arson ring, assassination ring, crime ring, subversive ring, etc.

brain ticklers: amphetamine or barbiturate pills

brainwashing: see **menticide**

Brandenburg: concentration subcamp west of Berlin

brank: leather or rubber head harness fitted with a gag and used to prevent a prisoner from shouting or talking

b-r-a-s-s: breathe, relax, aim, squeeze, shoot (the marksman's acronym)

brass knuckles: fist protector and knuckle guard sometimes used as a weapon by hoodlums and others

brass knucks: brass knuckles

Braunschweig: Nazi concentration camp located in what is now West Germany

breach of the peace: to agitate, to arouse, to assemble unlawfully, to awaken, to hinder, to incite to riot, to molest, to obstruct traffic, to trespass, etc.

bread: money

breadand: bread and water (prison fare for those in solitary confinement)

bread and water: traditional diet fed to difficult-to-handle prisoners as a form of punishment

bread and whiskey: last meal fed to prisoners held by the Republic of China before they are shot for the crime of dealing in narcotics

break-in: burglary

Breda: Italian semi-automatic shotgun

briar: hacksaw, a tool once considered useful in hacking one's way out of prison; modern alloys used in the construction of bars are resistant to most hacksaws

bribery: corruption of corporate or public officers by gifts of money or property or by the granting of certain favors

brick: compressed brick-shaped block of hashish, marijuana, morphine or opium; bricks usually weigh either one pound or one kilogram

bridewell: British synonym for a house of correction such as the infamous Bridewell described by Hogarth in *The Harlot's Progress*; the prison has disappeared but its site may be found on London's New Bridge Street between the Embankment and Fleet Street at what was St Bride's Well near the River Thames

Bridge House: detention home for juvenile delinquents of both sexes in Wilmington, Del.

briefcase buccaneer: white-collar pirate expert in preying upon shipping by altering documents, changing the names of ships and diverting cargoes and ships to places such as Greece or Lebanon or third-world countries where such operations may go undetected and the briefcase buccaneer may go unmolested due to the corruption of local bankers and government officials

brig: ship's prison (usually used to segregate unruly alcoholics and drug addicts or to hold stowaways until they can be turned over to immigration authorities)

Brigadier: 45-caliber pistol developed by the North American Arms Corp. of Canada

brig rat: convict; naval prisoner; shipboard prisoner

Brilab: bribery-labor (FBI investigation's code name)

brims: gang members wearing the same kind of hats

Brink's: Brink's Armored Car Service, used by many banks since 1859, when it was begun in Chicago by Washington Perry Brink

Bristol: prisons in Bristols in Connecticut, Colorado, Florida, Georgia, Indiana, New Brunswick, New Hampshire, Pennsylvania, Quebec, Rhode Island, South Dakota and Vermont as well as the Bristol shared by Tennessee and Virginia

britch: pickpocket's term—pocket; usually clearly defined as right britch or left britch—i.e., right-hand or left-hand pants pocket

Broadway Squad: New York City Police

Department group charged with the arrest of jostlers, flashers, etc.

broker: addict's term for a drug peddler

Bromberg: Nazi concentration camp in East Prussia close to the Vistula River

Bronx HTF: Bronx Homicide Task Force (New York City Police Department)

Brooklyn: Brooklyn Detention Center of the Immigration and Naturalization Service in New York City

Brooklyn HTF: Brooklyn Homicide Task Force (New York City Police Department)

brotel: hotel or motel that also functions as a brothel

brother officer: fellow policeman

brown: brownish heroin of Mexican origin; long-acting amphetamine sulfate capsule (sold in brown and other colors)

brown dope: brown or tan-colored heroin incompletely processed in Mexico

brown heroin trail: narcotics import route from Mexico to the United States

brownie: brown-capped amphetamine capsule such as a dexedrine spansule

Browning: American-designed automatic pistols now made in Belgium; Browning automatic rifle, designed by J.M. Browning, to fire 250 to 300 rounds per minute from its air-cooled barrel

Browning Gun Collection: located at 625 East 5300 South in Ogden, Utah's National Guard Armory; open to the public except on holidays

brown stuff: heroin made in Mexico; opium

brown sugar: Asian heroin (only 35 to 65 percent pure; often adulterated with substances such as caffeine and even the deadly poison strychnine)

Brownwood: State Home and School for Girls at Brownwood, Texas; Statewide Reception Center for Delinquent Girls at Brownwood, Texas

bruiser: brutish male

Brushes: Wormwood Scrubs Prison—*scrubs*, being the contraction of scrubbing brushes, explains the origin of this nickname for a London suburban penal facility

Brushy Mountain: Tennessee state prison, north of Knoxville and close to the Kentucky border and the Norris Dam

BSJ: *Baker Street Journal* (edited by Dr. Julian Wolff, 33 Riverside Drive, New York, NY 10023)

BSO: Black September Organization (q.v.)

BSP: Border Security Police (NATO); *Bureau de Sécurité Publique* (French—Bureau of Public Security) special police guarding buildings, communications facilities, highways, railways, etc.

BSS: British Security Service

BSSR: Bureau of Social Science Research

bt: bird turd—thus, inconsequential person; inconsequential remark

bto: big-time operator; gang chief

bt's: (prison) building tenders (porters, turnkeys, wing floor tenders, etc.)

bu: burglar(y)

bubble-gum machine: flashing or revolving light atop a police-patrol vehicle

bubblehead: champagne addict

bubble water: champagne

bubbling: killing by injecting air bubbles in the veins

bubbly: champagne

Büchenwald: Nazi concentration camp near Weimar, Germany where more than 100,000 persons from German-occupied countries died while working as slave laborers in nearby arms plants and quarries

bucket shop: office where nearly or completely worthless land or securities are promoted by mail or over the telephone (see also **telephone boiler room**)

buckle: belt-buckle knife designed to give service either as a buckle or as a knife

buffalo: bluff; deceive; swindle

Buffalo: Erie County Jail in Buffalo, N.Y.

bufotenine: intoxiccant snuff obtained from the pods and seeds of *Piptadenia peregrina*, a shrub found in northern South America and the West Indies

bug: auditory surveillance maintained by some electronic listening device; burglar-alarm protection; send to a mental hospital; firebug (arsonist or pyromaniac)

bughouse: insane asylum

bug trap: bed or cot in a jail or prison

build juice: ingratiate one's self

bull: police(man)

bullet: ace card; firearm projectile

bullet entrance wound: made by a bullet entering the body or head of the victim and leaving a neat round hole

bullet exit wound: made by a bullet leaving the body or the head of the victim; usually much larger than the bullet and often ragged or torn

bulletproof: bulletproof automobile (built to protect executives or dignitaries from bullets aimed at them by assassins); bulletproof document (free of legal loopholes); bulletproof vest (designed to protect the wearer from bullets)

bullets: capsules of heroin

bullhorn: hand-held voice-actuated loudspeaker (see also **bull roarer**)

bull jive: adulterated low-grade marijuana; bombastic statements

bull mastiff: powerful breed of guard dog

bullpen: common cell

bull roarer: electronic megaphone used to address crowds (see also **bullhorn**)

bummer: bad experience, especially a bad drug experience; bum customer

bumming: white-collar crime involving managers who forge company checks in favor of their personal accounts and then destroy the canceled checks when they are returned

bump-and-run: technique wherein two muggers run alongside an intended victim; as one knocks the victim to the sidewalk, the other snatches the victim's handbag or purse; then the muggers run away in opposite directions

bump off: murder

bum rap: undeserved arrest, conviction or reprimand

bum steer: false, inaccurate or misleading information

bum trip: unpleasant drug experience

bum wine: false or misleading information about drugs or drug pushers

Buna: forced-labor camp close to Auschwitz erected by the Nazis to aid in the production of artificial rubber also known as *Buna*

bunco artist: card sharper; confidence man or woman; swindler

bunco schemer: confidence man; professional swindler

bunco steer(ed): deliberately misdirect(ed) or misle(a)d

Bundeskriminalampt: (German—Central Criminal Council)—West German Interpol headquarters in Wiesbaden

bundle: bundle of bags of heroin; often a bundle contains 25 bags and is held together by a rubber band; pushers buy heroin by the bundle and then sell it to addicts a bag or two at a time

bundle of Benjies: bundle of $100 bills (see **Benjy**)

bun on: drunk; intoxicated

Bureau of Investigation: the FBI's forerunner, headed from 1921 to 1924 by Baltimore-born detective William J. Burns, who founded the Burns International Detective Agency, now known as Burns International Security Services Inc. (q.v.)

Bureau of Prisons: U.S. Department of Justice bureau administering U.S. penitentiaries, federal correctional institutions, and medical center for federal prisoners

burese: cocaine

burglarize: to break into, enter and steal

burglary: breaking into a building, home, office or other place where valuables are kept and entering it with the intent of stealing from it

burgle: burglarize

burgrep: burglary report

buried: serving a long sentence

burke: murder by suffocation (named for an Edinburgh murderer of the early 1800s, who sold his victims to anatomists, who needed cadavers to dissect for the instruction of medical students)

Burlington: Burlington County Jail east of Camden at Mount Holly, N.J.

burn: electrocute; smoke hashish or marijuana

burned: electrocuted; cheated, feeling cheated or wounded; wounded

burned out: debilitated and wasted away; prematurely aged

burn 'em: shoot them

burner: person cheating at games of chance

burnout: complete gutting by fire of an apartment, building, room or other enclosed space

Burns International Security Services Inc.: founded by William J. Burns in 1909; formerly called the Burns International Detective Agency

burn up the highway: indulge in dangerously fast driving

burpgun: small submachine gun

bury: betray a person to his or her enemies

bush parole: escape from confinement; escape from prison

bush smoke(r): marijuana smoke(r)

businessman's special: see **dimethyltryptamine**

bust: arrest or interrogation

bust a cap: fire a gun; take a narcotic

busthead: drunkard

busy air: airwaves cluttered with police or other radio calls (antonym of "quiet air," q.v.)

busy bee: another name for pcp or PCP (see **angel dust**)

Butcher of the Balkans: Andrija Artukovic, who ordered the death of thousands of Gypsies, Jews, and Serbs when he served as a minister in the Nazi puppet state of Croatia during World War II

Butcher of Lyons: Klaus Barbie, chief of police of Lyons during its German occupation, he arranged the deportation and massacre of thousands of Jews and others;

he was sentenced to life imprisonment in 1987

Butcher of Prague: Reinhard Heydrich—Hitler's Reichs-protektor of Bohemia

butchershop: hospital; operating room

butcherwagon: ambulance

Butner: Butner, N.C., near North Durham, site of the new mental health research center and the maximum-security prison built with escape-proof plastic window panes; although no gun towers surmount high walls, it is believed impossible for any prisoner to scale the two 12-foot-high fences separated by 20 feet of coiled barbed wire equipped with automatic sensors; prisoners are hard-to-rehabilitate repeat offenders compelled to work at prison jobs and to attend group discussions about all phases of prison life and outside life styles involving alcohol and drug abuse

butt: last period of a prisoner's sentence (may range from a few hours to a few weeks)

Butterworth: site of a Japanese prisoner-of-war camp close to Georgetown in Penang harbor where many Australians were held during World War II

buttlegger: person bootlegging cigarettes to avoid payment of taxes

button: peyote button

button man: low-ranking member of the syndicate given tasks such as beating people or taking their lives

Bu-Tyur: Butyrskaya Tyurma (Russian—Butyrki Prison)—a major prison in Moscow

Butyrskaya: north-central Moscow's block-long four-story prison hidden behind an eight-story department store on Novoslobodskaya Street; since czarist times common criminals as well as political prisoners have been held here for long periods of pretrial examination

buzz: ringing of the ears brought on by drugs or by being exposed to loud noises

buzzard: crochety, dirty or nasty old man

buzzed: arrested for a small charge

BVR: Bureau of Vocational Rehabilitation

BWC: Battered Women's Coalition

BWS: Battered Women's Service

bylow: big-bladed barlow-type knife often used as a weapon

bypass: wire device used by people who steal electric power by bypassing meters

by-the-hour hotel (or motel): place catering to the by-the-hour prostitution trade

C

C: abbreviation for cocaine; a hundred-dollar bill

ca: covert action

CAA: Congressional Assassination Act (q.v.)

caapi: caapi-vine tea (hallucinogen popular in Peru)

cabbage leaves: paper money

cab joint: whorehouse supplied with customers by taxicab drivers

CABLE: Computer-Assisted Bay Area Law Enforcement (q.v.)

CAC: Commission on Accreditation for Corrections

CACA: Central After-Care Association (British society handling prisoners on parole)

CACB: Council Against Cigarette Bootlegging

cache: (French—hiding place) place for concealing drugs, persons wanted by the police, stolen goods, etc.

CACJ: California Attorneys for Criminal Justice

cacodyl: garlic-like odoriferous poison used as an explosive because it ignites spontaneously in dry air; this is one of the deadliest and vilest substances mentioned in the *Anarchists Cookbook*

cactus: mescaline extracted from mescal or peyote

cactus juice: hard liquor

cadav: cadaver

cadaveric spasm: stiffening of the arms or hands at the time of death; persons who die with guns or knives in their hands will often clutch them tenaciously

cadet: new addict; pimp

CADPIN: Customs Automatic Data Processing Intelligence Network

cage: (a) jail; (to) imprison

CAGE: Convicts Association for a Good Environment

cage and key man: jailer; prison guard

calaboose: prison

CALEA: Commission of Accreditation for Law Enforcement Agencies

Caliente: the Nevada Girls Training Center correctional facility at Caliente

California Advocacy for Trollops: Los Angeles group advocating decriminalization of prostitution and legal protection of prostitutes

California Institute for Women: California's only state prison for women is also called Frontera as that is the name of the nearest town

California sunshine: LSD

callahan: policeman's nightstick

camarilla: cabal; clique; secret organization

Camarillo: Ventura Reception Center and Clinic at Camarillo, Calif.; the Ventura School for Girls at Camarillo, Calif.

camera eye: good witness with a memory for faces, facts and places

camisole: straitjacket (institutional euphemism)

CAMP: Campaign Against Marijuana Planting

camp: confinement and/or correctional facility, usually in a rural location

Campbellford: Ontario town containing the Warkworth Institution

Camp de Drancy: (French—Drancy Camp)—concentration and transit camp maintained by French collaborationists and the Gestapo in World War II in this northeastern suburb of Paris where many Jews and political prisoners died of malnutrition; survivors were shipped off to German and Polish camps where many more died in gas chambers

Camp Douglas: in the 1860s a prisoner-of-war camp near Lake Michigan and southwest of Holland, Michigan; many Confederates died here due to the cold and to inadequate nutrition

Campeche: prison in Campeche, capital of the state of Campeche, Mexico, located on the Yucatan peninsula, on the Bay of Campeche in the Gulf of Mexico

campfire boy: opium addict

Camp Iyar: prison camp in Israel where Adolf Eichmann was held while awaiting trial as a war criminal

Campo Alegre: Curaçao's red-light center close to the oil refineries and the port

Camp O'Donnell: American military encampment on Luzon in the Philippines where the survivors of the Bataan Death March were imprisoned during World War II by the Japanese

campus: nickname for prison grounds

Camp West Fork: juvenile correctional center near Warner Springs in southern California, close to San Diego

Camp Westway: juvenile detention center near Warner Springs, Calif.

CAMRC: Child Abuse and Maltreatment Reporting Center

Cam red: reddish-brown Cambodian marijuana

Cam trip: Cambodian trip weed (high-potency black marijuana from Cambodia)

can: one ounce of marijuana, also called a *lid*; a police station, with its detention cells

Canadian bouncer: seconal manufactured in Canada

Canadian black: Canadian-grown marijuana

canary: person who confesses or otherwise discloses information required by law-enforcement officers or other investigators

c & d: censorship and documents

c & h: cocaine and heroin

CANDLES: Children of Auschwitz Nazi's Deadly Lab Experiment Survivors

c & m: cocaine and morphine

candy: barbiturates

candyman: drug dealer

cane gun: steel walking stick concealing a deadly weapon

canhouse: whorehouse

canine shamus(es): dog detective(s)—used for their keen sense of smell in the war against drugs as well as in retrieving escaped prisoners

canna.: cannabinoid; cannabinol; cannabis

cannabinoids: compounds whose mind-altering effects resemble those produced by cannabis plants

cannabis: generic name for marijuana

Cannabis americana: low-grade marijuana grown in the United States and Canada

Cannabis indica: Indian hemp

Cannabis mexicana: marijuana commonly grown in many parts of Mexico

Cannabis sativa: botannical name for hemp or marijuana

cannabis tea: regular tea leaves boiled with those of a cannabis plant; also called *pot likker*

canned: intoxicated

canned sativa: hashish

cannery: prison of any kind

cannon: pickpocket

Canon City: Colorado Women's Correctional Institute at Canon City

can opener: tool used by safecrackers

Can Pen Ser: Canadian Penitentiary Service

cant: technical jargon; underworld language

cantharides: drug better known as Spanish fly, sometimes given to produce a supposed aphrodisiac effect

cantharidin: dangerous drug extracted from Spanish fly; used as an aphrodisiac

CANY: Correctional Association of New York (in New York City)

cap.: consumer account protection

cap: glycerine container used to hold narcotics and other drugs, notably LSD

CAP: Citizens Against Pornography; Community Advancement Program (providing nonresidential treatment for juvenile delinquents)

CAPE: California Association of Polygraph Examiners; Classification and Placement Examination

caper: criminal action, ranging from killing, robbing and setting fires to non-violent crimes

capital crimes: crimes punishable by death

capital punishment: the death penalty

CAPO: Chief Administrative Pharmaceutical Officer

Cap-Rouge: the Maison Notre-Dame de la Garde facility for juvenile delinquents at Cap-Rouge, Quebec

caps.: half bags of heroin capsules

captain: warden of a road prison with its road-gang guards and inmates

captured conversation: electronically recorded tape of conversation between two or more persons

capun: capital punishment

carbage: car-floor garbage (often contains bits of marijuana)

car bangers: thieves who steal from automobiles, recreational vehicles and trucks

Cárcel de Mujeres: (Spanish—Women's Prison—also name of the Instituto Nacional de Orientacion Femenina situated in los Teques Ejido Miranda in Venezuela

card mechanic: card cheat

cardsharp: person who cheats in card games

career criminal: individual who makes crime a way of life

CARES: Computer-Assisted Regional Evaluation System (q.v.)

cargo: load of drugs

Carl Gustaf: 9mm Swedish submachine gun

car-napper: automobile thief

carnie: carnival; carnival worker

carpet walker: long-time addict

carpilf: cargo pilferage

Carraca: La Carraca, Cadiz, Spain's infamous prison within its navy yard

carrie: cocaine

carrying: carrying drugs on one's person or in one's vehicle

carrying a heavy load: drunk

carry the difference: carry a concealed weapon

Carson: Nevada State Penitentiary in Carson City; Women's Prison in Carson City, Nev.

cartel: price-fixing agreement entered into by a number of parties and often controlled by a syndicate using legal or illegal means to gouge the public

car trap: automobile or automotive vehicle specially wired so that a bomb explodes when the engine is started

cartwheel: amphetamine tablet

CASA: Court-Appointed Special Advocate(s)

case knife: fishing or hunting knife carried in a leather or plastic case

caseload: total number of cases filed in a given court or before a given judicial officer during a given period of time

Casemates: Bermuda's prison island, formerly a fortress

case officer: espionage or law-enforcement officer supervising agents involved in a specific case

Caserta: women's prison just north of Naples, Italy

case the joint: (criminal slang) to survey a place before breaking in or holding it up; (law-enforcement term) to look a place over before entering to arrest its occupants

case note: one-dollar bill

casino: (Italian—little house) place where games of chance are played

casino cage: gambling establishment's control and security center where cash and chips are stored

Casino City: nickname shared by many gambling resorts, including not only Atlantic City, N.J. and Las Vegas, Nev. but also Freeport in the Bahamas, Macao in Portuguese China and Monte Carlo in Monaco

casketeer: racketeer undertaker who persuades the bereaved to order needlessly expensive caskets and funeral ceremonies

Castieau's hotel: nickname given the old jail in Melbourne, Victoria, Australia and honoring the jail's governor, JB Castieau

castor-bean poison: poison extracted from castor beans that is more deadly than cobra venom (see also **castored**)

castored: killed with a pinhead-size castorbean pellet shot from the tip of a cane, swagger stick or umbrella at close range

casual criminals: occasional criminals who most often are sane, law-abiding citizens who do not commit crimes for profit but to fulfill some pressing need

casusa: potent alcoholic drink made in Latin America by distilling chicha, an alcoholic fruit or grain fermentation

cat: boy or man; cat-o'-nine tails (whip used for flogging; traditionally made of nine knotted rawhide thongs attached to a handle)

CAT: California Advocacy for Trollops (q.v.)

cat burglars: thieves adept at breaking into and entering even "burglarproof" buildings by means of ropes and scaling ladders

catchup: drug-withdrawal process

Catete: former royal palace used as Rio de Janeiro's immigration prison

Catholic aspirin: amphetamine tablets bearing a cross-shaped scoring

cathouse: old-fashioned nickname for a brothel, especially a low-priced one

cattle prod: electric device often used to control violent people in mobs and riots

CAU: Child Abuse Unit (of police departments in many large metropolitan centers)

caught in a snowstorm: under the influence of cocaine

CBCII: California Bureau of Criminal Identification and Investigation

CBI: Central Bureau of Investigation

CBIS: Communist Bloc Intelligence Service

CBNE: California Bureau of Narcotics Enforcement

CB Radio Patrol: 30,000 citizen's band radio operators united to promote safety and discourage crime by means of a volunteer radio patrol

cbu: cluster bomb unit

cc: condemned cell

CC: Chief Constable; Circuit Court; County of City

CCA: California Correctional Association

CCB: Criminal Courts Building (New York)

CCC: Central Community Center (q.v.); Central Criminal Court; Crime and Correction Commission; Crime and Correction Committee; Customs Cooperation Council (to control smuggling and facilitate trade)

CCCJ: California Council on Criminal Justice

CCCP: Citizens Crime Commission of Philadelphia

CCCR: Center for Crime Control Research

CCD: Circuit Court Decision(s)

CCD: Criminal Conspiracy Division (q.v.)

CCD&C: Commission on Crime, Delinquency, and Corrections (Nevada)

CCETSW: Central Council for Education and Training of Social Workers

CCH: Computerized Criminal History (FBI's data file)

CCHS: Computerized Criminal Histories System (FBI)

CCI: Coastal Correctional Institution at Garden City, Georgia close to Savannah and the Savannah River; Connecticut Correctional Institution at Niantic on Long Island Sound

CCIB: Computerized Central Information Bank (q.v.)

CCINC: Cabinet Committee for International Narcotic Control

CCIPT: Canadian Center for Investigation and Prevention of Torture

CCJ: Center for Correctional Justice (Harvard Law School); Center for Criminal Justice (Washington, D.C.); Circuit Court Judge; Cook County Jail (Chicago); County Court Judge

CCOA: California Correctional Officers Association; County Court Officers Association

CCPC: Community Crime Prevention Center

CCPOA: California Correctional Peace Officers Association

CCPOST: California Commission on Peace Officer Standards and Training

CCPS: Certified Crime Prevention Specialist

CCR: Center for Constitutional Rights

CCRB: Civilian Complaint Review Board (of the New York City Police Department)

CCRKBA: Citizens Committee for the Right to Keep and Bear Arms

C Cr P: Code of Criminal Procedure

CCTF: California Correctional Training Facility

cctv: closed-circuit television (used in many banks and other public places as a security system)

ccu (CCU): correctional custody unit (q.v.)

ccw: carrying a concealed weapon

CCW: Citizens Crime Watch

CD: Corrections Department (New Mexico); Corrections Division (Hawaii, Oregon)

CDAP: Civil Defense Auxiliary Police

CDC: California Department of Corrections

CDC: Criminal Diagnostics and Counseling

cddd: comprehensive dishonesty, disappearance, and destruction (insurance policy)

CDJ: California Department of Justice

cdo (CDO): chronic drunkenness offender

CDRI: Central Drug Research Institute

CDS: Community Dispute Services

CDU: Civil Disobedience Unit

cdv: cadaver

ce: counterespionage (q.v.)

CEA: Captain's Endowment Association (police); Correctional Education Association

CEC: Correctional Economics Center (q.v.)

cecil: cocaine

cee: cocaine

Celery City Clink: Kalamazoo, Michigan's jail

celintrep: accelerated intelligence report

cement coffin: gangster invention consisting of fast-setting cement mixed in a bucket or tub big enough for a person to stand in; when the mix hardens the victim is dumped into a harbor, lake, river or swamp and the body disappears from sight

cement tomb: prison cell

centac: central tactical report (filed by law-enforcement officers)

Center City Detention Center: the Eastern State Penitentiary at 21st and Fairmount Avenue in Philadelphia, Pa.

center of mass: FBI term referring to the upper torso, where the heart, lungs and several arteries—all vital to life and thus lethal targets—are located

Central: North Carolina's Central Prison at Raleigh

Central Community Center: halfway house for released prisoners in Los Angeles

Central Detention Facility: District of Columbia's modern maximum-security prison, opened in 1976 and enlarged in 1980, for detainees and sentenced misdemeanants in Washington, D.C.

Centralia: the Maple Lane School for Juvenile delinquents at Centralia, Wash.

central nervous system depressants: alcohol, barbiturates (q.v.), nonbarbiturate sedatives (q.v.)

central nervous system stimulants: amphetamines (q.v.), caffeine, cocaine (q.v.), nicotine (q.v.)

century: $100 bill

CETHV: Council for the Education and Training of Health Visitors

CFA: Correctional Facilities Association

CFB: Consumer's Fraud Bureau

CFI: Committee on Foreign Intelligence (CIA)

C-4: anti-Castro Cubans who use terrorist tactics in their struggle to wrest Cuba from communist control

CG: Coast Guard

CGIC: Comisaria General de Investigacion Criminal (Spanish—Comissariat General of Criminal Investigation) Spain's Interpol headquarters in Madrid

C-girl: call girl

chain drinker: person who consumes one drink after another

chain and Ts: steel chain fitted with steel Ts at either end, used as nippers to restrain unruly prisoners; as the Ts are twisted, the chain applies increasing pressure on the prisoner's wrists

chain gang: convicts chained together during periods of outdoor work or transportation

chair: the electric chair

chalk: amphetamine tablets

chamber: the gas chamber

chamber music: off-the-record meeting of contending attorneys in a judge's chambers where they arrange for the accused to plead guilty to a minor charge and thereby save the cost of a time-consuming trial

champagne: nickname a call girl gives anyone who pays more than $100 for her services

Changi: Up Changi Road (Singapore's maximum-security prison)

channel: vein used for injecting a drug

Chaos: CIA's nickname for domestic security files and operations

charge: an injection of a narcotic drug; a marijuana cigarette

charged up: under the influence of drugs

charles: old nickname for cocaine

Charlestown: Charlestown, Mass. jail (where anarchists Sacco and Vanzetti were electrocuted Aug. 23, 1927)

charley coke: cocaine

charras: (Pushtu—hashish) smoking hemp of the type produced in Pakhtunistan, Pakistan

Charter Arms: American manufacturer of firearms, including the smallest, lightest .38-caliber special revolver

chaser: prison guard

chasing the bag: addicted to a drug

Château d'If: island prison off the port of Marseilles in the Mediterranean and the place where the *Man in the Iron Mask* and *The Count of Monte Cristo* were imprisoned

CHC: Chicago House of Correction

C-head: coke head (cocaine addict); user of LSD sugar cubes

CHEC: Citizens Helping Eliminate Crime

check bouncer: person writing checks not covered by supporting deposits

check fraud: issuance or passing of a check, draft or money order, signed by the legal account holder, with the foreknowledge that the bank or depository will refuse to honor it because the account has been closed or has insufficient funds

check out: commit suicide

Checks: Checks Anonymous (society for the rehabilitation of convicted check bouncers); Nebraska Penal and Correctional Complex, Lincoln, Neb.

Cheesebox: penitentiary at Statesville, Ill.

Chelmo: Nazi concentration camp near Lublin, Poland where some ninety thousand prisoners died during World War II

Chemical Shield: trade name for a disabling chemical spray available to law-enforcement officers in one-inch-wide, six-inch-long canisters; its use temporarily blinds and chokes its targets, such as rioters

cheracol: cough syrup containing codeine

Cherry Hill: nickname of the Philadelphia prison opened in 1829 on the site of an old cherry orchard; this was the historic Eastern Penitentiary designed to insure the solitary confinement of each of its many prisoners

Chetumal: prison in Ciudad Chetumal, capital of the Mexican territory of Quintana Roo, on the Caribbean coast at the border with Belize

Chicago leprosy: hypodermic-needle-induced abscesses

Chicago overcoat: coffin (mobster term dating from the 1920s)

Chicago piano: machine gun

Chicagorilla: Chicago-based gangster

Chicago style: gangster style

chicha: Latin American alcoholic drink made from fermented fruit or grain

chicken powder: amphetamine powder

chicken ranch: brothel

chickenshit: too small to be worthwhile

chicken queen: adult male homosexual engaging in homosexual activities with boys

chief: LSD

chief fence: another name for master fence (q.v.)

Chihuahua: prison in Chihuahua, capital of the northern Mexican state of the same name

child abndmnt: child abandonment

child abuse: physical mistreatment of children

child neglect: willful failure by the person(s) responsible for a child's well-being to provide education, clothing, food, shelter and supervision

child porn: pornography featuring children

Chillicothe: Training School for Girls at Chillicothe, Mo.; Chillicothe Correctional Institute at Chillicothe, Ohio (for males receiving psychiatric treatment)

chillum: Indian-style cylindrical pipe held vertically; used for smoking hashish

Chilpancingo: prison in the capital city of the Mexican state of Guerrero

Chinese connection: Chinese controlled and operated narcotic smuggling, extending from the Golden Triangle (q.v.) and Hong Kong to Amsterdam and to U.S., Canadian, Central American and Mexican airports and seaports

Chinese joint: Sing Sing, so nicknamed because of the pidgin-Chinese sound of its name

Chinese molasses: opium

Chinese saxophone: opium pipe

Chinese tobacco: opium

Chino: California Institution for Men at Chino; Chinese drug dealer

chins.: children in need of supervision

Ch Insp: Chief Inspector

chip: injecting drugs under the skin instead of into a vein

chipper(s): addict(s) who take drugs by injection under the skin instead of into the veins

chippie: prostitute

chippie joint: whorehouse

chipping: using drugs occasionally

chips: money

chips.: children in need of protection and services

CHiPs: California Highway Patrol cops (sometimes called Chippies by California motorists)

chirp: inform

chisel: cheat

chloracetophenone: tear gas

chloral hydrate: hypnotic or sedative, also known as trichloroacetaldehyde, but more popularly as joy juice, knockout drops or mickey finn

chlorethylmercaptan: highly-toxic substance used by Soviet authorities interested in war gases

chocolate chips: LSD

choke hold: device for handling unruly prisoners

chokey: punishment cell; solitary confinement

choky: (English slang—jail)—term believed to be derived from the Hindustani *chauki*, also meaning jail

cholley: cocaine

Cholo Town: nickname given to many Mexican-American ghettos

chopper: helicopter

chop shop: shop where criminals dismantle stolen vehicles and sell the parts for more than the original cost of the vehicles

chow hall: prison mess hall

chow line: prisoners lined up while waiting to be served food

CHP: California Highway Patrol

CHPA: California Highway Patrol Academy

Christianstadt: Nazi subcamp in what is now East Germany

Christmas trees: tuinal (composed of amobarbital and secobarbital)

chronophobia: fear of time (common psychiatric disorder among prisoners)

Ch Supt: Chief Superintendent

chuck horrors: big appetite in addicts who have stopped using narcotics

Chula Vista: Chula Vista Staging Center of the Immigration and Naturalization Service at San Ysidro, Calif., overlooking the Mexican border; many undocumented aliens are held there pending deportation

Chuna: Soviet forced-labor camp in Siberia about 150 miles (600 kilometers) from Bratsk and close to Kondratyevo on the river Chuna

chunk: hashish chunk

church key: one-piece can opener consisting of a metal handle terminating in a sharp-pointed triangular head, sometimes used by burglars as a jimmy

ci (CI): counterintelligence

ci: criminal informant

c-i: criminal investigation

CIA: Central Intelligence Agency; Correctional Industries Association

CIB: Central Intelligence Board; Criminal Identification Bureau; Criminal Intelligence Bureau; Criminal Investigation Bureau

CIC: Criminal Investigation Command (U.S. Army)

CICC: Criminal Injuries Compensation Commission

CID: Criminal Investigation Division (of many police departments)

CIEC: *Centre International d'Etudes Criminologiques* (French—International Center of Criminological Studies); located in Paris

cigarette-box bomb: bomb concealed in a cardboard cigarette box that explodes when anyone attempts to open it

cig gun: 22-caliber handgun concealed in a cigarette lighter

cig smug: cigarette smuggler, who smuggles cigarettes across national or state boundaries to avoid paying cigarette taxes

c-i info: criminal-investigation information

cins (CINS): children in need of supervision (see also **pins.**)

CIP: Citizens Involvement Project (q.v.)

CIPT: Canadian Institute for the Prevention of Torture

circumorbital hematoma: medical name for a black eye

circus grifting: type of short confidence game played with a circus as its background

CISC: Commission for Investigation of Special Crimes

CIT: Counterintelligence Team

Citizens Crime Watch: neighborhood non-profit organization in southern Florida that cooperates with local police by reporting crimes in progress, including details about crimes and suspects; has more than 75,000 members

Citizens Involvement Project: program to train civic leaders and sheriffs in the use of volunteers in jails

City College: slang for The Tombs prison in downtown New York City, close to the Criminal Courts

city watchhouse: police station; police station lockup

CIU: Criminal Intelligence Unit (police)

Ciudad Acuña: jail in Coahuila, Mexico, across the Rio Grande from Del Rio, Texas

Ciudad Victoria: prison in Ciudad Victoria, capital of the Mexican state of Tamaulipas south of Texas and the Rio Grande

Civic Center: Civic Center Jail in San Jose, Calif.

CIW: California Institution for Women at Frontera

CJ: Chief Justice; Civil Jail; Court of Judiciary

CJIE: Criminal Justice Information Exchange

CJIS: Criminal Justice Information System (Rhode Island)

C-joint: cocaine joint (place where cocaine is sold)

CKCJP: Center for Knowledge in Criminal Justice Planning

clam up: parry questions by refusing to talk

clandestine: conducted in secrecy

clandestine operations: intelligence term for the secret collection of information required by policy makers, also called espionage or covert actions

Clandestine Services: Directorate of Plans (CIA)

clanks: dt's (delirium tremens)

clap joint: brothel

CLAPS: Criminal Law and Public Safety

Clarkson Avenue: Kings County Hospital Prison Ward at 451 Clarkson Ave., Brooklyn, N.Y.

CLASP: Citizens Local Alliance for a Safer Philadelphia

class As: class-A drugs (addictive drugs such as opium and its derivatives)

class Bs: class-B drugs (slightly addictive drugs such as codeine)

classification center: unit within a correctional institution, or a separate facility, holding persons in custody while determining the correctional facility or program to which they should be committed

class Ms: class-M drugs (non-addictive drugs)

class-X crimes: armed violence of any sort

class Xs: class-X drugs (drugs such as cough syrups that contain almost non-addictive codeine)

clay pigeon: easy target

CLC: Citizens Legal Council

clean: not addicted; not carrying or hiding narcotics or stolen property; not in possession of firearms or other weapons; not involved in illegal enterprises such as prostitution; not wanted by the police or other law-enforcement officers

CLEAN: Commonwealth Law Enforcement Assistance Network (q.v.)

cleanskin: person without a criminal record

clean up: to break the narcotics habit

cleanup: attempt by police or vice squad to reduce crime in a specific area

CLEAR: County Law Enforcement Applied Regionally (q.v.)

cleared up: no longer addicted to drugs

clear light: trade name used by pushers of high-quality LSD also called window pane or windowpane acid

clear liquid: liquid LSD

CLEMARS: California Law-Enforcement Mutual-Aid Radio System

Clementina: nickname of the San Michele reformatory for boys 14 to 18; built in the time of Pope Clement XI (1700-1721) on Rome's Piazza di Porta Portese and still in use

cleptobiosis: aggressive stealing like that that often occurs during metropolitan blackouts (see also **lestobiosis**)

cleptomania(c): variant spellings of kleptomania(c)

CLES: Customs Law-Enforcement Service

CLETS: California Law Enforcement Telecommunications System

CLF: Chicano Liberation Front

client(s): person(s) on probation

client(s) of the correctional system: convict(s)

clink: jail

Clink: euphoniously named London prison formerly dominating the south bank of the Thames near London Bridge, where it was a well-known landmark in the days of Hogarth and Dickens; not only the generic nickname for all prisons but for brothels and the Southwark Fair depicted by Hogarth; only its name survives at its site on Clink Street

Clinton: Clinton Correctional Facility (for males) at Dannemora, N.Y.; Correctional Institution for Women at Clinton, N.J.

clip: metallic or plastic device for holding a series of cartridges so that they may be inserted easily into the magazine of a firearm; to take money from someone, especially a customer; roach clip (device for holding a marijuana cigarette so that it can be smoked to the end without burning the smoker's fingers)

clip artist: professional swindler

clip joint: place where customers are habitually overcharged and shortchanged

clipped: arrested

CLMDC: Citizens Legal, Medical, Dental Council

close call: narrow escape from being arrested, killed, robbed, etc.

close custody: constant supervision of prisoners likely to escape

CLSP: Center for Law and Social Policy

cluster bomb: lethal device, which when actuated springs open to release smaller bombs containing metal splinters or napalm gas or both

CM: Court Martial

CMP: Commissioner of the Metropolitan Police

CMS: Correctional Medical Systems

CN: chloroacetophenone (tear gas)

CNAEA: California Narcotic Addict Evaluation Authority

CND: Commission of Narcotic Drugs (United Nations)

CN-DM: combination of tear and vomiting gas

CNIN: California Narcotic Information Network

CNOA: California Narcotics Officers Association

CNPB: Canadian National Parole Board

CO: correctional officer

COA: Correctional Officers Association

Coalition of National Liberation Brigades: leftist Haitian terrorists

Coalition On Police: left-wing group dedicated to hampering police work

Coast Guard: naval force that combats smuggling as well as aiding vessels in distress; has jurisdiction over the construction and equipment of merchant ships as well as the licensing of their officers and seamen

coasting: enjoying a drug; feeling relaxed

coast-to-coast: long-acting amphetamine-sulfate capsules (available in many colors)

COB: Chief of Base (CIA)

cobbler: forger of birth certificates, paper money, passports, etc.

COBRAY: Cobra + Moray (anti-terrorist academy near Powder Springs, Ga.)

coca: leafy bush grown in the highlands of Java and in such Andean lands as Bolivia, Chile and Peru, where Indians mix the leaves with bird dung, cornstarch and lime and chew the mixture to release the cocaine it contains

cocaine: powerful stimulant drug

cocaine cowboys: drug smugglers, so nicknamed because bloody battles sometimes accompany the smuggling of drugs from across the border and overseas into the United States

cocainomania: craving for cocaine

cocaports: cocaine ports of South America

Code 4: no further assistance required

codeine: depressant drug often found in cough medicines; use sometimes causes nausea and stupor as well as pinpointing of the eye pupils

code name: cover name used by an informant, a secret operative or another wishing to conceal his or her identity

Code Napoleon: the French civil code promulgated during the reign of Napoleon, detailing all crimes and their punishments

Code of Hammurabi: Babylonian legal code compiled during the reign of Hammurabi, around 1950 B.C.; perhaps the oldest legal code, it emphasized the law of retaliation (an eye for an eye and a tooth for a tooth)

Code 7: time out to eat

Code 3: emergency call; proceed immediately using red or blue lights and siren

Code 2: urgent call; proceed immediately but without siren; red or blue lights optional

coffee: LSD; "*let's get some coffee*" is sometimes used as code language meaning *let's get some LSD*

coin: to counterfeit coins, paper money, securities, etc.

COINTELPRO: FBI-directed Counterintelligence Program

coke: cocaine

coked: intoxicated by cocaine

coked up: intoxicated by cocaine

coke-head: cocaine addict

cokesmoke: cocaine smoker; cocaine smoking

cokie: cocaine addict

colchicine: dangerous drug that asphyxiates its victims by paralyzing their muscles

cold and hot: cocaine and heroin mixture

cold busted: arrested for some crime such as drunken driving or vagrancy while carrying addictive drugs (see also **hot busted**)

cold meat: dead body or bodies

cold-meat box: coffin

cold turkey: abrupt or sudden withdrawal from alcohol, cigarettes or drugs

Colima: prison in Colima, Mexico

collabo: collaborator

collapsed veins: condition caused by excessively frequent injections; common among drug addicts

collar: arrest

college: reformatory

Collins Bay: Canadian penitentiary at Kingston, Ontario

Colombian: Colombian-grown marijuana, prized for its potency

Colombian Commandos: Colombian-trained pickpockets and shoplifters, active in many large coastal cities in the United States

Colombian connection: nickname for the network of Colombian brokers, farmers, gangsters, politicians and smugglers connected with the export of Colombian-grown cocaine and marijuana to Canada and the United States

Colorguard: trade name for a fabric-coated, pre-galvanized steel fencing system, which the Colorguard Corporation of Raritan, New Jersey claims cannot be penetrated by gun muzzles, knives, or rocks

Colt: Colt Firearms (q.v.); Colt pistol; Colt revolver

Colt Firearms: Colt Industries subsidiary engaged in the manufacture of firearms

Colt .45: Colt .45 automatic pistol or revolver

Columbus: Columbus Workhouse and Women's Correctional Institution in Columbus, Ohio

Com: Commissioner; Police Commissioner

combat-survival: appellation attached to many fighting knives

combat zone: section of downtown Boston, Mass., given over to use by massage parlors, pornographic bookstores and movie theaters, strip-tease bars and the like

Combinado: Combinado del Este (large prison outside Havana, Cuba)

combination guns: see **Savage combination** and **turkey gun**

combo: combination gun; safe, vault or padlock combination

combo lock: combination lock

come clean: confess; tell the whole story

Cominform: Communist Information Bureau (successor to the Communist International)

coming down: physical and emotional condition brought about as the effects of a drug wear off

comint (COMINT): communications intelligence

Comintern: Communist International Organization (q.v.)

commitment: admission of an adjudicated and sentenced adult, delinquent or status offender into a correctional facility

Commo: Office of Communications (CIA)

Commonwealth Law Enforcement Assistance Network: Pennsylvania's cumputerized file on criminals

Communist Combat Squads: offshoot of Italy's better-known Red Bregades

Communist International Organization: Moscow-directed organization active in aiding subversion of governments that oppose Soviet foreign policy

community facility: adult, juvenile or non-confinement facility from which residents are allowed to depart, unaccompanied by any official, to hold or seek employment or to go to school or treatment programs

Community Treatment Centers: halfway houses of the U.S. Bureau of Prisons, located in Atlanta, Ga.; Chicago, Ill.; Dallas, Texas; Detroit, Mich.; Houston, Texas; Kansas City, Mo.; Los Angeles, Calif.; New York, N.Y.; Oakland, Calif.; and Phoenix, Ariz.

comp (COMP): complainant

companionate crime: crime committed by two or more persons against another (as in a holdup or a mugging)

Company: euphemism for the Central Intelligence Agency (CIA)

company girl: call girl who is available to keep men company; some are paid to board cruise ships and overseas charter flights to entertain passengers

comparison microscope: optical device used by ballistic experts to identify bullets; if, when the ends of two bullets are brought together in a single fused image, their striations match, both were fired from the same weapon

compash: compassionate probation officer, prison chaplain or social worker

Compiègne: French concentration camp northeast of Paris controlled by the Gestapo during the years of German occupation in World War II

complaint: formal written accusation made by any person, often a prosecutor, and filed in a court, alleging that a specified person or persons committed an offense or offenses

compound a felony: accept a bribe or other valuable consideration in exchange for not prosecuting a felon (which is in itself a felony)

compulsive gambler: person who is addicted to gambling, much as alcoholics are addicted to alcohol

Computer-Assisted Bay Area Law Enforcement: criminal data file maintained by the police of San Francisco, Calif.

Computer-Assisted Regional Evaluation System: criminal data file kept in Massachusetts

computer cleaner: white-collar criminal adept at cleansing computer files, for a price, of unfavorable information regarding the character or the financial credit of others

Computerized Central Information Bank: system used by New York City Police Department to identify, track and arrest criminals with known records

comsab: communist sabotage; communist saboteur

con: confidence man; convict; to steer someone into a confidence scheme; consenting adult

con artist: person adept at making another believe almost anything

Conciergerie: (French—porter's lodge)— the great prison of Paris on the Ile de la Cité founded in 1392

Concord: New Hampshire State Prison at Concord

concrete overcoat: see **cement coffin**

concrete womb: prison

Condemned Rock: Macquarie Island, Tasmania's nickname for Grummet Island when it was a penitentiary for desperate criminals

conditional release: parole

confetti: machine-gun bullets

confinee: .prisoner

con game: confidence game; swindle

Congressional Assassination Act: law that makes killing or plotting to kill a member of Congress a federal crime

con job: swindle

conjugal visit: arrangement allowing a prisoner to enjoy a marital relationship with a spouse

conk a screw: club a guard

con man: confidence man; swindler

connect: to buy drugs; to find a call girl

CONNECT: Connecticut On-Line Enforcement Communication and Teleprocessing (computerized file on criminals)

connection: person receiving drugs from drug wholesalers and passing them along to smaller dealers or purchasers, at a considerable profit

Connoisseurs in Murder: see **Society of Connoisseurs in Murder**

conspiracy: agreement between two or more persons to commit any crime, or to indict another falsely and maliciously for any crime, or to commit any act injurious to public health and morals, or to pervert or obstruct justice

conspiracy of concealment: efforts to conceal or cover up any evidence of crime or wrongdoing

constructive sentence: sentence created to make the punishment fit the crime (as in San Diego, where juvenile criminals who snatched purses from elderly women were sentenced to work in convalescent homes for the aged)

contact: drug supplier; to meet someone to buy, sell or transmit some contraband, drug or secret information

contraband: smuggled goods, such as diamonds, narcotics, etc.

contract: (underworld one-word symbol—contract to murder) depending on the importance of the person to be murdered, a contract may cost from $50 to $50,000 or more; contracts to kill have also been repaid by favors as well as money

control unit: prison-within-a-prison solitary-confinement cell

Controlled Substances Act: law controlling the distribution of drugs prone to abuse

convict: person found guilty of a felony and confined in a federal or state confinement facility

convict goods: things produced by convict labor (automotive-vehicle license plates, mail sacks, school benches, etc.)

conviction: judgment of a court, based either on the verdict of a judicial officer or a jury or on the guilty plea of a defendant, that the defendant is guilty of the offense(s) for which he or she has been tried

convictional criminal: person whose ethical, religious, political or social ideas drive him or her to crime

convict labor: work performed by prisoners as part of their program of rehabilitation

con wise: wise convict (well-informed convict who knows what's going on behind prison walls; person wise to illicit operations within prison confines)

CoO (COO): Chief of Outpost (CIA)

cook: prepare drugs; prepare heroin by cooking or dissolving it before injecting it; smoke hashish or marijuana

cooker: small receptacle in which heroin is dissolved

coolie mud: low-grade opium

coon killer: (Ku Klux Klan slang) blackjack; bludgeon

coop: prison

coozie stash: drugs protected by a rubber balloon or a condom and inserted in the vagina to facilitate smuggling

cop: to buy drugs; to steal; nickname for policemen, as in the mid-19th century they wore large copper stars on their uniforms

COP: Coalition On Police (q.v.)

cop a broom: to leave in a hurry, like a witch atop a broom

cop a deuceway: buy a two-dollar packet of drugs

cop a drill: to leave at walking pace

cop a heel: to escape from the police or prison

cop a moke: escape from a correctional facility

cop a plea: to plead guilty to a lesser offense than that with which one is charged, and hence receive a lighter sentence than one would be liable to if he or she were to plead innocent and then be found guilty

cop a sneak: leave a place

cop a squat: to sit down

cop house: police headquarters; police station

copilot: person staying with another who has taken some drug such as LSD

copilots: amphetamines; dexedrine tablets

copman: supplier of narcotics

cop out: to rely on alibis, apologies, evasions and excuses

copper: policeman

Copper John: Auburn Prison near Syracuse, N.Y.

coppershop: police station

COPS: Concerns of Police Survivors

COPS: California Organization of Police and Sheriffs; Chief of Operations (CIA)

core city: congested and often depressed downtown area of any city (sometimes called the inner city)

corinne: cocaine

corn: corn whiskey (especially cheap whiskey)

corn mule: corn whiskey of mule-kick strength

Cornton Vale: Scottish prison

Corona: California Rehabilitation Center at Corona

coroner: medical examiner charged with determining the cause of any death where there is reason to believe the cause was not natural

corporal punishment: physical chastisement

correctional agency: federal, state or local criminal-justice agency charged with the investigation, intake screening, supervision, custody, confinement or treatment of adjudicated or alleged offenders

correctional custody facility: euphemism for brig, jail, etc.

correctional custody unit: U.S. naval euphemism for a ship's brig or jail

correctional day program: publicly financed and operated non-residential educational or treatment program for persons required, by a judicial officer, to participate

Correctional Development Centre: maximum-security facility in Laval, Québec

Correctional Education Association: publisher of quarterly *Journal of Correctional Education*

correctional facility: area(s), building(s) or structure(s) operated by a government agency for the custody and/or treatment of persons adjudicated and committed in criminal or juvenile court proceedings

correctional institution: generic name for long-term confinement facilities

correctional officer: prison guard

correctional restitution: requirement that criminals at liberty after punishment make restitution to their victims through work, thus making the criminals responsible for the society in which they live; Prof. Stephen Schafer advanced this concept in 1958; it is applied in restitution centers in Georgia, Iowa and Minnesota

Correctional Service Federation: U.S. representative of the International Prisoners Aid Association

correctional training school: modern term for reformatory

corrections caseload: total number of clients registered with a correctional agency or agent during a specified time period

corrective labor camp: euphemism for forced-labor camp of the type described by Solzhenitsyn in *The Gulag Archipelago*

Corrective Services: all of the gaols (jails) and prisons in Australia's New South Wales, managed by the Department of Corrective Services in Sydney

corrine: cocaine

corsair: pirate; politician of the sea, according to Ambrose Bierce's *Devil's Dictionary*

CORU: *Coordinacion de Organizaciones Revolucionarias Unidas* (Spanish—Coordination of United Revolutionary Organizations) anti-Castro underground operating in Latin America and the United States

CoS (COS): Chief of Station (CIA officer in charge of an overseas office)

CO(s): Correction Officer(s); Correctional Officer(s)

cosmetic surgery: plastic surgery; sometimes used to change a person's essential identity so that he or she finds it easier to elude the police

'cotics: narcotics

CO_2 gun: carbon-dioxide-activated gun; sometimes called an airgun

couch doctor: psychiatrist

count: prison population inventory taken as often as nine times a day to insure security and help detect escapes

counterespionage: detection and frustration of enemy espionage

counterfeit: to manufacture or attempt to manufacture a copy or imitation of a negotiable instrument with a value set by law or convention, or to possess such a copy without authorization, with the intent to defraud by claiming the genuineness of the copy; counterfeit items include bonds, coins, currency, food stamps, postage stamps and similar negotiables

counterforce cars: heavily armored, highpower automobiles, providing executives some security from terrorists

counterinsurgency: military action planned to oppose guerrilla underground efforts

counterintelligence: thwarting the intelligence activities of a foreign power attempting to gain information or to engage in sabotage

county cooler: county-supported mental hospital, often housing the criminally insane

county hotel: county jail

County Law Enforcement Applied Regionally: Cincinnati, Ohio's computerized file on criminals

county mounty: county police; sheriff's officer

courage pills: barbiturate pills; sedatives

cover: plausible false identity that gives an agent or undercover spy some good reason for being where he or she may be or doing whatever he or she may be doing

covert operations: intelligence community term meaning the undertaking of programs assisting policy makers in carrying out their policies

cover up: conceal evidence of crime; whitewash

cow: dilapidated prostitute

Cowansville: Quebec penitentiary at the town of the same name on the Yamaska River

Coxsackie: Coxsackie Correctional Facility, a medium-security prison in Coxsackie, N.Y., just south of Albany

COYOTE: Call Off Your Old Tired Ethics (organization urging legalization of prostitution)

Cp: Caucasian pimp; Chicano pimp; Chinese pimp

c-p a: cattle-prod approach (use of electric-shock batons to control crowds in mob situations)

CPA: Connecticut Prison Association

CPAS: Catholic Prisoners'-Aid Society

CPC: Crime Prevention Coalition

CPD: Chicago Police Department; county probation department

C-P D L: Christian-Patriots Defense League

CPF: Commonwealth Police Force

cpi (CPI): constitutionally psychopathic inferior (type of criminal)

CPIC: Canadian Police Information Centre

CPL: Council of Prison Locals

CPOA: California Peace Officers Association

CPPCA: California Probation, Parole, and Correctional Association

CPS: Canadian Penitentiary Service

CPSM: Colonial Prison Service Medal (British decoration)

CPU: Crime Prevention Unit (of any law-enforcement organization, such as a sheriff's office or a police department)

CPUSA: Communist Party of the United States of America

cr (CR): conditional release (parole)

CR: Cost Rican marijuana (Costa Rica is a major source of the drug; from there it is distributed throughout the Caribbean, Central American and many other parts of the Western Hemisphere, including Canada and the United States)

crack: neither an abbreviation nor an acronym but the name of a high-potency cocaine making a crackling sound when smoked; east-coast name for this deadly drug called *rock* on the west coast of the United States

crack: to break open a door, safe, vault or window; to falter emotionally and become mentally unbalanced; a whore

crack down: censure; descend upon; punish

cracked ice: diamonds

'cracker: safecracker

crackling shorts: breaking into automobiles for the purpose of stealing them or their contents

cracks: arrests

cracksman: burglar; housebreaker

crank: nickname for methamphetamine—a mind-altering drug

crank freak: person who is dependent on pills for digesting, evacuating, sleeping, staying awake, etc.

cranks: amphetamines

cranky hatch: cell reserved for mentally deranged prisoner(s)

Cranston: Adult Correctional Institution at Cranston, R.I. Juvenile Diagnostic Center at Cranston, R.I.

crap: low-quality drugs

crapehanger: mortician; undertaker

crapola: insincere conversation; misleading advertising

crap out: avoid or shirk responsibility

crapper dick: detective who searches public toilets for people engaged in illicit sexual activities or sales of illegal drugs

crash: escape from a prison or another correctional facility; fall asleep from the effects of alcohol or drugs; withdraw suddenly from alcohol or another drug

crash pad: bed; place to spend the night

crater: disfigurement resulting from repeated injections with hypodermic needles, which causes the skin over the vein to resemble a crater

crazy alley: cell block reserved for the mentally deranged

crazy hospital: psychiatric ward

CRC: California Rehabilitation Center (for drug addicts)

CRD: Civil Rights Division, U.S. Department of.Justice

creative conflict: euphemism for demonstration or riot

creative punishment: making the punishment fit the crime, the defendant and society

creative sentence: sentence created to fit the crime (for example, making graffiti artists clean the walls they have defaced)

credit-card crime: acquiring a credit card from another without the cardholder's or issuer's consent; using a forged or stolen credit card; incurring charges on credit cards without intending to repay them

credit-card fraud: use or attempted use of a credit card to obtain goods, money or services with the intention of avoiding payment

credit-card swindle: mail-fraud swindle in which people are urged to charge some attractive product to their credit cards; nothing is delivered but the charge is billed

creeper: pickpocket working in collusion with prostitutes

cremation: disposal of dead bodies by burning them and reducing them to ashes; killing people by setting them afire; suicide by setting oneself afire

crib: old-fashioned one-room shack occupied by a prostitute

crib job: easily accomplished crime

cribs: apartments used by drug addicts and prostitutes

crim: criminal; criminalism; criminalist; criminalistic; criminalistics; criminality; criminally; criminaloid, criminate; crimination; criminative; criminatory; criminologic; criminological; criminologically; criminologist; criminology; criminous(ly); criminousness

crime: anything forbidden by law and hence rendering the offender punishable

crime against nature: any sexual act deemed unnatural

crime-drug syndrome: when a drug's possession, sale or use is subject to law, the underworld breaks the law by supplying the drug to its users

crime in the suites: play on words recalling *crime in the streets,* referring to corporate embezzlement, fraud and security thefts by white-collar criminals in offices

crime lab(oratory): place where such evidence as bloodied clothing, bullet fragments, fingerprints, weapons, etc. are carefully examined to provide useful clues

crimeless: adjective indicating the absence of crime (this often means that no crime has been detected; crime may still exist)

crime of commission: criminal acts involving specific violations of laws (burglary, child beating, killing, etc.)

crime of omission: failure to fulfill a requirement imposed by law (failure of a father to support his family; failure to pay a tax, etc.)

crime of passion: murder incited by the infidelity of a lover or a mate; murder committed in the heat of anger or another passionate outburst

crime rate: number of reported crimes per a specified number (usually 100,000) of inhabitants

Crime Reduction Unit: unit carrying out the San Diego Police Department's program to reduce crime in areas infested by drug users, gamblers, massage parlors, etc.

crime tax: phrase referring to the fact that when vigorous law enforcement efforts are underway, the price or "tax" paid by all who deal with gamblers, gangsters, drug dealers and prostitutes is proportionately higher; this concept is often used by advocates of legalizing gambling, narcotics, prostitution, etc.

criminal: person violating a criminal law; in violation of criminal law

criminal adjudication: judicial decision ending a criminal proceeding by a judgment of acquittal, conviction or dismissal

criminal anthropology: Lombrosian criminology, which postulates that there are discernible and identifiable criminal types

criminal assault: physical attack against another person, typically involving actual or attempted sexual contact; rape

criminal associate: anyone interacting on a voluntary basis with a member of an organized crime group engaged in furthering illegal interests

criminal biopsychology: science investigating the psychosomatic personalities of criminals

Criminal Conspiracy Division: Los Angeles Police Department division dealing with criminal activities of extremist political groups such as the American Nazi Party and the Minutemen as well as gangsters of all types

criminal contempt: any act deemed disrespectful of the authority and dignity of the court

criminal court: court having the authority to try alleged offenders against the criminal law and to sentence them if they are found guilty

criminaldom: the realm of criminals; the underworld

criminal etiology: biological, physical, psychological and social agents making a behavior a crime and a person a criminal; criminal etiology is one of two major dynamic parts of criminology (the other is penology and correction), according to Prof. Stephen Schafer

criminal fence: place where stolen goods are exchanged for money or other valuable objects, such as arms or drugs; receiver of stolen goods

criminal history information: any information about a person's arrest record, conviction or non-conviction or correctional and release history

criminal homicide: killing another person without excuse or justification

criminal informant: individual providing information to law enforcement authorities whose relationships with associates of or members of organized criminal groups requires that his or her identity be kept confidential

criminalism: act, process or state of being criminal; criminal conduct

criminalist: expert in criminal law or in criminology

criminalistic: anything pertaining to the criminal

criminalistics: fact-finding process for detecting crime; police science; scientific detection and investigation of crimes

criminality: act or practice of being criminal

criminal law: branch of jurisprudence defining crimes, describing their nature and providing for their punishment

criminal lawyer: attorney specializing in matters having to do with criminal law

criminal offense: a specific crime

criminal of the upperworld: white-collar criminal protected by political or social position from the hazards faced by his or her underworld counterparts

criminaloid: person believed to have been born with criminal tendencies

criminal police: detective force

criminal sociology: science investigating social factors affecting and creating criminals

criminal sociopath: person who has failed to develop a conscience or understand the difference between right and wrong

criminal syndicalism: advocacy of force, terror and violence to bring about economic or political changes

criminal syndicalist: person committed to overthrowing the government by force and violence

criminal trespass: law defining trespass and empowering landlords, under certain circumstances, to enter their own property by force and eject squatters

criminal typologies: American criminologist Stephen Schafer's life-trend classification of criminals; according to Schafer, types of criminals include the **abnormal criminal**, the **convictional criminal**, the habitual criminal, the **occasional criminal** and the **professional criminal** (see also individual entries as indicated)

criminate: to charge with a crime; to incriminate

crimination: accusation; act of incriminating

criminative: involving accusation or incrimination

criminator: one who accuses or incriminates

criminatory: involving accusation or incrimination

criminogenesis: the origin of crime

criminogenic: crime-producing; criminogenic features of our society include alienation, the break-up of the family, excessive emphasis on materialism, impersonality, the lack of ethical standards or training, lawless abuse of alcohol and other drugs, slum environments, social disintegration, etc.

criminol: criminologic; criminological; criminologist; criminology

criminologist: student of crime and criminals

criminology: the study of crime, its causes, its detection and correction as well as its prevention; the study of crimes, criminals and victims

criminosis: psychoneurotic behavior marked by criminal acts or a tendency to engage in criminal activity

criminotechnol: criminological technology; the use of electronic and photographic devices and techniques to apprehend criminals and secure evidence needed for their conviction

criminotic: criminal neurotic; criminal psychotic

criminous: pertaining to anything criminal or having to do with crime

crimogenic: crime-productive; crimogenic elements of our society include poor training and compensation of policemen and understaffing and overloading of courts

crimp: to decoy or entrap a person or persons into maritime or military service; person engaged in crimping sailors or others by drugging them before putting them on board outbound ships

crimpage: money paid to crimps for their services

crimper: person engaged in decoying or entrapping persons into maritime or military service; crimp

crimp gang: press gang engaged in decoying or entrapping others for maritime or military service

crimping house: place where crimpers decoy and entrap persons for maritime or military service (often a bar or a brothel)

crim psych(ol): criminal psychology or criminal psychiatry

crim syn: criminal syndicalism; criminal syndicalist(s)

crink: metamphetamine

crip: crippler—gangster noted for crippling victims

Crips: Cripples, a black gang active in southern California; one can only become a member by crippling or severely injuring someone

cris: metamphetamine

crisis center: haven for teen-age runaways and others who have left home in emergency situations

cristina: metamphetamine

CRMT: Community Resources Management Team (parole and probation)

CRNPTG: Commission on the Review of the National Policy Toward Gambling (U.S.)

croak: die

croaker: physician favored by addicts because he will prescribe large doses of drugs they can resell as well as use; prison doctor

croaker joint: hospital

crock: (of baloney, crap or shit) blatantly false or exaggerated

crocked: intoxicated

crook: professional criminal; to cheat, steal or swindle

crooked: dishonest; illicit

crooker: an alcoholic

cross-bar hotel: prison

cross-examination: questioning of a witness by a lawyer representing the opposing side in a court case

crossroads: amphetamine tablets

CROWCASS: Combined Registry of War Criminals and Security Suspects

crowd engineer: euphemism for a police dog

CRP: Crime Restitution Program

CRS: Corps Republicain de la Securité (French—Republican Security Corps) anti-riot squads

CRS: Correction and Rehabilitation Squadron (U.S. Air Force)

crsp: criminally receiving stolen property

CRU: Crime Reduction Unit (q.v.)

cruiser: unmarked police car

Crumlin Road 14: address and nickname of one of Her Majesty's prison camps outside Belfast, Northern Ireland

crusher: policeman

crutch: device for holding a marijuana cigarette so it may be smoked to the end; hairpins and tweezers serve as crutches

cryptonym: name assigned to cover a secret operation or a secret operative; secret name

crystal: angel dust (pcp or PCP)

crystals: desoxyn or methedrine crystals

CSA: Controlled Substances Act (q.v.)

CSCA: Central States Corrections Association

CSCCL: Center for Studies in Criminology and Criminal Law (University of Pennsylvania)

CSCD: Center for Studies of Crime and Delinquency (of the National Institute of Mental Health in Rockville, Md.)

CSCJ: Center for Studies in Criminal Justice

CSD: Correctional Services Department; Corrective Services Department

C₁₇H₂₁NO₄: cocaine

CSF: Correctional Service Federation

CS-gas: civil(ian)-security or cyanide-simulating gas (Mace or tear gas, e.g.); gas causing temporary blindness, burning, tearing, coughing, vomiting and sensations of choking and stinging; used to control unruly mobs

CSM: Correctional Service of Minnesota (in Minneapolis)

CSNDA: Center for the Studies of Narcotic and Drug Abuse (National Institute of Mental Health)

CSNMDU: Center for the Study of Non-Medical Drug Use

CSO: Cargo Security Office (proposed organization designed to control cargo thefts and the hijacking of entire containers or other shipments); cargo security officer; community service office; community service officer

CSP: Connecticut State Police

CSS: Central Security Services (Department of Defense); Clandestine Services Staff (CIA)

CSSU: Crime Scene Search Unit

CS tear gas: see **CS-gas; Paralyzer**

CSTI: California Specialized Training Institute (for coping with terrorism)

csu: crime-suppression unit (of a law-enforcement organization), conducting, e.g., neighborhood cleanups and police sweeps

Ct Crim Aps: Court of Criminal Appeals

CTIA: Committee to Investigate Assassinations (of John F. and Robert Kennedy, Martin Luther King Jr. and others)

CUAV: Citizens United Against Violence

cubehead: habitual user of LSD-laced sugar cubes

cube juice: morphine

cubes: sugar cubes impregnated with LSD

cubo: conduct unbecoming an officer (pronounced *cue bow*)

cudgel: clublike weapon; heavy stick

CUE: Concentrated Urban Enforcement (gun-control program to take gun-carrying criminals off the streets)

Cuernavaca: prison in Cuernavaca, capital of the Mexican state of Morelos, in the mountains south of Toluca

cuff: handcuff

cuff-and-lead chain: single handcuff attached to a length of chain ending in a ring; used for leading prisoners or holding them to some stationary object

cuff case: leather case used by law-enforcement officers to carry handcuffs

cufflinks: handcuffs

cuffs: handcuffs

CUIP: Committee on Uniform Identification Procedures (for computer-user protection)

Culiacan: prison in Culiacan, capital city of the state of Sinaloa, on the Pacific coast of Mexico close to the Gulf of California and the U.S.-Mexican border

culpability: state of having committed an act liable to prosecution; guilt

Cummins: Cummins Prison Farm, a facility of the Arkansas State Penitentiary; holds girls and women convicted of illegal drug use and prostitution

Cupid's itch: any veneral disease

CURB: Campaign on the Use and Restriction of Barbiturates

CURE: Care, Understanding, Research (organization promoting the welfare of drug addicts)

curse of Venus: venereal disease

curtains: death

cush: cushion; goods, jewels or money obtained illegally and divided to give each criminal some ''cushioning'' for his or her participation in the crime

custodial officer(s): prison guard(s)

custody: see **close custody, maximum custody, medium custody, minimum custody** and **protective custody**

Customs Automatic Data Processing Intelligence Network: computerized data-bank system concerning known or suspected smugglers wanted by the U.S. Bureau of Customs

cut: to mix a drug, such as heroin, with powdered sugar or a sleeping powder in order to extend its bulk

cut: share of the profits; hence *to take a cut* means to take a share of the profits; to dilute drinks or drugs

cut down: teen-ager addicted to alcohol and/ or narcotics who begs or steals to support his or her addiction

cutlass: heavy, short sword, once popular with coast guardsmen, pirates and sailors; a heavy brass or steel handguard was characteristic

'cutor: prosecutor

cut out: depart; leave; retire; go-between in any clandestine operation (hyphenated)

CVCB: Crime Victims Compensation Board (New York)

CVLAI: Crime Victims Legal Advocacy Institute

CWAC: City-Wide Anti-Crime Unit (New York City Police Department group, sometimes called Quacks)

CWWC: Concerned Women in the War on Crime

cyanide: potassium cyanide (a deadly poison)

cyanide gun: assassination device powerful enough to penetrate any mucous membrane (eyes, lips, nostrils, et al.) and kill within seconds by releasing cyanide gas

CYC: Colorado Youth Center at Denver

cyc: cyclazogine (a narcotic antagonist used in curing addicts)

CZ: *Ceska Zbrojovka* (Czechoslovakian arms manufacturer)

CZ Pen: Canal Zone Penitentiary at Gamboa

D

D: dead; detective

DA: District Attorney

dab.: delayed-action bomb

dabble(r): irregular use(r) of narcotics

dacha: *Cannabis* plant grown and used in the Congo, where it is also called suma

Dachau: (Old German—marsh)—site of a large Nazi concentration camp near Munich

Dactek: trade name for an inkless fingerprinter as well as a line of field test kits for detecting the influence of such drugs as codeine, hashish, heroin, marijuana, etc.

dactyloscopy: technique of identifying people by their fingerprinnts

DAD: Drop A Dime (anti-drug association)

daddy tank: prison cell reserved for lesbians, to keep them from being attacked by other prisoners

dagga: *Cannabis* plant grown and smoked in many parts of Namibia (South-West Africa) and South Africa

Daisy International Air Gun Museum: on U.S. Highway 71 South, Rogers, Ark.

DALE: Drug Abuse Law Enforcement

Dallas: State Correctional Institution at Dallas, Pa.

Damon: Israeli medium-security prison for adult repeat offenders and Arab juvenile delinquents from 14 to 20 years old; built by the British in Mandate times and about halfway between Beersheba and the Dead Sea

damper: a safe-deposit box or a savings bank

Danbury: Federal Correctional Institution at Danbury, Conn.

dance: death by hanging (as the body tends to twitch and dance about during the execution)

dance-hall: cell or hallway leading to an execution chamber, where the condemned seems to dance when the current is applied to the electric chair

dance of death: hanging

dance on air: be executed by hanging

d & d: drunk and disorderly

Dane: Great Dane—very large and powerful breed of dog[s], often such as guard dogs

dangerous aliens: Canadian government designation of Japanese-Canadians in the post-Pearl-Harbor period; some 22,000 were evacuated from their homes, farms, and stores along the coast to inland places where they were used to help build a highway through the Rocky Mountains

dangle: offer the services of a double agent

Dannemora: Clinton Correctional Facility (for males) at Dannemora, N.Y.

darbies: handcuffs (nautical term current in the early 1800s when Herman Melville used it in *Moby Dick*)

DARE: Drug Abuse Research and Education; Drug Awareness Resistance Educattion

Darrington Unit: Texas penal facility begun in 1919 and holding maximum-security felons within its confines in Rosharon

dart: dart gun (q.v.); electronic dart; electronic dart gun

dart gun: gun that fires non-lethal, electronically-activated darts; when the dart makes contact it jolts the target with 50,000 volts of electricity, temporarily paralyzing him or her

DAS: Departamento Administrativo de Seguridad (Spanish—Security Administration Department) Colombian police agency

das (DAS): dextroamphetamine sulfate (a central nervous system stimulant)

dash: bribes

Datura: generic name for jimson weed or loco weed, found in the American Southwest, the Andes, India and Mexico; a beer whose effects are intoxicating is made from it

DAWN: Drug Abuse Warning Network (Drug Enforcement Administration)

daytimers: prostitutes working during daytime hours

Daytop: Daytop Lodge in Staten Island, N.Y., where male narcotics violators are offered treatment

db: dead body; dirty book

DB: Detective Bureau; Disciplinary Barracks

DBC: Detective Book Club

dbd: death by drugs (execution by lethal injection is legal in Idaho, New Mexico, Oklahoma and Texas)

DBHNT: Detective Bureau Hostage Negotiating Team (New York City Police Department)

dc: death cell

DC: District of Columbia Jail in Washington, D.C.

DCC: Deputy Chief Constable

DCCJ: Delaware Council on Crime (in Wilmington)

DCI: Director of Central Intelligence (CIA)

DCJ: Dade County Jail (Miami, Fla.); Department of Criminal Justice; District Court Judge

DCLE: Department of Criminal Law Enforcement (Florida)

DCS: Department of Correctional Services (formerly the New York Department of Correction); Domestic Contact Service (CIA)

D.C. WDC: District of Columbia Women's Detention Center

DD: Detective District; Detective Division

DDA: Dangerous Drug Act; Deputy Director of Administration (CIA)

DD&J: Deacons for Defense and Justice (q.v.)

DDCI: Deputy Director of Central Intelligence (CIA)

DDHA: Detective Division Homicide Assault Squad

DDI: Deputy Director of Intelligence (CIA)

DDO: Deputy Director of Operations (CIA)

D-dog: detector dog, used by the U.S. Customs Service to sniff out contraband such as cocaine, marijuana and other drugs

DDP: Deputy Director—Plans (overseas arm of the CIA's clandestine service)

DDS: Deputy Director of Support (CIA)

DDS & T: Deputy Director of Science and Technology (CIA)

ddw: displaying a deadly weapon

DEA: Detectives' Endowment Association; Drug Enforcement Administration

DEA: Drug Enforcement Administration

Deacons for Defense and Justice: a black vigilante group formed to combat the KKK and other racists in Alabama, Florida, Mississippi, Louisiana, North and South Carolina; organized in Bogalusa, La. in 1965

deadbeat: debtor whose debts are uncollectible

dead bolt: reasonably secure type of door lock

dead drop: place for depositing and collecting material or messages; a dead drop may be, for example, something taped under a bench or within a tree trunk

dead drunk: alcoholic state marked by coma—complete unconsciousness, depressed reflexes and subnormal temperature

deadfall: trap constructed to release a heavy weight—big logs or large stones, for example—once they have been tripped

dead-letter box: dead drop (q.v.)

deadly nightshade: nickname for belladonna

deadly weapon: any object, instrument or weapon capable of producing death or great bodily injury; a deadly weapon may be an automobile, a blackjack, a broken bottle, a cane, a farming implement, a household tool, an iron bar or pipe, a razor or a razor blade, a sock filled with salt or sand, an unloaded gun used as a bludgeon, etc.

Dead Man's Canyon: canyon leading from the Mexican border in the hills of Tijuana into the hills of San Ysidro, Calif., below San Diego; favorite route of many illegal aliens as well as smugglers of diamonds and drugs

Dead Man's Cove: nickname of the San Diego Police lockup at the end of the Pacific Highway

Dead Man's Island: North Coronado, off Tijuana, Mexico, whose outline resembles a shrouded corpse afloat in the Pacific; like South Coronado, it is a favorite transfer point for many smugglers attempting to bring contraband into the United States

dead marine: empty beer, whiskey or wine bottle

dead meat: carrion; rotten flesh

dead President: American paper money bearing the portrait of a dead President or an eminent statesman

dead soldier: empty beer, whiskey or wine bottle

deadwood: undercover law-enforcement officer posing as an addict to entrap drug pushers

deal: to deal in narcotics

dealer: supplier of illegal drugs

dealer loaders: multi-level sales-promotion schemes, unlawful in many American states

DEAN: Deputy Educators Against Narcotics

Dear John letter: written communication to a prisoner from a lover or wife informing him their romance or marriage is over

death penalty: punishment by death, imposed in any legal fashion

death rattle: sound often produced immediately before death, when air is forced through food or mucus lodged in the throat of the dying person

death row: cell block reserved for convicts awaiting execution

death's head: nickname of the deadly mushroom *Amanita nuscaria*

death ship: vessel deliberately destroyed, scuttled or wrecked by its owners so they can collect insurance and hence profit from their "loss," even though this may also involve the loss of the lives of its crew and passengers

debug: remove or render any wiretapping devices ineffective by electronic countermeasures

debugger: anti-wiretap device or technician

decap: decapitation

deck: small glassine envelope or folded paper packet containing heroin, morphine or cocaine

deck down: to adulterate and extend a narcotic by adding milk, sugar, or finely ground sleeping powders

decked: floored; hurled to the deck; knocked down

decks awash: intoxicated

deduction: logical form of inference whereby certain conclusions are reached from certain principles assumed to be true; many investigators apply deductive reasoning in solving crimes

Deer Lodge: Montana community southwest of Helena, site of the Montana State Prison

def (DEF): defendant

defective delinquent: criminally insane person

defendant: person against whom a criminal proceeding is pending

defenestration: suicide by throwing oneself out of a window; tossing a person or a thing out of a window

defense attorney: attorney representing the defendant in any legal proceeding

DEFY: Drug Education for You

DeHoCo: Detroit House of Correction

Delancey: Delancey Street Foundation in San Francisco, maintained for the rehabilitation of former addicts, convicts, murderers, prostitutes, thieves, etc.

Delancey Street Foundation: organization in New York City's lower East Side for rehabilitating drug addicts

delator: finger pointer; informant

delayed action bomb: timed explosive

delinquency: actions or conduct in violation of criminal law

delinquent: person convicted of having committed an illegal act

delirium tremens: toxic psychosis marked by hallucinations, insomnia and, sometimes, maniacal behavior; this is the dangerous phase of withdrawal from an addiction to alcohol

Delle Stinche: Florentine prison dating from the early 1300s famous for its advanced methods of inmate handling and segregation

demerol: synthetic opiate reportedly more addictive than heroin, used by many addicts who prefer it to morphine and began using it because they wrongly believed that it was non-addictive

demirep: demireputation (a demirep is a woman of loose morals and doubtful reputation)

demo: demonstration

dem pug: *dementia pugilistica* (Latin—punch drunk)

Denver: Denver County Jail in Colorado

dep: deputy; deputy sheriff

Department D: police department in charge of demonstrations

dependence: physical or psychological need to continue the use of a drug

Dep Insp: Deputy Inspector

depressant drugs: amytal, barbiturates, doriden, librium, luminal, miltown, nembutal, seconal and tuinal are some of the depressant drugs

deputy sheriff: law-enforcement officer employed by the county sheriff's department or office

De Quincy: Louisiana Correctional and Industrial School at De Quincy in Calcasieu Parish, north-northwest of Lake Charles

Deringer: Henry Deringer, American inventor and manufacturer of small arms; he refused to allow competitors to use his name, so they used Derringer instead, and capitalized on the fact that a Deringer was used to fire the fatal shot at Pres. Lincoln

Derringer: well-known American manufacturer of easy-to-conceal handguns

Des Moines Plan: innovative alternative to building new prisons, as less risky convicts are steered to programs allowing them to help themselves by working or attending school under probationary supervision

desperado: dangerous and reckless criminal of the type attracted to the American West in the post-Civil War era

Det: Detective

detained in federal custody: jailed in a federal penitentiary

detcom: detected communist

Detectionary: dictionary containing pseudonyms of detective-fiction authors (A.A. Fair-Gardner, Kyle Hunt-John Creasey, etc.)

detention: legally authorized confinement of a person subject to criminal or juvenile court proceedings until he or she has been committed to a correctional facility or released

detention center: jail housiing prisoners awaiting trial

detention facility: generic term for county farm, detention center, honor farm, jail, juvenile hall, road camp, work camp, etc.

detention glazing: chemically strengthened and plastically bonded glass used in place of bars or walls in modern penal facilities

Detention Headquarters: U.S. Bureau of Prisons detention headquarters, on New York's West Street facing the Hudson River waterfront and near Florence, Ariz.

detention hearing: a hearing by a judicial officer of a juvenile court to determine if a juvenile is to be detained or released while proceedings are pending for her or his case

detention screening: stainless-steel screening allowing air, light, and sound to enter but preventing the entrance of contraband such as drugs and weapons

detention windows: see **detention glazing**

deterrence: process of preventing crimes or their repetition

detox: detoxification; detoxification center (for alcoholic and narcotic addicts)

detoxcen: detoxification center (for alcoholics and others addicted to drugs)

detoxification: medical method of treating alcoholic and narcotic addicts; also called *disintoxification*; detoxification of a heroin addict, for example, is accomplished by substituting oral methadone for heroin and then gradually reducing the dose of methadone over a one- to three-week period

Det-Sup: Detective-Superintendent (Interpol)

Deuel: Deuel Vocational Institute, a medium-security penal facility at Tracy, Calif.

deviant: person living outside the conventions of society

devil's front porch: prison

Devil's Island: nickname of the penal settlement off the coast of French Guiana in northern South America

devil's testicle: nickname for mandrake, also called mandragora or Satan's apple

devil's trumpet: nickname for jimson weed, also called devil's apple or devil's weed

dew: hashish or marijuana

dewat: deactivated war trophy (often a deadly weapon any good mechanic can reactivate)

dexies: dexedrine capsules or tablets; dextroamphetamines

DFAR: Daily Field Activity Report (activities log kept by patrol officers)

DFLP: Democratic Front for the Liberation of Palestine (terrorist group formerly called PDFLP—Popular Democratic Front for the Liberation of Palestine)

DFS: *Direccion Federal de Seguridad* (Spanish—Federal Security Directorate) Mexico's famed *Federales*

dg: degenerate

DGI: *Directoria General de Inteligencia* (Spanish—Directorate General of Intelligence) office in Cuba responsible for information gathering and for the training of guerrilla terrorists invited to Havana from all parts of the world

DGSE: *Directorio General de Seguridad del Stado* (Spanish—Directorate General of State Security—Nicaragua's Secret Service)

DHC: Detroit House of Correction

DIA: Defense Intelligence Agency; Department of Institutions and Agencies (which governs New Jersey's prison systems)

diacetylmorphine: technical name for heroin

diagnosis center: see **classification center**

diamorphine: heroin prepared for smoking

diamorphine hydrochloride: heroin prepared for injection

dic: drunk in charge (of the joint, the office, the prison, the ship, etc.)

dice cappers: persons gambling with or making loaded dice

dicey: risky as playing dice

dick: detective; undercover investigator

dickless tracy: female law-enforcement officer (pejorative term derived from the fictional hero Dick Tracy)

die in the hot seat: be electrocuted

die of lead poisoning: be killed by lead bullets

die of throat trouble: be hanged

diet pills: amphetamine-filled pills used to reduce the appetite; diet pills are often used by those seeking a stimulant or so-called upper

digits dealer: numbers racketeer

dik: drug-identification kit

dilated pupils: enlargement of the pupils of human eyes, sometimes due to the action of stimulant drugs such as amphetamines and hallucinogens

dilauded: narcotic substitute for morphine

dimba: West African *Cannabis* plant smoked by the natives and sold to tourists and traders

dime bag: $10 bag or heroin or another drug

dimethyltryptamine: a synthetic drug producing effects similar to those of LSD but of shorter duration, and therefore nicknamed "businessman's special" or "lunchhour trip"

dip: to pick a person's pocket; pickpocket; a dipsomaniac (alcoholic)

dipco: diplomatic courier (who is protected by immunity and may sometimes be involved, perhaps unwittingly, in some illegal international transaction)

diphenylamine chlorarsine: Adamsite, or sickening gas, sometimes used to control unruly mobs

diplomatic pouch: oversize mailbag use by consulates and embassies for transporting mail and other objects; illicit uses of diplomatic pouches have included smuggling of narcotics as well as taxable items such as cigarettes and liquor

dipso: dipsomania(c)

dipsomania: insatiable craving for alcohol

dipsomaniac: alcoholic

dirk: dagger or short sword of Scottish design; any kind of dagger is a dirk legally, however

dirt: (prison argot) sugar

dirt grass: low-quality marijuana

dirty: containing seeds, stems and twigs (said of marijuana); carrying narcotics (as opposed to **clean**—not carrying narcotics)

dirty dishes: evidence planted to incriminate another or others

dirty pool: dishonest, unethical or unfair practices; underhanded schemes

dirty towel: prison barbershop

dirty tricks: disruptivve acts; schemes calculated to discredit or embarrass another cause or another person

discon: disorderly conduct; disorderly conduct charge; disorderly conduct conviction

discount justice: practice of allowing criminals to plead guilty to a lesser offense than the one with which they were originally charged, bearing a lesser sentence, and thereby saving the state the cost of a trial by jury

disinformation: false or misleading information leaked to an enemy so as to confuse its counterintelligence services or to stir up unrest resulting in revolution or rioting

disintoxification: detoxification (q.v.)

Dismas House: halfway house opened in St. Louis, Mo. in the 1950s

dismemberment: removal of a victim's arms and legs

dismissal: decision by a judicial officer to dismiss a case without determining the guilt or innocence of the defendant(s)

disorderly house: brothel

disulfiram: antabuse, used in the treatment of alcoholics, who find that alcohol plus antabuse produce difficulty in breathing, discomfort and, sometimes, nausea

ditchweed: nickname for Mexican marijuana, attesting to its low quality as compared to Caribbean and Colombian varieties

DIU: Diversion Investigation Unit (New Jersey's nine special police squads created to combat illegal drug peddling by doctors and pharmacists)

dive: low-class cocktail bar or saloon

diver: pickpocket

divert: steal from (popular euphemism used when the stealing is done by someone or some group considered friendly)

Division No. 1: modern name for Chicago's Cook County Jail

Division No. 2: modern name for Chicago's House of Correction

divorced moll: girl or woman with an imprisoned husband or lover

DJ: Department of Justice innvestigator; Don Jail (Don Mills, Ontario)

DJCP: Division of Justice and Crime Prevention (Virginia)

djoma: Central African hemp similar to marijuana, believed to have been introduced into the New World by African slaves

DLE: Department of Law Enforcement

DLPS: Department of Law and Public Safety (New Jersey)

D-man: drug-enforcement officer

dmt (DMT): dimethyltryptamine (q.v.)

DMV: Department of Motor Vehicles

DMV check: check of an automobile license by the Department of Motor Vehicles to find whether its owner is wanted by the police

DND: Division for Narcotic Drugs (United Nations)

doa (DOA): dead on arrival

do a bit: serve a sentence in jail

do a dime: serve a 10-year prison sentence

do a line: snort a small quantity of cocaine

do a nickel: serve a five-year prison term

do a pound: serve a five-year prison term

do a quarter: serve a 25-year prison term

Doberman (pinscher): medium-size to large dog often trained for police or protection tasks; named after the 19th-century German breeder Ludwig Dobermann and the Pinzgau area of Austria, where the breed was first raised

do bird: do time in prison; serve a prison sentence

D o C: Department of Correction (Arkansas, Connecticut, Delaware, Indiana, Massachusetts, North Carolina, Tennessee); Department of Corrections (Arizona, California, District of Columbia, Florida, Guam, Idaho, Illinois, Kansas, Kentucky, Louisiana, Maine, Michigan, Minnesota, Mississippi, Missouri, New Jersey, Rhode Island, South Carolina, Texas, Vermont, Washington, West Virginia); Division of Corrections (Utah, Wisconsin)

DOCS: Department of Correctional Services (New York)

dod (DOD): date of death
DoD: Department of Defense
DOD: Domestic Operations Division (CIA)
D of C: Department of Correction(s)
D of I: Division of Intelligence (Atomic Energy Commission); Division of Investigation(s) (of a police department)
D of L: Department of Law
Doftana: Bucharest's prison

dog detective(s): see **canine shamus(es)**
dogie: heroin
dognapper: dog kidnapper—some engage in dognapping for profit, perhaps stealing only pedigreed dogs, while others do it just to rid their neigghborhoods of barking dogs
dogtective: dog detective (trained to find dognapped or lost dogs)
D o I: Department of Institutions (Montana); Director of Institutions (North Dakota); Division of Institutions (Oklahoma)

dojee: heroin
doll: amphetamine or barbiturate pill
dolly: dolophine (q.v.)
dolo: dolophine (q.v.)
dolophine: methadone hydrochloride, used as a morphine substitute in withdrawing addicts from heroin
DOLPHIN: Dump Obsolete Laws—Prove Hypocrisy Isn't Necessary (acronym providing a name for an organization of prostitutes in Honolulu)
dom (DOM): 4-methyl-2, 5-dimethoxy-amphetamine (known popularly as STP)
dome: LSD tablet
domestic: American-grown marijuana

domestic violence: violence toward a family member, such as child abuse or wife beating
Don: crime boss; Don Jail (q.v.)
Don Jail: jail in metropolitan Toronto, Ontario
donnybrook: brawling fight, named after the fights once typical of the Donnybrook Fair outside Dublin
don't piss into the cash register: underworld way of warning *don't leave your fingerprints around*; also part of an old saying: *don't piss into the cash register—it runs into money*
doogee: heroin
D o P: Department of Prisons (Nevada)
dopadic(s): dope addict(s)
dope: drug or narcotic; person, also called *dopey*, who uses drugs; hence the saying *dope is for dopes*
dope fiend: drug addict
dope hop: narcotic addict
doper: habitual user of drugs
dope run: trip to buy and smuggle drugs
dope runner: person taking trips to buy and smuggle drugs; dope runners often pose as tourists and travelers
dopey: drugged; stupified by drugs
dopie: drug addicts; stupid person
dopium: opium
DOR: Department of Offender Rehabilitation (Georgia)
Dora: nickname for the Nazi concentration camp west of Leipzig, Germany at a place named Nordhausen; at the close of World War II advancing American and British soldiers found it filled with corpses as well as instruments of torture
Dorandordhausen: Nazi concentration camp near Buchenwald and west of Leipzig, Germany
dossing: drug-induced sleeping
dot: place LSD on a cube of sugar
do the book: serve a life sentence
do time: serve a prison sentence
double agent: espionage agent working for both the country or movement originally employing his or her services and its enemy
double-aught buck: double-O buckshot (.32-caliber buckshot shell used in police shotguns)
double-ceiling: placing two prisoners in the same cell (often necessary because prison populations usually expand much faster than new prisons are built or existing ones expanded)
double-cross: betray; cheat; deceive; inform upon

double Deringer: Great Western handgun built on the Deringer model and chambered to hold two .38-caliber bullets

double E: double eagle ($20 U.S. gold piece)

double payments: fraudulent device wherein two identical checks are written to suppliers but the second check is pocketed by the person(s) who requested or wrote the check

double trouble: tuinal (amobarbital sodium and secobarbital sodium)

down: imitation whiskey sold to customers in bars; depressant drug

down below: in New York City police parlance, this means any place south of 42nd Street in Manhattan, whereas **up above** means any place north of 42nd Street

down down home: (Afro-American slang) the Federal Penitentiary in Atlanta, Ga.

downer: depressant drug; hypnotic and sedative drug

down home: (Afro-American slang) the Tombs, also known as the Manhattan House of Detention, in New York City

downies: barbiturates or other tranquilizers

down south: Federal Penitentiary at Atlanta, Ga.

down the hatch: an informal toast; swallow your drink

down the toilet: destroyed, as evidence

down trip: bad experience with drugs

DPA: Discharged Prisoners Association (Great Britain)

DPAS: Discharged Prisoners' Aid Society (Great Britain)

DPC: Deputy Police Commissioner

DPI: disorderly persons investigation

DPR: Differential Police Response

DPS: Department of Public Safety

DPs: detention pens; specifically, the Manhattan Detention Pens at 100 Centre Street in New York City

DPSCS: Department of Public Safety and Correctional Services (Maryland)

dragger: shoplifter

Draper: Utah State Prison at Draper, some 15 miles south of Salt Lake City

DRC: Department of Rehabilitation and Correction (Ohio)

dream bead: opium pellet

dreamer: morphine; morphine or opium addict

dream stick: opium pipe

dream wax: opium

dressed in: just imprisoned and hence just dressed in prison clothing

drifter: hobo; nomad; restless person; vagrant

drive: sensation following the use of drugs

drive-out: person who fills his or her gas tank at a service station and drives away without paying

driving under the influence: driving under the influence of alcohol and/or another drug

dripper: eye dropper (sometimes used by drug addicts)

drop: to swallow a drug; clandestine hiding place for drugs, mail or ransom money; drug administered by mouth

drop a dime: inform; make a telephone call

drop bolt: secure type of door lock

drop money: bribe given law-enforcement officers

drop-off point: delivery point for a shipment of contraband such as alcohol, drugs, illegal aliens, etc.

dropout: person dropping out of society; person leaving school and not completing her or his education

dropped in the bucket: jailed

dropper: hired assassin; medicine dropper used to inject narcotics; dropout; drunkard; social outcast

drop reds: take red capsules or pills for their effect in producing feelings of elation or soaring

drop the hammer: fire the weapon; shoot

drug abuse: excessive and often compulsive use of drugs such as alcohol, the narcotics, the many sedatives, stimulants, tranquilizers, hallucinogens, etc., to the point of damaging one's health and ability to function socially or vocationally

drug addiction: defined by the World Health Organization (WHO) as "a state of periodic or chronic intoxication produced by the repeated consumption of a drug (natural or synthetic), which produces the following characteristics: (1) an overpowering desire or compulsion to continue taking the drug and to obtain it by any means; (2) a tendency to increase the dosage, showing body tolerance; (3) a psychic and generally a physical dependence on the effects of the drug; and (4) the creation of an individual and social problem."

drug dependence: condition following the repeated use of a drug, when an individual must continue to take the drug to avoid withdrawal symptoms and/or to gratify some strong emotional need

druggie: indiscriminate user of, or experimenter with, drugs

drughead: drug addict

drug subculture: the world of addiction—physiological or psychological—to drugs

drunk driving: driving under the influence of alcohol

drunkometer: popular name for an alcoholmeter, used to detect the percentage of alcohol in the breath of anyone suspected of being drunk

drunk tank: jail cell reserved for those arrested while under the influence of alcohol or other drugs

dry law: regulation forbidding the sale of alcoholic beverages as well as their transportation and use

dry out: detoxify from alcohol or another drug

Dry Tortugas: nickname of the U.S. military prison on one of the Dry Tortugas keys in the Gulf of Mexico west of Key West, Fla.

DSA: Department of Substance Abuse; Deputy Sheriff's Association

DS&T: Directorate of Science and Technology (CIA)

DSB: Drug Supervisory Body (UN)

DSCDP: Delaware State Central Data Processing

DST: *Defense et Securité du Territoire* (French equivalent of the FBI)

dt's: delirium tremens

dtx: detoxification

dubee: marijuana cigarette

dubok: respectable establishment used to conceal illegal or underground operations as well as loot and subversive literature or even weapons; a dummy corporation sometimes serves criminals or subversives as their dubok

Ducato Milanese: Milan, Italy's old prison

Dubrolag: complex of some 15 prison camps close to Potmu in the Moldavian Republic of the USSR

duck: sleeping sensation following use of many narcotics

dudgeon: wooden-handled dagger

duel: prearranged fight, usually with deadly weapons such as pistols or swords, between two persons wishing to settle an argument or seek redress for an insult; dueling is illegal and anyone who kills another during a duel is considered a murderer

DUF: Drug Use Forecasting (drug-control program)

dui: driving under the influence (of alcohol and/or drugs)

dujie: heroin

dumb gat: silencer-equipped handgun

dum dum bullets: expanding soft-point bullets of the type first made at the British arsenal in Dum Dum, India in the 1890s; prohibited by the Hague Convention of 1908; since then used illegally by many wishing to inflict serious wounds

dummies: counterfeit drugs, often sold to addicts and others

dummy: (prison argot) bread

dummy-up: appear to be dumb; refuse to talk

dump on: badmouth; speak disparagingly of

dump truck: depressed, slow-moving or torpid prisoner

dupe: duplicate (e.g., thieves can duplicate a stolen car by buying a similar wrecked car, stripping the stolen car of all essentials and rebuilding the wrecked car with parts from the stolen car; they then sell the rebuilt car legally, as they possess owner's papers and are seldom detected)

Durango: prison in Durango, capital of the mountainous Mexican state of the same name, close to Mazatlan on the Pacific

duress: actual or threatened force, imprisonment or violence, causing a person to agree to do something contrary to his or her will

Durham: the prison in Durham, N.C., as well as in smaller and less well known Durhams

dust: angel dust; heroin; money; to mix marijuana and heroin for use in cigarettes

duster: heroin-and-tobacco cigarette

Dutch act: suicide

Dutch cigars: cigars imitated in Indonesia (formerly the Dutch East Indies) and other places by smugglers who conceal addictive drugs inside their wrappers

Dutch route: suicide

dwba: direct-wire burglar alarm

dwi: ddriving while intoxicated

Dwight: the State Reformatory for Women at Dwight, Ill.

DYA: Department of Youth Authority (California)

dying of the measles: making a murder look like a natural death

dyna: dynamite

dynamite: cocaine-heroine mixture; nitroglycerin explosive; undiluted heroin

dyno: dynamite; undiluted drug(s)

DYS: Department of Youth Services (for juvenile offenders); Division of Youth Services (Florida)

E

E: eagle ($10 American goldpiece); efficiency; English; excellent

e: error(s)

ea (EA): enrolled agent

EAFB: Eglin Air Force Base (including the Counter-Insurgency School), near Pensacola, Fla.

Eagle Springs: the Samarkand Manor for female misdemeanants and juvenile delinquents at Eagle Springs, N.C.

East Indian Defense Committee: Asian organization active in Canada, where it combats racist antagonists and meets violence with violence

East Lake: Alabama State Training School for female juvenile delinquents at East Lake, near Birmingham

East 20th Street: 235 East 20th Street (New York City Police Academy)

easy: easily persuaded; easily seduced; of easy virtue

easy mark: easily deceived person; foolishly generous person

easy stuff: easy-to-loot-and-dispose-of-objects such as hi-fi systems, television sets, etc.

eater: person who takes drugs by mouth

Ebensee: Austrian concentration subcamp during World War II

ebt: examination before trial

e by i: execution by injection (q.v.)

ECAB: Early Case Assessment Bureau (of New York City's District Attorney's Office)

ECCP: European Commission on Crime Problems

ECEO: Economic Crime Enforcement Office (q.v.)

ECJ: Erie County Jail (Buffalo, N.Y.)

Economic Crime Enforcement Office: branch of the U.S. Department of Justice that oversees Economic Crime Units established nationwide to combat white-collar crimes such as corporate embezzlement, fraud and thefts of securities

ECS: Episcopal Community Services (job-reentry program for ex-offenders)

ECST: European Convention on the Suppression of Terrorism

Ecstacy: nickname of methylene-dioxy-methamphetamine

ect (ECT): electroconvulsive treatment (shock therapy)—see also **aversion therapy**

ECU: Economic Crime Unit (see **Economic Crime Enforcement Office**)

Eddyville: site of the Kentucky State Penitentiary east of Paducah in the western part of the state

Edison medicine: nickname for electroconvulsive shock treatments given by some prisoners

edp crimes: electronic data-processing crimes (offenses commited with the aid of computer technology)

EFEC: Efforts from Ex-Convicts (q.v.)

Efforts From Ex-Convicts: Washington, D.C.'s parole project

egg-sucking weasel: clever swindler

Eglin: Federal Prison Camp at Eglin Air Force Base, Florida

EIDC: East Indian Defense Committee (q.v.)

eighth: one-eighth ounce of heroin

eight-n: heroin (*h* is the eighth letter of the alphabet)

El Centro: El Centro Detention Center of the Immigration and Naturalization Service in El Centro, Calif., close to the Mexican border

elec app: electronic apparatus (hi-fi systems, radios, television sets, etc.)

electric cattle prod: device sometimes used to control violent people in mobs and during riots

electric Kool-Aid: soft drink "electrified" by the addition of LSD

electric teeth: police-controlled traffic radar (for detecting and recording automotive speeders)

electronic dart gun: see **dart gun**

electronic stimulation of the brain: technique used in the treatment of prisoners subject to violent rages as well as some epileptics

electronic surveillance: eavesdropping or wiretapping by means of electronic listening and recording devices

Electronic Theft Detection System: protection system often installed in libraries and other places vulnerable to theft

elevated: intoxicated

El Fatah: Arab guerrilla terrorist organization active in Israel and other Middle Eastern countries

elint (ELINT): electronic intelligence

Ellis Unit: maximum-security unit with a death row in Huntsville, Texas

Elmira: Reception Center at Elmira, N.Y. (for male prisoners)

El Paso: El Paso Detention Center of the Immigration and Naturalization Service in El Paso, Texas, on the Mexican border

El Reno: Federal Reformatory at El Reno, Okla.

El Sexto: (Spanish—The Sixth Book of Canonical Decrees—Lima, Peru prison noted for the Easter plays staged by its inmates and for its deadly riots

emancipist: person released from penal servitude

embalmed: intoxicated

embalming fluid: alcoholic beverage

embezzlement: illegal disposal, misapplication or misappropriation of legally-entrusted property with intent to defraud the intended beneficiary or the legal owner

embroidery: pattern of hypodermic-needle abscesses and puncture points

Eme: pronounced *ehm-may* (Spanish-American jail jargon) Mexican-American counterpart and rival of the Italian-American mafia

Emergency Service Unit: law-enforcement team responsible for handling shootouts as well as terrorists and other violent criminals

Emiliano Zapata Unit: Chicano underground group bearing the name of the Mexican revolutionary; has publicly claimed responsibility for bombings of banks and some government office buildings in California

emsel: morphine

Emerald Triangle: area encompassed by Humboldt, Mendocino, and Trinity counties in northern California where marijuana is grown

Endsville: an exciting place; best of all possible places; place convicts dream about when they imagine life outside of prison

Enfield: rifle originally designed and made in England; nickname of the 30-caliber American rifle modeled after it and used during World War I

enforcer: gangster hired to secure payment of drug or gambling debts or other unpaid obligations

Englewood: Federal Correctional Institution at Englewood, Colo.

Ensisheim: French penitentiary built near Mulhouse during the First Empire; it houses many lifetime and long-term convicts

entrapment: device used by some law-enforcement officers that involves encouraging suspects to commit crimes so that the officers can arrest them; entrapment is generally considered illegal

entrepreneurial ladies of the night: prostitutes

entry: breaking and entering; burglary

envelope: cash payment

EOD: Explosive Ordance Device; the bomb squad of the San Francisco Police Department is often referred to as the EOD Team

EPD: Excellent Police Duty citation

episodic excessive drinker: classification of alcohol user who becomes drunk up to four times a year

Equipes d'Action: (French—Action Teams)—against the traffic in women and children

erase: murder

ERC: Employment Rehabilitation Center(s)

ERC: Elmira Reception Center (for male prisoners) at Elmira, N.Y.

erector-set fraud: practice whereby an auto owner leaves an expensive car where it is stolen by prearrangement; the owner reports the "loss" to his or her insurance company, then "discovers" the skeleton of the car and buys it back from the insurance company for little or nothing; he or she then rebuilds the car with the parts his or her accomplices have stripped and sells it

ergot: see **ergotin tartrate**

ergotin tartrate: ergot fungus poison used to induce abortion, but also producing such side effects as diarrhea, convulsions, headache, nausea and vomiting; also used in manufacture of LSD

eros centers: brothels or harems

Erythroxylon coca: scientific name for the coca plant, whose leaves yield an alkaloid better known as cocaine

esb (ESB): electronic stimulation of the brain (q.v.)

escalated interpersonal altercation: (sociological jargon) murder

escape: unlawful departure of a lawfully confined person from a confinement facility or from custody while being transported

escort: pimp or procurer; in massage-parlor practice an escort acts as chauffeur and bodyguard for call girls making visits to homes, hotels, motels, etc.; also a girl or woman who, for a fee, will escort a client to parties, restaurants, clubs, etc.

ESD: Emergency Service Division (New York City Police Department)

Esmeralda: barkentine-rigged Chilean naval-training vessel used for a short time in 1973 as a prison holding left-wing activists

ESP: Eastern State Penitentiary (Philadelphia)

espionage: clandestine collection of information concerning the industrial, military, or political status of a nation or its people; espionage in the broader sense includes the full-scale analysis of another nation's newspapers, technical journals, television and radio broadcasts, etc.; spying

Essen: concentration subcamp operated by the Nazis during World War II close to the Rhine

Essex: Essex County Jail in Newark, N.J.

ESU: Emergency Service Unit (q.v.)

e/t (E/T): ergotin tartrate (q.v.)

ETDS: Electronic Theft Detection System

ethanol: ethyl alcohol

ethics: set of moral principles and values concerning what is right and what is wrong

ethnocentrism: feeling or idea that one's culture, group, race or religion is superior to all others

ethyl alcohol: depressant intoxicant found in beer, liquor and wine; concentrations of as little as 0.05 percent in the blood stream can impair one's driving ability, and concentrations of 0.5 to 0.8 percent are often fatal

euphorica: any drug diminishing or suspending the functions of emotion and perception

Euroterro: European terrorism; European terrorist

euthanasia: allowing people to die of natural causes rather than attempting to prolong their lives artificially is termed negative euthanasia; the practice of painlessly putting incurably ill people to death is called positive euthanasia and is illegal in many places

even-handed justice: democratic doctrine advocating equal punishment for criminals irrespective of their former position in society, their race or their wealth

evict: evaluation of intelligence-collection tasks

evidence tape: 3M's Scotch-brand tape designed to protect evidence from any tampering or seal breaking

evidentiary material: (Watergate-style jargon) evidence

ew's: edge weapons (daggers, cutlasses, knives, machetes, swords, etc.)

EXCEL: Ex-Offender Coordinated Employment Lifeline (q.v.)

excitantia: mentally-stimulating drugs

ex-con: ex-convict (former convict)

excusable homicide: intentional but justifiable killing of another or the unintentional killing of another by accident or misadventure without gross negligence—not usually considered a crime when committed by accident, in the heat of passion, when no undue advantage is taken, no dangerous weapons are used and the killing is not done in a cruel or unusual manner

ex det: explosives detector (q.v.)

execution box: container holding a body belt, a hangman's rope, a hood for covering the condemned person's head and restraining straps to fasten the limbs of the condemned

execution by injection: execution by injection of air or poison is carried out in many places; this technique is found to be far less complicated and far less costly than more conventional methods such as electrocution, hanging or shooting; abbreviated as e by i

execution pennant: small black flag flown over British prisons when an execution was taking place

execution shed: gallows area within a prison

Executive Action Group: undercover government-sponsored specialists in the permanent removal—by assassination and other means—of unfriendly foreign leaders

exercise in a cooler climate: translation of a Soviet euphemism for forced labor in northernmost Siberia

Exeter: HM Prison at Exeter in Devonshire, England; prisons in Exeters in California, Illinois, Maine, Missouri, Nebraska, New Hampshire, Ontario, Pennsylvania and Rhode Island

exhibitionism: compulsive or frequent exposure of one's body or genitals before others in public

EXIT: Ex-Offenders in Transit (q.v.)

exit plan: assassination plan; murder plan

Ex Med: Excerpta Medica

ex-offender: former offender who is no longer under the jurisdiction of any criminal-justice agency

Ex-Offender Coordinated Employment Lifeline: Indiana's parole project

Ex-Offenders in Transit: Maine's parole project

experimenters: name given to occasional users of dangerous or illegal drugs

explorer's club: circle of LSD users who claimed to be engaged in the exploration of the unconscious

explosives detector: anti-terrorist device, available in an executive-model attache case

exposé: (French—revelation) exposure of hidden facts or scandalous information

express cartridge: bullet fired at high velocity

expunge: purge or seal arrest, criminal or juvenile records

expungement: legal ablution of a criminal's record in an effort to assist in his or her social rehabilitation and to remove prejudice from the mind of potential employers

extortion: unlawful demanding or receiving of favors, money or property through the use of fear or force or the authority of office; blackmail, ransom demands and threats are forms of extortion

extradition: removal of fugitives from justice from the state or country where they are apprehended to the state or country where they may be tried for the commission of a crime or crimes committed there; many countries have specific treaties with others guaranteeing the extradition of wanted criminals

extras: massage-parlor parlance for sexual services

extreme penalty: death by execution

eye doctor: beggar, hard-luck-story teller or panhandler who is skilled at catching the eye of the people he or she is soliciting for funds or other help

eye in the sky: police-manned helicopter

eye-opener: first drink or first "fix" of the day for an alcohol or drug addict

eyes only: confidential material; letter to be read only by the addressee

EZU: Emiliano Zapata Unit (q.v.)

F

F: fifty-dollar bill

FA: Frankford Arsenal; small-arms ammunition made at the U.S. Army arsenal at Frankford near Philadelphia, Pa.

FAAPS: Fine Art, Antique, and Philatelic Squad (Scotland Yard)

FAAR: Feminist Alliance Against Rape

face-off: face-to-face confrontation

face the music: incur the penalty; pay the price demanded

FACFI: Federal Advisory Committee on False Identification

factory: laboratory or place where illicit drugs are manufactured and packaged for resale through pushers

fag factory: homosexual-filled prison

Fairbanks Institute: Northern Region Correction Institute at Fairbanks, Alaska

fair-weather revolutionaries: epithet applied by dedicated leftists to those who appear at demonstrations but run at the first rumors of danger to themselves

fal: fusil automatique legère (French—light automatic rifle) bears the initials "FAL;" made in Argentina, Australia, Austria, Belgium, Canada, India, South Africa and the United Kingdom; has been chambered to accept 7.62mm NATO ammunition

fall: be arrested

Fallbrook redhair: high-potency marijuana from the Fallbrook, Calif., region; also called *sensemilla*

fall dough: money held in reserve for use in case of arrest

fall guy: dupe; victim

fall out: depart; take leave; unconscious from a drug overdose

false-flag recruit: espionage agent who believes he or she is working for one country or party while actually working for another

family: group of gangsters under one head whose family name becomes the name of the mob; Mafia-controlled group in charge of underworld activities within a certain area of a city or a country

f & fp: fraud and false pretenses

farm: confinement and/or correctional facility, usually in a rural area

Farm: The Farm (CIA training school at Camp Peary near Williamsburg, Va.)

Farmingdale: Turrell Residential Group Center at Farmingdale, N.J.

fas: fetal alcohol syndrome (q.v.)

fascism: right-wing totalitarian rule glorifying the nation and the state and intent upon achieving control of the entire population; practiced by Franco in Spain, Hitler in Germany and Mussolini in Italy, as well as by lesser dictators such as Peron in Argentina

fascist: person believing in or sympathetic with facism (q.v.)

fat.: fire and theft

fat: having a good supply of drugs or narcotics

FATAH: from *Harakat-Tahrir Falastin* (Arabic—the name of the Palestinian terrorist underground organization) Arabic acronyms are characterized by inverted initials, as shown here

fatal: fatal accident

Father of Criminology: Cesare Beccaria (1738-1794), author of *Delitte e della Pene* (Italian—Crimes and Punishment)—advocated an end to capital punishment and called for wide-spread prison reform

Father of Penitentiary Science: Jean Jacques Vilain, who founded the Maison de Force built in Ghent in 1773

fatty: fat marijuana cigarette

f/B: female black

f-b: full-bore (greater than 22 caliber)

FBI: Federal Bureau of Investigation (U.S. Department of Justice)

FBI Museum: spectacular display of weapons plus extensive photographic gallery of underworld characters and many exhibits explaining how they were apprehended; within FBI headquarters in downtown Washington, D.C. at 9th St. and Pennsylvania Ave.

FBIRA: Federal Bureau of Investigation Recreation Association

FBIS: Foreign Broadcast Information Service (q.v.)

FBN: Federal Bureau of Narcotics (U.S. Treasury Department)

FBP: Federal Bureau of Prisons (U.S. Department of Justice)

FBPMC: Federation of British Police Motor Clubs

FCCD: Florida Council on Crime and Delinquency

FCF: Federal Correctional Facility

FCI: Federal Correctional Institution (these are located in Alderson, W. Va.; Danbury, Conn.; Fort Worth, Texas; La Tuna, Texas; Lompoc, Calif.; Milan, Mich.; Sandstone, Minn.; Seagoville, Texas; Tallahassee, Fla.; Terminal Island, Calif.; and Texarkana, Texas); Florida Correctional Institution (at Lowell)

FCIP: Federal Crime Insurance Program

FCIS: Foreign Counterintelligence System (FBI)

FCJ: Foreign Criminal Jurisdiction

FCPA: Foreign Corrupt Practices Act (q.v.)

FCR: Field Contact Report

FDA: Food and Drug Administration

FDC: Friends of Democratic Cuba (q.v.)

FDEA: Federal Drug Enforcement Administration

fd$_{50}$: median fatal dose

FDH: Federal Detention Headquarters (located in Florence, Ariz. and New York, N.Y.)

FDLE: Florida Department of Law Enforcement

fed: federal law-enforcement officer

fed.: federal narcotics agent

Federal Bureau of Investigation: investigative arm of the U.S. Department of Justice; has 59 field offices in principal cities and some 500 satellite offices; investigates violations of federal laws such as bank robberies, espionage, treason, kidnapping, interstate transportation of stolen property, organized crime, sabotage and white-collar crime; maintains more than 171 million fingerprint file cards useful in detecting criminals; compiles crime reports on all parts of the nation

Federal Center for Correctional Research: U.S. Bureau of Prisons facility in Butner, N.C.

federal crimes: acts prohibited by federal laws

Federal Probation Officers Association: founded in 1955 to build and maintain enlightened public interest in parole, probation and related services

Fed Ref: Federal Reformatory

Feebie: Federal Bureau of Investigation (FBI) agent

feel no pain: alcohol user's phrase for the pain-free euphoric state temporarily produced by the abuse of alcohol

Fellowship of First Fleeters: Australian society whose members must prove they are descended from the first convicts landed in Botany Bay in 1788

felon: any person who has committed a felony

felonious assault: assault with a deadly weapon

felonious murder: killing committed in connection with a burglary or other crime

felonry: prison-colony population

felon swell: upper-class convict

felony: a crime punishable by imprisonment for more than a year or by death

felony tank: jail cell reserved for felons

femicide: woman killer; woman who is killed; act of killing a woman

fence: device for buying and selling stolen goods; person buying and selling stolen goods; to buy and sell stolen goods in evasion of the law

fender bender: automotive vehicle accident involving damage to vehicle

FESIP: Fifth Estate Security Information Project (one of many controlled and sponsored by OC-5, q.v.)

fess: confess

'fession: confession

fetal alcohol syndrome: brought on by pregnant mothers whose abuse of alcohol increases the risk of their producing deformed or retarded children

fettered: restrained from escaping by the use of ankle or leg fetters or both

fetters: steel cuffs placed on the ankles or legs of prisoners to keep them from escaping

FFOPA: Federal Firearms Owners Protection Act

fi: female impersonator

FI: Field Interview (usually recorded on a 3'' x 5'' card or a slip of paper)

fi (FI): Foreign Intelligence Advisory Board

fi/ci (FI/CI): foreign intelligence-counterintelligence

fiend: one who indulges compulsively or excessively in drugs or sex

fiery cross: terroristic device used by the Ku Klux Klan at the climax of ceremonial meetings; also used to identify and frighten its victims

Fiesta de la Merced: (Spanish—Mercy Fiesta)—celebrated on September 24, also known as Prisoners' Saints Day

FIF: Friends of Irish Freedom

FIFSP: *Fédération Internationale des Functionnaires Supérieurs de Police* (French—International Federation of Senior Police Officers)

fifth column: traitorous elements within a country

Fifth Estate: organized crime—international conglomerates and syndicates, often aided by corrupt public officials, unlawful labor leaders and bribable politicians

FIJ: *Fédération Internationale de Judo* (French—International Judo Federation)

file: pickpocket

Filthy Few: elite corps of assassins working within the Hell's Angels gang of motorcyclists; noted for their filthy personal habits and their murders

filthy pictures: pornographic movies; pornographic postcards

fin: five-dollar bill

fine: court-imposed penalty requiring a convicted person to pay a specific sum of money

fine stuff: finely-cut marijuana; marijuana whose stems have been removed before it is cut

finger: to inform on another person; to point the finger at a person to be arrested, beaten or killed

fingerprints: see **latent fingerprints; plastic fingerprints**

finger wave: anal examination for concealed drugs

finishing school: slang term for women's prison

fink: to give information to the police or other law-enforcement officers; informer; detective; police officer

finski: five-dollar bill

FIPP: *Fondation Internationale Pénale et Pénitentiaire* (French—International Penal and Penitentiary Foundation)

fire apparatus: fire-fighting equipment such as engines, pumpers and other vehicles as well as extinguishers, hooks and ladders, etc.

firearms: weapons that use a gunpowder charge to hurl bullets and other projectiles

Firearms Museum: see **National Rifle Association Firearms Museum**

fireball: explosive-filled projectile

fire blanket: fireproof or flameproof heavy cover used to smother fires

fireboat: vessel equipped for fighting fires on or near the water, e.g. in ports and rivers or on the open sea

firebomb: destroy by setting off fire bombs

fire bomb: incendiary device such as a Molotov cocktail

firebrand: bit of burning wood used to kindle a fire; impassioned person adept at kindling strife or unrest

firebreak: barrier constructed of cleared or plowed land used to check the progress of forest fires, prairie fires, etc.

fire brigade: body or group of firefighters

firebug: arsonist; pyromaniac

fire control: extinguishment of a fire; fire protection

firecracker: a paper-wrapped explosive detonated by merrymakers, and sometimes by criminals wishing to create a diversion

fire door: fire-resistant door

fire engine: apparatus equipped to extinguish fires

fire escape: device for facilitating the escape of people within a building on fire; often used by burglars to gain access to apartments

fire fight: exchange of gunfire; gun fight

firemanic: pertaining to firefighters or firefighting

fire plug: large opium pellet

fire prevention: program aimed at the prevention and suppression of fires

fires: firearms (police jargon)

firetrap: building or other structure deemed dangerous in the event of fire; these are sometimes set on fire to collect insurance

firewall: fire-retarding structure

fire warden: officer charged with the authority to extinguish or prevent fires

firewater: alcoholic drink; liquor

firing squad: detachment of armed men assigned to execute a condemned person

Firlands: Minimum Security Facility at Firlands, Wash.

first-degree manslaughter: killing committed without express or implied malice

first-degree murder: killing with malice aforethought; premeditated murder is sometimes punished by death

first-generation money: cash; currency

first, second and third degree: in police parlance the first degree is arrest, the second is transportation to a jail or other place of detention and the third degree is interrogation by the police or other arresting authority

FIS: Facial Identification Systems

fish: (male homosexual slang) woman; (prison slang) prisoner just incarcerated or *dressed in;* pimp

Fishkill: Fishkill Correctional Facility near Beacon-on-Hudson, N.Y.

fish story: lie; improbable tale

five: five-milligram tablet of amphetamine or benzedrine

five finger: pickpocket; thief

five percenter: fixer who, for a five percent fee, arranges profitable (and not necessarily legal) transactions between business and government

five spot: five-dollar bill; five-year prison term

fix: to bribe someone for legal or police protection; to inject a narcotic addict; a shot of heroin or some other drug

fixed: bribed; under the influence of drugs

FKL: Frauen Konzentration Lager (German—Women's Concentration Camp)—Hitler-era prison

flag: blood appearing in an eyedropper or a hypodermic syringe when a vein is punctured, as in injecting drugs

flagitious: outrageous, scandalous or villainous

FLAIRS: Fleet Locating and Information Reporting System (for police-patrol vehicles)

flake: cocaine; crazy person; person under the influence of cocaine

flak(e)y: dreamy; hazy; odd because of perceptions and values different from most others'; surrealistic; under the influence, or appearing to be under the influence, of cocaine or other drugs

flamethrower: lethal device for shooting a burning stream of liquid or semiliquid fuel

flaps-and-seals man: expert in opening and closing letters and packages without being detected

flash: sensation occuring when heroin enters the body

flashback: repetition of an earlier drug experience without taking the drug

flashers: exhibitionist(s)

flash house: hostel patronized by criminals

flat: LSD tablet

flat bit: prison sentence for a definite period of time (see also **split bit**)

flat burglar: thief specializing in robbing apartments and private homes

flea powder: greatly diluted heroin

Fleetsie: nickname of the Federal Law Enforcement Training Center in Brunswick, Georgia

FLETC: Federal Law Enforcement Training Center

Fleury Mérgois: Europe's largest prison and France's largest high-security facility, on the outskirts of Paris; it is often spoken of as prison city

flex-cuf ties: all-purpose flexible plastic ankle cuffs or handcuffs for trussing prisoners or suspects

flick-knife: switchblade knife

flimflammer: confidence man; fast talker; sleight-of-hand artist

flip: to inform; to tell all

float: be intoxicated by drugs

floating crap game: crap game that moves from place to place to avoid the police or another authority enforcing laws that forbid gambling

floating hells: British prison ships bound for Australia and Tasmania during the late 18th and early 19th centuries; French prison ships bound for Algeria, French Guiana, and New Caledonia during the same era and to the convict colony in French Guiana as recently as 1950

flopper: accident faker feigning having been hit by a vehicle so insurance can be collected

Florence: Federal Detention Headquarters at Florence, Ariz.

Flossenbürg: German prison and town near Nürnberg but closer to the Czechoslovakian frontier; Admiral Wilhelm Canaris was executed here by Himmler's Gestapo as they believed he was a British agent

FLQ: Front de Libération Québecois (French—Front for the Liberation of the people of Quebec) bomb-planting terrorists intent in forcing the separation of French-speaking Canada from the rest of Canada by violent means

flunky: one who obtains drugs by carrying them for drug pushers

fly a kite: smuggle a letter out of prison

fly bait: dead body

fly cop: policeman

fly dick: detective

flying: under the influence of drugs

Flying Handcuffs: symbol of Security Air Transport (q.v.)

fly in the sky: police-manned helicopter

fly the coop: escape from prison

f/M: female Mexican

FN Browning: Belgian-made Browning semi-automatic pistol

f/O: female Oriental

F of I: Fruit of Islam (q.v.)

FoI (FOI): Fruit of Islam (q.v.)

FoIA: Freedom of Information Act

foil: tinfoil-wrapped package of drugs

folding stuff: paper money

fold up: drug-withdrawal process

Foley Square: downtown New York City's federal court building, where offices of the FBI are also located

Folsom: California State Prison at Folsom

fool: gangster term for a person who is not a member of a gang and, hence, vulnerable

foolish powder: heroin

football: football-shaped pill containing synthetic opiates such as dilaudid or diphetamine

footbath: mobster technique of forcing a victim to put his feet into a bucket of quick-setting cement before being tossed overboard from a dock, motorboat, etc., and declared missing

FOP: Fraternal Order of Police

force option: elite group of anti-terrorist commandos trained to deal with terrorists holding hostages or threatening civilian populations

Foreign Broadcast Information Service: CIA-administered radio monitoring activity

Foreign Corrupt Practices Act: law designed to prevent American businessmen from bribing foreign officials

foreign intelligence: espionage

forensic ballistics: science of detecting and identifying lethal bullets and the firearms from which they were fired

forensic chemistry: chemistry applied to questions by law

forensic medicine: the application of medical knowledge to legal problems such as determining the cause of death

forensic odontology: investigative branch of dentistry often used to identify cadavers and bite marks, just like fingerprints, since no two people's bite marks are the same

forensic psychiatry: psychiatric knowledge applied to questions of law, as in the determination of insanity

forensics: art of argumentative discourse; application of science to the solution of legal problems

forge: to counterfeit or reproduce checks, currency, passports, securities, works of art, etc. for fraudulent purposes

forger: counterfeiter; person committing forgery or skilled in the alteration or fabrication of documents and their signatures

forgery: alteration or creation, with the intent to defraud, of a printed or written document that, if validly executed, would constitute a record of a legally-binding transaction; counterfeiting or otherwise creating imitation currency (minted metal or paper money), securities (bonds and stock certificates), signatures, works or art, etc.; something counterfeit or forged, such as a check bearing a forged signature

fork: pickpocket

Fort Apache: former nickname of the 41st police precinct station in New York, south of Boston Road and the Bronx River, where walking on the street is unsafe at almost any hour; because of the high rate of arson and the number of gutted tenements and vacant lots where gutted tenements once stood, the precinct station is now nicknamed "the Little House on the Prairie"

Fort Dimanche: Haiti's infamous prison close to Pétionville

Fort Help: National Center for Solving Special Social and Health Problems (which welcomes abusers of alcohol and other drugs to its San Francisco headquarters)

Fort Jefferson: former military prison on an island in the Dry Tortugas near Key West, Fla.; Dr. Samuel Mudd was held here after the Civil War because he treated Lincoln's assassin, John Wilkes Booth, who stopped at his home while fleeing from Federal troops

Fort Leavenworth: U.S. Diciplinary Barracks at Fort Leavenworth, Kan.

Fort Madison: Iowa State Penitentiary at Fort Madison

Fort Margherita: old Sarawak prison near Kuching on the island of Borneo or Kalimantan; it served as a Japanese detention camp for Australian and British prisoners of war during World War II

Fort Montluc: old prison in Lyon, France, which during World War II was used as Gestapo headquarters by occupying Germans, who shipped many prisoners from there to concentration camps

Fort Riley: U.S. Army Correctional Training Facility at Fort Riley, Kan.

Fort Worth: Federal Correctional Institution at Fort Worth, Tex.; U.S. Public Health Hospital at Fort Worth, Texas (many narcotic addicts are treated here)

forwards: amphetamines and other pep pills

Fossoli di Carpi: transit camp built by Mussolini's Black Shirts in north-central Italy just north of Modena as a collecting depot for Jews and others en route to concentration camps where many died or were killed

foul play: criminal action; treachery; unfair action

found in the bay: found drowned (usually as the result of a gang-inflicted homicide made to look like a drowning)

Fountain: Fountain Correctional Center at Atmore, Ala.

four sheets to the wind: intoxicated

14-n: narcotics, as *n* is the 14th letter of the alphabet

four-time loser: criminal convicted four times of felonies and hence imprisoned for life under the New York State statute called the Baumes Law

four-way check: character information obtained from the files of state police records as well as local, state and federal records

Fox Lake: Wisconsin Correctional Institution (medium-security prison between Green Bay and Madison)

fp: flat-point bullet

FPBs: Fast Patrol Boats

FPC: Federal Prison Camp (these are located at Allenwood, Pa.; Eglin Air Force Base, Fla.; Lompoc, Calif.; Marion, Ill.; Montgomery, Ala.; and Safford, Ariz.)

FPCC: Fair Play for Cuba Committee (communist-controlled organization disbanded after the assassination of Pres. John F. Kennedy by one of its members and organizers, Lee Harvey Oswald)

FPI: Federal Prison Industries

fp merchants: people operating under false pretenses

FPOA: Federal Probation Officers Association

fps: feet per second (unit of muzzle velocity)

FR: Federal Reformatory (these are located in El Reno, Okla. and Petersburg, Va.)

fractured: intoxicated

frag: to attack, bomb, kill or wound—especially an unpopular officer—with a fragmentation grenade; a fragmentation bomb or grenade

fragmentation grenade: popular underground weapon capable of exploding many deadly shrapnel fragments once its safety pin has been pulled

frame: arrange for responsibility for a crime to rest on an innocent person; victimize

frame-up: act of making an innocent person appear guilty: *it was a frame-up—she's innocent*

Framingham: Massachusetts Correctional Institution for female felons, misdemeanants, defective delinquents, drug and alcohol addicts at Framingham, Mass.

Franchi: Italian semi-automatic shotgun

Frankie Brown: (underworld nickname) the Federal Bureau of Investigation (FBI)

FRAT: Free Radical Assay Technique (heroin-morphine test)

fratricide: murder of one's own brother or sister; one who takes the life of his or her brother or sister

fraud: illegal use of concealment, deceit and misrepresentation, by individuals or groups, to obtain money, property or services or to secure business, personal or political advantage

freak: anyone engaging in odd or unusual sexual activities; frequent user of drugs

freaking freely: acting freely and spontaneously when under the influence of LSD

freak-out: drug-induced hallucinations, violence or withdrawal

freak out: lose contact with reality

free-base: smokeable form of cocaine sometimes purified with ether and hence highly flammable

free-base parties: cocaine-smoking parties

freebie: freeloader

freebooter: pirate; plunderer

free clinic: usually a public health service clinic aiding in the control and eradication of communicable diseases; many cases of veneral disease are cured by visits to such free clinics; some free clinics offer help to alcoholics and drug addicts

free for all: fight wherein all present participate

Freeport: gambling capital of the Bahamas on Grand Bahama Island, about 80 miles east of Lake Worth, Fla., below Palm Beach

free world: outside prison walls

freeze: turn doown a sale of contraband such as arms or narcotics

French blade: the guillotine

French connection: international drug-distribution syndicate based on heroin made in Marseilles

French leave: act of slipping away secretly

Frentes Abiertos: (Spanish—Open Fronts) minimum security prisons scattered throughout Cuba

fresh and sweet: just out of jail

fresh fish: new prisoner

Fresnes: southern suburb of Paris, location of a great French penitentiary of the same name

fried: badly burned; electrocuted; intoxicated

friendly house: upper-class British euphemism for a house of prostitution

Friends of Assata and Sundiata: underground prison-support movement active in New York City

Friends of Democratic Cuba: right-wing exile support group active in Miami

Frisco speedball: San Francisco-style mixture of cocaine, heroin and LSD

frisk: search a body, dead or alive, for concealed weapons, contraband, drugs, gemstones, etc.

frisker: pickpocket active in crowded places, like buses and subways, often working as teams but sometimes as individuals

frog's march: nickname for a method of conveying hard-to-handle prisoners—four officers each grab an arm or leg and carry the prisoner along face downward

Frontera: California Institution for Women at Frontera

front money: advance payment for goods or services

front the bread: put up money for something prior to its delivery

Frontón: Peruvian maximum-security offshore prison on an island close to Callao; its name brings to mind the high-walled court where jai-alai is played

frozen: frozen pupils (pinpoint-size eye pupils sometimes brought on by abusive dosages of narcotics)

fruit(er): male homosexual

fruit machine: coin-operated slot machine for gambling

Fruit of Islam: Black Muslim storm-troop disciplinary corps

fruit salad: teenager's game, sometimes played with fatal results, in which players agree to swallow one of each kind of pill found in their parents' medicine cabinets

FRW: Federal Reformatory for Women (in Alderson, W. Va.)

fry: electrocute; burn badly

ftA: fuck the Army (to hell with the rules); also appears as FtA and FTA

F-13: drugs; narcotics

fund-raising racket: organization in which professional fund raisers take up to 90 percent of the contributions they solicit

funked out: under the influence of alcohol or other drugs

funny farm: insane asylum; psychiatric ward

Futility Hill: prisoner's graveyard at San Quentin, Calif.

fuzz: detective(s); law-enforcement officer(s); police; etc.

fuzz-buster: radar device used by some motorists to give them warning of speed traps set up by the police

fuzzled: intoxicated; under the influence of alcohol, drugs, etc.

fuzzy bear: country sheriff (in the American Southwest)

fuzzy tail: police(man)

f/w: female white

FYC: Federal Youth Center (these are located in Ashland, Ky. and Englewood, Colo.)

G

G: a $1,000 bill

GA: Gamblers Anonymous (q.v.)

gaff: cheat; shortchange

gaffer: person who operates mechanically controlled gambling devices, such as roulette wheels and slot machines

gage: marijuana

gag law: law restricting freedom of the press or of speech

Galef: importer of handguns located in downtown New York

gallery: place where an addict can rent and use injection equipment (also called a **shooting gallery)**

Gallery 13: graveyard for prisoners

gallows: metal or wooden framework used for the execution of criminals by hanging

gallows bird: criminal

Gamblers: Gamblers Anonymous (q.v.)

Gamblers Anonymous: peer group helping compulsive gamblers identify their self-destructive habit

gambler's rose: card-player's shuffle

gamble with death: attempt to commit suicide

gamble: hazard or speculate money or property on an uncertain outcome such as a bet, or a dog or horse race, the fluctuation of a stock market, etc.

gambling table: table used for any form of gambling

Gamle: Swedish prison on a Baltic inlet near Vastervik

GAMMA: Guns and Magnetic Material Alarm (q.v.)

gang: group of people organized to achieve some common goal; criminals often pool their talents by joining or organizing gangs to control traffic in alcohol, cigarettes, drugs, money lending, pornography, prostitution, etc.

gang bang: gang-inflicted rape

gang hit: gang murder

gangster: one of marijuana's many nicknames

Gang Task Force: division of the San Francisco Police Department established in response to a wave of gangster killings and terrorist attacks

ganja: Jamaica-grown hashish or marijuana

gaol: (British spelling) jail

gaolage: a gaoler's fee (demanded more than a century ago and now replaced by bribes)

gaoler(s): British—jailer(s)

garand: M-1 semi-automatic rifle named for its developer, John C. Garand

garbage: low-quality drug such as hashish, heroin or marijuana

Garbage Dump: nickname of the Great Meadow Correctional Facility at Comstock, New York and of California's San Quentin Prison

gargle: a beverage; to drink

garlic and glue: convict's or vagrant's slang term for beef stew

garnish(es): bribe(s) given prison guards by inmates

garrison state: military dictatorship

garrote: a capital-punishment device of Spanish origin that strangles the prisoner with an evertightening iron collar; to execute with a garrote

garroted: strangled

gas chamber: specially built chamber or room where prisoners are executed by poison gas

gas chromatograph intoximeter: device for measuring the degree of intoxication of drunk drivers

gas mask: face-covering device protecting wearers from deadly and injurious gases; gas masks filter and purify the air their wearers breathe

gasphyxiation: gas + asphyxiation (death resulting from exposure to poisonous gas)

gas pistol: silent weapon loaded with deadly cyanide gas

Gasre: Tehran, Iran's great prison also called Ghasre or Qsar; up to its storming by militant Moslem mobs on February 11, 1979 it held some 11,000 inmates, including common thieves, drug pushers, pimps, prostitutes, and political prisoners

gassed: intoxicated; executed in a gas chamber

gassing: execution in a gas chamber

gas tank job: smuggling contraband such as drugs by means of an automobile or truck gas tank modified to conceal an inner compartment

gat: gun (named after the Gatling machine gun, invented by an American, R.J. Gatling)

gavar: pick pockets; snatch luggage

gay bashing: beating and robbing homosexuals

gay hustler: male prostitute

Gaylord: New York manufacturer of Chic Gaylord handgun holsters

gayola: payments made by homosexual establishments to crime syndicates in exchange for protection

gazer: federal law-enforcement agent

gazooney: inexperienced or innocent person; unit of any foreign currency

gazump(er): cheat(er)

gb (GB): code name for sarin (a chemical warfare agent of high toxicity; its chemical formula is $C_4H_{10}FO_2P$)

gb'd: goofballed (drugged)

GBI: Georgia Bureau of Investigation (q.v.)

gbi: great bodily injury

gcg: gas-chamber green (nickname given a bilious green prevalent on the walls of many penal institutions, where inmates complain about the depression induced by gcg)

gci (GCI): gas chromatograph intoximeter (q.v.)

GCP: Glasgow City Police

GD: Gaol Delivery

G de CR: *Guerrilleros de Cristo Rey* (Spanish—Guerrillas of Christ the King) right-wing terrorists active in Spain

Gds: Guards

geezin a bit of dee gee: (motorcycle-gang slang) injecting a bit of heroin

Geisenkirchen: Nazi subcamp in what is now West Germany

gelignite: nitrate-and-wood-pulp-base dynamite often exploded by underground terrorists

gemprint: laser-beam photograph taken of a gem to provide security, as no two gems are exactly alike

Geneva: Illinois State Training School for Girls at Geneva; Girls Training School at Geneva, Neb.

genocide: crime of destroying intentionally and systematically, an ethnic, racial, national or religious group

George Jackson Brigade: underground black extremists responsible for many bank robberies and bombings as well as the courtroom shoot-out during the 1970 trial of Angela Davis in Marin County, near San Francisco

Georgia Bureau of Investigation: state-supported crime detection and investigation group called the GBI and modeled after the FBI

geriatric institution: nickname of an old prison

geronticide: abandoning or killing off relatively helpless people who are too old to work

get a gift: obtain narcotics

get down: get down into the vein (inject intravenously)

get off: get high on heroin or another drug

get the goods on: produce conclusive evidence

get the wind: take leave

get the works: be sentenced to death

G-4: undercover anti-terrorist group within the Royal Canadian Mounted Police organization

GGI: Guided Group Interaction

ghetto: poor section of any city where for a combination of economic, racial or religious reasons some minority group lives in segregated and often squalid conditions; ghettos are often viewed as breeding places for criminals

ghost: LSD-25

ghosting: procedure whereby prisoners are spirited away during the night from one prison to another for the purpose of breaking up protest movements or hampering outside inquiries about allegations of beatings and riots

Ghost Shadows: juvenile gang in New York City's Chinatown that threatens owners of various enterprises if they fail to pay protection money to the gang

ghost train: late-night railroad train used to transport prisoners from one place to another

ghoul: person reputed to feed on corpses; person whose habits are detestable

gibbet: gallows with a projecting arm from which prisoners are hanged

giggle smoke: smoke produced by burning hashish or marijuana; hashish or marijuana

giggle water: champagne

giggle weed: hashish or marijuana

Giglio: Italian isle of exile in the Tuscan Islands within the Tyrrhenian Sea northwest of Rome; a special law, enacted in post-World-War-II Italy, permitting judges to exile suspected criminals to remote places such as Giglio if it is felt prolonged isolation will bring about rehabilitation; natives of islands such as Asinara off Sardinia, Filicudi off Sicily, and Giglio near Rome protest such action as being inimical to their personal safety and to the tourist trade they try to cultivate

gigolo: male who escorts women to social affairs and provides them with sexual services

GII: Georgia Industrial Institute at Alto; it holds more than 1,000 felons in maximum security

Gila Bend: Indian reservation in southwestern Arizona that was used after Pearl Harbor as a relocation center for Japanese-Americans

gillette (one's) way out: commit suicide by slashing one's wrists with a razor blade

gimmick: drug-injecting equipment; sales-promotion device; tricky device

ginhead: alcoholic; compulsive gin drinker

gin mill: bar; place where liquor is sold

GIPA: GI Project Alliance (q.v.)

girl: cocaine

girls' school: nickname for a reformatory for young female offenders; such places are usually given names suggesting that they are select schools for young girls

Girls' Town: correctional facility for misdemeanants at Tecumseh, Okla.

GIRU: General Intelligence and Reconnaissance Unit (Israel's anti-terrorist commando force is called GIRU 269)

give a permanent wave: electrocute

give wings: instruct another in injecting heroin

GJB: George Jackson Brigade (q.v.)

GK: Gaol Keeper

glad rag: rag saturated with quick-drying airplane glue used for sniffing; usually results in altered perception and may cause some organic damage

glass eyes: drug addict

Glass House: the glassed-in Los Angeles County jail

glassy-eyed: under the influence of alcohol or other drugs

gleep a cage: (motorcycle-gang slang) steal an automobile

glop: unappetizing prison food

glowing: highly elated as the result of being drugged

glue: arrest

glued: suffering from venereal disease

gluer: airplane-glue sniffer

glue sniffing: sniffing volatile airplane glue; often affects the central nervous system and shows itself in the eyes as well as the muscular action of the sniffer; glue sniffing may result in death through suffocation

G-man: special agent of the FBI

GNTP: Georgia Narcotics Treatment Program

go: a purchase of narcotics

goa: gone on arrival

GOA: Gun Owners of America

go bail: advance the money required as security to free a person until trial

go belly up: cooperate with law-enforcement officers in detecting crime and apprehending criminals

goblet of jam: hashish confection popular in North Africa, where its Arabic name is *m'jun-i akbar*

godfather: among Mafia mobsters and other Sicilian-American gangsters the godfather is the boss of all bosses of organized crime and prototype of the fictionalized *Godfather*; the last so-called godfather, who died in late 1976, was Carlo (Don Carlo) Gambino, who succeeded Vito (Don Vitone) Genovese

Godfather of International Terrorism: Dr. Wadi Haddad, who helped found the Popular Front for the Liberation of Palestine (PFLP) and its foreign operations chief until his death in 1978; his underground cells forged strong links with the Baader-Meinhof gang in West Germany and with the Red Army in Japan; he had a flare for disguises and false passports as well as high-risk operations involving abduction and assassination

go down: completion of a narcotics deal

God's own medicine: nickname for opium because of its power to temporarily relieve mental and physical distress

go into the sewer: inject a drug into a vein

gold: see **Acapulco gold**

goldberg: pejorative term for a Jew

gold dust: cocaine

gold duster: frequent user of cocaine

golden grain: Lebanese hashish grown around the ruins of Baalbek and sold in Beirut for export as well as local use

Golden Grove: correctional facility of St. Croix in the U.S. Virgin Islands

Golden Triangle: opium-growing area in Laos, Cambodia and Vietnam

goldfinger: synthetic heroin

gold-plated gillette: cocaine user's razor blade worn as a neck charm and also employed to cut lumpy powder finely so that it may be inhaled more readily

GOMA: Good Outdoor Manners Association (an anti-vandalism group)

gong: opium pipe

gong beater: opium smoker

goods: drugs; stolen goods

good secrets: secrets protecting the identities of intelligence sources whose work is vital to national security

good stuff: high-class heroin or any other drug

good time: time taken off a prisoner's sentence for good behavior

good trip: pleasant experience with narcotics or psychedelic drugs

goofball: cocaine-heroin mixture; amphetamine-barbiturate mixture

goofing: dreaming; heavily drugged

goof off: be absent without a good reason; lie down on the job; pretend to work

goon: hired hoodlum; usually goons are hired by people engaged in labor disputes to intimidate others by acts or threats of violence

goon squad: platoon of hoodlum terrorists

go over the hill: escape; take leave

go over the wall: escape from a correctional facility

Goree Unit: Women's Prison at Huntsville, Texas

goric: paregoric (an opiate narcotic)

gorilla: person acting aggressively or with hostility

gorilla pills: barbiturates or other sedatives

go stir bug: to go crazy while imprisoned

got beat: bought a bag containing no heroin

goulash joint: illegal gambling casino

go under: die

government men: Australian euphemism for former convicts

Governor: British penal equivalent of U.S. warden

gow: opium

gowhead: opium addict

goya & kod: detective initialism meaning one can best complete an investigation by getting off your ass and knocking on doors (to interview people)

GQS: General Quarter Sessions

grabber: pickpocket; purse snatcher

graffiti: scratchings, scribblings and sprayings of initials, names, phrases or words, cartoons or pictures on building walls, public toilets, mass transportation vehicles, etc.; often the messages are indecent and vulgar as well as unsightly

graft: payment made by politicians for non-existent jobs or services in exchange for partial kickbacks (see also **honest graft**)

grain alcohol: ethyl alcohol (never to be confused with poisonous wood alcohol)

grand jury: body of citizens selected and sworn to investigate criminal activity and the conduct of public officials as well as to hear evidence against accused persons to determine if there is sufficient evidence to bring such persons to trial

grand larceny: grand theft (q.v.)

grand theft: stealing of property having a value more than that decreed by laws as the maximum for petty theft

grape parfait: LSD

grapevine: informal word-of-mouth communication

graphologist: handwriting expert

grass: marijuana

grass brownies: brownies containing hashish or marijuana

grass-eaters: policemen or politicians who accept bribes but who do not demand them (as contrasted with meat-eaters—policemen and politicians who demand bribes)

grassed: turned in by an informer

gravity knife: German-designed two-edged knife enclosed in a case and released for use when held upside down; the heavyweight model is used for stabbing and the lightweight model for slashing; some spring-loaded versions of this design come from Japan and from Spain

gravy: coagulated mixture of a heroin addict's blood and heroin; once reheated it is often injected back into the same or another vein

graybar hotel: jail

gray propaganda: mixture of distortions, half-truths and untruths

grease: bribe

grease gun: submachine gun

greasy junkie: indolent drug addict who obtains drugs by begging or by rendering sexual services

Great Meadow: Great Meadow Correctional Facility—a maximum-security prison north of Albany at Comstock, N.Y.

Great Western: American manufacturer of handguns and importer of foreign handguns

greefa: marijuana cigarette

green: greenish Mexican marijuana; low-grade marijuana

greengoods: paper money

greengoodsman: counterfeiter or passer of counterfeit money

greengoods racket: swindle wherein a dishonest victim buys a device he or she plans to use in making counterfeit paper money and later finds that he or she has purchased a bogus device

Green Haven: Green Haven Correctional Facility—a maximum-security prison near Stormville, N.Y., northeast of Beacon in Dutchess County

green ice: emeralds

greenies: oval-shaped amphetamine-sulfate tablets

green money: paper money

greens: marijuana

green stuff: paper money

green triangle: criminal identification badge worn in concentration camps controlled by the Nazis in World War II

Greenville: Federal Prison Camp at Greenville, S.C.

grefa: marijuana

grenade: explosive missile thrown by hand or projected from a launcher such as a rifle

griefo: Indian hemp (*Cannabis sativa*)—also spelled *griffo*

griffo: see **griefo**

grift: dirty money; money made dishonestly

grill: question closely and intensively

grog: hard liquor

grog blossom: red face or red nose produced by excessive drinking

grogged: intoxicated

groghound: alcoholic

grogmill: cheap cocktail bar; low-class saloon

grogshop: saloon; waterfront dive selling hard liquor

Gross Rosen: Nazi concentration camp known for the number of forced-labor slaves it furnished German industry during World War II

ground animal meat: prison nickname for hamburgers, hot dogs, sausages

ground animals: prison nickname for hamburgers, hot dogs and any sausages

Group 4: British security guard service used by many businesses and governments

group home: non-confining residential facility for adjudicated adults or juveniles (see also **halfway house**)

grower: person who grows marijuana

Gruenheld: East Berlin's great prison

GS: Garda Siochana (police force of Ireland's twenty-six southern counties); General Sessions (court)

GSG 9: *Grenzschutzgruppe Neun* (German—Border Protection Group 9) West Germany's anti-terrorist commandos

GTF: Gang Task Force (q.v.)

gtT: gone to Texas (one jump ahead of the sheriff)

G-2: military intelligence section of the U.S. Army or the U.S. Marine Corps; military intelligence office(r)

Guadalajara: Mexican prison in Jalisco's capital city of Guadalajara

guage butt: marijuana cigarette

Guanajuato: prison in Guanajuato, capital of the Mexican state of the same name, close to Queretero

guardhouse: military jail or lock-up

Guaymas: prison in Guaymas, a Mexican port on the Gulf of California

guerrilla: (Spanish—little war) underground; underground war(fare)

guerrilla war(fare): fighting between irregular underground troops and organized forces who are trying to hold or protect some territory where the guerrillas may have the support of many of the natives

guest of the city: prisoner confined in a city jail

guest of the governor: prisoner confined in a state penitentiary

guest of the nation: prisoner confined in a federal penitentiary

guest of the realm: prisoner in HM gaols (jails) and penitentiaries

guest of the state: prisoner held in a state penal institution

Guevarist: guerrilla tactics of the type advocated by Ernesto (Che) Guevara, who was Castro's chief collaborator in the Cuban Revolution

guide: person who cares for and guides another person who is taking drugs for the first time

guillotine: device for beheading criminals; named for Dr. Joseph Guillotin, who advocated the use of this device, which was invented during the French Revolution by Dr. Antoine Louis

gumfoot: policeman

gumshoe: detective

gun: firearm; hypodermic syringe

gunga: Indian hemp

gunk: nickname for aerosols, glues and solvents used for inhaling

gun lobby: representatives of arms and munitions makers as well as the National Rifle Association

gunpoke: gunman

gunport: opening in the front of an automobile made to be invisible from the outside that enables the driver or security guard to fire at approaching antagonists; turret fitted in an armored truck permitting the driver or guard to fire at assailants

gunpowder: dynamite-strength narcotic

Guns and Magnetic Material Alarm: an anti-hijacking device

gunsel: catamite (boy used for pederastic purposes); armed criminal

gunshot wound: penetrating or perforating injury caused by a bullet; usually the entrance wound is smaller than the exit wound if the bullet left the body of the victim

gun-shy: cowardly

gunslinger: gunman

gunsmith: skilled designer and maker of firearms

guru: (Hindi—teacher; spiritual master) expert LSD user who guides a first-time user through his or her trip

Gusen: forced-labor camp run by the Nazis in Austria

gutbucket: cheap cocktail bar; low-class saloon

guthook: knife used for cutting, gutting and skinning; to be guthooked is to have your guts hooked out with such a weapon

gut shot: gunshot wound in the abdominal cavity, often causiing a lingering death due to severe internal injuries

guzzled: arrested

guzzler: alcoholic; fast drinker

gw: guerrilla warfare (q.v.)

gya: got you again (slang for caught you again)

gyp: cheat; deceive; swindle

gyp artist: accomplished cheater or swindler

gyp joint: place where cheating and overcharging are standard operating practice

gyp moll: female accomplice in confidence games and similar swindles

gypsy cab: simulated taxicab without a taximeter, making its driver free to charge whatever he thinks he can get from gullible customers

Gypsy Squad: police group assigned to keep an eye on Gypsies

gyve: marijuana cigarette

gyves: handcuffs or fetters

H

h (H): heroin; husband

hab. corp.: habeas corpus (q.v.)

habe: habeas corpus (q.v.)

habeas corpus: (Latin—may you have the body) prisoner's right to be brought before a court so its judge may decide on the legality of his or her detention

habit: alcoholic or drug addiction

habit forming: causing addiction through continued use

habitual excessive drinkers: classification of alcohol users who become intoxicated more than 12 times a year or who are under the influence of alcohol more than once a week

habitual offender: consistent lawbreaker

habituation: psychological dependence on drugs, whether alcohol, caffeine, marijuana, narcotics (analgesic pain killers and opiates), nicotine, sedatives, stimulants, tranquilizers or hallucinogens

hack: prison guard; taxicab; taxicab driver

Haddam: Connecticut Justice Academy at Haddam (and, within, its old jail, built in 1786)

haiduk: Balkan bandit guerrilla

hailer: bullhorn

Halawa: Halawa Jail at Aiea on Oahu, Hawaii

half a stretch: six month's imprisonment

half-corned: intoxicated

half piece: half an ounce of cocaine, heroin or morphine

half seas over: intoxicated

half shot: semi-intoxicated

half under: semi-intoxicated

halfway house: non-confining residential facility for adjudicated adults or juveniles; facility providing an alternative to confinement for persons not suitable for probation or needing a period of readjustment to the community after confinement

Hall: Hall of Justice

Hallowell: the Stevens School for female juvenile delinquents at Hallowell, La.

hallu: hallucinate; hallucinating; hallucination(s); hallucinogen(ic)(s)

hallucinogenic: producing hallucinations

hallucinogens: hallucinogenic drugs; continued use may result in chromosomal breakdowns or damage to the brain

halter: hangsman's noose

Hamilton: Hamilton County Jail in Cincinnati, Ohio

hammer and sickle: communist symbol

hammerless: revolver in which the hammer is shrouded to facilitate its quick draw from its owner's pocket

Hammerli: Swiss manufacturer of handguns

h & c: heroin and cocaine

handcuff: arrest, check or make powerless by putting on handcuffs

handcuffed and fettered: held or restrained by handcuffs and fetters

handcuffs: adjustable metal bracelets connected by a chain and used to restrain prisoners

handgun: any gun made so it can be fired with one hand

H & H: Holland & Holland (British gunmakers)

handmark: fingerprint; palmprint

handprint: impression left by a hand on a solid surface

H & R: Harrington and Richards (revolvers and shotguns)

H & S: Health and Safety (Code)

Hands Off This Car: anti-theft program underway in Boston, sponsored by the American Legion Auxiliary Auto and Travel Club

hand-to-hand: hand-to-hand fighting; person-to-person delivery of drugs

hand-to-hand go: purchase of narcotics wherein the dope is passed directly from one person to another

hand tools: lockpicks and screwdrivers

hanger hooks: hook-like devices sewn to the inner lining of clothing worn by shoplifters

hanging: slang term meaning distress caused by lack of narcotics

Hanging Judge: Judge Roy Bean of Langtry, Texas ("The Law West of the Pecos"); nickname of other judges noted for the number of criminals they eliminated by hanging

hangman: executioner

Hangman's Day: Friday (customary day for hangings)

hang one on: get drunk

hangout: meeting place

hangup: habit or idea found to be distasteful or uncomfortable; psychological block

hanky panky: adultery; double dealing; swindling

Hanoi Hilton: nickname of Hanoi's Hoa Lo prison in North Vietnam

haphim: Pakistani dialect word meaning morphine sulfate tablets of the type smuggled from the Northwest Frontier to spots as distant as Denmark and the United States

happy dust: cocaine

Harbison: Harbison Correctional Institution for Women at Irmo, S.C.

hard drugs: physically-addictive drugs such as heroin, morphine, opium and the like

hard labor: sentence involving imprisonment plus useful labor such as road building or maintenance

hard liquor: liquors of high alcoholic content

hard narcotics: opiates such as heroin and morphine

hard stuff: nickname for heroin

hardware: guns; weapons

Hardwick: Georgia Rehabilitation Center for Women at Hardwick; felons and misdemeanants 17 years of age and up are sent to here

HARM: Humans Against Rape and Molestation

harness bull: police(man)

Harrington & Richards: American manufacturers of revolvers and shotguns (H & R)

Harris: Harris County Juvenile Detention Center (Houston, Texas)

Harrison Narcotic Act: federal regulations providing prison terms for the illegal sale or use of drugs

harry: heroin

Hartford: Connecticut State Prison at Hartford

hash: hashish

hashish: (Arabic—Indian hemp) marijuana-type drug popular throughout Europe, North Africa and the Middle East as well as other parts of the world where it is valued by drug users because of its very high THC content

hashish bar: saloon selling hashish as well as alcoholic beverages

hashish oil: see **hash oil**

hash oil: extremely potent extract of hashish; often used in conjunction with tobacco cigarettes by placing a drop at one end or along the paper cover; also known as red oil or THC oil

hash pipe: hashish pipe (for smoking hashish)

hassle: irritate; quarrel with; squabble; tease

hatchet: combination axe and hammer sometimes used as a weapon; hatchet murder(er)

hatchet man: hired assassin

hatpin: effective weapon consisting of a long pin used to fasten a hat upon a woman's head; the pin's blunt end usually is a bulbous glass bead or a simulated pearl

have a ball: have a good time

have a snoot full: have a snoot full of liquor; be intoxicated

haven house: shelter for families of violent alcoholics

Hawaiian sunshine: LSD

hawkshaw: nickname for detectives derived from a comic strip, *Hawkshaw the Detective*

hay: marijuana

haymaker: heavy blow with the fists rendering the recipient unconscious; smashing success

hbd: has been drinking

hc: habitual criminal; hot and cold

H-caps: heroin-filled capsules

HCCJ: Harvard Center for Criminal Justice

HCN: House (of Representatives) Committee on Narcotics

H Ct: High Court

head: person dependent upon alcohol or drugs; toilet (especially on a ship)

headache department: liquor counter in a store

headache house: cocktail bar; liquor store; any establishment selling alcohol by the glass or by the bottle

headcrusher: one who beats or kills others on orders from a gang leader

head drug: psychologically addictive drug; psychological stimulant such as an amphetamine or a hallucinogen

headhunter: a hired killer

headkit: drug user's collection of injection impedimenta (hypodermic needle, rubber tube, syringe, etc.)

headpiece: person dependent on alcohol or drugs

headshop: store or section of a store where the paraphernalia of drug users such as cigarette paper, incense, opium pipes, psychedelic posters, "roach clips" and waterpipes are displayed and sold

head shrinker: psychiatrist or psychologist

hearing: proceeding whereby arguments, evidence or witnesses are heard by an administrative or judicial officer

hearts: amphetamines

heat: attention directed against underworld people by the police or the press or both; *the heat's on* means the police or the press, or both, are on the alert and active in crime suppression and exposure

heat artist: person skilled in refining solidified alcohol (such as Sterno) and drinking it without suffering from poisoning

heat up: causing suspicion when police or other law-enforcement officers are around

heave: vomit

heave ho: ejection

heavenly blues: hallucinogenic morning-glory seeds

heavenly dust: cocaine

heaven 'n' hell: nickname for pcp (PCP)

heavy: man hired by a prostitute to give physical protection or even to commit a murder

heavy drugs: hard drugs (q.v.)

heavy man: person possessing narcotics

heavy stuff: hard drugs such as cocaine and heroin

Heckler and Koch: West German manufacturer of firearms

heel: to assault or attack; a sneak thief; a low-down person

heeled: armed; possessing drugs; possessing money (as in the expression *he is well-heeled*)

heesh: hashish

heip: high-explosive incendiary plug

heisd: high-explosive incendiary self destroying

Heiser: Herman Heiser Saddlery of Denver, Colo., maker of handgun holsters

heist: to steal; a hold-up

heistman: hold-up man

Helena: the Mountain View School for female juvenile delinquents at Helena, Mont.

helicoptered: executed by being thrown out of a helicopter

hell-bender: drunken binge

hell house: pawnshop or warehouse maintained by receivers of stolen goods

Hell's Angels: militant motorcycle gang terrorizing many American metropolitan communities in California and on the East Coast; chapters of the gang exist in other parts of the country as well as in Australia, Germany and Switzerland; assassinations are carried out by an elite group calling themselves the Filthy Few; the Hell's Angels make their living trafficking in drugs

hemp: common name for the cannabis plant used to make hashish and marijuana

hempen four-in-hand: hangman's noose

hemp stretcher: nickname for a hangman

hen house: brothel

Hennigsdorf: Nazi subcamp close to Berlin and larger concentration camps

hen pen: girl's school; reformatory for females

henry: heroin

her: cocaine

herb: marijuana

herder: prison guard

herion: (Afro-American slang) heroin

Hermosillo: Sonora state prison in Hermosillo, Mexico

heroin: physically addictive drug derived from morphine but five times stronger

Heroin Supermarket: nickname of the open-air sidewalk formerly used by drug pushers plying their trade along Eighth Avenue between 116th and 117th streets in Harlem; the New York City Police Department finally arrested so many of them that they were forced to abandon their operations and go elsewhere

hero of the underworld: heroin, in the opinion of so many underworldlings who benefit from its sale and use

Herrera Family: drug ring controlled by the Herrera family of Durango, Mexico; more than 2,000 members push drugs in big American cities as well as in Caribbean resorts such as Puerto Rico

Herstedvester: Danish psychiatric prison in a western suburb of Copenhagen; world-famed for its advanced methods, said to result in reduced recidivism

he-she: male transvestite prostitute dressed and padded to resemble a female on the prowl

HFC: Human Freedom Center (q.v.)

HFSSA: Historical Firearms Society of South Africa (in Cape Town)

hick dick: rural detective or policeman

hideaway: secret place of refuge and retreat

hide out: evade law-enforcement officers

hideout: hiding place

high: exhilarated, intoxicated or turned on by the use of alcohol or drugs

high as a kite: extremely intoxicated; highly elated by drugs

highbinder: hoodlum; criminal

high-profile crime: one committed in broad daylight and in full view of many people (see **low profile crime**)

high roller: person willing to risk large sums of money during a visit to a gambling establishment

high sign: secret signal; *don't go until I give you the high sign*

hijack: to seize a vehicle such as an airplane, automobile, motorboat or truck

Hilton Head: old Federal prison holding many Confederate prisoners of war in the 1860s

him: heroin

hinkey: suspicious

hip-hugger: handgun holster

HIRE: Hooking Is Real Employment (association for prostitutes)

hi-sp: high-speed bullet

Hi-Standard: American manufacturer of handguns

Hi-Standard Derringer: two-round 22-caliber minimum-size pistol named for its original designer (who spelled his name Deringer)

Hi Stan 22 plus: High Standard .22-caliber automatic plus silencer (also known as the *assassin's special*)

hit: arrest or be arrested; get into a vein; be rejected for parole; inhale from a marijuana cigarette; an assassination; potential customer's approach to narcotics pusher

HIT: Health Inca Tea (tea containing coca leaves)

hit-and-run: a hit-and-run accident is one in which the driver fails to stop to identify herself or himself; term may also apply to such a driver

Hitler: Adolf Hitler (1889-1945), Austro-German founder of the reactionary National Socialist German Workers (Nazi) Party, which under his direction took over Germany and, with the aid of the German armed forces and their allies, almost all of Europe until their defeat and his suicide in 1945, following the mass killings of untold millions of people

hit list: listing of persons to be harassed, maimed, or murdered

hitman: professional killer

hit murder: killing performed by a hit man or hit men

hit the bottle: drink alcohol habitually

hit the fence: escape from prison

hit the mattress: go into hiding

hit the pipe: smoke opium

hit the pit: be jailed

hit the sidewalk: be released from jail or other place of detention

hit the steam: smoke opium

hitting the stuff: under the influence of drugs

hit up: inject drugs; burglarize

hit with a shoe: kick

HIU: Hypnosis Investigation Unit (q.v.)

HK: Heckler and Koch (q.v.)

hl: hard labor

HLPR: Howard League for Penal Reform

HMBI: Her (His) Majesty's Borstal Institution

hmc: heroin-morphine-cocaine mixture

HMG: Her (His) Majesty's Gaol

HMP: Her (His) Majesty's Penitentiary; Her (His) Majesty's Prison

HO: Home Office

'ho': whore

hoak: alter inventory records to cover theft or illegal sale of merchandise

Hoa Lo: downtown prison in Hanoi, Vietnam, nicknamed the Hanoi Hilton

hobble: walk with leg irons attached

hobo: vagrant sometimes engaged in temporary tasks such as gathering crops and sometimes subsisting on charity and petty thievery

hock: pawn

hockshop: pawnshop

HOCPC: Home Office Crime Prevention Center

hocus: marijuana or another drug

hocus-pocus: swindle

HOFSL: Home Office Forensic Science Laboratory (London)

hogleg: American frontier-era six-shooter revolver

hog(s): addict(s) with a big habit

hoist: to hang (a person); to rob

hoister: shoplifter

hokeypokey: deception; hocus-pocus; trickery

hold: carry drugs on one's person; hold drugs for sale or personal use, whether on one's person, in one's automobile or in one's home

hold the bag: be left with incriminating evidence; be left with all the responsibility; *they left me holding the bag*

hold-up: action of a criminal in holding a victim at the point of a gun or other weapon during the execution of a robbery or other crime; robbery

hole: solitary-confinement cell; promiscuous female; prostitute

hole up: hide

holiday headache(s): alcohol-or-drug-induced ailment(s), usually

Holland & Holland: British gunmakers, also known as Holland's

hollow point: bullet designed to expand dramatically on impact; some states prohibit their use by the police or other law-enforcement officers

holmes: (prisoner's jargon) brother, friend, partner

Holmes: short form for Sherlock Holmes, the legendary detective created by Sir Arthur Conan Doyle; Holmes Electric Protective, incorporated in New York as Holmes Protection in 1858, when it featured the first central-office burglar-alarm system, devised by its founder, Edwin Holmes

Holmesburg: prison in Philadelphia's industrial suburb of Holmesburg

holocaust: destruction by fire; policy of total physical annihilation of a nation or a people, as of the Jews under Nazism

Holy Three of Criminology: Enrico Ferri, Raffaele Garofalo and Cesare Lombroso

Holzminden: German maximum-security prison northwest of Göttingen

home free: having escaped arrest, indictment, trial, conviction, sentencing, fine or imprisonment

home-grown: domestically-cultivated marijuana

homicide: killing of one person by another (see also **criminal homicide, excusable homicide, justifiable homicide** and **willful homicide**)

homicide hours: midnight to 1:00 a.m. and 1:00 a.m. to 2:00 a.m., respectively, according to New York City's Police Department statistics concerning these time periods, when most murders are committed

homrep: homicide report

honest graft: phrase coined by Tammany Hall chieftain George Washington Plunkitt to describe the profit made by politicians who have advance notice of public plans and purchases and are thus able to make or suggest profitable moves to others—for a fee

honeyman: pimp

honeytrap: counterintelligence snare bated with a sexually attractive female or male, as required

honked: drunk

honky: (Afro-American slang—white person) black pejorative equivalent of the white pejorative *nigger*

honky-tonk: low-class frontier or waterfront cocktail bar, dance hall or saloon

hooch: homemade alcoholic drink made of fruit and sugar or potato peelings

hooch hound: an alcoholic

hood: hoodlum; gangster

'hood: neighborhood (usually gang-controlled when so contracted)

hook: fasten (handcuffs)

hookah: Middle Eastern or Oriental smoking pipe designed so the smoke bubbles through a bowl of perfumed water before it is inhaled via a long flexible tube; often used for smoking hashish and marijuana; also known as a hubble-bubble pipe or narghile or by its Turkish name, *nargile*

hooked: addicted to dangerous drugs

hook 'em: hook them (fasten with handcuffs)

hooker: prostitute

hookshop: hooker('s) shop (a whorehouse)

hooligan: hoodlum; juvenile delinquent; vandal

Hooper Home: Issac T. Hooper Home, the first halfway house in the United States, opened by the Society of Friends or Quakers in New York City in 1845

hoosegow: jail; slang term believed to be derived from the Spanish *juzgado* (court of justice)

hoosier: prison visitor

hootch: hooch (q.v.)

hop: opium

Hope Halls: halfway houses for ex-convicts sustained by the Volunteers of America from 1896 through the 1920s

hophead: narcotic addict

hopped up: drugged; intoxicated

hoppie: narcotics agent

hopstick: opium pipe

horizontalist: euphemism for prostitute

horn: sniff cocaine or another drug

horrors: delirium tremens

horse: nickname for heroin

horse brine: caramel-colored alcohol supposed to pass for whiskey

horse doctor: prison doctor; veterinarian

horse room: betting or bookmaking place

horse trank: horse tranquilizer (pcp or PCP)—an animal tanquilizer used by some drug pushers as a substitute for the much-harder-to-obtain tetrahydrocannabinol (thc or THC), the active ingredient of hashish or marijuana; an overdose of horse trank can produce coma and death

hose: beat with a length of hose; gun down with high-pressure water hoses used to quell public disturbances and riots

hostage: person held for the payment of a ransom or the performance of an act such as the release of imprisoned terrorists

Hostage Negotiating Team: New York City Police Department's group responsible for foiling terrorists and obtaining the release of their hostages

hot: wanted by the police; stolen

hot and cold: heroin (a depressant) and cocaine (a stimulant)

hot area: place where there are police

hot arts: hot art dealers (who traffic in stolen works of art)

hot busted: arrested for carrying addictive drugs discovered during a police roundup (see also **cold busted**)

HOT Car: Hands Off This Car (q.v.)

Hotel Detail: branch of a police department's burglary squad specializing in hotel and motel thefts

hot ice: stolen diamonds

hot seat: electric chair or its metaphoric equivalent

hot sheet: card containing current list of stolen vehicles

hot-sheet trade: short-time hotel and motel guests who use their beds for an hour or less but pay for a full night's lodging

hot shot: container of pure heroin or heroin-and-poison mixture used to kill an informer

Hot Shot: Hot Shot Products Company, manufacturer of the Sabre-Six electric cattle prod used to control violent individuals

hot squat: electric chair

hot stick: marijuana cigarette

hot wire: electrical jumper wire used to start an automotive vehicle without using an ignition key; used by many automotive vehicle thieves

house: police-station house; whorehouse

House 33: Soviet secret-police prison in Rostov-on-Don

housebreaker: criminal who makes forcible entry into an apartment or house with the intention of robbing or molesting its inhabitants

house connection: drug dealer operating out of a private apartment or house, where coming and going is more or less taken for granted and not subject to surveillance

house dick: house detective (as in a hotel, office, plant or store)

house of assignation: Victorian euphemism for a whorehouse; originally an assignation was simply a lover's secret meeting place

House of C: House of Correction

House of Correction: in Philadelphia, Pa., for male and female felons, misdeameanants and untried juveniles and adult females

House of D: Women's House of Detention in New York City

house of darkness: prison

house of detention: jail; lockup

house of ill fame: brothel

House of Metamorphosis: San Diego drug-abuse treatment center helping addicts quit heroin and other addictive drugs

Howard: Rhode Island town containing most of the state's correctional facilities, such as the Providence County Jail, now called the Admission and Orientation Unit; the Rhode Island State Prison, now called the Maximum Custody Facility; the Medium-Minimum Facility, formerly the Reformatory for Men; the Rhode Island Training School for Girls; and the Rhode Island School for Boys

hpc: history of the present complaint

hua: head up ass (reckless driving)

Hubert Street: New York City Police Academy at 7 Hubert Street in lower Manhattan

hubble-bubble: hookah (q.v.)

Hudson: Hudson County Penitentiary in New Jersey; the New York School for Girls at Hudson, N.Y.

Hudson Street: alimony jail on the lower west side of Manhattan; inmates were imprisoned for their failure to pay alimony

hulk: prison ship—usually an old vessel unfit for sailing on the high seas but adequate as a floating prison

Hull: HM Prison at Hull, England; prisons in Canada's Hull, opposite Ottawa, and in Boston's suburb of Hull, on Massachusetts Bay

Human Freedom Center: group organized in Berkeley, Calif. to aid cultists in breaking away from cults, such as the People's Temple of the late Rev. Jim Jones

hummer: false arrest; person giving inaccurate information

humpback: nickname of the Browning automatic shotgun

hung over: suffering a morning-after alcohol-induced headache

hungry croaker: doctor whose need for money causes him to prescribe drugs for addicts, even in amounts large enough for them to resell the drugs to others

hungup: distressed by lack of narcotics

hung up to dry: hanged

hunt down: track down with intent to arrest

Huntsville: Goree Unit Women's Prison at Huntsville, Texas

hush-hush: confidential; quiet; secretive

hush money: bribe given to induce someone not to give evidence or to testify before a congressional committee or in a court of law

hustle: to get alcohol, drugs or money by stealing or whoring

hustler: person obtaining alcohol, drugs or money by stealing or whoring

hustling drawers: specially fitted underwear worn by professional shoplifters for the concealment of stolen goods

hut: prison cell

hydrogen cyanide gas: see **blue pellets**

hype: drug peddler; hypodermic; hypodermic injection; hypodermic needle; hypodermic syringe; drug addict

hype stick: hypodermic injection; hypodermic needle

Hypnosis Investigation Unit: unit of Los Angeles Police Department using hypnotic techniques to help victims, witnesses and others recall what happened at the time of the crime

hypnotic: sleep-producing drug

hypnotica: sleep-producing drugs

hypnotic drugs: central nervous system depressants such as barbiturates, used in large doses to induce sleep and in small ones to reduce nervous tension

hypnotic sedatives: hypnotic drugs (q.v.)

hypo: hypodermic injection; hypodermic needle

I

IAAI: International Association of Arson Investigators (q.v.)

IABTI: International Association of Bomb Technicians and Investigators

IAC: Intelligence Advisory Committee (q.v.) of the CIA

IAC: International Anticounterfeiting Coalition

IACCI: International Association of Credit Card Investigators

IACP: International Association of Chiefs of Police (q.v.)

IAD: Internal Affairs Division (of the Los Angeles Police Department and the New York City Police Department)

IAF: International Abolitionist Federation (for the abolition of prostitution); International Association of Firefighters

iafd: intentionally administered fatal dose(s)

I&NS: Immigration and Naturalization Service (U.S. Department of Justice)

IAPA: Inter-American Police Academy; International Association of Police Artists

IAPIP: International Association for the Protection of Industrial Property

IAPL: International Association of Penal Law

IAPP: International Association of Police Professors

IAWP: International Association of Women Police (q.v.)

ib: illegal behavior

IB: Intelligence Branch

IBI: Illinois Bureau of Investigation

ibogaine: drug obtained from the African shrub *Tabernanthe iboga* and used to combat fatigue; in large doses it produces excitement, hallucinations, intoxication and mental confusion

IBPI: International Bureau for Protection

IBSTP: International Bureau for the Suppression of Traffic in Persons (engaged in prostitution)—founded in 1899

ICA: Institute of Criminal Anthropology

ICAP: Integrated Criminal Apprehension Program (q.v.)

ICC: International Control Commission (of the Comintern and the Cominform)

ICCC: International Center for Comparative Criminology (q.v.)

ICCD: Information Center on Crime and Delinquency (of the National Council on Crime and Delinquency)

ICCS: International Center for Criminological Studies

icebox: prison coroner's laboratory and office

ice creamer: occasional user of drugs

ice cream habit: practice of using drugs sporadically

iced: jailed

iceman: diamond thief

icepick: bar or kitchen utensil consisting of a long sharp-pointed spike fitted into a heavy handle; used to chip ice and sometimes to inflict lethal wounds or to slash rubber tires; used by many murderers because it causes internal bleeding not readily apparent to bystanders or victims; also, to puncture or slash the air-inflated tire of an automotive vehicle with an icepick or similar instrument

ice-water doctor: unsympathetic doctor refusing to prescribe drugs to addicts suffering withdrawal symptoms

ICFPW: International Confederation of Former Prisoners of War (Paris, France)

ICND: International Commission on Narcotic Drugs (UN)

ICPA: International Commission for the Prevention of Alcoholism; International Conference of Police Associations (q.v.)

ICPC: International Criminal Police Commission (Interpol)

ICPI: Insurance Crime Prevention Institute

ICPO: International Criminal Police Organization (Interpol)

ICSPPR: International Centre of Sociological, Penal, and Penitentiary Research (Messina, Italy)

IDAA: International Doctors in Alcoholics Anonymous

idb: illicit diamond buying

ID bracelet: plastic identification bracelet tag held fast to evidence or to prisoners by sets of double-headed grip fasteners

IDC: Intelligence Documentation Center (of OC-5, q.v.)

i/d/d: illicit diamond dealer

IDEA: International Drug Enforcement Association

identification-paper racket: scam in which an auto thief buys the wreck of a very expensive car such as a Cadillac or an import just to obtain its identification papers, buys license plates for the wreck, insures it for good-condition market value, reports it stolen and collect the insurance

identification parade: police lineup of prisoners held for identification by eyewitnesses or victims

Identi-Kit: identification device consisting of 536 photographic transparencies enabling investigators to assemble a human face from its components—beard, chin, eyebrows, eyes, hairline, headgear, lips, moustache, nose, scars, etc.; the components are available on easy-to-assemble 4-by-5-inch films; the Identi-Kit was invented by a former Los Angeles law-enforcement officer, Hugh C. McDonald, a man with more than 40 years experience in tracking down criminals

IDF: Israeli Defense Force (also known as the Israeli Secret Service or Zahal)

idiot chart: city map consulted by amateur burglars with such care that it soon becomes apparent that they are busy casing a neighborhood before breaking into and entering homes or offices

idiot juice: nutmeg-and-water combination used in prisons as an intoxicant

idiot pills: barbiturates

IDLE: Idaho Department of Law Enforcement

idm: illicit diamond mining

id racket: identification racket; false-document business offering people phony birth certificates, death certificates, driver's licenses, military discharge papers, school and college diplomas, social security cards, passports, etc.

ids: illicit diamond smuggling

IDSO: International Diamond Security Organization

ied: improvised explosive device

IFA: International Footprints Association (q.v.)

IFIF: International Foundation for Internal Freedom (q.v.)

IfK: Institut for Kriminologi (Norwegian); *Institut für Kriminologie* (German)

IFNE: International Federation for Narcotic Education

IFSPO: International Federation of Senior Police Officers (q.v.)

IFSSE: International Fire, Security, and Safety Exhibition

i/g/d: illicit gold dealer

IHHA: International Halfway House Association (q.v.)

ii: illegal immigrant

iid: infrared intrusion detection (burglar alarm); interior intrusion device (burglar's tool)

IIDS: Interior Intruder Detection System

IIP: Indian Imperial Police

IJA: International Journal of the Addictions

IJOA: International Juvenile Officers Association (q.v.)

IJR: Institute for Juvenile Research (concerning delinquent children)

IKPK: International Kriminal-Polizei-Kommission (German—International Criminal Police Commission)

ILAAS: International League Against Anti-Semitism

Ile du Diable: (French—Devil's Island, q.v.)

illegal: contrary to law; an espionage agent posing as a citizen of the country where he or she is spying; an illegal alien

illegal gun: a shotgun with a barrel less than 18 inches long from breech to muzzle or an overall length less than 26 inches, or a rifle with a barrel less than 14 inches long

illegit: illegitimate

illicit: contrary to ethical, legal or moral standards and hence unethical, illegal or immoral

illuminated: intoxicated

ILSR: Institute for Law and Social Research

im: intramuscular injection

IME: Institute of Makers of Explosives (q.v.)

IMI: Israeli Military Intelligence

imm: impairing a minor's morals

immoral: illicit, indecent, obscene or without redeeming social implication or value

immurement: confinement within walls

impaired physician: doctor impaired by addiction to alcohol and/or drugs

importer: importer of dangerous drugs

impound: imprison

impulse crimes: assaulting, mugging, raping, shoplifting, stabbing, tire slashing, vandalizing, etc.

imqc: imported merchandise quantity control (U.S. Customs Service program)

INCB: International Narcotics Control Board (Geneva, Switzerland)

incendiarism: agitation and subversion; malicious burning

incendiarist: agitator; arsonist

incendiary: fire-productive bomb or other explosive; malicious burning; person stirring up discontent and strife or setting fires

incendiary bullet: projectile igniting upon impact; in the United States these are often color-coded by their blue-painted tips

inco: incorrigible

incog: incognita; incognito

incognita: (of a woman) living under an assumed name and/or disguised

incognito: (of a man) living under an assumed name and/or disguised

in cold blood: without compassion or mercy

in cold storage: in the grave(yard)

incorrigible: person who will not be corrected, reformed or made to conform to social standards

incriminate: charge with a crime; involve in a crime

indecent assault: personal violation; rape

indecent exposure: act committed by a person who willfully and lewdly exposes his or her private parts in any public place where others are present

index crimes: crimes reported in the Crime Index of the *Uniform Crime Reports* compiled by the Federal Bureau of Investigation (FBI)

Indiana Girls School: at Indianapolis, for female juvenile delinquents from 12 to 18 years old

Indianapolis: euphemistic name often used when referring to the Indiana Girls School in Indianapolis or to the prison there

Indian hay: marijuana derived from Indian hem (*Cannabis indica*)

Indian hemp: hemp-type plants from which hashish and marijuana are derived

indictment: formal written accusation made by a grand jury and filed in a court, alleging that a specific person or persons committed a specific offense or offenses

Indio: Indio Branch of the Riverside County Jail in California

individual confinement: solitary imprisonment

industrial prison: workshop type of penitentiary where inmates produce useful things such as mail bags and vehicle license plates

inebriantia: alcoholic beverages causing cerebral excitation followed by depression

inebriate: an alcoholic

Inebriate Reception Center: place where non-violent abusers of alcohol and other drugs accept coffee and counseling in lieu of being jailed; pilot facility in San Diego, Calif.

INEOA: International Narcotics Enforcement Officers Association

infanticide: killing of newborn babies

Infernal Revenue Service: nickname of the Internal Revenue Service, most often applied by those who come out second best in bouts with the tax collector

info: information

informant: person giving information to law-enforcement officers to be used in the investigation of criminals

infrared heat sensor: device used by the U.S. Border Patrol to detect persons attempting to come from Mexico into the United States

infrared intrusion detection: burglar-alarm system

in front: money handed over before the narcotic is passed to the purchaser

inhaler: person who inhales airplane glue, cleaning fluids, gasoline or other psychotoxic intoxicants

in high: under the influence of alcohol or drugs

inmate: person in a confinement facility; prisoner

inner city: congested and often depressed area of any city, sometimes called the core city

INR: Intelligence and Research (U.S. Department of State)

INS: Immigration and Naturalization Service

insanity: lunacy; mental deficiency, disease or incompetence

inside job: crime committed by an employee or an inhabitant

inside the tall walls: inside prison

Inspr: Inspector; Inspectorate

Institute: The Sybil Brand Institute for Women (a Los Angeles prison)

Institute for Scientific Information: publisher of the *Social Sciences Citation Index*

Institute of Makers of Explosives: organization of companies that make blasting caps and blasting machines, commercial explosives, detonating cords, safety fuses and special tools; it cooperates in preventing the misapplication of explosives by bank robbers and other criminals, such as terrorists

institutional capacity: officially determined number of inmates a correctional facility is designed to house

institutional superintendent(s): warden(s)

Insular Penitentiaty: in Rio Piedras near San Juan, Puerto Rico

insurgency: underground warfare

insurgent: guerrilla; underground fighter

intake unit: government agency receiving juveniles from the police or other agencies and screening them so petitions may be filed in juvenile courts, so they may be referred to care and supervision or so their cases may be closed

Integrated Criminal Apprehension Program: computerized system seeking out criminals according to the types of crimes they commit (see also **STAR**)

Intelligence Advisory Committee: the CIA's guiding committee, abbreviated IAC and concerned with overall policy

intelligence community: consists of organizations such as the CIA, the FBI, the ONI and other intelligence-gathering organizations in the United States and their counterparts in other countries

intelligence-gathering: collecting, analyzing, recording and disseminating information needed in advance of initiating a course of action (by diplomatic, law-enforcement, military or other agencies or groups)

intelligence investigation: data compilation wherein the immediate objective is not arrest or prosecution

Intelligence Resources Advisory Committee: includes representatives of the CIA, the Department of Defense, the Department of State and the Office of Management and Budget

Intensive Care Unit: locked unit for juvenile offenders

Interarmco: International Armament Corporation (q.v.)

interdict: intelligence detection and interdiction countermeasures

interior intrusion annunciator: burglar alarm

intermediate-term adult penal institutions of the U.S. Bureau of Prisons: these are located in Danbury, Conn.; Fort Worth, Texas; La Tuna, Texas; Lexington, Ky.; Milan, Mich.; Sandstone, Minn.; Terminal Island, Calif.; and Texarkana, Texas

internal exile: Soviet euphemism for imprisonment in some remote part of the USSR

Internal Revenue Service: corporate and individual income-tax collecting division of the U.S. Treasury Department

International Armament Corporation: supplier of arms to law-enforcement agencies worldwide and to certain paramilitary groups; maintains American offices and some warehouses along the waterfront of Alexandria, Va.

International Association of Arson Investigators: publisher of *Fire and Arson Investigator* bimonthly

International Association of Chiefs of Police: publisher of *Police Chief* monthly and *Journal of Police Science and Administration* quarterly

International Association of Women Police: formerly the International Policewomen's Association; issues brochure on *Women in Law Enforcement*

International Center for Comparative Criminology: a UN and UNESCO consultant in Montreal, Quebec

International Conference of Police Associations: represents more than 200,000 police officers; publishes *Law Officer* bimonthly

International Council for the Investigation of Narcotics: see *JIFE*

international disposal man: hired killer working for a government espionage agency and ordered to eliminate a counterspy or other enemy agent

International Federation of Senior Police Officers: based in Muenster, West Germany; publishes *International Police Chronicle* bimonthly in English and French

International Footprints Association: organization dedicated to improving knowledge of law-enforcement problems

International Foundation for Internal Freedom: drug experimenter's society founded by former Harvard professors Richard Alpert and Timothy Leary

International Halfway House Association: publisher of *Directory of Residential Treatment Centers*

International Juvenile Officers Association: organization founded in 1951 to assist law-enforcement agencies to work with youngsters

International Penal and Penitentiary Commission: founded in 1872, in 1950 it became a part of the United Nations; originally known as the International Penitentiary Commission

International Police Academy: Washington, D.C. school sponsored by the Agency for International Development (AID)

International Police Chronicle: bimonthly publication of the International Federation of Senior Police Officers (q.v.)

International Prisoners Aid Association: publisher of *Directory of Prisoners Aid Agencies*

International Shooting Union: overseas counterpart of the National Rifle Association in the United States

international terrorism: terroristic actions of groups or individuals that are not confined to one country

Interpol: 114-nation International Criminal Police Organization whose secretariat is in the Parisian suburb of Saint-Cloud; before World War II it was in Vienna, but all its files disappeared during the war

Interpol Washington: National Central Bureau in the Treasury Department in Washington, D.C.

in the chips: to have lots of gambling chips; to have lots of money

in the clear: relieved of all guilt or responsibility

in the grinder: in jail; in prison

in the nick: Cockney English—in jail; in prison

in the well: in jail

in the wind: (motorcycle-gang slang) under the influence of alcohol or a drug

in tight: trusted, as by a narcotics dealer

IntMilPol: International Military Police (NATO)

intox: intoxicant; intoxicate; intoxicated; intoxication

intoxication: physical state wherein coordination and speech are impaired noticeably or general behavior is altered as a result of drinking alcoholic beverages

intravenous injection: injection into a vein

intruder detector: burglar alarm

inventory shrinkage: euphemism for losses due to pilfering or shoplifting

invisible crimes: unrecorded crimes

Invisible Empire: Knights of the Ku Klux Klan, a racist organization with a history of violence toward minority groups, particularly blacks

invisible government: governmental agencies charged with conductinng the espionage and secret operations needed to gather intelligence for carrying out policies at home and overseas

invitation: police summons to appear in court

IOB: Intelligence Oversight Board (CIA)

IOCI: Interstate Organized Crime Index

Ionia: Ionia State Reformatory between Grand Rapids and Lansing, Mich.

Iowa Training School for Girls: at Mitchellville, Iowa; holds girls from the ages of 12 to 18

IPA: Institute of Propaganda Analysis (exposes many underground groups); International Police Academy (q.v.); International Police Archives (Manchester Central Library); International Police Association; International Psychoanalytical Association

IPAA: International Prisoners Aid Association (q.v.)

IPC: Intelligence Priorities Committee (CIA)

ipecacuanha: nausea-producing drug used by some aversion therapists in the treatment of alcoholics and drug addicts; must be used with great caution as emetine, its main ingredient, is a deadly toxic drug

IMP: Institute of Police Management

IPPC: International Penal and Penitentiary Commission

IPPF: International Penal and Penitentiary Foundation

IPS: Indian Police Service

IPS: Institute for Policy Studies (leftist think tank)

IPS: Intensive Probation Supervision

IRA: Irish Republican Army (q.v.)

IRAC: Intelligence Resources Advisory Committee

IRC: Inebriate Reception Center (q.v.)

IRGDLP: International Research Group on Drug Legislation and Programs (Geneva, Switzerland)

Irish: Irish whiskey

Irish confetti: bricks or brick fragments suitable for hurling

Irish dew: whiskey

Irish Republican Army: outlawed underground group that has taken credit for many bombings and killings in Northern Ireland as well as Britain; paramilitary movement dedicated to ousting the English from Ireland along with England's supporters in the Protestant section of Northern Ireland (see also **Ulster Defence Association**)

Irish Republican Committee: American fund-raising organization of the Irish Republican Army (IRA)

Irmo: Harbison Correctional Institution for Women at Irmo, S.C.

iro: in rear of

iron: firearm; revolver

iron betsy: military-service rifle

iron house: jail; lockup

ironmongery department: nickname for Her (His) Majesty's prison

iron out: assassinate; murder

iron society: another name for the mafia or other criminal organizations of mobsters and racketeers

IRS: Internal Revenue Service (q.v.)

IS: Identification Section (New York City Police Department)

ISC: Institute for the Study of Conflict; International Society of Criminology

ISD: International Security Division (U.S. Department of Justice)

ISDD: Institute for the Study of Drug Dependence (London, England)

ISI: Institute for Scientific Information (q.v.)

ISIT: Institute for Studies in International Terrorism (State University of New York)

Isla de la Juventud: (Spanish—Isle of Youth)—new name for the Isla de Pinos (Isle of Pines), where many Cuban political prisoners are held

Islamic Marxists: Iranian guerrilla group active in the Middle East

Island: Parkhurst Prison on the Isle of Wight in the English Channel off Southampton; Rikers Island in New York City's East River between the Bronx and Queens; any other island that holds prisoners

isolation tank(s): solitary-confinement cell(s)

isolator: Soviet penal colony specializing in solitary confinement; many in distant parts of the Siberian Arctic and in the White Sea east of Kem on the Solovetski Islands

Isole Eolie: (Italian—Aeolian Islands)—the Lipari Islands off the north coast of Sicily that serve as penal colonies

ISOO: Information Security Oversight Office

ISP: Idaho State Penitentiary; Indiana State Police; Industrial Security Program; Institute of Social Psychiatry of Indiana

ISS: Israeli Secret Service (also known as the Israel Defense Force or Zahal)

ISSC: Institute for the Study of Social Conflict; International Social Science Council

IST: In-Service Training (within California state prisons)

ISTD: Institute for the Study and Treatment of Delinquency

istom: interstate transportation of obscene matters

ISU: International Shooting Union (q.v.)

ISV: Institute for the Study of Violence (Brandeis University)

ITA: International Temperance Association

Italian football: bomb; incendiary explosive

itar: interstate and foreign travel (or transportation) in aid of racketeering enterprises

ITB: International Theft Bureau (for the protection of private aircraft)

Ithaca: American firearms manufacturer

itom: interstate transportation of obscene matter

ITRC: International Terrorist Research Center (El Paso, Texas)

itsa: interstate transportation of stolen aircraft

itsb: interstate transportation of strike-breakers

itsc: interstate transportation of stolen cattle

itsmv: interstate transportation of stolen motor vehicle(s)

itsp: interstate transportation of stolen property

IUPA: International Union of Police Associations

iv: intravenous injection (of drugs)

Iver Johnson: American manufacturer of handguns

iv needle: intravenous needle

ivories: dice

I Wor Kuen: Maoist-oriented underground movement in the United States, where it works closely with the Black Workers Congress and the Puerto Rican Revolutionary Workers Organization to overthrow the capitalist government

ixey: morphine

J

J: jack (money)

j: joint (of marijuana)

jab: inject(ion)

jab a vein: inject heroin or any other drug

jabber: hypodermic needle

jacker-upper: inflationist; price-ripoff expert

jacket: prisoner's case-history dossier or file

jacketed bullet: expanding bullet encased by a gilded or thin metallic jacket

jackleg: dishonest or low-grade lawyer

jack out: pull a gun from its holster

jackroll: rob; rob a person of his or her bankroll

Jackson: world's largest walled prison, enclosing more than 57 acres near Jackson, Mich.

Jack the Ripper: unknown killer and mutilator of many Whitechapel streetwalkers; although he terrorized London in 1888 he is still spoken of as almost contemporary

jack up: increase the price; inflate the cost

jackup: maximum-possible prison sentence

Jacobi: Jacobi Morgue (at Abraham Jacobi Hospital in the Bronx, at Eastchester Ave. and Pelham Pkwy.)

JADPU: Joint Automatic Data-Processing Unit (shared by the Home Office and the Metropolitan Police of London)

jag: drug habit; under the influence of alcohol or a drug

jagged: intoxicated

jag off: slow injection of narcotics

jail: confinement facility usually administered by a local law-enforcement agency; city jails are usually run by local police departments, whereas county jails are usually run by sheriff's offices

JAIL: Justice Against Identification Laws

jailage: see **gaolage**

jail bait: a person whose illegal activities indicate that he or she will be in jail sooner or later; an attractive girl who has not reached the age of consent

jailbird: ex-convict; prisoner; recidivist

jail delivery: clearing a jail of its inmates by bringing them to trial and then releasing them or sentencing them to prison

jail distemper: jail fever (typhus often due to overcrowding); sickness brought on by incarceration or fear of incarceration

jaileress: female jailer

jailhouse(s): building(s) used as jail(s)

jailhouse lawyer: legally well-informed prisoner

jailhouse punk: anyone who becomes a homosexual while in jail

jail limits: area or district surrounding a jail where debtors may be at large under a bond of security

jail plant: narcotics concealed on a person sent to jail or visiting a jail

Jalapa: prison in Jalapa, capital of the Mexican state of Veracruz, northwest of the Gulf of Mexico port of Veracruz

Jamaica ganga: Jamaica-grown marijuana

Jamejala: Soviet psychiatric hospital charged with isolating political prisoners on the pretext of insanity

jammed: intoxicated

jammed up: overdosed on a dangerous drug

jamocha: java + mocha (prison argot—coffee)

JANIS: Joint Army-Navy Intelligence Surveys

Japanita: Santa Anita Assembly Center's nickname during World War II when the racetrack stables were used for the incarceration of Japanese-Americans

Jay: Florida State Prison at Jay, where 37 lives were lost during a fire set by inmates in July 1967

jay: marijuana cigarettes

J-bird: jailbird (q.v.)

jbt: jail(ing) before trial

J. C. Higgins: trade name of Hi-Standard handguns marketed by Sears, Roebuck

jd: juvenile delinquent

JDC: Juvenile Detention Center

JDI: Juvenile Delinquency Index

JDL: Jewish Defense League (q.v.)

Jefferson: Jefferson County Jail in Birmingham, Ala. (both men and women are held there); Jefferson Parish Jail near New Orleans

Jefferson City: Missouri State Penitentiary in Jefferson City

jelly bean: pep pill

jenny barn: female quarters in a United States Public Health Service hospital

Jersey green: New-Jersey-grown marijuana

Jessup: Maryland Correctional Institution for Women at Jessup; Maryland House of Correction at Jessup

Jewell Manor: Jewell Manor Girls Center at Louisville, Ky.

Jewish Defense League: militant organization responding to anti-Semitic attacks and participation in support for Israel

JGWTC: Jungle and Guerrilla Warfare Training Center (U.S. Army)

JHA: John Howard Association (q.v.)

JHAH: John Howard Association of Hawaii (q.v.)

JHDF: Juvenile Hall Detention Facility

jhj: jail-house juvenile delinquent

jib: jibaro (Spanish—peasant farmer) Puerto Rican

JIC: Joint Intelligence Committee (of the Joint Chiefs of Staff of the U.S. Department of Defense)

JIFE: Junta Internacional de Fiscalizacion de Estupefacientes (Spanish—International Council for the Investigation of Narcotics)

jiggery pokery: deception; trickery; swindling

jig is up: end is near; situation is hopeless

jimmy: metal lever, usually sharpened at one end, used to pry open doors and windows; a jimmy may be a crowbar, a screwdriver or a tire iron

jimsonweed: the loco weed of the American Indians, who used it to cause violent excitation before going into battle or to aid witch doctors in diagnosing a person's ailments

jingler: an alcoholic

JIS: Jail Inspection Service

jive: lie

jive stick: marijuana cigarette

JJC: Juvenile Justice Center (q.v.)

JJCCJ: John Jay College of Criminal Justice (q.v.)

JJSC: Juvenile Justice Standards Committee

JLS: Jail Library Service (California State Library)

jnb: jail no bail (see **preventive detention**)

JND: Juvenile Narcotics Division (Los Angeles Police Department)

JOE: Juvenile Opportunities Extension (for delinquents)

Joe Bananas: nickname of the late New York Mafia chief Joseph Bonannos

Joey: man who takes a prisoner's place at home while the convict is imprisoned

john: customer of prostitutes; toilet

John Barleycorn: cartoon figure or literary personification of alcohol and alcoholic beverages

John Doe: fictitious name used in a legal action where the true name is unknown; if more than one such name is needed, Philip Poe may be used, as well as Jane or Mary Doe, Richard or Susan Miles, Richard or Susan Roe, John, Jane or Mary Stiles, and others selected by the court

John Howard Association: organization founded in 1901 and named after an 18th-century English prison reformer; provides professional consultative services; always meets in Chicago

John Howard Association of Hawaii: Honolulu prisoner-service agency named after the English prison reformer John Howard

John Jay College of Criminal Justice: general liberal arts and police training school occupying what was once De Witt Clinton High School at 59th St. and 10th Ave. in New York City

john law: law-enforcement officer; police

John Sites Gunshop: museum of gunsmith tools in Arrowrock, Mo.; open from June through August

Johnson's Island: Civil War prison on Johnson's Island in Lake Erie north of Sandusky, Ohio

John Woodman Higgins Armory: museum of arms, armor and related art objects at 100 Barber Avenue in Worcester, Mass.

joint: home-rolled cigarette filled with hashish or marijuana; low-class bar, cabaret, dance hall or similar place of entertainment; prison

Joliet: Illinois State Penitentiary at Joliet

jolly: confederate of swindlers or thieves

jolly roger: black flag sometimes displayed by pirates, usually adorned with a white hourglass or a white skull-and-crossbones device

jolt: alcoholic drink; heroin injection

jones: habit; heroin addict; heroin habit

Jonestown: Jonestown Peoples Temple, named for its fanatical founder, the Rev. Jim Jones of San Francisco, who settled more than 1,000 Americans near Port Kaituma in northwestern Guyana near the Venezuelan border; rather than submitting to a congressional investigation, he ordered the murder of visiting American investigators and the enforced suicide of his cultist followers; on Nov. 18, 1978 more than 900 Americans were shot or poisoned in and around Jonestown; Jones himself perished with them in the tropical jungle commune he had run like a concentration camp

jostle: pickpocket's action in placing a hand on a person's pocket or handbag or crowding him or her when a third person's hand is already near the prospective victim's pocket or handbag

jostler: pickpocket

Joyceville: Ontario Penitentiary near Kingston

joy juice: chloral hydrate or knock-out drops

joy pop: injection into an arm or leg muscle instead of a vein

joy popper: amateur heroin user; person who believes he or she can control his or her drug habit

joy popping: irregular drug habit

joy powder: morphine

joyrider: reckless driver

joy riding: the reason juvenile delinquents often give for stealing automotive vehicles

joy smoke: hashish or marijuana

joy stick: marijuana cigarette

J-pipe: pipe for smoking marijuana

JPS: Juvenile Probation Services

jri: jail release information

JSA: Jewelers' Security Alliance

J-smoke: marijuana cigarette

J-stick: marijuana cigarette

J-2: intelligence section of a joint military staff

'juana: marijuana

Juarez: nickname of a Mexican prison in Ciudad Juarez, opposite El Paso, Texas

judas: warden's peephole in a prison-cell door; permits the observation of prisoners without their being aware of it

judas slits: prison-door peephole used by guards to check on prisoners

judge: judicial officer appointed or elected to preside over a court of law

judgment: statement of the decision of a court indicating that a defendant is acquitted or convicted of the offense(s) with which he or she was charged

judicial execution: execution in response to a court order

judicial hanging: hanging performed in response to a court order (as opposed to a lynching)

judicial murder: derogatory term for capital punishment as defined by its opponents

judicial officer: anyone exercising judicial powers in a court of law

judo: (Japanese—art of gentleness or weakness) mastered art that uses rapid movements to overthrow an opponent

judy: prostitute

jug(s): jail(s); prison(s)

jugged: intoxicated; under the influence

jugger: an alcoholic

juggler: pusher of dangerous drugs

jughead: alcoholic addict

jug heavy: person adept at breaking into safes and vaults

jug tank(s): prison cell(s) reserved for drug addicts

juice: alcohol; an alcoholic drink; electric current; electricity; a high interest rate obtained by threatening the borrower's life; to lend money at excessive interest rates

juiced: intoxicated; under the influence of alcohol or drugs

juice dealer: person charging excessive interest on money loaned

juice freak: alcoholic

juicehead: alcoholic

juice man: underworld loan collector

juicer: alcoholic; heavy drinker

jujitsu: Japanese self-defense method based on the use of the strength of the adversary

juju: marijuana cigarette

juke: cheat; deceive; swindle

jukehouse: whorehouse

julia: jewelry

JUMIP: Juror Utilization and Management Incentive Program

jump: attack; mug; rape; *he jumped her in the alleyway*

jump bail: forfeit bail by not appearing in court at the time directed or by failing to comply with some other condition set before bail was granted

jumper: piece of metal or short length of wire used to bypass or close a circuit; jumpers or jump wires are used by automotive vehicle thieves and by persons stealing electric power; amphetamine tablet

Juneau: the South Eastern Region Correction Institute at Juneau, Alaska

Jungfernhof: extermination facility near Riga where many Austrian Jews were transported before being murdered by their Nazi captors

jungle: depressed, disorderly and lawless section of a city

jungle juice: alcoholic drink made from cleaning fluids or any liquid containing some alcohol

junior jumper: (Afro-American slang) rapist under 16 years old

juniper juice: gin (so nicknamed because it

is flavored with juniper berries)

junk: narcotic drugs, especially heroin; to remove brass, copper, lead and wrought iron from buildings, homes and public parks for the purpose of selling it to junk dealers

junked: under the influence of narcotics, especially heroin

junker: heroin addict; automobile almost ready for junking

junkhound: narcotic addict

junkie: drug vendor or addict

junkie pro: drug-addicted or drug-vending prostitute

junk pusher: narcotic dealer

junk tank: prison cell(s) reserved for drug addicts

jurimetrician: attorney skilled in solving legal problems by scientific methods

jurimetrics: solution of legal problems by scientific methods

JURIS: Justice Retrieval and Inquiry System (U.S. Department of Justice); Juvenile Referral Information System (q.v.)

jury: persons selected according to law and sworn to determine certain matters of fact in a criminal action and then to render a verdict of guilty or not guilty

jury trial: trial wherein the jury determines the issues of fact in a case

Justice: U.S. Department of Justice

justifiable homicide: a murder is called justifiable homicide when it is committed while the murderer is resisting any attempt to kill him, her or another person or in defense of his or her family, home or property; in many states very strict laws are enforced to make certain that such homicides are, in fact, justifiable

juve: juvenile

juve delinq: juvenile delinquent

juve gang: juvenile gang(ster)

juvenile adjudication: juvenile court decision ending an adjudicatory hearing and decreeing either that the allegations made in the petition were not sustained or that the juvenile is a delinquent, a dependent or a status offender

juvenile court: court having jurisdiction over people alleged to be dependent, delinquents or status offenders

juvenile delinquency: criminal behavior exhibited by adolescents and children

juvenile hall: holding facility for juvenile delinquents

juvenile-justice agency: government agency whose functions include the adjudication, care, confinement, investigation and supervision of juveniles

Juvenile Justice Center: agency in Los Angeles, Calif., designed to cope with the growing problem of juvenile criminals

juvenile record: official record containing information concerning juvenile court proceedings and all applicable correctional and detention processes ordered

Juvenile Referral Information System: St. Louis, Missouri's criminal data file on juvenile delinquents

juvie: juvenile delinquent; juvenile hall; juvenile law-enforcement officer

K

K: kilo (of marijuana)

K-9 Corps: Canine Corps

Kaiserwald: Nazi concentration camp in Latvia during most of World War II when Germany occupied this area close to Riga

kakistos: kakistocrats (gangsters, mob leaders, syndicate chiefs, venal politicians, etc.)

kakistocracy: (Latin—rule by the worst) control by gangsters, mob leaders, syndicate chiefs, venal politicians, etc.

kamp: known as male prostitute (acronym used in New York City Police Department reports)

k & r: kidnapping and ransom (insurance)

kanga(s): kangaroo(s)—Australian prison warden(s)

kangaroo court: prisoners' court imposing contributions, fines and work tasks on convicts brought before such a body; nickname of any small court that is harsh on alcoholics, beggars and vagrants

Kansas State Industrial Farm for Women: at Lansing, Kan.; women from age 16 up are held there

KAP: initials stand for Chinese Ministry of Public Security, the external counter-intelligence and internal secret police force of the People's Republic of China

KAR: Karabine (German—carbine)

karate: (Japanese—empty hands) method of self-defense that originated on the island of Okinawa; elbows, feet, knees and open-hand slashes are aimed at vital nerve centers, and can paralyze or kill an attacker

katar: short dagger of Indian design

katyusha: katyusha rocket (Russian weapon used by Cuban and Palestinian guerrillas)

katzenyzammerer: an alcoholic

Kaufering: forced-labor subcamp in the south of Germany close to Dachau

KBI: Klan Bureau of Investigation (underground arm of the Ku Klux Klan)

KBW: Klan Border Watch (q.v.)

KC: Jackson County Jail in Kansas City, Mo.

KCJ: Kings County Jail in Seattle, Wash.

keelhaul: subject to a (now illegal) naval punishment wherein a rope was rigged from yardarm to yardarm and passed under the keel of the ship; the culprit was made fast to one end of the rope and hauled beneath the keel from one side of the vessel to the other; many delinquents did not survive keelhauling; they either drowned while being keelhauled or bled to death as the result of being cut by too many sharp-edged barnacles on the ship's hull and keel

keester plant: hollow suppository made of metal, plastic, rubber or even wood and used to conceal drugs, money or uncut diamonds within the rectum

keester stash: anything hidden in the rectum

Kendall: juvenile-delinquent rehabilitation center at Kendall, Fla., near South Miami

kenten: small lamp for cooking opium pills before they are smoked

Kentucky Manpower Development: agency responsible for a program of prisoner rehabilitation

Ketchikan: Ketchikan State Jail and Detention Home in Ketchikan, Alaska

key: kilogram of hashish, marijuana or another drug

KGB: Komitet Gosudarstvennoye Bezopastnosti (Russian—State Security Committee) Soviet secret police

KGWP: Kitty Genovese Women's Project (q.v.)

kha: killed by hostile action

khai: Indo-Chinese mixture of aspirin, morphine base and the remains of smoked opium; the mixture is heated in a metal can and its fumes are inhaled

khat: amphetamine-like drug

Kholmogori: Arctic death camp established by Lenin's men near Archangel in 1921 for political prisoners in the Soviet Union

ki: one kilogram (2.2 pounds) of any drug; kilogram of marijuana, usually compressed into a brick-shaped form

kick: stop using a drug or indulging in a bad habit

kickback: usually illegal referral fee; *venal politicians get rich on kickbacks*

kick party: social gathering characterized by hashish or marijuana smoking

kick stick: marijuana cigarette

kick the bucket: to die; originally, to commit suicide by standing on an overturned bucket, tying a noose around one's neck, and then kicking the bucket

kick the gong: to frequent places where narcotics are sold

kick the gong around: smoke hashish, marijuana or opium

kick the habit: overcome a habit such as drinking, smoking or using drugs

kidnap: transport a person unlawfully without her or his consent or, if she or he is a minor, without the consent of her or his guardian or parent

kife: cheat

kifi: North African opiate

kike killer: (KKK slang) blackjack; bludgeon

kike sticker: (KKK slang) dagger

killer weed: phencyclidine (PCP) mixed with parsley so that it can be smoked

killing power: strength of a bullet or other deadly weapon

kilobrick: compressed brick of marijuana leaves, seeds and stalks measuring about 2.5" x 5" x 12"

kilo connection: distributor of heroin who adulterates it to half strength or less before selling it to other pushers

kilo man: drug wholesaler who deals by the kilo

kimona: coffin

kindergarten of vice: epithet applied to many county jails

king kong: ape-size heroin habit likened in dimension to the fictional ape of the movies; prison-distilled gin

king-kong pills: barbiturates or other sedatives

Kings: Kings County Jail in Seattle, Wash.

Kingston Pen: Kingston Penitentiary (and mental hospital) just west of Kingston, Ontario in the suburb of Portsmouth, at the northeast end of Lake Ontario

Kinston: Dobbs School for Girls (the State Training School for Girls) at Kinston, N.C.

kiq (KIQ): key intelligence questions asked by intelligence-gathering operatives

kirkbasher: petty thief or pickpocket operating in places of worship, where collection plates, donation boxes and the pockets of the faithful are pilfered while they pray

kirkbuzzer: another knickname for a kirkbasher

kit: drug-injection equipment

kite: increase the amount of a company's or a customer's checks; obtain or sustain credit by rapidly transferring funds from one bank to another so as to produce the illusion that ample funds are in several banks at the same time or what appears to be the same time

Kitty Genovese Women's Project: anti-rape group named for a New York City barmaid who was stabbed to death in 1964 in front of nearly three dozen witnesses, who explained they did not wish to become involved

kj: killer judo

kk: killer karate

KKK: Ku Klux Klan (q.v.)

KKKK: Knights of the Ku Klux Klan (Louisiana-based splinter group of the KKK)

KKKUK: Ku Klux Klan in the United Kingdom

Klan: Ku Klux Klan (q.v.)

Klan Border Watch: plan of the Ku Klux Klan to get favorable publicity by volunteering the manpower of its members in assisting the U.S. Border Patrol in the task of preventing illegal aliens from entering the United States along the more than 1,900-mile-long border with Mexico

klavern: (klan + cavern) local KKK group

kleagle: (klan + eagle) head of a statewide KKK organization

klepto: kleptomania(c)

kleptomania: abnormal desire to steal, even if the object to be stolen is of little or no value or well within the purchasing power of the kleptomaniac

kleptomaniac: person suffering from kleptomania

kleptophobia: abnormal dread of stealing or thieves

KL: Konzentrationslager (German—concentration camp) prisoners contracted this to *KL*

klondike: solitary prison cell

kloran: (klan + koran) the KKK's book of duties, obligations, passwords and prayers

kloxology: the KKK's ideology of bigotry and racial and religious hatred

Kluxer: Ku Klux Klansman

KMCI: Kettle Moraine Correctional Institution (near Duluth, Minn.)

KMD: Kentucky Manpower Development (q.v.)

kneecapping: form of torture performed by shooting a bullet or running an electric drill through a kneecap to cripple the victim for life

knifesmith: skilled designer and maker of knives

Knights of the Ku Klux Klan: a branch of the Ku Klux Klan (q.v.)

knock cold: strike a blow resulting in unconsciousness

knocked out: drugged; intoxicated

knock on the door: (of an addict) to attempt to reenter decent society by staying away from other addicts and addictive drugs

knock-out drops: see **chloral hydrate**

knock the habit: stop drinking, taking drugs or smoking; take a cure forcing one to abstain from alcohol, drugs or tobacco

knout: a Russian lash made of dried rawhide thongs interspersed with wire hooks capable of tearing the flesh of anyone struck with it; to strike with a knout

knowledge factory: prison school

knuckle dusters: brass knuckles (q.v.)

knuckle-duster knife: Japanese weapon combining a short bayonet blade and an offensive hand guard

knucks: brass knuckles

ko or **KO:** knockout blow, usually delivered by the fist of a prizefighter or another person adept in pugilistic assault

kokomo: narcotic addict

Kolyma: USSR penal camp north of the Arctic Circle near a Soviet city and river of the same name

Komsomol: (Russian—Young Communist League)

Kona (Coast) gold: nickname for marijuana grown on the *kona* or lee side of any Hawaiian or Polynesian island; any Hawaiian-grown marijuana

kong: cheap low-grade whiskey; homemade whiskey

kook: odd and unusual person

KOPS: Keep Our Precinct Safe

Korsakoff's psychosis: condition of alcoholic addicts afflicted with muttering delirium, disorientation, hallucinations, illusions, insomnia and pain; also called Korsakoff's syndrome

Korydallos: prison in Athens, Greece

KPM: King's Police Medal (British decoration)

Krag: Krag-Jorgensen 30-caliber rifle of Norwegian design and Danish manufacture; used by the U.S. Army between 1894 and 1904

Kragshovhede: Danish open-type prison built without high enclosures or walls; the type of detention is said to result in reduced recidivism among former in-

mates; the prison is near the Skagen or Skaw in northernmost Denmark

KRIM: not an acronym but the made-up name for the Danish association for penal reform

Krems: site of a World-War-II concentration camp on the Danube northwest of Vienna

Kresty: Leningrad's central prison

kris: double-aged serpentine-bladed dagger designed for killing by thrusting and used by the Malays of Indonesia and Malaya; pronounced *creese*

KROM: not an acryonym but the contrived name of the Norwegian association for penal reform

Krome Avenue: address and nickname of the immigration and naturalization detention camp on Krome Avenue in Miami, Florida

KRUM: not an acronym but a made-up word standing for the Swedish association for penal reform

Krupp: German firm of armament and ordnance makers

Kryukovo: USSR prison colony/psychiatric hospital northwest of Moscow

Ktr: Katorzhane (Russian—compound) prison compound reserved for people sentenced to hard labor

Kuibyshev: Soviet transit prison

Ku Kluxer: member of the Ku Klux Klan (q.v.)

Ku Klux Klan: violent underground organization incorporated in 1915; espouses hatred of blacks, Jews and Catholics

Ku Kluxism: pseudo-Americanism cloaking racism and religious bigotry (see **Ku Klux Klan**)

kukri: favorite fighting knife of the Gurkhas of Nepal and the Iban headhunters of Borneo

kung fu: (Chinese—boxing principles) karate-like art of self defense

Kunie: old French penal colony in the Southwest Pacific southeast of New Caledonias; also called the Isle of Pines but not to be confused with a Cuban penal colony of the same name

kuttar: double-edged Indian dagger consisting of a blade attached to two parallel bars fitted with a crosspiece that is held by the hand, directing the knife's slashes and deadly stabs

KY: Kentucky (U.S. Public Health Service Hospital for addicts seeking a cure for their drug addiction); this health facility is located in Lexington, Ky.

L

L: law (the police, the task force, the vice squad, etc.)

l: liter (of blood, gasoline, liquor, etc.); loser

l (L): loop (fingerprint description)

laam (LAAM): levoalpha acetylmethadol

lab boys: law-enforcement officers' nickname for forensic anthropologists, odontologists and serologists whose efforts often aid them in securing convictions of criminals who otherwise would be released for seeming lack of evidence

labor racketeering: corrupt practices involving organized crime and organized labor

La Cabaña: (Spanish—The Cabin)—old Spanish prison at the entrance to Havana harbor and still in use

La Catena: (Italian—The Chain) international underground gang devoted to helping extremist right-wing causes by robbing banks; this is the so-called sewer gang active in France, where two big banks were entered via the sewers; allegedly the gang is headquartered in Turin, Italy

LACJ: Los Angeles County Jail

lady snow: cocaine

La Force: top-security prison of Paris in the late 1700s and early 1800s

lag: convict; transported convict

Lager Westerbork: transit camp established in the Drenthe province of the Netherlands by German occupation forces during World War II off the Hooghalen-Rolde road (see **Durchgangslager**)

lagging: serving a three-year sentence in a British prison; transportation by sea of convicts sent from overcrowded jails in the British Isles to those in Australia and Tasmania

Lagoinha: Brazilian jail in Belo Horizonte some 467 kilometers (290 miles) north of Rio de Janeiro

La Grange: Kentucky State Reformatory at La Grange

Lahti: 9mm Swedish pistol long popular in Finland

laid out: intoxicated

Lake Butler: another name for Florida's state prison at Starke

Lambda Alpha Epsilon: see **American Criminal Justice Association**

lame: not a drug or alcohol user; not in the know; straitlaced; uninformed

La Mesa Penitenciaria: (Spanish—La Mesa Penitentiary) Baja California's major prison; located in eastern Tijuana

LAMPS: (Center for the Study of) Legal Authority and Mental Patient Status

lamp trap: kerosene lamp whose coal oil or kerosene is replaced with high-octane gasoline; when the lamp is ignited a massive incendiary explosion results

lamster: escaped convict; person hiding from the police

Lancaster: jails in places such as Lancaster, Pa. and in smaller towns in 15 other states and two Canadian provinces

L & SA: Law and Society Association

Landsberg: fortress prison on the Lech River in Upper Bavaria about 22 miles (35 kilometers) south of Augsberg; Hitler was imprisoned here in 1923 for plotting the overthrow of the Social Democratic government of Germany during the Munich Beer Hall Putsch; he served only nine months of his five-year sentence but during his incarceration wrote *Mein Kampf*

Langholmen: Swedish prison close to Stockholm

Langley: headquarters of the Central Intelligence Agency (CIA) in Langley, Va., just northwest of Washington, D.C.

Lansing: State Industrial Farm for Women at Lansing, Mich.

LAPD: Los Angeles Police Department

La Pica: (Spanish—the stonecutter's hammer, the pike or the long lance of the epicador)—nickname of Venezuela's central penitentiary of Oriente

larceny: theft; taking away another's property with intent to deprive the owner of its possession

lard: law-enforcement officers; police

lar rep: larceny report

La Roquette: Parisian prison for prostitutes or other female offenders

LAS: Legal Aid Society

La Salle: French semi-automatic shotgun

Las Colinas: Las Colinas Girls' Facility in Santee, Calif., east of San Diego; facility includes maximum-security cells for hard-to-handle female convicts; *colinas* is Spanish for cabbages

laser-aimed weapons: weapons whose laser-equipped aiming makes accurate shooting as simple as pointing a flashlight; a red spot projected by the laser pinpoints the target; assault rifles, revolvers and shotguns are fitted in this fashion; produced by the Newport Research Corp. of Fountain Valley, Calif.

last laugh: a bullet shot through the heart often produces a laugh as its first effect—the victim's last laugh

last mile: euphemism for the short walk from a prison cell to the place of execution

last waltz: condemned prisoner's march to the electric chair, gas chamber or other place of execution

Las Ventas: (Spanish—The Stalls)—Madrid's old municipal prison

Latchmere House: a remand center in Surrey, England

latent fingerprints: fingerprints that are invisible but detectable by several techniques

lathi: long metal-tipped police stick used in India to control crowds

latino: person of Hispanic or Hispanic-American origin: Cuban, Mexican, Puerto Rican, South American, etc.

latrinogram: latrine rumor

La Tuna: Federal Correctional Institution at La Tuna, Texas

l-a turnaround: long-acting amphetamine capsule

laudanum: opium solution in general use since the early 1500s; past addicts include many British writers, the American author-editor-poet Edgar Allen Poe, the Russian composer-pianist Modest Moussorgsky and a host of French literary lights

laughing gas: nickname for nitrous oxide

launder: invest money gained illegally through such ventures as narcotics traffic, prostitution and rackets in legitimate business enterprises

laundered man: Sicilian killer who is smuggled into another country, where he is taught something of its customs and language before being used as a killer by gangster bosses; if he is apprehended or his life is lost, the local police will not be able to identify him, as he has no record locally

laundered money: illegally-obtained funds transferred by banking and other third-party transactions until the original source of the money is no longer evident

Laurel: maximum-security juvenile facility near Laurel, Md.

Laval: Laval Institution (Canadian maximum-security facility at Ville de Laval, Quebec)

law: rules of conduct and order set up in any organized society, where they are enforced by the threat of fines, imprisonment or other forms of punishment, sometimes exile and death

LAW: Legal Aid Warranty

LAW: Lawyers Against Wigs

law-enforcement agency: federal, state or local criminal-justice agency charged with the apprehension of alleged offenders as well as crime detection and prevention

law-enforcement center: Dubuque, Iowa's euphemism for the local jail

Law Enforcement Intelligence Unit: founded in 1956, this private organization is a network of 277 local and state law enforcement agencies in the United States that exchange records and information on criminal suspects, organized crime and terrorism

law-enforcement officer: peace officer or policeman sworn to carry out law-enforcement duties; sworn employee of a prosecutorial agency primarily concerned with investigation as well as the arrest and suppression of offenders

Lawrence: George Lawrence of Portland, Ore., a manufacturer of handgun holsters

Law West of the Pecos: self-appointed Judge Roy Bean, who ran a combined billiard hall, courtroom and saloon called the Jersey Lily, honoring his favorite actress, Lily Langtry, for whom he also named the west Texas town of Langtry, on the Rio Grande opposite Mexico; whenever a man was killed in the area—and fatal shootings were quite frequent there in the 1880s and 1890s—he did not go to the trouble of impaneling a coroner's jury until he and his pistol-packin' cronies had decided the answer to the question, "should the deceased have departed?"; at least two old mesquite trees used for hangings are within a lariat's throw of the Jersey Lily, and give mute testimony to the character of frontier justice and law west of the Pecos

lawyer: counsel or attorney

lay down: smoke opium while reclining to avoid nausea and vomiting

lay low: remain in hiding; *lay low until the investigation is completed*

lay on the hip: smoke opium

lay the hypo: take a shot of narcotics

lay the note: give short change

lazaretto: hospital for contagious diseases; place of quarantine; betweendecks storeroom sometimes used as a hospital or even as a lockup if a vessel is without a brig

LC: London Club (q.v.)

LCB: Liquor Control Board (Canada)

LCBBC: Liquor Control Board of British Columbia

LCBM: Liquor Control Board of Manitoba

LCBO: Liquor Control Board of Ontario

LCBS: Liquor Control Board of Saskatchewan

ld: lethal dose

LDF: Legal Defense Fund of the National Association for the Advancement of Colored People (NAACP)

LEAA: Law Enforcement Assistance Administration (U.S. Department of Justice)

lead: metal most often used in the making of bullets

lead poisoning: bullet wound(s)

LEADS: Law Enforcement Agencies Data System (Illinois' computerized file on criminals)

leaflet bomb: explosive device designed to scatter leaflets over crowds of people

LEAP: Law, Education, and Participation

leaper: amphetamine pill

LEAPS: Law Enforcement Agencies Processing System (Massachusetts' computerized file on criminals)

Leavenworth: U.S. Penitentiary at Leavenworth, Kan.

lebake: Swazi and Zulu name for a *Cannabis* plant

Lebanese: Lebanon-grown brownish-red hashish

LECLU: Law Enforcement Civil Liberties Union (for the protection of the civil, constitutional and political rights of law-enforcement officers)

Lecumberri-Hilton: nickname of Mexico City's Lecumberri prison

LEEGS: Law Enforcement Explorer Girls (Los Angeles Police Department program connected with the Boy Scouts of America, intended to promote the reporting of possible crimes)

leepers: amphetamines

Lefortovo: prison in Moscow described in *The Gulag Archipelago* by one of its inmates, Aleksander I. Solzhenitsyn

left-handed wife: concubine

leftie: left-winger

LEG: Law Enforcement Group

legacy of terror: see **survivor syndrome**

legal beagle: astute attorney; trial lawyer skilled in uncovering evidence and presenting facts as well as opinions

legal eagle: astute attorney

legal weapon: so-called legal weapons, available to otherwise defenseless citizens, include aerosol sprays, kitchen knives, nail files, umbrellas and whistles; many believe a woman's best defense is a loud and prolonged scream; threatening an assailant with a hammer or a hatchet may also be effective

legat: legation-based secret operative—an espionage agent operating under diplomatic cover

legbreaker: an enforcer who beats people to enforce a gang's wishes

legend: complete cover story used by an espionage or law-enforcement secret agent

legger: bootlegger

leg holster: handgun holster designed to be strapped to a leg of its user so the weapon may be concealed

legit: legitimate

legitimate racket: gangster Al Capone counted anti-trust violations, business theft, consumer fraud, embezzlement and malfeasance in office as legitimate rackets run by businessmen and politicians

legster: ankle or leg holster

legume: peyote bean or button

LEIU: Law Enforcement Intelligence Unit (q.v.)

lemonade: diluted heroin or another drug made less potent by dilution or extension

LEOPARD: Law Enforcement Operations and Activities to Reduce Drugs (U.S. Army Criminal Investigation Command)

LEP: Labor Education Project (of OC-5)—see **OC-5**

LEPA: Law Enforcement Planning Agency

LERC: Law Enforcement Research Center

lestobiosis: form of cleptobiosis in which aggressive plundering is replaced by covert stealing

LETAC: Law Enforcement Training Advisory Council

lethal dosage: amount of a drug needed to cause death (see also **abusive dosage, maximal dosage, minimal dosage and toxic dosage**)

lethality: capability of killing

Lethbridge: Royal Canadian Mounted Police headquarters for Alberta

lethiferous: deadly

let it all hang out: confess fully; give all the facts

letter bomb: explosive concealed in an envelope designed to detonate when opened

lettuce: paper money

level four: death-dealing dose or injection of barbital or another drug causing stoppage of breathing

levoalpha acetymethadol: a synthetic opiate used in treating addicts

Lewes: a small jail in the Delaware River fishing port of Lewes, just inside the Delaware River Breakwater

lewd conduct: indecent behavior such as displaying one's genitals in public, making sexual solicitations in public or using obscene language

Lewis: air-cooled machine gun named for its inventor, I. N. Lewis

Lewisburg: U.S. Penitentiary at Lewisburg, Pa.

Lewisburg Plan: the plan of the Lewisburg Penitentiary, also called the telephone-pole design, providing for maximum- and medium-security cells, inside and outside, respectively; there are dormitory blocks with honor rooms for inmates who have earned special treatment (see **telephone-pole design**)

Lexington: U.S. Public Health Service Hospital in Lexington, Ky. (drug detoxification facility)

lezzie: lesbian—short form popular in girl's detention and rehabilitation facilities

l/f: left front

lfd: least fatal dose

LGC: Laminated Glass Corporation (see **detention glazing**)

LGD: London Gaol Delivery

libel: written defamation (as opposed to slander—spoken defamation)

Liberation News Service: press association representing the viewpoint of revolutionaries and terrorists

Liberty Street: nickname of the city jail on Liberty Street in Louisville, Ky.

library birds: vagrants who find shelter in public libraries

librium: tranquilizer whose excessive use results in addiction

lic: license

LICA: *Ligue Internationale Contre le Racisme et l'Antisemitisme* (French—International League Against Racism and Anti-Semitism)

lid: one ounce of marijuana; also called a *can*

lid poppers: amphetamines

lie down: smoke opium

lifeboat: commutation of a death sentence or a prison sentence; judicial order for a retrial

lifer: prisoner sentenced to life imprisonment

lift: steal

light artillery: hypodermic needle used to inject drugs

light-fingered: inclined to steal

light stuff: "soft" drug such as marijuana; called *light* because it is not physically addictive, although it exerts a psychological hold on many users and hence could be called partially addictive

light up: to light up a marijuana cigarette

likkered up: casual spelling of "liquored up" (intoxicated; under the influence of alcohol)

limo: limousine

limp: intoxicated

limpet: see **audio wall probe**

Lincoln: jails in some 51 American cities named "Lincoln," including the capital of Nebraska, where the Nebraska State Penitentiary is located

Lindbergh Law: U.S. statute making the kidnapping and transportation of a person across state lines punishable by imprisonment for life; enacted in 1932 after the kidnapping of the only child of Charles A. Lindbergh and his wife, Anne Morrow Lindbergh

line: money; to inject heroin into the big vein of one's arm; a small quantity of cocaine shaped into a "line" to be inhaled

lineup: police-conducted parade of prisoners, arranged to facilitate identification by complainants and other victims of crime or by eyewitnesses

linoleum knife: sharp, stiff blade terminating in a hooked point; used from time to time by killers and slashers

Lipton tea: poor-quality drugs

liquidate: assassinate; kill

liquid bread: beer

liquid hashish: hash oil (q.v)

liquored: intoxicated; under the influence of alcohol

liquored up: intoxicated

liquor laws: legislation prohibiting or regulating and restricting the manufacture, sale and use of alcoholic beverages

LISC: London Institute for the Study of Conflict

Liszt: Franz von Liszt (1851-1919), cousin of the composer of the same name; best remembered for this theories about what he called the global science of criminal law (*Gesamte Strafrechtswissenschaft*) and the twofold division of criminals into criminals of the moment (*Augenblicksverbrecher*) and chronic criminals (*Zussandverbrecher*)

lit: drunk

LITE: Legal Information Through Electronics

little duke: 12- to 13-year old youngster who is addicted to alcohol and/or drugs and who may beg or steal the money needed to support his or her addiction

Little House on the Prairie: nickname for the 41st police precinct station in the south Bronx area of New York City; the precinct itself has been called Fort Apache because of the high crime rate in the area, where tenement after tenement has been gutted by arsonists and leveled by bulldozers; as a result the station now stands amid many vacant lots

lit to the gills: intoxicated

lit up: under the influence of alcohol or drugs or both

Llama: Spanish .22 and .32 caliber automatic pistols, scaled down from a .45 automatic

lmg (LMG): light machine gun

LMP: London Metropolitan Police

L-note: $50 bill

LNS: Liberation News Service (q.v.)

load: to load a firearm or other weapon to place materials or messages in a dead drop or dead-letter box; to overcharge customers, enter or ring up the correct amount and then pocket the difference; a shipment of contraband

loaded: drugged; intoxicated; possessing great amounts of money or sexual charm

loaded stick: two-foot-long stick loaded with a lump of lead at one hollow end; this weapon is quite popular in the British Isles, where it is often concealed in coat sleeves

loan shark: person who lends money at high rates of interest and uses the threat of physical violence as a means of enforcing repayment

local bears: local police

local lockup: usually the local police station or the county sheriff's prison

lock: mechanical device for keeping others from breaking into and entering one's home or property, whether to steal or to trespass and violate one's privacy

lockup: usually a small jail or prison

loco weed: *Datura stramonium* or jimson weed, found in the American Southwest; when made into beer, its action as an intoxicant is very powerful and may cause those who consume it to become very violent

log: marijuana cigarette

loid man: celluloid man (thief who uses a strip of celluloid, such as a credit card, to open spring-locked doors)

Lombroso: Cesare Lombroso (1835-1909), Italian criminologist, often called the Father of Modern Criminology and one of the Holy Three of Criminology, best remembered for his books such as *Delinquent Man* and *The Female Offender* as well as *Crime, Its Causes and Remedies*

Lompoc: Federal Correctional Institution at Lompoc, Calif.; Federal Prison Camp at Lompoc, Calif.

London: state prison farm near London, Ohio, west-southwest of Columbus

London Club: criminologists, freelance writers, reporters, etc., who are concerned with controversial trial verdicts and unsolved crimes

long arm: long arm of the law; law-enforcement agency or agent; *look out for the long arm*

long-arm inspection: medical examination of an erect penis

long bid: long prison term

Long Branch: Canadian arsenal near Toronto; managed by Canadian Arsenals Ltd.

Long By: Sydney, New South Wales, Australian prison setup of its Corrective Services Department, including the Central Industrial Prison, Her Majesty's Training Center, and the Parramatta Gaol

long-fingered: one who steals from family, friends or fellow convicts

long green: paper money

long gun: rifle or shotgun

long hitter: alcoholic; heavy drinker

Long Lane: Long Lane School for Girls at Middletown, Conn.

long rod: rifle or shotgun

long stretch: long prison sentence

look: be in search of a drug pusher

looker: good-looking person

loop belt: restraining device used in handling and transporting unruly prisoners

looped: intoxicated

loose price: unit price of any drug

loot: money; stolen goods

Lophophora williamsii: scientific name for the peyote cactus, which yields mescal or mescaline; grows in many parts of the American Southwest and northern Mexico

Lorton: District of Columbia Correctional Complex at Lorton, Va.

Los: (Caio or Mexican-American truncation) Los Angeles, Calif.

Los Guilucos: Los Guilucos School for Girls at Santa Rosa, Calif.

lost luggage racket: smuggling method in which a smuggler loads personal luggage—but not hand luggage—with contraband before checking it on a flight to another country; at the destination the smuggler's hand luggage only is checked by the customs inspectors; in a few hours the smuggler telephones the airline to claim that the checked baggage must have been lost, as it was not at the terminal after debarkation; the airline baggage-master discovers the so-called lost luggage and, after making apologies, has it delivered to the smuggler's address without having it examined by customs inspectors

louisette: beheading device perfected by Dr. Antoine Louis of Paris at the suggestion of his colleague Dr. Joseph-Ignace Guillotin, who argued before the French National Assembly that culprits should be executed by a simple mechanism such as a heavy blade falling by its own weight along two vertical runners to decapitate the victim; because Dr. Guillotin won the argument, the resulting device is called the guillotine rather than the louisette

Louvain: Belgium's central prison to the east of Brussels

love weed: marijuana

lowball: deceptively lowcost estimate made by an unethical firm or one of its sales representatives; e.g., drug pushers like to tell prospective clients they can buy whatever they want for just a few pennies

Lowell: Florida Correctional Institution at Lowell

lowered pistol: handgun whose muzzle is pointed downward

low profile: almost out of sight; *keep a low profile and you'll never be detected*

low-profile crime: crime committed in the absence of eyewitnesses (see also **high-profile crime**)

Lowry: 3320th Retraining Group of the U.S. Air Force at Lowry Air Force Base, Colorado

l/p: listening post

LP: Liverpool Prison

LPCM: London Police Court Mission

L-pill: lethal potassium-cyanide pill (deadly if ground between the teeth but harmless if swallowed, as it has an indigestible plastic coating; at Nuremberg Nazi Hermann Goering took an L-pill rather than submitting to hanging)

l/r: left rear; lower right

l.s.: locus sigilli (Latin—place for the seal)

lsd (LSD): see LSD-25

LSD-25: d-lysergic acid diethylamide tartrate 25, made from rye ergot or synthetically; its manufacture in the United States is illegal and brings long prison sentences

LSF: Lock Security Force (Panama Canal)

LSM: Liberation Support Movement (q.v.)

LTI: Louisiana Training Institute (branches are located at Baton Rouge, Monroe and Pineville)

LTs: *Legal Times*

lubange: East African name for hashish, hemp or marijuana

lubed: lubricated (intoxicated)

Lubianka: Moscow headquarters of the Ministry of the Interior—the Soviet secret police whose combination office and prison back on Dzerzhinsky Square is named for the founder of the Cheka and its many successors—the Lubianka is one block from the Kremlin

Lublin: concentration camp in Poland close to the extermination camps of Maidanek and Sobibor

lubricated: intoxicated; under the influence of alcohol or drugs

luck out: be fortunate; be successful

Lucky: Charles (Lucky) Luciano, originally Salvatore C. Luciana; long the boss of bosses governing La Cosa Nostra (the Mafia) and, hence, big gambling, loan sharking, narcotics, prostitution and related criminal activities

lude: quaalude (depressant drug)

lude out: become intoxicated on alcohol and quaaludes

Luger: 9-millimeter automatic pistol designed and made by Luger in Germany; 30-caliber pistol also made by Luger

Luger parabellum: recoil-operated self-loading pistol devised in 1893 by the Austrian arms designer George Luger and later used in the German army and navy and emulated by many other arms makers

luminal: trade name for a barbiturate called phenobarbital; taken by many people as a means of committing suicide; also known by its slang nicknname—purple hearts

lunacy: old-fashioned legal term for a psychotic person

lunatic: old-fashioned legal term describing mental illness

lunatic soup: cheap wine

lunch hour trip: see **dimethyltryptamine**

lush: alcoholic; heavy drinker

lushed up: intoxicated

lush roller: pickpocket preying upon alcoholics

lush worker: pimp, prostitute or other person who robs patrons who are under the influence of alcohol or other drugs

Lyman: gun sight manufacturer based in Middlefield, Conn.

lynch: hang a suspected criminal on the basis of mob action rather than legal procedure; named for Capt. William Lynch, also called Judge Lynch

lynching: executing someone by mob rule rather than by the rule of law; freeing a suspect in police custody (slang definition describing encounters between gangs or mobs and police)

lynch law: situation wherein people take the law into their own hands and kill or punish anyone they believe to be a criminal

Lynwood: Lynwood Girls Center at Anchorage, Ky.

M

M: marijuana; morphine

M-2: Match-Two (program matching volunteers from a community, called sponsors, on a one-to-one basis with prison inmates; sponsors write to inmates and visit them regularly with the aim of establishing warm and meaningful relationships and providing convicts with references and job support after they are paroled)

MAAB: Manufacture d'Armes Automatiques Bayonne (French—Bayonne Automatic Arms Factory) maker of a 9mm parabellum 15-round pistol

MAB: Metropolitan Asylums Board (British group responsible for administration and policy of all sorts of asylums, including those for the criminally insane)

mac: maquerau (French—mackerel) pimp

McAlester: Oklahoma State Penitentiary at McAlester

McCain: North Carolina Prison Sanatorium at McCain

mace: spiked club in use since the Middle Ages; some consist of a spike-faced iron ball attached to a handle by a chain and are designed to penetrate armor and inflict serious wounds

Mace: spray used to control mad dogs and rioters, as it causes dizziness, nausea and tears; to mace means to spray with Mace; not to be confused with the spice

machine pistol: European name for a machine gun

machinery: drug-injecting equipment

machismo: (Spanish—maleness) toughness; virility

machona: Brazilian marijuana

mack: a pimp or procurer; to pimp; term more often used in Europe than in the United States

mackman: pimp

McLaughlin Youth Center: Anchorage, Alaska's diagnostic-program reception center for delinquents

McNeil Island: U.S. Penitentiary at McNeil Island, Wash.

macon: West African marijuana-like hemp

maconha: Brazilian type of marijuana believed to have been brought from Africa in slave times, as there it is known as *macon*

mad: mind-altering drug

madam: brothel keeper; whoremistress

MADD: Mothers Against Drunk Driving

Madsen: Danish firearms manufacturer formerly known as *DISA*, for *Dansk Industri Syndicat*

MAFIA: Morte Alla Francia Italia Anela (Italian—Death to France is Italy's Cry) acronym devised when the secret society was first organized in the 1860s to combat French forces threatening the freedom of Italy; the society later became less concerned with patriotism and more concerned with power and profit

mafiosi: (Italian—gangsters; Mafia members)

mafioso: (Italian—gangster; Mafia member) pertaining to the Mafia and its criminal operations

mag cap: magazine capacity (number of bullets or shells the magazine of a firearm will hold)

Magdalene: a reformed prostitute

Magdeburg: concentration subcamp southwest of Berlin

magic mushroom: psilocybin, a hallucinogenic drug that produces a sense of unreality and, sometimes, a sense of anxiety or panic and retching or vomiting

mail fraud: usiing the mails to defraud the public

Mail Fraud Division: division of the U.S. Postal Service investigating complaints involving the use of the U.S. mail to perpetrate frauds

mail-order flimflam: using the mails to defraud the public

mainline: inject a drug into a major vein

maintain: maintain a level of drug use

Maison Gomin: correctional facility for women at St. Cyrille, Quebec

Maison Notre-Dame de la Garde: home for Catholic juvenile delinquents from 14 to 18 years old at Cap-Rouge, Quebec

Maison Tanguay: Montreal's facility for women prisoners

Majdenek: Nazi concentration camp near Lublin, Poland and second only to

Auschwitz in size; at the Nürnberg war-criminal trials it was estimated more than 1,500,000 perished here and another 2,750,000 at Auschwitz

majoon: candy eaten for its psychedelic effects; known throughout the Arab world as *ma'jun*

major trauma unit: ambulance

make: buy narcotics from someone; inform on someone; recognize someone; steal from someone

make a buy: purchase drugs

make a connection: become introduced to a drug source such as an illegal laboratory, a pusher, a smuggler or, more often, a dealer or distributor

make a croaker: deceive a doctor into prescribing narcotics

make a hit: make a purchase of narcotics; make a killing

make a killing: steal, win or otherwise obtain a large amount of money

make a meet: make a purchase of drugs or other contraband

make a reader: deceive a doctor into writing a perscription for dangerous drugs

make a run: take an automobile, motorcycle, plane or ship to another country with the object of returning with drugs and eluding inspection

make a scene: buy narcotics

make a strike: obtain drugs

make bones: assassinate; murder

make bush: escape from jail or prison

make off with: run away with; steal

make the fur fly: create a commotion

make the turn: withdraw from alcohol or drugs

make up: to prepare narcotics for injection, often called cooking

Makindye: Uganda's military prison

making little ones out of big ones: see **rock crushers**

Malagambas: members of the Malagamba Gang of Cuban hoodlums from northern New Jersey, who maintain a foothold in Atlantic City's illicit market in cocaine, marijuana and prostitution

Malang: women's prison in eastern Java south of Surabaya, Indonesia

Malayan National Liberation Front: Peking-based underground movement active in Malaysia and Singapore

Malchow: North German concentration camp northwest of the Elbe River

MALDEF: Mexican-American Legal Defense and Education Fund

malefactor: person guilty of committing a crime

malice aforethought: the intention to commit a felony, especially murder

Malines: Belgian transit camp near the French border and the North Sea built by German occupying forces during World War II as a way station for concentration camp prisoners; also known as Mechlin

mama bear: policewoman

Man: drug pusher; the police; or simply a form of address, as in *hey, man*

manacle: to handcuff

manacles: handcuffs

Manbarco: Man Barrier Corporation of Seymour, Connecticut engaged in manufacturing electronic detection systems and physical barriers made of coils of barbed wire and knife-edged wire used to keep prisoners within bounds

Manchester: places of detention in cities named Manchester in Connecticut, Georgia, Iowa, Kentucky, Massachusetts, New Hampshire, New York, Ohio, Tennessee, and Vermont

Mandan: North Dakota Industrial Farm at Mandan

mandatory sentence: statutory requirement that a certain specific minimum penalty shall be imposed and executed upon those convicted of certain offenses

m & c: morphine and cocaine

Mandogs: shepherd dogs trained by Mandelyn Kennels of Bakersfield, Calif. to detect contraband such as dangerous drugs, explosives and weapons as well as to serve as patrol or security guardians

man down: someone who is drunk, hurt or sick

Mandragora officinarum: botanical name for the European solanaceous herb called mandrake and prized by some addicts for its dream-inducing narcotic properties

mandrake: nickname for *Mandragora officinarum* (q.v.) also called devil's testicle or Satan's apple

Manhattan Homicide Task Force: New York City Police Department unit assigned to solve major murders occuring in the borough of Manhattan

Manhattan House of Detention: Tombs Prison in lower Manhattan, known to some as "Down Home"

manhunt: hunt organized to catch a criminal, an escapee, a fugitive from justice or a person who is lost

manicure: remove dirt, seeds and stems from marijuana

manipulator: professional card or dice player who sees to it that suckers are fleeced of their earnings and their winnings

manita: milk-sugar heroin adulterant

Mann Act: the White Slave Traffic Act (q.v.), passed through the efforts of James Robert Mann in 1910

mannite: another name for milk sugar, used to adulterate heroin

Mannlicher: Austrian-designed firearms named for their designer, Ferdinand Mannlicher; the automatic pistol and the breechloading five-cartridge rifle have been used by the Austrian and German armies during several wars

Mannlicher-Carcano: 6.5-millimeter rifle of Austrian design and Italian manufacture; weapon allegedly used by Lee Harvey Oswald to assassinate Pres. John F. Kennedy

MANO: Movimiento Argentina Nacional Organizado (Spanish—National Organized Movement of Argentina) terrorist group

man of respect: ranking gangster; senior member of a crime syndicate

man. one: first-degree manslaughter

manor: policeman's beat (English underworld slang)

Manor: English slang for London or its prisons

Mansfield: Ohio State Reformatory at Mansfield

Mansions: The Mansions in Brisbane, Queensland—Australia's name for its Prison Department

manslaughter: accidental killing of a human being; unlawful killing of a human being without malicious intent, as in many automobile and industrial accidents (see also **negligent manslaughter, vehicular manslaughter** and **voluntary manslaughter**)

Manson Family: terrorist group headed by Charles Manson and responsible for butchering actress Sharon Tate and four of her friends as well as attempting the assassination of Pres. Gerald R. Ford

man. two: second-degree manslaughter

manufactured lightning: electrocution

Manzanar: American relocation center for Japanese-Americans detained in this camp in southern California's Owens Valley between Independence and Lone Pine

Manzanillo: prison in Manzanillo—a Mexican seaport on the Pacific southwest of Guadalajara

MAOF: Mexican-American Opportunities Foundation (which supports a program to rehabilitate juvenile Chicano recidivists)

MAP: Mutual Agreement Programming (for parolees)

MAPA: Mexican-American Political Association

Maple Lane School: in Centralia, Wash.; for juvenile delinquents

maq: maquereau (French—mackerel) a pimp

Marathon: call-girl's date involving going out to dinner and visiting several nightclubs before going to bed with her client, who pays all the way and may spend as much as $500 in three hours

Marble Hill: Bollinger County jail at Marble Hill, Mo.

marble orchard: cemetery

Marian Hall: home for English-speaking Catholic juvenile-delinquent females at Beaconsfield, Quebec

mariholic: marijuanaholic (addict)

marijuana: leaves, flowering tops or stems of cannabis plants such as *Cannabis americana, C. mexicana* or *C. sativa;* usually dried, smoked or eaten (cooked in foods such as cookies); its effects vary, but some users lose contact with reality; addiction is psychological rather than physical; also called bhang, dagga, gangi, hay, hemp, mary jane, pot, tea, et al.

marijuana bar: see **hashish bar**

Marina Street: San Juan, Puerto Rico's district jail on Marina Street, where it was opened in 1837

Marine Interdiction Program: (U.S. Customs Service) program designed to detect and interdict smuggled contraband in water boundary areas, whether lakes, rivers or ports

Marion: Federal Prison Camp at Marion, Ill.; Marion County Detention Home, holding juvenile delinquents in the Indianapolis area; U.S. Penitentiary at Marion, Ill., replacing Alcatraz in San Francisco Bay

maritime law: branch of international law dealing with matters affecting seamen shipowners and ships

mark: easy mark; gullible person

market price: current price quoted by prostitutes for sexual services

Marlin: American firearms manufacturers

Marquette: maximum-security Marquette Branch Prison at Marquette, Mich. (where, in a survey, some nine out of 10 prisoners told an investigator they had learned new tricks and improved their criminal expertise by watching crime programs on TV)

martial arts: defensive and offensive techniques used in handling criminals, mobs, rioters, unruly persons, etc.; some forms include aikido, fencing, judo, jujitsu, karate and kung fu

martial law: order enforced by military forces during periods of local or national emergency

Martin: J.H. Martin of Calhoun City, Miss., maker of handgun holsters

Martinez: Contra Costa County Juvenile Hall in Martinez, Calif., northeast of San Francisco

mary: morphine

mary ann: marijuana

mary jane: marijuana

Marysville: Ohio Reformatory for Women at Marysville

mary warner: marijuana

MASCA: Middle Atlantic States Correctional Association

MASH: Multiple Accelerated Summary Hearing (for deporting undesirable aliens)

masher: man who molests women

masochism: sexual abnormality where pleasure follows physical maltreatment such as beating, punching or slapping

masochist: person deriving sexual pleasure from being beaten, dominated or hurt, physically or psychologically

massage parlors: often disguised whorehouses offering sexual services disguised as therapeutic massage; many massage parlors are telephone outposts for call girls, who make their dates over the phone and split their fees with the massage parlor operators

MAST: Metropolitan Arson Strike Team; Michigan Alcoholism Screening Test

master fence: remote over-the-telephone operator managing the sale of stolen goods via neighborhood fences, better known as neighborhood connections

master key: key specially cut to open a series of locks rather than just one lock

mastermind: a gang leader; a master plotter; to engage in master plotting; *who'll mastermind the operation?*

Mata Hari: seductive World War I spy whose real name was Gertrud Zelle but who used this alias meaning ''Eye of the Morning'' in Malay; she was on German Col. Nocolai's books as Agent H 21; she was caught by the French and executed by a firing squad in 1917

matchbox: enough marijuana to make about six cigarettes

matricide: mother murder(er); daughter or son who takes her or his mother's life

matron duty: tasks assigned policewomen such as caring for abandoned or lost children, guarding female material witnesses, strip searching and guarding female prisoners who might otherwise hide evidence as well as drugs and weapons

Matsqui Institution: British Columbia's minimum-security facility for drug addicts at Abbotsford

Mattachine: member of the Mattachine Society, founded in the late 1940s by Henry Hay to defend the rights of homosexuals

Matteawan: Matteawan State Hospital (for the criminally insane) near Beacon-on-Hudson, N.Y.

maui waui: Hawaiian-grown marijuana (pronounced *mau-wee wau-wee*)

Mauser: firearms made in Germany and used during World Wars I and II; originally designed by Peter Paul and Wilhelm Mauser

Mauthausen: Austrian Nazi concentration camp near Linz; some 200,000 inmates were gassed here during World War II

Maxim: machine gun named for its designer, the American-born inventor Sir Hiram Stevens Maxim; gun silencer named for its inventor, Hudson Maxim, younger brother of Sir Hiram

maximal dosage: maximum amount of a drug needed to produce a therapeutic effect without accompanying symptons of poisoning (toxicity) (see also **abusive dosage, lethal dosage, minimal dosage** and **toxic dosage**)

maximum custody: keeping of prisoners in institutions built with tool-proof bars and cells as well as high walls; maximum-security prisons are manned by many guards and are fun on a plan of rigid discipline

Maximum John: Chief Judge John J. Sirica, federal judge nicknamed for giving maximum sentences, as in the Watergate Trials

maximum security: applied to inmates considered very dangerous to correctional officers, to others, and to themselves; such inmates often have a history of jailbreaks and violent conduct; prisoners awaiting the death penalty are also kept under maximum security

max out: complete a maximum sentence

May Day: the first day of May; international holiday commemorating the martyrdom of the anarchists whose demands for an eight-hour day resulted in the Haymarket Square riots in Chicago on May 4, 1886; since then anarchists, communists and socialists as well a many trade unions have celebrated May Day

mayhem: unlawfully and maliciously depriving a human being of a member of his or her body, or disabling, disfiguring or rendering it useless; cutting or disabling another's tongue, putting out an eye or slitting the nose, ear or lip

Mazatlán: prison in Mazatlán, Mexican resort and seaport on the Pacific, southwest of Durango

m/B: male black

mbangi: South African name for hashish or marijuana (sometimes written *mbanji* or *mbanzhe*)

mbt: murder before treason (rationale used by many underground terrorists)

mc: metal-case bullet

MCA: Massachusetts Correctional Association (in Boston); Medical Correctional Association; Minnesota Corrections Authority

MCC: Metropolitan Correctional Center (in Chicago; a barless prison of the latest design)

MCCW: Miami Citizens Crime Watch

MCDC: Montgomery County Detention Center (in Maryland, near Washington, D.C.)

MCI: Massachusetts Correctional Institution (Framingham)

mcid: multipurpose concealed intrusion-detection (device)

MCJCC: Mayor's Criminal Justice Coordinating Council (in the City of New York)

MCO: Michigan Corrections Organization (of prison wardens)

mCp: my Cadillac payment (abbreviation current among many debt-ridden blacks and others attempting to live beyond their means; sometimes they are forced to resort to crime just to meet "my Cadillac payment")

mda (MDA): methyldiamphetamine (stimulant)

MDC: Minnesota Department of Corrections

mdma (MDMA): methylene - dioxy-methamphetamine (nicknamed Adam or Ecstacy)

ME: Medical Examiner (often called a coroner)

meat-eater: grafter; policeman or politician accepting or extorting graft

meat salesman: pimp

meat wagon: prison van

MECHA: *Movimiento Estudiantil Chicano de Aztlan* (Spanish—Chicano Student Movement of Aztlan) in Spanish Aztlan is a mythical land northwest of Mexico to which the Aztecs departed—possibly California, where MECHA has many members who are active in demonstrations and vandalism

mechanic: criminal skilled in some specialty such as assassination, bombing, safe-cracking, etc.

meconism: opium addiction

meconist: opium addict

med: medic; physician or surgeon

media: popular truncation of mass media (a term not defined in most dictionaries, but referring to radio, the press and televison)

medical addict: patient receiving authorized maintenance doses of any of several opium-like drugs prescribed for pain relief

medical fraud: perpetrated by physicians arranging to receive kickbacks from specialists they have unnecessarily recommended to their own patients and from druggists and laboratories whose medicines and services are used without being needed

medical hype: drug addict who became addicted during medical treatment requiring narcotics; person obtaining drugs with a legal prescription

medical jurisprudence: medical knowledge applied to legal questions

medico—legal medicine: medical knowledge applied to questions of law

medifraud: medical fraud (q.v.)

meditation: solitary confinement

medium custody: prisoners who are less dangerous and less hardened are often kept in panal institutions of this sort, which are designed to give them more freedom of movement and greater scope for self-direction than do maximum security institutions

megabucks: slang unit of money equal to a million dollars or to any very large sum of money

Meinhof-Puig Antich Group: terrorists active in France and in West Germany

mellow: amiably intoxicated

mellows: strong drugs

mellow yellow: nickname for fried banana skin scrapings sold to the gullible by drug pushers

meltout: escape technique used in some modern prisons, where certain types of doors and windows can be melted out by prisoners wishing to escape confinement

Memphis dominoes: dice

Mems: 9mm Argentine parabellum machine gun popular with counterinsurgency forces and their guerrilla opponents

Menard: Illinois State Penitentiary at Menard

Mendelsohn: Benjamin Mendelsohn, contemporary Romanian-born behavioral researcher and lawyer who first suggested the establishment of the science of victimology

Mendoza: Mexican machine gun named for its developer, Rafael Mendoza

menticide: brainwashing; implanting ideas normally rejected but made to seem attractive by the brain-washers; some people, when charged with a crime, claim they were brainwashed—the victims of menticide

MERAG: Middle-East Research and Action Group (q.v.)

merchandise: contraband; drugs; stolen arms or other things

merchant of death: nickname sometimes given to one who sells alcohol, tobacco, armaments, drugs or other merchandise that may result in the death of its purchasers

mercy killing: euthanasia (killing a hopelessly injured or sick animal or person)

meretricious traffic: prostitution

Merida: prison in Merida, capital of the Mexican state of Yucatan, just south of the seaport of Progreso on the Gulf of Mexico

meritorious good time: promise of parole for good behavior on the part of convicts wanting to get out of prison and turn over a new leaf

MESA: Mining Enforcement and Safety Administration (q.v.)

mesc: mescal; mescaline

mescal: Mexican alcoholic beverage distilled from the fermented sap of agave plants

mescal buttons: see **peyote**

mescaline: hallucinogenic drug produced from mescal buttons; called *peyote* by American and Mexican Indians, who use it during religious rites as it induces a trance-like state

mess with it: dilute it

Met: Metropolitan Correctional Center in downtown San Diego, Calif.

metal case: metal-case bullet consisting of a lead core enclosed in a gilding metal jacket

metal knuckles: brass knuckles (q.v.)

metal point: metal-point bullet consisting of

a lead core with a gilding metal jacket over its nose; this gives increased penetration of the projectile

metanoia: change of heart and mind necessary for the rehabilitation of a criminal

meter jumper: device for stealing electric power from a public utility

meter maid: female member of the police force assigned to checking parking meters and giving tickets to parking violators; sometimes nicknamed Dickless Tracy

meth: methamphetamine (q.v.)

methadone: synthetic opiate often used in the treatment of narcotic addicts

methadyl acetate: drug used for relieving the symptoms of withdrawal from heroin without producing any euphoria, as does methadone

methamphetamine: amphetamine stimulating the central nervous system and producing rapid heartbeat and restlessness and, sometimes, anxiety and irritability

methhead: habitual user of methamphetamine

methedrine: potent amphetamine also known as *speed* because of its stimulating effect; its use is sometimes fatal

meth freak: methedrine addict

meths: methylated spirits (methanol-denatured ethyl alcohol); sometimes imbibed by alcoholic addicts, usually with fatal results

methylmorphine: pharmacological name for codeine

Met Pol: Metropolitan Police

Metropolitan Arson Strike Team: typically consists of fire department arson investigators and police department detectives; known in many places as MAST

Metropolitan Correction Centers: U.S. Bureau of Prison penal facilities in Chicago, Ill.; Detroit, Mich.; New York, N.Y.; and San Diego, Calif.

Mexican brown: Mexican marijuana, superior to Mexican green (q.v.)

Mexican chickens: Mexican children who are sexually exploited

Mexican green: green marijuana of low potency and value

Mexican horse: brownish heroin made in Mexico

Mexican locoweed: jimsonweed (q.v.); scientific name is *Astragalus mollissimus*; its effects are intoxicating to both beast and man

Mexican mud: brown Mexican heroin usually made from opium grown in the

Sierra Madre mountains and taken to Durango, where it is refined into morphine and then into Mexican mud

Mexican mushroom: psilocybin (*Psilocybe mexicana*), a mushroom whose extracts produce hallucinogenic effects lasting up to six hours

mezz: marijuana

mezzrole: highly potent marijuana cigarettes named for those once made and sold by Harlem jazz musician Mezz Mezzrow

M-15: British secret service charged with counterespionage and security at home and overseas

M-14: 7.62mm ammunition and rifle used by NATO military forces

mg: machine gun(ner)

MHP: Missouri Highway Patrol

MHTF: Manhattan Homicide Task Force (New York City Police Department)

MI: Military Intelligence (British)

mia: missing in action

MIB: Military Intelligence Branch (see also **Military Intelligence Division**)

Michigan City: Indiana State Prison at Michigan City

michoacan: bright-green marijuana cultivated in the Mexican state of Michoacan

mickey finn: see **chloral hydrate**

Mickey Mouse ears: police-car siren lights

microdot: lsd (LSD) tablet

microdot process: microphotographic reproduction system wherein a page of printed matter can be reduced to the size of a dot so security and transmission are facilitated; a high-power microscope is used to read the microdot message

MID: Military Intelligence Division (q.v.)

Middle-Eastern connection: phrase describing the flow of narcotics from Iran and Turkey through local laboratories via Iranian and Turkish traffickers to Austria, France, Italy, the Netherlands and West Germany as well as to Canada, Mexico and the United States

Middle-East Research and Action Group: anti-Zionist pacifist and libertarian organization in London

midget: 10- or 11-year-old youngster who is addicted to alcohol and/or narcotics and busy begging or stealing the money needed to support his or her habit

Midtown North and Midtown South: police precincts in New York City's midtown Manhattan, where pornography and prostitution are accompanied by assaults and robberies

MI-5: Military Intelligence 5 (British internal intelligence organization)

mighty mezz: oversize marijuana cigarette

mike: microgram; microphone

Milan: Federal Correctional Institution at Milan, Mich.

Milford: Delaware facility for juveniles from the ages of 8 to 18 at Milford; also called Stevenson House

milieu therapy: treatment given to aid convicts in returning to society, such as halfway houses, pre-release guidance centers, tranquilizing drugs, etc.

military execution: execution by a military firing squad

Military Intelligence Division: America's intelligence service begun in 1885, but not really organized until 1898, when Capt. Ralph H. Van Deman took over what by World War I had become the MIB—the Military Intelligence Branch

milk: drain of profits or resources

milk sugar: lactose crystals resembling heroin and used in its dilution

milk wagon: police or sheriff's van for transporting prisoners

Millhaven: Millhaven Institution at Bath, Ontario (maximum-security Canadian prison)

Miltown: trade name for a meprobamate tranquilizer

Milwaukee: Milwaukee County Jail in Milwaukee, Wis.

Mimico: Mimico Correction Centre (for males) in Toronto, Ontario

min: policeman; policewoman

M-in-C: Matron-in-Chief

mindblower: drug or experience that upsets a person's emotional equilibrium

Mineola: Nassau County Jail in Mineola, N.Y.

mini-cannon: number-10 can filled with plastic explosive and topped with a tight-fitting concave steel projectile

minimal dosage: minimum amount of a drug needed to produce a therapeutic effect (see also **abusive dosage, lethal dosage, maximal dosage** and **toxic dosage**)

minimum custody: honor dormitories, prison camps and prison farms that offer inmates as much freedom from restraint as possible while preventing their escape

Mining Enforcement and Safety Administration: agency charged with safe handling and safekeeping of explosives as well as mine safety

mini-nuke: miniature nuclear-explosivve device

mini-streamer: tear-gas-filled spray container used to fend off mad dogs, muggers, rapists, etc.

Minneapolis pimp: pimp who is notorious for rounding up stray teen-age girls and sending them to New York, where they are forced into prostitution

Minnesota Strip: nickname for the section of Eighth Avenue in the Times Square area of New York City populated by streetwalkers from Minnesota

mins (MINS): minor(s) in need of supervision (see also **pins.**)

minute of angle: accuracy capability of ammunition and firearms

MIP: Marine Interdiction Program (q.v.)

Miporn: Miami pornography (FBI code name for its investigation of a billion-dollar pornographic racket)

miracle-drug racket: selling so-called miracle drugs through the mails; such drugs may purport to cure anything from cancer to epilepsy, from cardiovascular disorders to constipation

MIRACODE: Berkeley, California's computerized criminal data bank, set up for ready reference by law-enforcement officers

Miranda card: a card-size printed statement used by law-enforcement officers when they outline the legal rights of criminal suspects they arrest; name derived from a decision of the Supreme Court of the United States defining the legal rights of criminal suspects when they are apprehended

misdemeanant: person convicted of committing a misdemeanor

misdemeanor: any crime less serious than a felony and hence not punishable by death or more than a year's imprisonment

MI-6: Military Intelligence 6 (British external intelligence organization)

misprision: concealment of a felony or of treason by anyone who is aware of either, although not a participant; seditious conduct; cover-up; wrong performance of official duty

miss: inject a drug outside a vein; miss the vein

miss emma: morphine

Missouri Uniform Law Enforcement System: the state's computerized criminal data file

Mister Whiskers: federal law-enforcement agent(s)

Mitchellville: Iowa Training School for Girls at Mitchellville

mj: marijuana

MJ: Ministry of Justice

mld: median lethal dose (enough to kill)

MLN: Movimiento de Liberacion Nacional (Spanish—National Liberation Movement) Uruguayan terrorists, also known as Tupamaros

m/M: male Mexican

MMP: Military Mounted Police

MMTP: Methadone Maintenance Treatment Program (for narcotic addicts)

M'Naghten: M'Naghten Case, Rule or Test, defining criminal insanity, and thus responsibility; named for a 19th-century English trial of a man named M'Naghten

MNLF: Malayan National Liberation Front (q.v.); Moro National Liberation Front (q.v.)

M-note: $1,000 bill

m/O: male Oriental

m.o. (mo; MO): modus operandi (Latin—manner, method or mode of operating; way of working) pattern of criminal operation often repeated by the same culprit and frequently leading to his or her detection and arrest

moa: minute of angle (q.v.)

Moabit: Berlin's great prison in the Tiergarten section of the metropolis, dating back to the time of the kaisers

mob: criminal syndicate or gang

mobile crime: police van equipped to gather evidence and take pictures

MOCCC: Massachusetts Organized Crime Control Council

moderation: reasonable conduct with respect to drinking alcoholic beverages

mohasky: hashish or marijuana

mohoska: marijuana

mojo: narcotic addict

Mole: The Mole—nickname of James Earl Ray, the convicted murderer of the Rev. Martin Luther King Jr.; so named because of his eight escapes from various prisons

mole: member of the intelligence organization of one country who is in fact a secret agent for another, hostile or potentially hostile nation and hence is able to divulge the first country's secrets and to expose its counterintelligence forces

moll: female gangster

moll buzzer: pickpocket adept at stealing or removing money from women's pocketbooks, purses, handbags and wallets

Mollies: Molly Maguires (q.v.)

Molly Maguires: Irish-American secret terrorists active in the anthracite coal mines of Pennsylvania between 1865 and 1877; organized in Ireland in 1843 to resist government evictions and called Molly Maguires because members disguised themselves as women

Molly Pitcher: nickname of Mary McCauley, who, at the Battle of

Monmouth in 1778, carried pitchers of water to weary and wounded soldiers; she took over the firing of her husband's cannon when he fell mortally wounded

Molotov cocktail: incendiary bomb made by filling a bottle with some flammable fluid such as gasoline and inserting a wick to be ignited just before the bomb is tossed; developed during the Spanish Civil War to destroy tanks; named for former Soviet foreign minister V. M. Molotov

Monadnock: Monadnock Lifetime Products (police clubs and accessories)

Monday boy: man who steals from clotheslines; derisive term for a petty thief

Monday girl: woman who steals from clotheslines; petty thief

money laundering: concealing source of funds or evading federal reporting requirements

M-1: 15-round 30-caliber carbine; eight-round Garand semi-automatic rifle used by American troops during World War II

Mongols: rival motorcycle gang to the Hell's Angels, who also engage in assault, burglary, drug dealing and other crimes

Mongoose: Mongoose Gang (secret police in the West Indian island of Grenada)

moniker: underworld nickname

monkey off your back: formerly drug-addicted

monkey on your back: presently drug-addicted

Monowitz: forced-labor subcamp close to Auschwitz, Poland's extermination camp

Monroe: Washington State Reformatory at Monroe, northeast of Seattle

Monte Carlo: gambling capital and resort city in Monaco, on the Mediterranean some 10 miles east of Nice, France; its subjects are not permitted at its gambling tables

Monterrey: prison in Monterrey, capital of the state of Nuevo Leon in northeastern Mexico

Montey: Allenwood Federal Prison Camp at Allentown, Pa., near Montgomery

Montgomery: Federal Prison Camp at Montgomery, Ala.

Montluc: French greystone prison in Lyons where during World War II Nazi Gestapo held many before shipping them off to concentration camps and gas chambers in Germany

Montreal: the Maison Tanguay, a correctional facility for women prisoners in Montreal, Quebec

Montrose School for Girls: at Reistertown, Md.

moocah: old nickname for marijuana

mooch: beg; borrow

moola: money

Moon Crescent: Singapore's minimum-security prison taking its name from the moon crescent in the island nation's flag

moonshine: homemade whiskey

moonshiner: person engaged in the illicit distillation of whiskey

moonshine victim: alcoholic

MOOP: Ministerstvo Okhranenia Obshehestvennogo Poriadka (Russian—All-Union Ministry for the Preservation of Public Order) latest in a long line of Soviet secret police agencies, which began with the Cheka and the GPU or OGPU

Moor: The Moor—Dartmoor Prison near Princetown in Devonshire, England

mooter: old nickname for a marijuana cigarette

MOPSS: Multispectral Opium Poppy Sensor System

moragrifa: marijuana

moral holidays: occasions when enforcement of the laws is relaxed and the police are indulgent, as during many athletic events, election celebrations, fraternal conventions, the Mardi Gras, New Year's Eve, etc.

moral turpitude: legal term describing a crime found shocking to the sense of decency or the morals of a community

Morelia: prison in Morelia, capital of the Mexican state of Michoacan, to the west of Mexico City

morf(ie): morphine

morgue: public building provided with refrigerated chambers for holding unidentified bodies pending their identification and the investigation of their deaths

morning-glory seeds: source of a hallucinogen used by American Indians and others

Moro National Liberation Front: Libyan-backed Filipino terrorists demanding self-rule in Mindanao and the Sulu Islands, two largely Islamic areas in the Philippine Islands

morph: morphine

morphia: morphine

morphine: alkaloid of opium; taken in excess, it often results in respiratory failure and death; less potent than heroin but often just as fatal

morphine base: morphine sulfate

morphine sulfate: morphine base product used by many heroin addicts when no heroin is available

morph injec: morphine injection (death

brought about by an injection of morphine)

morpho: morphine

Morrison: the Mount View Girls School at Morrison, Colo.

Moscow connection: airport exchange point between Oriental sources of narcotics flown westward via low-cost Soviet airlines and many Occidental outlets beyond the Iron Curtain

Mossad: Israel's intelligence service

Mossberg: American firearms manufacturer

Mossberg 500: shotgun often used by law-enforcement agents

Most: Johannes Most, late 19th-century German-American anarchist who invented the letter bomb and advocated the assassination of all bearing responsibility for the servitude, exploitation and misery of the people

mother: nickname for a drug pusher, especially a homosexual drug pusher; madam of a brothel

Mother of Prison Reform: Dorothea Lynde Dix (1802-1887), American reformer active in Massachusetts and other states

mother's day: day when welfare checks arrive; the checks are sometimes used by addicted mothers and other to buy drugs

Mothers in Prison Projects: organization affiliated with Women in Jails and Prisons

motive: reason for the commission of a crime; *whatever was the motive for killing him?*

motorcycle mama: female member of a predominantly male motorcycle gang; as their *mama* she is expected to give them sexual services whenever demanded, and only attains the title of *mama* when she has had intercourse with every member of the gang

Motorola: Motorola Teleprograms (Chicago-based firm producing films and manuals covering all aspects of the terrorist threat, as well as instructions on how to handle the kidnapping of executives)

motor vehicle theft: unlawful taking, or attempted taking, of a motor vehicle owned by another, with intent to deprive her or him of it permanently or temporarily

Moundsville: West Virginia Penitentiary at Moundsville, on the Ohio River just south of Wheeling

mountain dew: moonshine whiskey

Mountain View School: for juvenile-delinquent females at Helena, Mont.

Mounties: members of the Royal Canadian Mounted Police

Mount View Girls School: at Morrison, Colo.

mouthpiece: lawyer; legal representative

mouth worker: drug user who swallows drugs

move in on: attack

movement: *the movement* can refer to a labor movement, radical movement, underground movement, et al.

mp: metal-point bullet

Mp: Minneapolis pimp (q.v.)

MPC: Model Penal Code (published by the American Law Institute in 1962)

MPD: Metropolitan Police Department

mpd: maximum permissible dose

MPI: Movimiento Pro-Independencia (Spanish—Pro-Independence Movement) for the liberation of Puerto Rico

MPLA: Movimento Popular de Libertacao de Angola (Portuguese—Popular Movement for the Liberation of Angola) communist led and supported movement

MPP: Mothers in Prison Projects

MPU: Missing Persons Unit (of a police department)

MR: Michigan Reformatory in Ionia, in the central part of the state, where many young offenders are housed

MR: Mobilizacion Republicana (Spanish—Republican Mobilization) pro-Castro political party active in the Nicaraguan underground

MRC: Minnesota Restitution Center (see also **restitution center**)

MRCP: Maoist Revolutionary Communist Party

mrt: mid-range trajectory (of a bullet in flight)

ms: morphine sulfate

MSC: Metropolitan Special Constabulary

MSI: Movimento Sociale Italiano (Italian Social Movement) neo-fascist right-wing gangs

MSPU: Massachusetts State Prostitutes Union (prostitutes seeking the decriminalization of their profession)

MSS: Maximum Security System

MTU: Michigan Training Unit (reform school)

M-2: 15-round 30-caliber automatic carbine; Match-Two (program matching volunteers from a community, called sponsors, on a one-to-one basis with prison inmates; the sponsors write to the inmates and visit them regularly, with the aim of establishing meaningful and warm relationships and providing the convicts with references and job support after they are paroled)

mu: marijuana user; hashish or marijuana

muckraker: one of the American critics, journalists and novelists who, in the early 1900s, exposed the crimes committed by some businessmen and politicians; Upton Sinclair, Lincoln Steffens and Ida Tarbell are some of the best-remembered muckrakers; hence, anyone—especially a writer—who exposes official or corporate wrongdoing

mudslinger: libeler; slanderer

mug: (American slang) a face; (English slang) a whore's client (used by whores as a term of contempt); to assault with the intent to rape, rob or kill the victim

muggle: marijuana cigarette; dried, unshredded marijuana leaf

mug shot: facial portrait; police-file photograph of a criminal's face, full-view and side-view

mulct: a fine; to punish an offender by fining

mule: person used to transport drugs or contraband such as heroin or weapons from one place to another, especially across the Mexican border

Mulege: Mexican prison camp on the Gulf of California, southeast of Santa Rosalia

MULES: Missouri Uniform Law Enforcement System (q.v.)

mule's ear: hidden device for controlling the movement of a roulette wheel

multiprisoner transportation unit: paddy wagon; police patrol van

munchies: peanuts, popcorn and similar snack foods; hunger brought on by marijuana

Muncy: State Prison for Women, near Williamsport in central Pennsylvania

murder: the intentional killing of one human being by another (murder is legally indefensible except in the carrying out of capital punishment, the performance of any law-enforcement or military duty, in self-defense or in the defense of someone whom it is one's duty to defend); to kill another human being intentionally

Murder City: media nickname applied to any city sustaining the greatest number of murders in any one year

murderee: actual or intended victim of a murderer

murderer: anyone, especially a male, legally guilty of killing another person; killer of a living creature

murderess: female murderer

Murder, Incorporated: nickname of a band of professional killers who worked for the Mafia during the 1930s and 1940s in many parts of the United States

murder in the first degree: killing with

malice aforethought; premeditated murder may be punished by death

murder in the second degree: killing committed during the course of a quarrel and in the heat of passion

murder merchandise: addictive drugs and lethal weapons

murder one: murder in the first degree (q.v.)

Murphy game: confidence game wherein money is taken from a customer—often by a pimp—to pay a prostitute who never shows up

muscle: take drugs via intramuscular injection

muscleman: strong-arm bully or gangster

muscle relaxer: barbiturate

mushroom: so-called ''sacred mushroom'' containing psilocybin, producing excitation and hyperactivity plus restlessness and, in some cases, irritability, anxiety, depression and hallucinations

musical execution: execution performed to the roll of a field drum or tenor drums; usually a military execution with the drum roll starting with the command to aim and finishing with the firing by the firing squad, with the last note accented sharply

Muskegon: Michigan's medium and minimum-security correctional facility at Muskegon

musta: marijuana

Mustang Branch Ranch: one of Nevada's largest legal brothels; after a 50-50 split of earnings with the managers, it is estimated that the prostitutes working there make $300 to $600 a week

muta: Mexican word for marijuana

mutineer: sailor or soldier who has revolted or is revolting against his officers

mutinous: hard to handle; prone to revolt

mutiny: sailors' or soldiers' revolt against their officers

mutual welfare league: convict-self-government system introduced by Warden Thomas Mott Osborne at Sing Sing; later introduced at the U.S. Naval Prison at Portsmouth as well

muzzler: petty thief; small-time operator

mv: muzzle velocity

MVP: Most Valuable Player (award given to FBI agents assigned especially hazardous tasks)

m/w: male white

MWA: Mystery Writers of America

MWL: Mutual Welfare League

N

n: narcotic; no; note (banknote); nothing

N: Navy; Negro

NA: Narcotics Anonymous (q.v.); National Academy (of the FBI)

naa (NAA): neutron-activation analysis (q.v.)

NAACO: North American Arms Corporation of Canada

NAAWS: North American Association of Wardens and Superintendents

nab: to arrest; a law-enforcement officer who makes an arrest

NAB: National Alliance of Businessmen (whose members seek to give ex-convicts a chance by giving them a job)

NACCC: National Association of Citizens Crime Commissions

NACDL: National Association of Criminal Defense Lawyers (q.v.)

NACHEPO: National Advisory Commission on Higher Education for Police Officers

NACLA: North American Congress on Latin America

naco: night-alarm cutoff

NACRO: National Association for the Care and Resettlement of Offenders

NADA: National Association of Drug Addiction (London)

NADDIS: Narcotics and Dangerous Drugs Information System (computerized criminal file)

NADPAS: National Association of Discharged Prisoners' Aid Societies

NAFF: National Association for Freedom (right-wing British extremists)

Nafha: Israel's top-security prison opened in 1980 but the smallest of all its correctional institutions

NAFI: National Association of Fire Investigators (q.v.)

NAFS: National Association for Forensic Sciences

nail: a hypodermic needle; to arrest

nail bomb: nail-covered explosive stick designed to scatter the nails in every direction, often with fatal results

NAILS: National Automated Immigration Lookout System

NAJ: National Association for Justice

NAJC: National Assessment of Juvenile Correction (University of Michigan)

NAJCA: National Association of Juvenile Correctional Agencies

NAJJ: National Assessment of Juvenile Justice (University of Michigan)

naked: without weapons; unarmed

NALA: National Association of Legal Assistants

NALP: National Association for Law Placement

NAM: New American Movement (q.v.)

Nambu: Japanese-made automatic pistol

NAME: National Association of Medical Examiners (in some communities they are called coroners)

nanny-goat sweat: low-grade whiskey

NAP: Neighborhood Awareness Program (q.v.)

NAP: Nuclei Armati Proletari (Italian—Armed Proletarian Nucleus) terrorists in and out of prison, where they began their organization

NAPAN: National Association for the Prevention of Addiction to Narcotics

NAPCRO: National Association of Police Community Relations Officers (q.v.)

NAPD: Natinal Academy of Police Driving

NAPLP: National Association of Para-Legal Personnel

NAPO: National Association of Probation Officers

NAPRC: National Association for the Prevention of Rape by Castration

NAPV: National Association of Prison Visitors

NARA: Narcotic Addict Rehabilitation Act

narc: narcotics agent or any law-enforcement officer

narco: narcotics agent; nickname of the U.S. Public Health Service Hospital in Lexington, Ky., where addicts are treated

NARCO: United Nations' Narcotics Commission

narco card: narcotic-addict registration card

narco fuzz: narcotics law-enforcement officer

narcomania: abnormal craving for drugs offering relief from pains, actual or imaginary

Narconon: Narcotics Anonymous (q.v.)

narcot: narcotic; narcotize(d), narcotiz(ing)

narcotest: test made to determine if someone is or was under the influence of narcotics

narcotic: pain-killing drug such as demerol, heroin, methadone, morphine or opium; an overdose of any may produce death; all tend to impair judgment

narcotic antagonist: drug used in the treatment of narcotic overdose that tends to neutralize the effects of opiates; cyclazocine and Nalline (nalorphine) are fairly well-known narcotic antagonists

Narcotics Anonymous: nationwide addicts' group patterned after AA—Alcoholics Anonymous

narcotism: condition brought about by the use of narcotics; narcotic addiction

narcs: narcotics; narcotics agents; narcotics hospitals; narcotics officers; narcotics treatment centers

narghile: Turkish-type water pipe

nark: narcotics agent or law-enforcement officer

NASAR: National Association of Search and Rescue

Nashville: Tennessee Prison for Women at Nashville; Tennessee State Vocational School for Girls at Nashville

NATB: National Automobile Theft Bureau

National Academy of Police Driving: Dallas, Texas school where law-enforcement officers are taught how to avoid disaster during the pursuit of escaping vehicles

National Association of Criminal Defense Lawyers: formerly the National Association of Defense Lawyers in Criminal Cases; publishes *Criminal Defense Magazine* quarterly

National Association of Fire Investigators: organization aiming to increase knowledge and improve skills of persons responsible for investigating arson, explosions, fires, etc.

National Association of Police Community Relations Officers: acts as a consultant aid; gives technical assistance; maintains library in Washington, D.C.

National Association of Training Schools and Juvenile Agencies: organization created by the merger of the National Association of Training Schools and the National Conference of Juvenile Agencies

National Association of Volunteers in Criminal Justice: formerly National Forum on Volunteers in Criminal Justice

National Border Patrol Council: citizens' organization advocating stricter control of immigration and illegal entrants

National Cargo Security Council: organization concerned with cargo thefts and the hijacking of entire containers

National Clearinghouse for Criminal Justice Planning and Architecture: maintains a 10,000-volume library at the University of Illinois at Champaign

National Correctional Recreation Association: sponsors prison postal weight-lifting contests for inmates in Canada and the U.S.

National Crime Panel Survey Reports: (often shortened to National Crime Panel Reports) criminal victimization surveys made for the LEAA by the Bureau of the Census

National Crime Prevention Institute: functions through the School of Police Administration of the University of Louisville in Kentucky; issues printed information about home burglar alarm systems available

National Detective Police: espionage and anti-subversive organization of the Federal government during and after the Civil War

National Firearms Freedom Fund: priority project of the Citizens Committee for the Right to Keep and Bear Arms

National Jail Association: presents annual award for the outstanding jailer and jail matron; publishes *Jail Forum* quarterly

National Jail Managers Association: has established historical archives, an information clearinghouse and a library in Eugene, Ore.

National Juvenile Detention Association: publisher of *Counterpoint* (bimonthly) and the *Directory of Juvenile Detention Homes*

National Liberation Front of Cuba: underground terrorist organization manned by specially-trained commandos who seek out and destroy Castro's spy ships off the coast of Cuba close to Florida

National Organization for the Reform of Marijuana Laws: members assert that it is their constitutional right to be left alone and to enjoy their bodies as they see fit—i.e., to use marijuana

National Police and Fire Fighters Association: 41,000-member fraternal organization that publishes the *National Police and Fire Journal*

National Police Officers Association of America: 32,000-member organization; maintains the Police Hall of Fame and

Museum; publishes *Enforcement Journal* quarterly

National Prison Project: the American Civil Liberties Union's program aimed at fixing prison sentences and improving the lot of prisoners

national razor: French nickname for the guillotine

National Rifle Association: organization of gun enthusiasts and sportsmen who wish to defend their right to bear arms and who are concerned with the national defense and self-defense; the NRA's headquarters are in Washington, D.C.

National Rifle Association Firearms Museum: museum in which more than 1,000 firearms are displayed; located at 1600 Rhode Island Ave. NW in Washington, D.C.; open daily, except holidays, from 10:00 A.M. to 4:00 P.M.; includes exhibits from all parts of the world

National Rural Crime Prevention Center: located at Ohio State University in Columbus; its studies reveal that rural crime is on the increase, with most suspects in the 16- to 19-year-old group; encourages rural dwellers to become more security-minded and to report suspicious activity or persons to county sheriffs, as rural crimes can usually be solved when ordinary citizens notice such activity or persons and report them instantly

National Sheriffs Association: 65,000-member organization that publishes *National Sheriff* bimonthly

National Socialist White People's Party: formerly the American Nazi Party

National States Rights Party: Georgia-based, racist-oriented political group

National Task Force on Prostitution: organization seeking the decriminalization of prostitution; formerly called COYOTE (Call Off Your Old Tired Ethics)

NATSJA: National Association of Training Schools and Juvenile Agencies (q.v.)

Natzweller: forced-labor concentration camp close to the Rhine in eastern France, south of Strasbourg

natural euthanasia: death by starvation

NAVCJ: National Association of Volunteers in Criminal Justice (q.v.)

Navigators' Islands: former name of Samoa islands in the South Pacific

Naxas: Naxalites (Maoist extremists active in India)

NBDC: National Burglar and Fire Alarm Association

NBPA: National Black Police Association

NBPC: National Border Patrol Council (q.v.)

NCA: Narcotics Control Act (enacted in 1956 in response to the increase in the use of drugs after World War II); National Council on Alcoholism (headquartered in New York City)

NCAI: National Clearinghouse for Alcohol Information (United States Public Health Service)

ncb: narcotic-centered behavior

NCCAN: National Center on Child Abuse and Neglect

NCCCD: National Center for Computer Crime Data

NCCD: National Council on Crime and Delinquency

NCCG: National Council on Compulsive Gambling

NCCH: National Council to Control Handguns

NCCJ: National Coalition for Children's Justice

NCCJPA: National Clearinghouse for Criminal Justice Planning and Architecture (q.v.)

NCCL: National Council for Civil Liberties

NCCPL: National Council for Civil Liberties

NCCPV: National Commission on the Causes and Prevention of Violence

NCCVD: National Council for Combating Venereal Diseases

NCDA: National Center for Drug Analysis; National Council on Drug Abuse

NCDC: National Center for Disease Control; National Communicable Disease Center; National Council on Crime and Delinquency

NCIC: National Crime Information Center (Washington, D.C. computer operation)

NCJA: National Criminal Justice Association

NCJISS: National Criminal Justice Information and Statistics Service

NCJRS: National Criminal Justice Reference Service

NCLR: National Council of La Raza

NCOC: National Conference on Organized Crime

NCMEC: National Center for Missing and Exploited Children

NCP: National Customs Police (Philippines)

NCPA: National Crime Prevention Association

NCPI: National Crime Prevention Institute (q.v.)

NCPPL: National Committee on Prisons and Prison Labor

NCPV: National Commission on the Prevention of Violence

NCRA: National Correctional Recreation Association (q.v.)

NCROPA: National Campaign for the Repeal of the Obscene Publications Act (British effort)

NCSC: National Cargo Security Council (q.v.)

NCSRC: National Centre for Social Research and Criminology (Cairo, Egypt)

NCTR: National Center for Toxicological Research (Jefferson, Ark.)

ND: Narcotics Division (of the New York City Police Department)

NDAA: National District Attorneys Association

ndd: narcotic-detection dog

NDI: National Death Index

NDP: National Detective Police (q.v.)

NDPs: Narcotic Detention Pens at 111 Centre Street in New York City

NDSB: Narcotic Drugs Supervisory Body (United Nations)

neb: nembutal (q.v.)

nebbies: numbutal capsules

NECCC: New England Correctional Coordinating Council

neck oil: whiskey

necktie: hangman's noose

necktie hanger: gallows

necktie party: lynching; lynch mob

needle capsule: air-propelled poisonous capsule used to penetrate the clothing and skin of the victim, who may be yards away from the assassin; the capsul enters the body much in the manner of an insect's sting; in less than a dozen hours, the victim dies of what appears to be heart failure, as all traces of poison disappear in 60 seconds or less; by then the assassin is far from the scene of the crime, beyond the reach of the law

needle freak: drug addict who enjoys using hypodermic needles

Needle Park: nickname of Sherman Square in New York City, at the intersection of Amsterdam Avenue and Broadway on West 71st Street, where many drug addicts formerly congregated

negative sanction: punishment or threat of punishment; the death penalty, for example, is a negative sanction

negligent manslaughter: causing the death of another by gross negligence or recklessness

Neighborhood Awareness Program: program in which local police enlist citizens who pledge to report all suspicious activities to law-enforcement agencies

neighborhood connection: fence dealing in small amounts of stolen furs, hi-fi sets, jewelry, radios, television sets, etc. (see also **master fence**)

nembutal: hypnotic barbiturate used as a quick-acting sedative

nemish: nembutal (q.v.)

nemmies: nembutal capsules

nep: nude-encounter parlor (legal dodge devised to mask a massage parlor)

NEST: Nuclear Emergency Search Team (q.v.)

Neuengamme: main concentration camp near Hamburg during the Hitler regime

neuroleptic: tranquilizer drug used to reduce anxiety and tension

neutralize: assassinate; kill

neutron-activation analysis: method of determining the composition of many items, including bullets, knives and other weapons

Neve Tirza: Israeli maximum-security prison for women

New Albany: minimum-security jail in New Albany, Ind., just across the Ohio River from Louisville, Ky.

New American Movement: communist-directed leftwing group founded in the fall of 1971

New Dawn Collective: Berkeley-based California distributor of underground literature advocating over-throw of the government by force

Newgate: long the principal prison of London, adjacent to the Central Criminal Courts (better known as the Old Bailey) on Newgate Street, across from the General Post Office

Newgate's Angel: Elizabeth Gurney Fry, a lay visitor well known to Newgate's prisoners in the early 19th century

Newgit: nickname for London's old Newgate Prison

new police: bullet noted for its stopping power

Newport Research Company: a Fountain Valley, Calif., firm whose products include laser-aimed assault rifles, revolvers and riot shotguns

New Queens: newer section of the Riker's Island Penitentiary in New York City's East River, just north of the La Guardia Airport in the borough of Queens

New Scotland Yard: see **Scotland Yard**

New Westminster: Canadian maximum-security facility at New Westminster, British Columbia, adjacent to Vancouver

New York City Police Museum: narcotics and police exhibits open to the public from Monday through Friday free of charge;

reference library available to law-enforcement officers and college students; both at 235 East 20th Street in New York City

New York School for Girls: at Hudson, New York

New York's Finest: nickname for New York City's policemen

NF: National Front (British racist party active in London and other metropolitan centers)

NF: Nuestra Familia (Spanish—Our Family)

nfd: no further description

NFE: National Front of England (racists advocating immediate deportation of all non-whites to wherever they originated)

NFFF: National Firearms Freedom Fund (q.v.)

NFPCA: National Fire Prevention and Control Administration

ng: no good

NGC: National Gambling Commission

NIA: National Intelligence Authority

NIAAA: National Institute on Alcohol Abuse and Alcoholism

Niantic: Connecticut Correctional Institution at Niantic

NIC: National Institute of Corrections

nick: steal; arrest

nickel (bag): $5 bag of heroin; $5 bag of marijuana—enough to make from 5 to 8 cigarettes or joints

nickel note: $5 bill

nickel's worth: five dollars worth of drugs

Nicotiana glauca: (Latin—green nicotine) one of many names given marijuana

nicotine: central nervous system stimulant found in tobacco; because of its very poisonous alkaloidal nature it is often used as an insecticide

NIDA: National Institute on Drug Abuse

NIE: National Intelligence Estimate

nigger sticker: (KKK slang) dagger

night-chuk: trade name for a Oriental-type riot baton found very effective in controlling crowds or violent people

night house: English euphemism for a whorehouse

nightingale: informer

nightscope: see **quickpoint**

nightstick: police baton

NIJ: National Institute of Justice

NIJRs: National Institute of Justice Reports

nik: narcotic identification kit

NILECJ: National Institute for Law Enforcement and Criminal Justice

nimbies: nembutal tablets

nimby: nembutal (q.v.)

NIN: Narcotics Intelligence Network; National Information Network

NIO: National Intellience Officer

nip.: nipper; not in possession

NIPE: National Intelligence Programs Evaluation

nippers: chain-grip-actuated handcuffs

NIS: National Institute of Science; National Intelligence Survey; Naval Intelligence Survey; Naval Intelligence Service (U.S. Navy's FBI-like organization); Naval Investigative Service

nitro: nitroglycerin (a powerful explosive)

NIWW: National Institute for Working Women (prostitutes)

nixon: adulterated, low-quality, low-potency drug, especially when sold as a pure, high-quality, high-potency drug

NJA: National Jail Association (q.v.)

NJCCC: New Jersey Casino Control Commission

NJDA: National Juvenile Detention Association (q.v.)

njemu: *Cannabis* plant grown and smoked in East Africa

NJLC: National Juvenile Law Center (University of St. Louis)

NJMA: National Jail Managers Association (q.v.)

NJMP: New Jersey Marine Police

NJRW: New Jersey Reformatory for Women (Clinton)

NJSP: New Jersey State Police

NLADA: National Legal Aid and Defender Association

NLF: National Liberation Front

NLG: National Lawyers Guild

NLJ: National Law Journal

NLW: National Lawyers Wives

nmi: no middle initial

nmn: no middle name

nobbler: person hired by gamblers to drug racing dogs or horses to improve their track performance

Noble Experiment: Pres. Herbert Hoover's description of the Constitution's 18th Amendment, concerning the prohibition of alcohol (ratified Jan. 16, 1919 and repealed by the 21st Amendment, effective Dec. 5, 1933)

NOBLEE: National Organization of Black Law Enforcement Executives

NOCC: New Orleans Crime Commission

nod: doze off, as when under the influence of alcohol or a drug

nod.: night observation device

noise: heroin

NOISE: National Organization to Insure Support Enforcement (in divorce actions)

noiseless assassin: any lethal weapon whose

action is silent, such as a dagger, stiletto, switchblade, etc.

no-knock provision: law allowing law-enforcement officers to enter a premise forcibly, without announcing their presence before entering, under certain circumstances

Nome: Nome State Jail for males and females at Nome, Alaska

nomology: the science and study of law

nonbarbiturate sedatives: central nervous system depressants such as chloral hydrate, Doriden, Equanil (meprobamate), Miltown (meprobamate), paraldehyde and Placidyl

nonchaku: chain-connected or cord-connected set of hardwood or metal rods used as a weapon for strangling or swinging; of Oriental design; outlawed in many states

non-confinement facility: see **community facility**

nondiscernible microbionoculator: concealed poison-dart gun

non-negligent manslaughter: accidentally causing another's death

nonsecrets: declassified intelligence or technical reports once secret but now public knowledge

NOPA: National Organization of Police Associations

NORC: National Opinion Research Center (University of Chicago)

Norfolk: Norfolk City Jail in Norfolk, Va.; Norfolk Prison Farm in Chesapeake, Va.

norm: guideline or rule generally recognized within a culture

NORML: National Organization for the Reform of Marijuana Laws (q.v.)

Northern Region Correction Institute: Alaskan facility at Fairbanks for felons, misdemeanants and juvenile delinquents

North West Assassination Research Committee: communist-oriented San Francisco group that insists that the assassinations of Pres. John F. Kennedy, Sen. Robert F. Kennedy and the Rev. Martin Luther King Jr. were directed by the CIA; they also send out material from the Black Panthers, who claim that the CIA was responsible for the murders and mass suicides in Jonestown, Guyana

Norwich: jails in Norwich, Conn. and smaller American places named Norwich

nose candy: cocaine

nose paint: alcohol, so nicknamed because its prolonged use breaks the arteriols of the skin and leaves the nose reddened

nose powder: any drug powdered so it may be sniffed or snorted (cocaine, hallucinogens such as MDA, and heroin are often snorted)

noser: police informer; spy

Nou: island prison of New Caledonia in the South Pacific within the harbor of Nouméa

Nouvelle Calédonie: (French—New Caledonia)—penal colony from 1864 to 1894, when its prisoners were shipped to French Guiana

Nova Scotia School for Girls: at Truro, Nova Scotia

NP: Naval Prison

np: new police (q.v.)

NPA: National Police Agency (Japan)

NPB: National Parole Board (Canada)

NPC: National Police Computer

NPCC: Nebraska Penal and Correctional Complex

NPFFA: National Police and Fire Fighters Association (q.v.)

NPI: National Paralegal Institute

NPI: National Penitentiary Institute

NPOAA: National Police Officers Association of America (q.v.)

NPP: National Prison Project (q.v.)

NPPAJ: National Probation and Parole Association Journal

NPPR: Nationalist Party of Puerto Rico

NPROA: National Police Reserve Officers Association

NPS: Narcotics Preventative Service (Hong Kong)

NPSB: National Prisoner Statistics Bulletin

NRA: National Rifle Association (q.v.)

NRC: Newport Research Company (q.v.)

NRCPC: National Rural Crime Prevention Center (q.v.)

NRG: National Resurrection Group (extreme right-wing terrorists who claimed responsibility for many bombings in Athens; member Apostolos Protopapas was Greece's most wanted man until captured by the police in March 1979)

NRO: Narcotic Rehabilitation Officer; National Reconnaissance Office (Department of Defense)

NRS: National Runaway Switchboard

NRTI: National Rehabilitation Training Institute

NSA: National Security Agency (U.S. Department of Defense); National Sheriffs Association (q.v.)

NSA/CSS: National Security Agency/Central Security Service

NSAM: National Security Agency Memorandum

NSBISS: NATO Security Bureau/Industrial Security Section

NSC: National Security Council

NSCID: National Security Intelligence Directive (these are called *en-skids*)

NSDF: National Sex and Drug Forum

NSLF: National Socialist Liberation Front (Nazi student organization in the United States)

NSP: Nebraska State Patrol

NSPCA: National Society for the Prevention of Cruelty to Animals

NSPCC: National Society for the Prevention of Cruelty to Children

NSPI: National Society of Penal Information

NSRP: National States Rights Party (q.v.)

NSWP: New South Wales Police

NSWPP: National Socialist White People's Party (q.v.)

NSY: New Scotland Yard

NTA: Narcotics Treatment Administration (Washington, D.C.)

NTF: Narcotics Task Force

NTFP: National Task Force on Prostitution (q.v.)

NTS: Narodnyi Trudovoy Soyuz (Russian—National Labor Union) anti-communist Russian exile group

Nuclear Emergency Search Team: U.S. government agency organized to combat nuclear terrorism

NUL: National Urban League

number: marijuana cigarette

number-one diet: bread and water

numbers pool: numbers racket (q.v.)

numbers racket: illegal lottery whose winner is determined according to some arbitrary number, such as the number of shares traded on the stock market on a given day

No. 2 sale: second conviction for selling narcotics

nunchaku: alternate spelling of nonchaku (q.v.)

Nuremberg: forced-labor subcamp in the south of Germany close to the site of the Nuremberg Trials of war criminals

Nuremberg Laws: anti-Semitic legislation passed by the German *Reichstag* on Sept. 15, 1935, about a year after the appointment of Hitler as chief of state and commander-in-chief of Germany's armed forces; by July 16, 1937, the Buchenwald concentration camp had been opened

Nuremberg Tribunal: war crimes trials of Hitler's top aides held at Nuremberg, Bavaria at the end of World War II; the defendants were charged with crimes against humanity and sentenced to death by hanging, to life imprisonment or to long prison terms

nut: bribe given a public official

NUTAT: Nordisk Union for Alkoholfri Trafic (Nordic Union for Alcohol-free Traffic)

nut factory: mental hospital; psychiatric ward; section of a prison where criminally insane convicts are held

nuthouse: insane asylum; psychiatric ward

nutmeg: aromatic East Indian seed of the *Myristica fragans* tree; sometimes it is used as a drug because its myristicin content can produce hallucinations

nutpicker: psychiatrist

NVC: National Violence Commission

NVRC: National Victims Resource Center

nvd: night-viewing device(s)

n-v device: night-viewing device

NWARC: North West Assassination Research Committee (q.v.)

NWCTU: National Women's Christian Temperance Union

NWLEE: Northwest Law Enforcement Equipment

NWRO: National Welfare Rights Organization

NYCCCC: New York City's Citizens Crime Commission

NYCCIW: New York City Correctional Institute for Women

NYCDC: New York City Department of Correction

NYCPM: New York City Police Museum (q.v.)

NYHD: New York House of Detention

Nykøbing: Danish prison near the Jutland port of the same name, close to the Limfjorden in northwest Denmark

NYMCC: New York Metropolitan Correctional Center

nympho: nymphomaniac; male form is satyr

NYPD: New York City Police Department

NYRM: New York Reformatory for Men

NYRW: New York Reformatory for Women (Westfield Farm)

NYSCC: New York State Department of Correctional Services

NYSDCS: New York State Department of Correctional Services

NYSNACC: New York State Narcotic Addiction Control Commission

NYSNC: New York State Narcotics Commission

NYSP: New York State Police

NYU: New York underworld (abbreviation used in law-enforcement circles, although it also stands for New York University)

NZPS: New Zealand Police Service

O

O: opium

OACA: Ontario Arms Collectors Association (in Beamsville, near Toronto)

OADAP: Office of Alcoholism and Drug Abuse Prevention

OAG: Office of the Attorney General

Oakalla: prison in Burnaby, a suburb of Vancouver, British Columbia

Oakdale: Iowa's Security Medical Facility at Oakdale

OAR: Offender Aid and Restoration (q.v.)

OAS: Organisation Armée Secrete (French—Secret Army Organization) Algerian-based French-colonial forces that fought for many years to retain Algeria for France

OAS: Organization of American States (offshoot of the Pan-American Union); not to be confused with the French *OAS* (q.v.)

Oaxaca: prison in Oaxaca, capital of the Mexican state of the same name, in the Sierra Madred del Sur mountains

obc: old brutal con (older convict who uses his experience and physical prowess to intimidate younger less experienced prison inmates)

obit: obituary

Oblatos: jail in Guadalajara, Jalisco, Mexico, where many American and Mexican drug smugglers are held

Obregon: 45-caliber Mexican pistol, named for soldier-politician-president Alvaro Obregon

obscene: abhorrent to morality; depraved or disgusting; inciting to depravity or lust; repulsive; tending to corrupt public morals—*all these definitions tend to vary from place to place and from time to time; many manisfestations of the obscene could more properly be called in bad taste, repulsive or ugly*

obscenity: pictures, speech, or writing disgusting to the senses and designed to incite depravity or lust

OBSP: Old Bailey Sessions Papers

obstitute: part-time prostitute

OBTS: Offender-Based Transaction Statistics

o/c: organized crime; overcharge

OCA: Office of Consumer Affairs

Ocala: Alyce D. McPherson School for Girls from 11 to 17; at Ocala, Fla.

OCC: Oklahoma Crime Commission; Organized Crime Control (New York City Police Department)

occasional criminal: person committing a crime only under immediate pressure of desire, emotion or need

OCCC: Organized Crime Control Commission (q.v.)

OCD: Office of Collection and Dissemination (CIA)

OCF: Ossining Correctional Facility (Sing Sing)

OC-5: Organizing Committee for a Fifth Estate (q.v.)

ochlocracy: mob rule

OCI: Office of Current Intelligence (CIA)

OCIB: Organized Crime Intelligence Bureau (of the State of California); Organized Crime Intelligence Bureau (New Jersey State Police)

OCID: Organized Crime Intelligence Division (Los Angeles Police Department)

OCIS: Organized Crime Information System (FBI)

OCP: Office of Consumer Protection

OCPCJR: Office of Crime Prevention and Criminal Justice Research

OCRSF: Organized Crime and Racketeering Strike Force (U.S. Department of Justice)

OCS: Organe de Controle des Stupefiants (French—Narcotic Drug Control Supervision)

October League: Marxist-Leninist revolutionary organization in the U.S.A.

od: overdose

ODALE: Office of Drug Abuse Law Enforcement

ODESSA: Organisation Der Ehemaligen SS Angehoerigen (German—Organization of Former Members of the SS) organization for simulating suicides and arranging new names, occupations and places of residence for war criminals who served Hitler; some 59 members are alive and well in the United States, according to Howard Blum's book *WANTED! The Search for Nazis in America*

112

ODI: Office of Defense Investigation (U.S. Department of Defense)

Odom: Jackson, North Carolina penal facility for felons in close security

ODOTS: One-Day One-Trial System (for jurors)

ODS: Office of Defender Services

Off: Officer

offender: person convicted of a criminal offense

Offender Aid and Restoration: conducts CIP (Citizens Involvement Project) to educate and train civic leaders and sheriffs in the use of volunteers in jails

offense: act committed or omitted in violation of the law

Office of Juvenile Justice: Chicago-based organization that conducts the National Youth Gang Survey

Office of Professional Responsibility: FBI office charged with investigating the bureau's alleged transgressions

Office of Strategic Services: American espionage, sabotage and subversion organization active during World War II, when it helped organize underground resistance groups in many enemy-occupied countries

off limits: area that is restricted

off the habit: no longer using drugs, alcohol, tobacco or any other addictive substance

off the pigs: kill the cops; kill the police

off the wagon: (off the water wagon) drinking alcoholic beverages again after stopping temporarily; *he's off the wagon again*

Ogden: Utah State Industrial School at Ogden

OH: Omega House (q.v.)

Ohio State: Ohio State Penitentiary in Columbus on the Scioto River; also called *River House*

Ohrdruf: Thuringian town just south of Gotha in central Germany, site of a notorious concentration camp as well as the underground headquarters of the German army during World War II

OICJ: Office of International Criminal Justice

oil: bribe

oiled: intoxicated

oilhead: alcoholic

oil of palm: bribe(s)

OIPC: Organisation Internationale de Police Criminelle (French—International Criminal Police Organization) also known as Interpol

OiT: Officer in Training; rookie policeman or policewoman

OJARS: Office of Justice Assistance, Research, and Statistics

OJDYD: Office of Juvenile Delinquency and Youth Development (U.S. Department of Health, Education, and Welfare—Social and Rehabilitation Service)

OJJ: Office of Juvenile Justice (q.v.)

ojt: on-the-job training

OL: October League (q.v.)

OLAS: Organization of Latin American Solidarity (q.v.)

Old Bailey: most famous of London's criminal courts, with jurisdiction over the trials for all treason, murders, felonies and misdemeanors committed within the City of London, adjacent and nearby counties, as well as offenses committed on the high seas

old hand: Australian euphemism for a former convict

Old Horse: Bridewell Prison's nickname

old lag: person serving a three-year sentence in a British prison

Old Newgate Prison: penological museum on Newgate Road in East Granby, Conn.; open from June through October

Old Queens: older section of the Riker's Island Penitentiary in New York City's East River, just north of La Guardia Airport in the borough of Queens

old smokey: electric chair

Old Sparkey: Florida's natural-oak electric chair, used to execute criminals sentences to capital punishment

Old Territorial: Old Territorial Penitentiary in Santa Fe, N.M.; it was built when New Mexico was still a territory; the city fathers chose to build this penitentiary rather than to fund a state-supported university

OLEP: Office of Law Enforcement and Planning

Omega House: Okinawa-based organization for revolutionary subversion within the U.S. Navy

Omega 7: terrorist arm of the Cuban Nationalist Movement in the United States, where it has taken credit for a number of assassinations and bombings

OMS: Otdel Mezdunarodnykh Svyazey (Russian—International Relations Section) network of Comintern and Cominform agents overseas

Omsk: czarist prison close to the borders of Kazakhstan on the Irtysh River; the terrible punishments inflicted on prisoners here are described in Dostoevski's *Notes from the House of the Dead*

ONE: Office of National Estimates (CIA)

one-armed bandit: coin-operated, hand-actuated slot machine popular in gambling casinos, where their owners can set them to retain a specific percentage of profit; modern models are made to receive dollar bills and are electronically powered

one percent: (motorcycle-gang slang) the top one percent of the gang

One Police Plaza: see **Police Plaza**

one-spot: $1 bill

ONI: Office of Naval Intelligence (U.S. Navy)

on ice: imprisoned

ONMSS: Office of Nuclear Material Safety and Safeguards (Nuclear Regulatory Commission)

Ontario: Youth Training School at Ontario, Calif., east of Los Angeles

on the bricks: out of jail; on the streets

on the erie: eavesdropping

on the ground: out of jail

on the lam: escaping from, evading or hiding from the police or other law-enforcement agents

on the make: seeking sexual contact(s); pursuing some goal aggressively

on the needle: addict who injects his or her narcotics with a hypodermic needle

on the nod: doped or sleepy as a result of the influence of narcotics

on the prowl: seeking clients, drugs or loot that can readily be converted into money; most drug addicts and most prostitutes are usually on the prowl

on the qt: on the quiet; secretly

on the run: moving from city to city or place to place to avoid arrest or detection

on the shake: criminally involved

on the shelf: in solitary confinement

on the street: in search of drugs; seeking sexual companionship; out of jail; (of a truant) away from home or school

on the take: accepting bribes, favors, gifts and/or money; accepting graft

on the up and up: decent; honest; legal

on the wagon: (on the water wagon) refraining from drinking alcoholic beverages; *she's on the wagon—thank goodness*

Ont Pen: Ontario Penitentiary

ooloo: Eskimo skinning knife

ooze out: sneak away

op: opium

OPC: Office of Policy Coordination (CIA)

ope: opium

open city: nickname of any place that is free from territorial monopoly by any one gang or underworld group

open fire: begin attacking; begin shooting

open prison: penal facility built without bars on the windows, locks on the doors or walls surrounding the prison

operate: sell narcotics; sell one's body

Operation Artichoke: a former CIA program for experimenting with drugs and exotic poisons used to control behavior and mental patterns

Operation Condor: plan to cut down the production of drugs such as cocaine, heroin, opium and marijuana in Mexico using federal forces, including the air force and army

Operation Drugs: New York City Police Department's drive against pushers of drugs

Operation Identification: crime-deterrent system in which homeowners mark all items of value so that if they are stolen they may more readily be recovered by the police

Operation Q: gun control enforcement in several major American cities (statistics there reveal a subsequent drop in the number of crimes committed with handguns)

Operation Sinsemilla: federal, state and local law-enforcement crackdown on pot growers whose high quality marijuana may sell for $175 or more per ounce (*sinsemilla*)

operations officer: intelligence officer charged with management tasks

OPI: Office of Protective Intelligence (U.S. Secret Service)

opiate: drug derived from the juice of the opium poppy's unripe seed pods; such drugs include codeine, heroin and morphine

opioid: synthetic opiate

opium: narcotic extracted from the seeds of the oriental poppy (*Papaver somniferum*), which is also the source of codeine, heroin and morphine; highly-addictive drug used to relieve pain, quiet coughs and treat intestinal disorders

opium of the poor: *Cannabis* (source of hashish and marijuana)

opium-poppy sensor: multispectral device for spotting opium-poppy fields by aerial reconnaissance

OPP: Ontario Provincial Police

OPR: Office of Professional Responsibility (q.v.)

Optimum Record Automation for Courts and Law Enforcement: criminal data file kept by Los Angeles, Calif.

or. (OR): (released from bail or jail on her or his) own recognizance (and promising to return to court when summoned)

ORACLE: Optimum Record Automation for Courts and Law Enforcement

orange: orange-colored heart-shaped dexedrine tablet

orange wedge: LSD

Oranienburg: concentration camp near Berlin erected in 1933, just a few months after the opening of Dachau

orderly revolution: predominantly non-violent takeover of a government, as achieved by Gandhi and his followers in India

Ordinary of Newgate: Chaplain of Newgate Prison

ordinary transportation: on-foot transportation of prisoners

Ordot: Guam's penitentiary at Ordot, southeast of Agana

Oregon: the Wisconsin School for Girls at Oregon

Organization of Latin American Solidarity: Castro-controlled group

organized crime: underworld society operating outside the control of any government; supplies illegal goods and services such as gambling, loansharking, narcotics, pornography and prostitution; coordinated and structured on an international as well as national scale to ensure maximum financial gain; investigators estimate organized crime rakes in twice as much money as all other types of criminal activity combined; organized crime generally involves the Mafia and Mafia-like syndicates

Organize Crime Control Commission: California organization that conducts hearings and compiles information concerning the magnitude and scope of organized crime in the state

Organizing Committee for a Fifth Estate: communist-controlled organization involved with the assassination of Athens-based CIA chief of station Richard Welch; has offices in downtown Washington, D.C.

Oriente: Oriente federal holding institution for prisoners in Mexico City

Orient Express: the route of narcotic products extending from the opium-rich Golden Triangle at the intersection of Burma, Laos and Thailand to Amsterdam, one of Europe's foremost dope distribution centers; an express train linking Paris and Vienna to Istanbul

ORPA: Office of Regional and Political Affairs (CIA)

o-r release: own-recognizance release (legal device freeing responsible citizens from going to jail or posting bail bond until their cases come to court for hearing)

ORW: Ohio Reformatory for Women

OSAP: Office of Substance Abuse Prevention within ADAMHA (Alcohol, Drug Abuse, and Mental Health Administration)

OSI: Office of Special Investigation (U.S. Air Force)

OSPAAL: Organization of Solidarity with the Peoples of Africa, Asia, and Latin America (communist led and supported organization)

OSR: Office of Strategic Research (CIA)

OSS: Office of Strategic Services (q.v.)

ossified: intoxicated

Ossining: Ossining Correctional Facility, formerly known as Sing Sing, at Ossining, N. Y.

Oświęcim: Polish name for Auschwitz, site of one of World War II's worst concentration camps operated by the Nazis

Otay Mesa: site of a new California prison south of San Diego, on the Mexican border, close to Tijuana and its airport

OTB: offtrack betting

other prisoners: prison guards

other side of the tracks: ghetto; poor section; slum

Otisville: new federal prison some 50 miles northwest of New York City, near Middletown, southwest of Newburgh

otMs: other than Mexicans (in detention centers, jails, etc.)—statistical abbreviation

oubliette: secret dungeon into which inmates are lowered via a trapdoor in its roof

ounce man: small dealer in narcotics who buys his drugs by the ounce

outcall massage parlor: business often employing prostitutes and using business cards in hotels and motels as well as advertising to solicit customers

outfit: drug-injecting equipment

Outlaws: militant motorcycle gang, rivals to Hell's Angels (see also **Hell's Angels and Mongols**)

out of action: not dealing in drugs; not practicing prostitution

out of bounds: restricted area

out of one's mind: under the influence of drugs

out of the woods: in the clear; out of danger

out of town: in prison

outside: outside of prison

overamp: take an overdose of any drug

overamped: overdosed with amphetamines

over-and-under gun: double-barrelled gun whose barrels are stacked one above the other; some over-and-under guns combine rifle and shotgun barrels

overcharge: charge a defendant with a separate offense for every violation connected with the original offense, so as to gain an advantage during any subsequent plea bargaining

overdose: to take, or to have taken, too much of a drug; overdoses often result in death

overjolt: overdose

overkill: capability of destroying an enemy with more force than is needed

overrecommend: recommend a more severe sentence than would normally be imposed for a given offense so as to gain an advantage during any subsequent plea bargaining

over the blue wall: confined to a hospital for the criminally insane

over the hump: completely withdrawn from alcohol or any other addictive drugs

Owsley's acid: LSD

Oxford: Federal Correctional Institution at Oxford, Wis.; jails in some 20 other American places named Oxford

oz: ounce of any drug, especially marijuana

P

P: penny; peyote
P: police; policeman; policewoman
p: pimp; penny
PA: Pardon Attorney (U.S. Department of Justice); Prosecuting Attorney; Parents Anonymous (q.v.)
PAA: Prisoners Aid Association
PAAM: Prisoners Aid Association of Maryland (in Baltimore)
pAc: pure Argentinian cocaine
Pachuca: prison in Pachuca, capital of the Mexican state of Hidalgo, near Mexico City
pack rat: petty thief
packy: sneak thief who specializes in interrupting the flow of merchandise that is being unloaded from a truck and stealing some part of the cargo without being caught in the act
pad: apartment; home; sleeping room
paddy wagon: police van for transporting prisoners or suspects
PADPAO: Philippine Agency Detective Protective Association Organization (security guard service)
pad room: place where drugs are taken or opium is smoked
PAIGC: Partido Africano da Independencia da Guine e Cabo Verde (Portuguese—African Party of Independence of Guinea and the Cape Verde Islands) communist-led and supported group
paint remover: strong alcoholic drink of any kind
PAIRS: Private Aircraft Inspection Reporting System (q.v.)
Paki bashing: attacks on Indians or Pakistanis, especially by British or Canadian racists
Paki busting: see **Paki bashing**
Pakistani black: high-grade *Cannabis* resin that is sometimes smuggled from Pakistan into Canada, the United Kingdom and the United States concealed in chunks of carved onyx
PAL: Police Athletic League
p-a-l: prisoner-at-large
palace revolution: non-violent takeover of a government, especially from within

Palais de Justice: (French—Palace of Justice)—Parisian court and prison
Palestinian Armed Struggle Command: underground group controlled by El Fatah
Palestinian Liberation Army: paramilitary terrorists who have claimed responsibility for many assassinations, bombings and other acts of terror
palimony: alimony payable to former live-in lovers
palm oil: bribe(s)
palm sap: shot-loaded blackjack or billy designed to fit in the palm of one's hand
pamphlet bomb: explosive device designed to scatter leaflets or pamphlets over crowds of people
PAN: Parents Against Narcotics
Panama gold: Panama red (q.v.)
Panama red: high-grade marijuana grown in Panama
panatella: oversize marijuana cigarette
pancake: easy-to-conceal handgun holster
P & C: Pickpocket and Confidence Squad (of a police department)
pander: a person furnishing clients for prostitutes; a person supplying boys or men or girls or women for sexual services; to pimp; to procure
p & q: peace and quiet (solitary confinement)
panhandler: beggar
Pan-Hellenic Socialist Commune: militant underground organization active in Greece and the Greek Isles, where they traffic in weapons
panic: heroin shortage at the street level, where it produces panic among addicts
panic man: addict deprived of or unable to get drugs
panic woman: female counterpart of a panic man (q.v.)
Pankrác: Prague's great prison
panopticon: prison where all cells are visible from a central point
pantopan: narcotic substitute for morphine
PAODAP: President's Action Office for Drug Abuse Prevention
papa bear: policeman

Papenburg: Nazi concentration camp west of Bremen, Germany

paper: blank checks, especially blank payroll checks; narcotics packed within a fold of paper

paperhanging: forging checks; passing bad checks

paper pusher: person passing counterfeit money

paper trip: obtaining false identification papers and using them to evade the law

paper war: device used by attorneys to avoid or delay a trial by attempting to drown the other side in counter-suits, motions, etc.

paralyzed: intoxicated

Paralyzer: CN tear-gas weapon often supplied in a 4 1/2-inch (115-millimeter) aerosol container fitted with a spring clip just like a pen; when released the gas produces burning and tearing of the eyes and difficulty in breathing and makes the victim's skin feel as if it has been doused with hot acid; many women buy this as a defense weapon and keep it handy in case of attempted muggings or rapes

parang: straight-edged knife popular in Malay countries such as Indonesia, Malaysia, the southern Philippines and Singapore

paraphernalia: papers, pipes, tiny scales, and tiny spoons used by narcotics addicts

paraquat: crop-destroying chemical sprayed from airplanes in Mexico in order to kill marijuana crops

parboiled: intoxicated

Parchman: Mississippi State Penitentiary at Parchman

pardon: exemption from punishment for a crime or for a pending criminal conviction granted by a state or national executive

paregoric: medicinal preparation containing a small amount of opium extract; often used to treat diarrhea by deadening the abdominal pain it causes; sometimes abused by drug addicts

parenticide: killing one's parents; parent-killer

Parents Anonymous: organization set up to combat child abuse by parents, as well as juvenile alcoholism, delinquency, drug addiction, etc.

Parkhurst: top-security prison near Newport on the Isle of Wight off England's south coast below Southampton

Park Row: Metropolitan Correctional Center in downtown New York City at 150 Park Row

Parkside: New York State Correctional Facility in Manhattan

parole: conditional release of an offender from a confinement facility before the expiration of his or her sentence; the released offender is usually placed under the supervision of a parole agency or officer

parole agency: correctional agency supervising adults or juveniles placed on parole

parole authority: correctional agency or officer having authority to release adults or juveniles committed to confinement facilities on parole, to discharge them from parole or to revoke parole

parolee: person conditionally released from a correctional institution before the expiration of his or her sentence and placed under the supervision of a parole agency or officer

parole violation: a parolee's failure to conform to the conditions of his or her parole; such a violation usually results in a return to prison and loss of parole

parricide: father killer; killing one's father

parrot's perch: suspended horizontal pole to which a prisoner's ankles and wrist are strapped while his body dangles beneath; torture device used in many African, Asian, Latin American and Levantine prisons

partisan: underground saboteur or irregular soldier fighting invaders or occupiers in any way possible

Part I Crimes: aggravated assault, burglary, criminal homicide, rape, larceny, theft, motor vehicle theft, robbery (see also **Part II Crimes**)

Part II Crimes: lesser crimes, as defined by the FBI Uniform Crime Reports (see also **Part I Crime**)

party: to take drugs with other addicts

PAs: Parents Anonymous (q.v.)

PASC: Palestinian Armed Struggle Command (q.v.)

PASOK: Pan-Hellenic Socialist Commune

pass: to let an addict or a criminal go free instead of making an arrest

Passage to Marseille: melodramatic 1944 motion-picture commentary on the old French penal colony in French Guiana; features Humphrey Bogart, Peter Lorre, Sydney Greenstreet, and others

passive infrared intrusion detector: device used by law-enforcement officers to observe movements of burglars, smugglers and other law evaders

pass the queer: pass counterfeit money or securities

pass-through point: contraband distribution point; drug distribution point

PATRIC: Pattern Recognition and Information Correlation (q.v.)

patricide: murder of one's father or parent; daughter or son who takes the life of a parent

Pattern Recognition and Information Correlation: police computer used in Los Angeles to track the mo—modus operandi—of criminals and to identify suspects on that basis

Patton: California State Hospital (for the criminally insane) at Patton, near San Bernardino

Patuxent: Patuxent Institution for the Crimanally Insane (Patuxent, Md.); Patuxent Institution for the Defective Delinquents

PAU: Police Airborne Unit

Paul Revere Associated Yeomen: heavily-armed paramilitary group of right wing terrorists

pavement pounder: streetwalker

pavement princess: prostitute; streetwalker

payoff: division of loot or money obtained illegally; petty graft extracted from business people by corrupt officials as well as racketeers

payola: bribe(ry)

PB: patrol boat; police boat

pb: petrol bomb (Irish-style Molotov cocktail); poor bastard (dim-witted or easily-fooled person)

PBA: Patrolmen's Benevolent Association

p B c: pure Bolivian cocaine

PC: Police Constable; Police College; penal code

PCA: Police Complaints Authority

PCC: *Partido Comunista de Cuba* (Spanish—Communist Party of Cuba)

PCC: Pennsylvania Crime Commission; Poison Control Center

p C c: pure Colombian cocaine

PCCNY: *Penal Code of the City of New York*

p Ch c: pure Chilean cocaine

PCI: *Partito Comunista Italiano* (Italian Communist Party)

PCI: Program of Correctional Institutions (Puerto Rico)

pci: potential criminal informant

PCL: Police Crime Laboratory

PCOB: Permanent Central Opium Board (United Nations)

PCOP: President's Commission on Obscenity and Pornography

pcp: pimp-controlled prostitution

PCP: *Partido Comunista Portuguesa* (Portugese Communist Party)

pcp (PCP): phencyclidine, a dangerous drug also known as angel dust, busy bee, crystal, elephant tranquilizer and superjoint; hundreds of accidental deaths as well as murders and suicides have been linked to the use of this drug

PCR: *Partido Comunista Revolucionario* (Spanish—Revolutionary Communist Party) of Chile

PCU: Protective Custody Unit

PD: Police Department; public defender (q.v.)

PDA: *Polizeiliches Durchgangslager Amersfoort* (German—Police Concentration Camp—Amersfoort, Netherlands)—staging area for the transport of Dutch prisoners to Nazi concentration camps and extermination centers

pda: personal death awareness (often manifested by potential victims and transmitted to assassins, muggers and other aggressors)

P del E: *Penitenciaria del Estado* (Spanish—State Penitentiary)

PDFA: Partnership for a Drug-free America

PDID: Public Disorder Intelligence Division (Los Angeles Police Department)

PDP: Petty Delinquency Detention (juvenile crime-correction program)

PDR: *Physicians' Desk Reference*—some addicts call this illustrated reference work *the book*

PDSOC: Police Department Superior Officers' Council

PDTS: Police Detective Training School

pe: private eye (private investigator)

PEA: Policewomen's Endowment Association

peace: LSD

peace and quiet: maximum-security cell

Peacemaker: original model of a semi-automatic Colt revolver whose large and unjacketed soft-nosed lead bullets were famous for smashing the bones and tearing the tissue of any person or animal in their way

peace pill: pcp (phencyclidine)

peace tablet: LSD

peaches: benzedrine tablets

peanuts: barbiturates

peashooter: handgun of less than magnum caliber and hence less lethal

p E c: pure Ecuadoran cocaine

peccadillo: slight offense

pecul: peculate(d); peculating; peculation; peculator (an embezzler)

peculiar service: espionage

peddler: pusher of drugs

pedigree: criminal record

pedophile: adult who molests children sexually

Peeler: a Bobby, a member of London's first corps of metropolitan police, who were nicknamed after British Home Secretary Sir Robert Peel, who founded the organization in 1829

peep: undercover photographer; clandestine photograph taken by an espionage or other undercover agent

pee-wee wino: 6-to-9 year-old child addicted to wine, and often begging or stealing the money needed to support the habit

pellet: capsule of LSD

pen: penitentiary

penal isolation: solitary confinement

penal servitude: imprisonment combined with hard labor

penalty: punishment for a particular offense

Pence Springs: West Virginia State Prison for Women at Pence Springs

Penetang: Penetanguishene Provincial Establishment for the Criminally Insane on Georgian Bay, Lake Huron, 80 miles north-northwest of Toronto, Ontario

pen gun: pen-shaped 22- or 38-caliber handgun, as easy to conceal as a pocket pen

peniatrist(s): prison doctor(s); prison psychiatrist(s)

peniatry: branch of medical science dealing with penal establishments and their prisoners

penitentiary: house of correction or rehabilitation center where offenders are confined for detention, discipline, reformation, rehabilitation, or punishment, if they are forced to labor; in the United States a penitentiary is a maximum-security penal facility designed to hold prisoners serving long sentences

Pennsylvania System: see **solitary system**

pennyweighting: substituting fake gems or jewelry for the genuine article

penol: penological; penologist; penology

penologist: social scientist concerned with penal institutions and the deterrent effect of punishments decreed by law

penology: scientific study of penal institutions, the deterrent effect of punishments decreed by law, the consequences of crime and the means of changing lawbreakers into law-abiding citizens and repairing the damage done to victims of crime

pensioner of the Crown: Australian euphemism for a former convict

Pent: The Pent (nickname for Pentonville Prison completed in 1842 in the outskirts of London's Islington Parish)

Pentridge: Melbourne, Victoria's prison well known to many Australians concerned with crime

pen trap: ballpoint pen converted into a lethal weapon; when its plunger is depressed, it detonates a charge of explosive tetryl and kills the user

People's Coalition for Peace and Justice: communist-directed organization once known as the Committee for Action/Research on the Intelligence Community or CARIC

people's crime: shoplifting

People's Temple: see **Jonestown**

pep.: personal effects protection

PEP: Parent Effectiveness Program (aimed at guiding youngsters before they become juvenile delinquents); Preventive Enforcement Patrol (New York City Police Department)

pep pill: stimulant drug in pill form

percodan: oxycodone hydrochloride, a drug derived from morphine and long popular with heroin addicts

PERF: Police Executive Resource Forum

perjury: the crimee of affirming or swearing falsely; giving false or misleading testimony when under oath

perks: nickname for percodan (q.v.)

Perm: Soviet labor camp region 700 miles (1127 kilometers) east of Moscow and not far from the Urals

perpetrator: police euphemism for criminal or suspect

personal protection dog: dog trained to attack on command

personal violation: rape

persuader: short hand weapon sometimes augmented by a tear-gas cartridge

Peruvian perfume: cocaine

perv: perversion; pervert; perverted

peteman: safecracker

peter blower: safecracker

Peterhead: prison near Aberdeen, Scotland

Petersburg: Federal Reformatory at Petersburg, Va.

pethidine: synthetic narcotic also known as meperidine

petrified: intoxicated

Petros: Tennessee penitentiary northwest of Knoxville in a valley of the Cumberlands, close to the village of Petros

petty larceny: synonym for petty theft

petty theft: theft of property having a value less than a specific figure decreed by law

petty treason: old English term for husband-killing

Pewee Valley: Kentucky Correctional Institution for Women at Pewee Valley

peyote: cactus plant (*Lophophora Williamsii*) native to northern Mexico and the American Southwest, where many Indians use it for its narcotic effect in the performance of their religious ceremonies; peyote is the source of the intoxicant mescal as well as mescalin powder

PF: Police Foundation

PFA: Policia Federal Argentina (Spanish—Argentine Federal Police)

PFF: Police Field Force

PFF Inc: Police-FBI Fencing Incognito (Washington, D.C. traffickers in stolen goods—dummy corporation set up to trap the traffickers)

PFI: Police Foundation Institute

PFIAB: President's Foreign Intelligence Advisory Board

PFJM: Policia Federal Judicial Mexicana (Spanish—Mexican Federal Judicial Police) long arm of the law south of the border, often involved in bribery and extortion scandals

PFLP: Popular Front for the Liberation of Palestine (q.v.)

PFLP—GC: Popular Front for the Liberation of Palestine—General Command

PFOC: Prairie Fire Organizing Committee (q.v.)

pg: paregoric; pure gin

phantastica: hallucinogenic drugs and substances

pharmaceutical experimenting: taking addictive drugs experimentally

phd: panty-hose distributor (pornographer)

P-head: pinhead; small-minded person; user of phenobarbital

phencyclidine: PCP (q.v.)

pheno: phenobarbital; phenobarbital user

Phoenix: Arizona Girls School at Phoenix; this correctional facility is for juvenile delinquents from 8 to 21 years of age

Phoenix House: drug rehabilitation program in New York City

phone freak: white-collar criminal guilty of bypassing a telephone toll-collecting device or system; sometimes written *phone phreak*

phonoscopy: study of voice prints; voice-print analysis and identification

phony: person making obscene telephone calls; person pretending to be something he or she is not; false or misleading

phony money: counterfeit money

photint: photographic intelligence

photo money: counterfeit money

photint: photographic intelligence

photo surveillance: surveillance of the movements of possible suspects provided by photographic devices such as cameras, which sometimes provides pictures useful in apprehending offenders

PHP: Preventive Health Programs

PHS: Prison Health Services (providing a complete system of health services to prisons)

physiological dependence: addiction

pi: (pronounced *pee-eye*) a pimp

pi (PI): private investigator

PIA: Prison Industry Authority

PIB: Prison Industry Board

PICA: Police Insignia Collector's Association (q.v.)

picking oakum: picking apart pieces of tarred rope for use in caulking wooden ships (a century ago this was still the task given many prisoners confined to jails along the coast of Britain as well as the United States)

pickled: intoxicated

pickler: an alcoholic

Pickle Works: nickname of the building occupied by the CIA in Langley, Va.

pickpocket: sneak thief skilled in removing the contents of other people's handbags, pockets and purses

pickup: arrest for a minor crime

pickup point: delivery point for a shipment of contraband such as drugs, illegal entrants, etc.

PICL: President's Intelligence Checklist

picture gallery: file of photographs of criminals

picture-taker: radar-equipped police car

PID: Police Intelligence Detail

piece: ounce of heroin; pistol or other gun; piece of meat (sexually attractive female); piece of missing information essential to understanding other information already at hand

piece of the business: mobster slang for a part of the profits

pie-eyed: intoxicated

pig: highway patrolman; law-enforcement officer; policeman; policewoman; prostitute

pigeon: an informer; a victim of a confidence game or other fraudulent scheme (most frequently an older or retired person on a fixed income)

pig outfit: fly-by-night portable laboratory for processing drugs such as PCP

pigsticker: bayonet or sword

piki: opium smoker

PILCOP: Public Interest Law Center of Philadelphia (q.v.)

pilferage: repeated stealing of goods on a large scale, as from a storeroom or supermarket

pillhead: addicted drug user

pillow: black polyethylene heat-sealed bag containing amphetamines or barbiturates

pill popper: frequent user of addictive pills

pimp: man who finds customers for prostitutes

Pimp Squad: seven-man New York City Police Department squad battling prostitution in Manhattan

pin: hypodermic needle; thin cigarette filled with marijuana

PIN: Police Information Network (North Carolina)

Pinal: Pinal County Jail at Florence, Ariz.

pinch: arrest; steal

Pinchgut: prisoner's nickname for Fort Denison Prison in Sydney Harbour, New South Wales, where in the early days of settlement they complained about the very small allowance of food

pineapple: hand grenade

pine box: coffin

Pine Street: Baltimore, Md. jail on Pine Street

Piney Point: alcoholic rehabilitation institute of the Seafarer's International Union at Piney Point, Md., on the Potomac near Leonardstown

pingponging: medical fraud in which a physician unnecessarily recommends that patients see a number of specialists

pink: nickname for detective derived from the Pinkerton detective agency

Pinkerton's: world's largest security service, organized in Chicago in 1850 by Glasgow-born Allan Pinkerton to provide protection for express companies, mines and railroads as well as others preyed upon by the underground as well as the underground as well as the underworld

pink(o): leftist

pinks: barbiturates; seconal

pins. (PINS): person(s) in need of supervision (juvenile and pre-juvenile curfew violators, delinquents, incorrigibles, runaways, truants or vagrants)

pin yen: opium

pipe: a club made from a short length of pipe; an easy-to-inject vein; an opium pipe; to club with a piece of piping

pipe bomb: short length of pipe capped at both ends and drilled at one end to accept a fuse, which is used to detonate an explosive concealed within the pipe

pipeline: source of supply of drugs

pipe trap: explosive concealed in a smoking pipe and detonated when the smoker lights the pipe or attempts to clean it

pipped: intoxicated

pip off: steal

piracy: robbery attempted or committed in the air or on the high seas by force of arms and intimidation; pirates are punishable wherever they may be caught, no matter where their felonious acts were committed

pirid: passive infrared intrusion detector (q.v.)

pissed: intoxicated

pistol range: area reserved for law-enforcement officers and others to practice the use of handguns

pistol safe: steel compartment for safeguarding handguns and other weapons

pistol-whip: to hit with or threaten with a pistol

pit: main vein leading from the arm to the heart

Pithiviers: concentration and transit camp in north-central France northeast of Orleans

PIU: Public Inspection Unit (vice squad)

pixilated: intoxicated

PJ: Police Judiciare (French-criminal investigators; detective division)

PK: Principal Keeper

pk: probability of kill

PKI: Partai Kommunis Indonesia (Indonesian Communist Party)

PLA: Palestinian Liberation Army (q.v.)

plain wrapper: unmarked police car

Plankinton: South Dakota Training School at Plankinton

plant: materials arranged by an arsonist to cause or start a fire; a hiding place for drugs; the introduction of false evidence; an undercover agent; to kill

PLAP: Port of London Authority Police

plastered: intoxicated

plastic bomb: explosive device sometimes mailed to its victims, who are killed when they try to open the letter addressed to them that contains the plastic bomb

plastic connection: plastic surgery used to change someone's essential identity so that he or she may find it easier to elude the police

plastic fingerprints: fingerprints left on soft surfaces such as dirt or wax, which are readily detectable

Plaszow: Nazi concentration camp northwest of Cracow, Poland

platform pushers: criminally insane persons who push others from the platform to the tracks of a railway or subway as the train is pulling into the station

play back: feed false information; replay a tape recording to learn its meaning

play chickee: to be a lookout for customers or for the vice squad

play dirty: deal unfairly; fight unfairly or viciously

player: pimp

play vandalism: destruction of property during the course of play, as in the destruction of athletic equipment such as goal posts

plea: defendant's formal answer to charges

plea bargaining: exchange of judicial or prosecutorial concessions, such as a lesser charge, dismissal of other pending charges, a prosecutor's recommendation of a reduced sentence or a combination thereof in return for a plea of guilty by the defendant

plead the fifth: plead the fifth amendment to the Constitution, i.e., refuse to answer questions on the grounds that answers might be self-incriminating

plead the Gaming Act: (British expression) tell a creditor that a debt will not be repaid (the Gaming Act states that the government will not enforce any debt arising from gambling)

plea minor: plead guilty to a minor charge (see **chamber music**)

Pleasanton: Federal Correctional Institution at Pleasanton, Calif., an all-female facility serving felons with sentences of five years or less

Pleasantville: federal minimum-security facility at Maxwell Air Force Base in Alabama; no fences, gates or walls divide its stucco buildings from the golf course at the Air Force base; its best-known inmate was former Attorney Gen. John Mitchell of Watergate notoriety

PLI: Pacific Law Institute

plinker: handgun or rifle designed for casual shooting; plinkers are usually of low weight, minimum price and simple design; Saturday-night specials are also known as plinkers

PLO: Palestine Liberation Organization

PM: *Pistol Makarov* (Russian—Makarov pistol); *Policia Metropolitana* (Spanish—Metropolitan Police)

PMA: Police Management Association

PMAD: Public Morals Administrative Division (of the New York City Police Department)

p M c: pure Mexican cocaine

pm specialists: paramilitary specialists

PMS: Prison Management Systems (health-care plan offered in the United States); Prison Medical Services (under the Home Office in the United Kingdom)

PNCC: President's National Crime Commission

PO: parole officer; police officer; probation officer

POA: Police Officers Association; Prison Officers Association

poach: take fish or game illegally from another person's property

POAG: Peace Officers Association of Georgia

POC: Prison Officer's Club

pocho: Mexican-American or Mexican-border Mexican, usually speaking a mixture of English and Mexican Spanish

pocket: pocket uncollected wages

pocket pistol: usually a .22-caliber or a .25-caliber automatic or the .38-caliber pocket pistol first made by Henry Deringer and turned out in more recent years by other American gunsmiths, such as Great Western and Remington

pod: marijuana

poetic punishment: matching the punishment to the crime

poison: any chemical agent productive of deadly or injurious effects

Poison Act: nickname for the federal narcotics laws

Poison Gang: self-assumed name of extortionists who demanded diamonds in exchange for data about food items they had laced with cyanide in several San Diego, Calif. supermarkets in 1980; they also demanded large sums of money in Colorado Springs, Colo., where similar tactics were used

poke: to puff on a marijuana cigarette; a roll of paper money

pokey: jail

pol: political prisoner; politician

POLA: Prostitutes of Los Angeles (protective association)

Pol Col: Police College

Pol Com: Police Commissaire (Interpol); Police Commissioner

poleax: battle ax or slaughterhouse ax used in killing animals; to kill with a poleax

Pol Fed: Police Federation (London)

Pol Found: Police Foundation (Washington, D.C.)

poli: politician

police: law-enforcement agents charged with arresting criminals, detecting and preventing crime, protecting people and their property, controlling traffic, keeping records pertaining to all the foregoing, etc.

police action: military action taken against aggressors or other violators of law and order such as bandits, guerrillas, mobs, pirates, etc.

police artist: person trained in creating composite sketches of wanted criminals from random descriptions; these drawings are often essential in the identification and arrest of criminals

police brutality: excessive use of physical force by law-enforcement officers

police commissioner: appointed civilian official charged with the control, discipline and regulation of the police department

police corruption: misuse of police power in return for favors or gain

police court: court of record in charge of handling minor offenses such as breaches of the peace or traffic violations but also having the power to detain suspects and turn them over to higher courts

police department: governmental division charged with the administration of the police force and the preservation of law and order in the community it serves

police dog: usually a German shepherd dog trained to protect the people and the property within its territory; sometimes trained to lead the blind or to smell out contraband such as marijuana being smuggled across a border; also used to control mobs and track criminals

policedom: police system; the world of the police

police force: body of professionally-trained officers entrusted with the duty of maintaining public peace and order as well as detecting and preventing crime

Police Insignia Collector's Association: organization whose members collect such police memorabilia as badges, buttons, hats, shoulder patches and uniforms

police inspector: high-ranking police officer commanding other law-enforcement officers and reporting to a superior such as a police commissioner, a chief of police or a superintendent of police

police justice: magistrate of a police court

police lineup: identification parade of criminals before eyewitnesses and victims

police magistrate: judge of a police court

policemanship: action or character typical of an effective police force

police matron: policewoman charged with the care of children or women held in a police station

police offense: minor offense handled by a police court and not requiring trial by jury in a higher court

Police Plaza: One Police Plaza, a 15-story brick building in New York's lower Manhattan, near the approach to the Brooklyn Bridge; the headquarters of the New York City Police Department

police reporter: newspaper, radio or television reporter specializing in arrests, crimes, etc.

police reserve officer: uniformed volunteer who assists regular police officers

police science: fact-finding process for detecting crime; also called criminalistics

police state: nation controlled and under the surveillance of the secret police by governments that find it necessary to suppress groups and individuals critical of the ruling party and its officials

police station: local or precinct headquarters of the police, where criminal suspects are brought

police sweep: concentrated effort to clean up a crime-prone neighborhood by making mass arrests of drug pushers, muggers, pimps, porno vendors and vagrants

political: political prisoner

politico: political prisoner; politician

polluted: drunk

polyg: polygraph; polygrapher; polygraphic(al)(ly); polygraphy

polygraph: lie-detection apparatus

POME: Prisoner of Mother England (also called a Pommy when in early colonial days convicts were shipped to Australia)

Ponar: site of a Nazi concentration camp near Vilna in what is now Soviet Lithuania

ponce: (British slang) pimp

pong machine: pinball machine

poniard: slender dagger of French design

Ponte del Sospiri: (Italian—Bridge of Sighs)—heavily barred, stone-covered, two-storied bridge arching a Venetian canal, the Rio di Palazzo, and connecting the Doge's Palace with the state prisons and dungeons

PONY: Prostitutes of New York (protective association)

Ponzi scheme: confidence game named for Charles Ponzi, who in 1919 defrauded some 20,000 gullible individuals in New England, New York and nearby states with his get-rich-quick schemes; money is collected from investors and part of it is paid back to encourage them and others to give the swindlers increasing amounts for manipulation before they disappear

poogie: jail

poor man's cocaine: sobutyl nitrite, whose immediate effects are similar to those of amyl nitrite; it may bring on headaches, heart attacks, nausea and damage to the liver and lungs

poormouth: plead poverty as a defense or as an excuse for criminal conduct; speak disparagingly of another

pop: to inject drugs; to pop pills into one's mouth; to arrest

pope stopper: (KKK slang) dagger

pop-out blade: spring-loaded stiletto

popped: intoxicated

popper: amyl nitrate, taken to enhance sexual pleasure and, reportedly, to prolong orgasms

poppy: opium

Popular Front for the Liberation of Palestine: Arab-supported guerrilla organization largely financed by Iraq and Libya and sharing its manpower, money, training and weapons with terrorists around the world, in places as remote as Ireland, Japan and Latin America; cooperation is based on such ideological considerations as forming a common front against capitalism, colonialism, imperialism and Zionism; according to the Israeli military command, the PFLP is headed by Dr. George Habash; it has taken credit for many terroristic acts in all parts of the world, including the hijacking of an Air France jetliner to Uganda in June 1976

population-control equipment: euphemism for riot-control equipment such as rubber bullets and tear gas

population movement: entries and exits of adjudicated persons, or persons subject to judicial proceedings, into or from correctional facilities

PORA: Peace Officers Research Association

PORAC: Peace Officers Research Association of California

Pork Dump: Clinton Prison near Utica, N.Y.

pornography: sexually-stimulating art, books, magazines, motion pictures, photographs, etc.

pornokitsch: pornographic kitsch (sexually-oriented artistic rubbish or junk art of the type displayed in pornographic advertising, cinema, posters, publications and other media)

pornoshop: pornographic bookstore or shop vending pornographic paraphernalia

Porn Squad: Pornographic Publication Squad (of Scotland Yard or other metropolitan police force)

porridge: (English slang) jail

Portage La Prairie: Correctional Center for Women at Portage La Prairie, Manitoba

prisoner at large: naval prisoner confined to the barracks or the ship

Port Arthur: Australia's principal penal colony was in Port Arthur off Storm Bay below Hobart, where from 1834 to 1853 only one convict escaped; this nearly escape-proof prison was in Tasmania, then known as Van Diemen's Land; today a museum and visitor's center replace the convicts' quarters

Port Blair: capital of the Andaman and Nicobar Islands in the Bay of Bengal; once the headquarters of a penal settlement dating from the Sepoy Rebellion of 1857 but discontinued in 1945; in *The Sign of Four* by Conan Doyle it is mentioned several times

Porte d'Enfer: (French—Gate of Hell)—convict's nickname for the prison gate at Saint Laurent du Maroni in French Guiana where one of the world's most horrible penal colonies was headquartered

Port Isabel: Border Patrol Academy of the U.S. Department of Justice at Port Isabel, Texas, where agents are taught the use of firearms, self-defense and Spanish, including Mexicanisms and criminal slang; Port Isabel Detention Center of the Immigration and Naturalization Service in Port Isabel, Texas close to Brownsville across the Rio Grande from Mexico

Port Laoise: prison southwest of Dublin, Ireland

Port Macquarie: Australian convict colony in New South Wales it bore this name in the early 1800s

Portsmouth: New Hampshire port, long the site of the U.S. Naval Prison

posse: group of able-bodied men deputized by a county sheriff to assist him in pursuing a criminal or a band of criminals or in quelling a riot

Post Care Program: for adult felons 16 years and up

post mortem: (Latin—after death) medical examination of a corpse to determine the cause of death

Poston: former Indian reservation in southwestern Arizona; after Pearl Harbor it was used as a detention camp for Japanese-Americans

pot: marijuana; term believed derived from a Mexican Indian word, *potaguaya*, equivalent to marijuana

Pot Air Line: nickname for the Mafia-financed fleet of airplanes engaged in smuggling choice Colombia marijuana into the United States

potato masher: hand grenade

potato water: alcoholic drink made by convicts from fermented potato peelings

pothead: frequent user of hashish or marijuana

pot likker: regular tea leaves boiled with marijuana leaves; also called *cannabis tea*

Potma: reputed to be the Soviet Union's largest forced-labor penal colony, in the Ural Mountains 500 miles (800 kilometers) southeast of Moscow

potter's field: pauper's burial ground (sometimes called Aceldama, the place where Judas was believed to have died)

pound: $5; $5 worth of heroin

pow (POW): prisoner of war

pox: police (journalist's abbreviation)

Pozsony: Czech name for Bratislava, site of an old prison built during the days of the Austro-Hungarian Empire

Pozzi: old Italian prison in Venice; generations of prisoners have complained about the dampness of its cells

pp & p's: perverts, pimps, and prostitutes

PPC: Positive Peer Culture (for the treatment of juvenile offenders); Practical Pistol Course

p P c: pure Peruvian cocaine

PPCAA: Parole and Probation Compact Administrators Association

PPCS: Personnel Protection and Communication Services (British anti-terrorist organization)

PPL: Police Protective League

PPS: Pennsylvania Prison Society (in Philadelphia)

pq: punishment quarters (isolated section of many penitentiaries and reformatories)

pr (PR): Panama red marijuana

Prairie Fire Organizing Committee: active in San Francisco, where its veteran Communist Party members recruited for and supported the Weather Underground, allegedly responsible for many bombings and acts of terrorism in the 1970s; sponsor of a 90-minute film entitled *Underground*, made in cooperation with Weather underground fugitives in 1975

PRAY: Paul Revere Associated Yeomen (q.v.)

PRC: Palestine Red Crescent (q.v.)

preserved: intoxicated

Pressburg: German name for Pozsony, also known as Bratislava, and site of an old prison in Czechoslovakia

press gang: see **crimp gang**

preventive detention: denying bail to persons who might commit more crimes or fail to appear in court for trial

Prime Minister of the Underworld: Frank Costello, New York aide of Lucky Luciano, deported for his criminal activities concerning prostitution

Prince Albert: location of the Provincial Penitentiary as well as headquarters of the Royal Canadian Mounted Police for central and northern Saskatchewan

Prince George: British Columbia penitentiary some 300 miles north of Vancouver

principal agent: master espionage agent or spy controlling and paying others engaged in espionage or undercover investigation

printmaster: fingerprint and palm-print inker

prints: fingerprints; footprints; voice prints

prior: prior conviction

prior record: information about any law enforcement, court or correctional proceedings occurring before a current investigation of or proceedings against a person or persons

prison: confinement facility with custodial authority over adults sentenced to confinement for more than a year

prison bird: recidivist; prisoner who has been in prison before

prison break: an escape from prison involving force and violence

Prison Camps: the U.S. Bureau of Prisons maintains camps at Allenwood, Pa.; Eglin Air Force Base, Fla.; Montgomery, Ala.; and Safford, Ariz.

prison coffin: plain wooden box fitted with rope handles and perforated with many large holes facilitating disintegration once the coffin is buried

prisoner: person in custody in a confinement facility or in personal custody of a criminal-justice official while being transported to or between confinement facilities (see also **population movement**)

prisoner at large: naval prisoner confined to the barracks or the ship

Prisoners' Chorus: the finale of Act I of *Fidelio*, Beethoven's only opera, is an appeal from political prisoners longing for the scent of open air as they know their prison is a tomb

prisoners of the Crown: old Australian euphemism meaning convicts

Prisoner's Union: publishes *Outlaw* bimonthly; seeks to end economic exploitation of prisoners and redress for convicts' grievances

prison fever: typhus (usually due to overcrowding)

prison house(s): prison(s)

prison hulk: prison ship

prison labor: work carried on by convicts such as producing furniture for public schools, road building and repairing, stamping out automobile license plates, etc.

prisonment: imprisonment

prison pallor: bloodless yellow pallor of many prisioners deprived of fresh air, sunshine, and vitamins

prison psychosis: psychotic reactions of criminals and others fearing actual or anticipated imprisonment

prison sentence: penalty of commitment to the jurisdiction of a confinement facility

prison simple: mentally deranged by imprisonment

prison van: black maria or paddy wagon, used to transport prisoners from court to prison or vice versa or from the place of arrest to a jail or lockup

prison within a prison: solitary confinement cells

privacy: the right of groups, individuals or institutions to determine for themselves how, to what extent and when information about themselves may be communicated to others

Private Aircraft Inspection Reporting System: system set up to monitor all general-aviation aircraft arriving in the United States from foreign countries

private dick: private detective or investigator

private eye: private detective or investigator

prl: pick-resistant lock

prld: pick-resistant locking device

pro: professioal, especially a professional prostitute

proactive police work: acting to prevent crimes from occuring (opposite of reactive police work)

prob: probation(ary); probation officer

probable cause: set of circumstances or facts sufficient to induce a reasonably intelligent or prudent person to believe an accused person committed a crime

probation: conditional suspension of imprisonment of a convicted offender, who must stay in the community under the supervision of a probation officer

probation agency: correctional agency supervising adults and juveniles placed on probation and investigating adults and juveniles to prepare predisposition and presentencing reports, which assist courts in determining sentences

probation officer: employee of a probation agency or probation department

probation sentence: court requirement that a person fulfill certain conditions of behavior and accept the supervision of a probation agency or department

probation violation: a probationer's nonconformance to the conditions of his or her probation

probie(s): probationer(s)

problem child: euphemism for a juvenile delinquent

problem drinker: alcoholic

procurer: a panderer; a pimp

procuress: a madam; a female panderer

professional associate: in the underworld this refers to one whose professional services are employed by a member of organized crime on a continuing basis in furtherance of illegal activity

professional criminal: person making a career out of crime, whether as an individual or as a member of a syndicate; black-marketeer, confidence man or woman, racketeer or white-collar criminal using his or her financial or social power to commit crimes

professional torch: member of an arson-for-profit ring operating in many big cities, where slumlords find it more profitable to set fire to their tenements than to keep them in repair

PROFILE: Utah's computerized criminal data file

prohibition: legal prevention of the manufacture, sale or transport of alcoholic beverages; was in effect in the United States from Jan. 16, 1919 to Dec. 5, 1933; widespread public contempt for liquor laws led to large-scale underworld activities concerned with the smuggling and supplying of illegal liquor and the corruption of the police and many public officials

Project Haven: the Internal Revenue Service's ongoing investigation of tax evasion by means of offshore numbered bank accounts held in places such as the Bahamas and the Cayman Islands in the West Indies

Project Sister: organization founded in Los Angeles in 1972 to help victims of rape

promenade of the prostitutes: main prostitution thoroughfare of many big cities

promenade princess: streetwalker

PROMIS: Prosecution Management Information System (q.v.)

proof: measure of the alcoholic strength of any hard liquor; liquor that is 100 proof is 50 percent alcohol by volume, one that is 90 proof is 45 percent alcohol, one that is 80 proof is 40 percent alcohol, etc.

PROOF: Parole Resource Office and Orientation Facility (Jersey City, N.J.)

prop: lie; made-up story

PROP: Preservation of the Rights of Prisoners

propaganda: dissemination of information; in many underground operations it consists of both **black propaganda** and **gray propaganda**

probaganda bomb: see **leaflet bomb, pamphlet bomb**

probaganda by deed: 19th-century terrorist slogan used to describe assassinations and bombings; still used by some activist groups

pro. per.: in propria persona (Latin—acting as one's own attorney)

property crime: auto theft, burglary, larceny, etc.

Pros Atty: Prosecuting Attorney

Prosecution Management Information System: criminal data kept in computerized files by the U.S. Attorney's Office in Washington, D.C.

prosecutor: attorney employed by a government agency to initiate and maintain criminal proceedings on its behalf against persons accused of committing criminal offenses

Prosecutor: trade name of the Monadnock PR-24 two-handle baton, used for crowd control and family disturbances

prosecutorial agency: criminal-justice agency engaged in the prosecution of alleged offenders

pross: prostitute(s)

prossie: prostitute

prostitute: woman (or man) receiving profit from sexual service

protected point: expanding bullet

protection: protection money; sums paid to gangsters who offer protection from bodily harm, from having one's business sabotaged, etc.

protective custody: detention of persons by law-enforcement agencies to protect them from reprisal by criminal elements

protective patrol force: usually a euphemism for a vigilante patrol

Protect the Innocent: anti-crime lobby founded in Indiana

Provies: Provisional IRA (outlawed paramilitary organization that has claimed credit for many bombings and killings in Liverpool, London and Northern Ireland)

Provos: Provisionals (Provisional Irish Republican Army nationalists who use terrorism as a device to reunify Ireland); (Dutch slang—Provokers) militant youth staging riots to provoke the police and undermine order in big seaport cities such as Amsterdam and Rotterdam

prowl car: radio-equipped police car; squad car

PRP: People's Revolutionary Party (Tanzanian terrorists)

PRp: Puerto Rican pimp

PRRWO: Puerto Rican Revolutionary Workers Organization (q.v.)

PRS: Property Recovery Squad (of a police department); Protective Research Section of the United States Secret Service, responsible for preventive work in protecting the life of the President and other high officials

PRSP: Puerto Rican Socialist Party (q.v.)

PRT: Prison Reform Trust

PRT: Partido Revolucionario de los Trabajadores (Spanish—Revolutionary Party of the Workers) Mexican section of the SWP (Socialist Workers Party), active in protesting the deportation of illegal aliens and demanding the return of all territory lost by Mexico to the United States in 1847

Prune Pickers: Californians

pruno: (prison jargon) intoxicant often made by prisoners, who ferment a mixture of bread, food and fruit scraps and sugar; *pruno* is Spanish for plum

PS: *Pubblica Sucurezza* (Italian—Police)

PSA: Pretrial Service Agency

PSAMPP: Philadelphia Society for Alleviating the Miseries of Public Prisons (founded by Benjamin Franklin, William Rush and others)

PS & SC: Public Service and Safety Committee (concerned with crime in the streets)

PSAODAP: Presidential Special Action Office for Drug Abuse Prevention

PSC: Police Staff College

PSD: Public Safety Division (Texas)

pse (PSE): psychological stress evaluator (q.v.)

pshr: pusher

PSI: Personnel Security Investigation

Psilocybe: generic name of hallucinogenic fungi or sacred mushrooms used by some American and Mexican Indians as well as by others

psilocybin: hallucinogenic substance extracted from the fungi known to botanists as *Psilocybe mexicana*

PSP: Policia de Segurança Pública (Portuguese—Public Safety Police)

PSS: Personal Security System

PSTD: Prison Service Training Depot (Pretoria, South Africa)

P-stuff: pcp (PCP)

PSU: Public Security Unit (Ugandan secret police)

psychedeli: (psychedelicatessen) store selling drug paraphernalia

psychedelia: collective term for the world of mind-altering drugs and drug takers as well as related paraphernalia

psychedelic: anything enhancing or expanding the conscious state

psychedelic drugs: LSD-25, mescaline, psilocybin, etc.

psychedelic experiences: heightened and often inappropriate emotional reactions, mood changes of an extreme character, tactile and visual distortions and vivid hallucinations are among them

psychiatric abortion: one performed because the sanity of the mother is endangered

psychic dependence: repeated use of drugs to achieve a so-called normal state

psycho: psychotic

psychological stress evaluator: voice-analysis lie detector

psychopath: person suffering from mental aberrations and disorders, especially one who perceives reality clearly except for his or her own social or moral obligations and seeks instant gratification in criminal or otherwise abnormal behavior

psychopathic hospital: insane asylum

psychopathic personality: (penological parlance) criminal, especially a criminal psychopath

psychopathology: science and study of mental abnormalities

psychopharmacology: study of the psychological and social effects of drugs

psychoprison: psychiatric hospital/prison in the USSR

psychoquack: unqualified would-be psychiatrist or psychologist

psychotomimetics: psychotomimetic drugs—alkaloidal substances capable of altering consciousness; also called psychedelic drugs

psychotoxic: (of drugs) capable of changing human behavior by mood modification; alcoholic beverages and narcotics are psychotoxic

psychotropics: drugs affecting behavior and moods without depression of the central nervous system or general stimulation; psychotropics include antidepressants, halucinogens, hashish and marijuana and tranquilizers

psycho ward: psychopathic ward

psycho-weapon(ry): psychological weapon(ry)—the fear of death or great bodily harm implanted by terrorists, who intimidate hostages and other victims

psywar: psychological warfare

PTA: Prevention of Terrorism Act (providing for seven days' detention of suspects in Great Britain and Northern Ireland)

P-38: German 9mm service pistol (used in World War II)

PTI: Protect the Innocent (q.v.)

PTJ: (Cuerpo) Tecnico de Policia Judicial (Spanish—Technical Corps of the Judicial Police) Venezuelans call its members *Petejotas*

ptp: part-time pimp

PTU: Psychiatric Treatment Unit

PU: Prisoner's Union

pu & d: pickup and delivery (of contraband, narcotics or other illicit material)

public defender: attorney appointed by a court to defend anyone unable to pay for the legal services of a counsel; also the nickname of an electric dart gun called the taser

public defender's office: government criminal-justice agency representing defendants who are unable to hire their own attorneys

Public Enemy Number One: gangster Al Capone's nickname

public house: old-fashioned term for a whorehouse

Public Interest Law Center of Philadelphia: watchdog organization concerned with exposing police brutality charges

Puebla: prison in Puebla, capital of the Mexican state of the same name, about halfway between Mexico City and Veracruz

Puerto Rican Socialist Party: communist-led organization that maintains an office in Havana

puff bamboo: smoke opium

puffer: opium smoker

pugging: fighting

pukeweed: *Lobelia inflata* (a toxic weed)

Pul-i-charki: prison in Kabul, Afghanistan

pull a score: mug someone; strangle or threaten to strangle someone; victimize

during an assault
pull in: arrest
pull jive: ghetto slang phrase meaning to drink alcoholic beverages
pull the pin: pull the grenade pin; retire
PUMA: Prostitutes Union of Massachusetts
puncture wounds: wounds inflicted by bullets, daggers, knives, nails or needles; these often become infected because they do not bleed freely and the point of entry seals rapidly
punji sticks: sharp-pointed stakes carefully concealed in the ground so they will pierce the feet of trespassers threatening the hideouts of fugitives or crops such as hashish and marijuana; originally made of bamboo by the Viet Cong
punk: boy homosexual; coward; hoodlum; petty criminal; whore
Punxey: Punxsutawney, Pennsylvania
Purdy: Purdy Treatment Center for Women (one of America's most advanced facilities for female offenders; just outside Tacoma, Wash.)
pure: pure heroin
purge: complete removal of arrest, criminal or juvenile record information from a records system
purloin: steal
purple: see **Zacatecas purple**
purple barrels: LSD
purple haze: LSD
purple heart: dexamyl (amytal and dexedrine) pill, so named because of its purple color and heart shape
purple owsley: LSD
purple ozoline: LSD
push: to sell dangerous drugs such as narcotics
pusher: illegal vendor of drugs (also nicknamed bagman, candy man, dealer, junker, mother, peddler, player, trafficker, travel agent et al.)
pushing up the daisies: dead and buried

push shorts: cheat; sell lesser amounts of drugs than specified
push the queer: pass counterfeit money
pussy patrol: vice squad
pussy posse: roundup of prostitutes
pussy squad: vice squad
put away: put away in prison; put away from society
put down: arrest
put in the hole: put into a solitary-confinement cell
put out a contract: Mafia phrase meaning to hire an assassin to kill someone in return for a stated sum of money
put the arm on: arrest; physically detain
put the chill on: kill
put the finger on: identify a criminal or a suspect
put to sleep: murder
put up: encapsulate powdered drugs
put-up job: frameup; prearranged deal; something plotted to insure its outcome
Puyallup: assembly center for Japanese-Americans brought in from other parts of Washington after Pearl Harbor; in this small town southeast of the Seattle-Tacoma area many were housed in former pigpens
PVA: Prison Visitor's Association
PVR: Police Volunteer Reserve
pw: prisoner of war
PWA: Prison Wardens Association
pyramid: pyramid investment scheme (organized to gull the gullible)
pyramid franchise: multi-level sales-promotion scheme also known as a dealer loader
pyrolagnia: sexual pleasure derived from setting fires; many pyromaniacs have been found to be afflicted with pyrolagnia
pyromania: compulsion or mania to set things on fire
pyromaniac: person with an abnormal and malicious mania to set things afire
pyrostat: heat- or smoke-actuated fire alarm

Q

Q: queen; queer; queer money; queer securities; queer sexual habits; prison at San Quentin, Calif.

q & a: question(s) and answer(s)

q & a session: question-and-answer session held when a suspect is first interrogated by the police

QC: Queen's Counsel (during the reign of a queen; during the reign of a king there is the King's Counsel—KC)

QCPSA: Quaker Center for Prisoner Support Activities (q.v.)

QCSR: Quaker Committee on Social Rehabilitation (in New York City)

qd: questioned document; quick detachable (weapon or weapon accessory quickly assembled or disassembled and hence easily concealed)

QJSA: Quarterly Journal of Studies in Alcohol

QPA: Queensland Police Academy (Brisbane)

QPM: Queen's Police Medal (British decoration)

QPP: Quebec Provincial Police

Qsar: Teheran, Iran's great prison, pronounced *Gasre* (also called Ghasre)

qt: quiet (*the crime was committed on the qt*)

quaal: quaalude (q.v.)

quaalude: trade name of methaqualone (hypnotic and sedative)

quack: a charlatan or fraud pretending to be a physician or other professional and gaining a living by illegal practices; many people in all ranks of society are fleeced by quacks charging high prices for make-believe cures, medicines and treatments of little or no value; to inform the police

Quacks: CWACs (members of the City-Wide Anti-Crime Unit of the New York City Police Department)

quad: prison; prison quadrangle; prison yard

quaffer: alcoholic

quail roost: women's dormitory in a house of detention

quaker: quaker gun (dummy gun used to intimidate prospective victims of a holdup)

Quaker Center for Prisoner Support Activities: conducts non-violent training workshops for prisoners

Quantico: Quantico, Virginia's FBI Academy and U.S. Marine Base

quarantine: enforced isolation of animals, persons, places, plants or vessels suspected of carrying or harboring some communicable disease

quarry cure: forcing addicts to work in stone quarries far from sources of alcohol and narcotics

quarter bag: $25 bag of marijuana

quarter piece: one-quarter ounce of cocaine, heroin or morphine

quarter stretch: three-months' sentence

quas: methaqualone (also called quacks or quads)

queen: British colloquialism for prostitute

queen's bus: prison van (slang term heard in many parts of the British Commonwealth)

Queens Homicide Task Force: New York City Police Department detectives assigned to solve major murders committed in the Borough of Queens

queer: counterfeit, as in the expression *passing the queer*

queer bird(s): jailbird(s)—expression goes back to Elizabethan times

queer-ken: prison (term goes back to Elizabethan times)

Quent: San Quentin (California State Prison)

Queretero: prison in Queretero, capital of the Mexican state of the same name

Questore: Italy's security service and the National Central Bureau of Interpol in Rome

Quetelet's hypothesis: no two persons possess the same physical measurements, insisted the Belgian statistician Lambert Adolphe Jacques Quetelet (1796-1874), whose work is the basis of all Bertillon measurements once used to identify criminals; these measurements are no longer used because in 1903 Warden McCloughty of Leavenworth discovered that two black prisoners who looked alike and had the same Bertillon measurements had different fingerprints; from that day forward the Bertillon System was abandoned, along with Quetelet's hypothesis

quick entry: no-knock entry made by law-enforcement officers

quick on the draw: quick in drawing a gun out of its holster; ready for quick action

quick on the trigger: ready to shoot without warning

quickpoint: a gun sight eliminating the need to sight down the barrel of a weapon; if one looks through the sight one sees a pink dot directly in the center of the target; sometimes called a nightscope

quick push: easy mark; person easily victimized

quiet air: airwaves undisturbed by police radio calls (antonym of **busy air**)

quill: folded matchbook cover used for holding, smoking or sniffing drugs

quinine: drug used to adulterate heroin, as its bitter taste is like that of heroin; also used in the treatment of malaria

quis: quisling (term for traitor derived from Vidkun Quisling, who, during World War II, headed Norway's puppet government set up by the German invaders)

quit: died

quitter: suicide

quod: prison

R

r: racket(eer)

R: rogue (letter branded on the left shoulder of convicts transported to various British colonies from 1619, when the first were landed in Virginia, until 1868, when the last arrived in Western Australia)

rabbit fever: desire to break parole or leave an honor camp before completing a sentence

rabbitfoot: escaped prisoner

racehorse charlie: old user of morphine

rack: maximum-security cell

racket: business or criminal operation in which quick profits are produced by deceiving the customers; many so-called sporting events linked to large-scale gambling are legalized rackets

Racketeer-Influenced and Corrupt Organization: federal act providing for the prosecution of loan-shark racketeers and mobsters

racketeering: exploitation for personal profit, and by means of violence or the threat of violence, of business and employee organizations as well as individual businesses, whether legitimate or otherwise; U.S. government and law-enforcement agencies estimate no less than $48 billion a year is taken in the racketeers, whose enterprises range from cigarette bootlegging to gambling, hijacking, loan sharking, narcotics, pornography and prostitution; gambling is the main source of revenue, followed by loan sharking and narcotics, pornography and prostitution; gambling is the main source of revenue, followed by loan sharking and narcotics

radar speedalyzer: automatic radar-controlled automotive-vehicle speed analyzer, used to detect speeders on highways and streets

Radical Alternatives to Prison Plan: British program abbreviated as RAPP

radiclib: radical liberal

radint: radar intelligence

radsab: radiator sabotage (puncturing the radiator of an automotive vehicle; if initially undetected, this will cause the radiator to lose fluid and the engine to overheat and stall)

RAF: *Rote Armee Fraktion* (German—Red Army Faction) underground terrorist group

Rahway: Rahway State Prison at Woodbridge, N.J., southwest of Newark

Raiford: Florida State Prison at Raiford, northeast of Gainesville

railroad: to send a person to jail without benefit of a trial or proof of guilt

rainbow: red and blue capsule of tuinal, containing amytal and seconal barbiturates

rainy-day woman: marijuana cigarette

raised pistol: handgun with its muzzle pointed upward

raisinjack: alcoholic drink made by prisoners, who save raisins and ferment them

rake-off: special commission or cut of the receipts

Raleigh: Correctional Center for Women at Raleigh, N.C.

RAM: Revolutionary Action Movement of the Black Liberation Front of the U.S.A.

Ramla: Israeli maximum-security prison built by the British in 1934, between Jerusalem and Tel Aviv-Yafo

ranch: confinement and/or correctional facility for older boys, run as a school by the Probation Department of San Diego (California) County at Campo, where the isolated and rockbound Mexican border discourages escapees, as do the Mexicans across the line

Rancho del Rayo: juvenile correctional facility for younger boys in Campo, Calif. on the site of an Italian prisoner-of-war camp during World War II

rasphuys: (Flemish—rasp house)—Ghent's workhouse-type prison bilt by its burgomaster, Jean Jacques Philippe Vilain, in 1773, where prisoners grated wood to powder as penance and to carry out the motto *only those who work will eat*—the French call this a *maison de force (workhouse)*

R & CC: Ross and Cromarty Constabulary

R & PA: Rifle and Pistol Association

r & r: rape and robbery (common type of crime); rate and rhythm (pulse); rest and recreation or rest and rotation (of military personnel); rock and roll (popular music); rock and rye (whiskey)

Ranger: Ranger Arms, Inc. (American firearms manufacturer)

Rangers: Texas Rangers

rap: from the French *repartir*, meaning to retort with witty comments; in current slang meaning to talk frankly and freely about anything; conversation (a rap session); prison sentence (a bad rap is a long and severe sentence)

RAP: Release Aid Program (to help recently-released inmates adjust to society)

RAP: Radical Alternatives to Prison

rape: unlawful sexual intercourse with a female by force or without factual or legal consent (see also **statutory rape** and **rape without force or consent**)

rape without force or consent: sexual intercourse with a female who is legally of the age of consent but who is unconscious or whose ability to judge or control her conduct is impaired by mental defect or intoxicating substances such as alcohol or drugs

rapee: rape victim

rape rep: rape report

rapist: person who rapes

rapo: rapist

RAPP: Radical Alternatives to Prison Plan (British program)

rap parlor: euphemism for a massage parlor; place where clients can go to establish conversational rapport or where they can telephone for someone to come and talk with them; subtle device to evade laws requiring that women working in massage parlors have actual training in therapeutic massage techniques and not just in sexual services

RARE: Rehabilitation of Addicts by Relatives and Employers

rat: inform(er)

Rathmore Road: nickname derived from the address of Cork Prison in the south of Ireland

rat on: inform against; *be careful, he'll rat on you*

rat row: segregated prison cells reserved for informers to guarantee their safety

Raul Sendic International Brigade: French terrorists named for the founder of the Tupamaros (q.v.)

Ravensbrück: Nazi concentration camp north of Berlin where some 92,000 women died during World War II; this camp is famous for the medical experiments performed on its prisoners

Rawlins: Wyoming State Penitentiary at Rawlins

Raymond Street: Raymond Street Jail, formerly the best known in Kings County, N.Y.; close to the Criminal Courts in the Borough Hall section of Brooklyn

razor ribbon: razor-edged stainless-steel security fencing

razzle: razzle-dazzle game (almost-impossible-to-win game of chance enriching carnival operators and ripping off the gullible public)

RCC: Rape Crisis Center (Washington, D.C.)

RCCP: Royal Commission on Criminal Procedure

RCG: Reception Guidance Center

RCMP: Royal Canadian Mounted Police

RCP: Revolutionary Communist Party (q.v.)

RCYB: Revolutionary Communist Youth Brigade (Trotskyite)

rd (RD): red devil (seconal)

REACH: Rape Emergency Aid and Counseling for Her

REACT: Radio Emergency Associated Citizens Team

reactive police work: taking action after a crime or something else bad has happened (opposite of proactive police work, q.v.)

reader: sneak thief specializing in trailing delivery clerks, reading the address on any valuable-looking package and rushing ahead to that address, where they appear in the guise of the impatient recipient, quick to unburden the delivery person of the package

Reading: HM Prison at Reading in Berkshire, England, where Oscar Wilde was imprisoned and where he wrote *The Ballad of Reading Gaol*; jails in Readings in Kansas, Massachusetts, Michigan, Minnesota, Ohio, Pennsylvania and Vermont

REAL: Rape Emergency Assistance League

Reception and Diagnostic Center for Children: at Bon Air, Va., for juvenile delinquents from 8 to 18 years of age

reception centers: World War II euphemism for the concentration camps set up to hold some 110,000 Americans of Japanese descent until they could be relocated away from the West Coast and until the Pearl-Harbor-attack-induced paranoia of other citizens could be overcome; many Japanese-Americans lost their homes, their farms, and other businesses, as well as personal contacts and many possessions

recid: recidivist

recidivism: person habitually returning to crime; person serving a second, third or fourth prison sentence (a habitual prisoner); some recidivists spend most of their lives in prison

record purge: complete removal of arrest, criminal or juvenile record information from a records system

red: Mexican red (barbiturate sleeping capsule)

Red: old-fashioned term applied to an anarchist, communist or socialist and, often, one who was in fact a political liberal

red and blue: tuinal tablet

Red Army: traditionally the army of the USSR; more recently the name taken by Japanese terrorists who claim their enemies include imperialsts and Zionists; Japanese Red Army terrorists have engaged in airplane hijackings and airport bombings as well as demanding multi-million-dollar ransoms

Red Army Faction: official name of the Baader-Meinhof terrorists, active in West Germany and elsewhere; some intelligence officers believe they receive funds and training from Soviet forces anxious to discredit democracy in West Germany

red biddy: red wine fortified with methyl alcohol, often fatal to its drinkers

redbird: secobarbital capsule

Red Brigades: Italy's terrorist movement—*Brigatas Rossa*

red chicken: Chinese heroin

redcoat: member of the Royal Canadian Mounted Police

red devil: red-colored gelatine capsule containing secobarbital or its sodium derivative

red-dirt marijuana: uncultivated marijuana

red eye: low-quality liquor

red flag: red flag of communism, of danger, of revolution or of warning

Red Flag 74: terrorist organization in the United Kingdom

Red Guards: teenage Chinese followers of Chairman Mao active in the late 1960s

Red Guerrilla Family: black terrorists active in California; they support the Black Liberation Army, the *Frente de Liberacion Chicano*, the *Fuerzas Armadas de Liberacion Nacional de Puerto Rico*, the New World Liberation Front, the Symbionese Liberation Army and the Weather Underground organization,

according to a statement they made when they attacked the Alcohol, Tobacco and Firearms Bureau offices of the Treasury Department in San Francisco, causing $100,000 in damages and terrorizing the staff

red-handed: in the act (of doing something wrong or illegal; *they caught him red-handed*)

red herring: false issue raised to confuse the real issue

red ink: red wine

red-lamp district: British equivalent of the American red-light district

red light: red lamp displayed from the last car of a railroad train; illuminated by oil, they were carried by railroad men enroute to or from their trains; some were hung on the porches of brothels they visited when away from home—hence the term "red-light district"

Red Light Abatement Act: California law enabling officials to control prostitution and related crimes

red-light district: section of any city or town filled with brothels; formerly, a red light in the window of a house meant that it was a house of prostitution; today such houses have been largely replaced by call girls for hire, massage-parlor and rap-parlor girls in order to circumvent anti-prostitution laws

red oil: see **hash oil**

red telephone: hot-line telephone network linking top law-enforcement officials in Austria, Italy, Switzerland and West Germany in their fight against terrorism

Reeducation of Attitudes and Repressed Emotions: treatment program for sex offenders

reefer: marijuana cigarette

reefer butt: the butt end of a marijuana cigarette, also known as a roach

reefer man: marijuana pusher

reentry: returning to normal after a psychedelic "trip"

ref: reformatory

reflection cell: maximum-security cell

reformatory: house of correction or penitentiary designed to encourage prisoners to reform

regicide: (Latin—king killer) person who assassinates a head of state

Regina Coelli: (Latin—Queen of Heaven)—Rome, Italy's great prison well known to convicts and to Italian moving-picture fans

regulator: vigilante

rehab: rehabilitate; rehabilitation

rehabilitation: changing the offender's character, intent, and motivation toward law-abiding conduct

rehabilitation camps: Vietnam's prison camps for political prisoners opposed to the communist regime in that country

rehabilitation laboratory: euphemism for any modern prison

Reidsville: Georgia's maximum-security prison, about 50 miles west of Savannah

Reistertown: the Montrose School for Girls at Reistertown, Md.

Release Aid Program: see **RAP**

relocation center(s): internment camp(s) where Japanese-Americans were confined shortly after the attack on Pearl Harbor when it was generally believed Japan would invade the United States

remand: to send, or the act of sending, a prisoner back to court for a continued or further hearing; a remand prison holds people awaiting their return to the court where their crimes will be judged

remand center: British term for a borstal or juvenile jail, holding 8- to 18-year-old delinquents pending a period of rehabilitation, often followed by parole and release

remand home: remand center

remand institution: European term for a jail or prison

Remington Arms: Dupont subsidiary engaged in the manufacture of ammunition and arms

Remington Gun Museum: display of firearms from the 1840s to the present; free and open to the public daily from 9:00 a.m. to 9:00 p.m.; at Hoefler Avenue in Ilion, N.Y.

Rem-UMC: Remington-Union Metallic Cartridge Co.

Reno: El Reno, Okla. (federal detention reformatory just west of Oklahoma City); Reno, Nev. (divorce and gambling center on the Truckee River, long known as the Divorce Capital of America)

drent-a-cop: hired guard; security guard

rent boys: British teenage male prostitutes serving *punters* (prostitute customers)

rep: representative; reputation

repeaters: loaded dice; repeating rifles

repressive terrorism: criminal act(s) committed to eliminate informers, rivals or anyone failing to conform to the demands of the terrorists

reprieve: executive order temporarily suspending the execution of a sentence imposed on a criminal

reserve officer: uniformed volunteer police reserve officer

resilient cell: padded cell designed to prevent prisoners from injuring or killing themselves

resin: hashish or marijuana resin, containing the drug tetrahydrocannabinol

respectable pushers: those doctors, pharmacists and other professionals who are looked up to in their communities but who peddle a cornucopia of illicit drugs

REST: Routine Execution Selection Table

restitution: restoring something to its rightful owner or reimbursing him or her for its loss; many juvenile offenders are paroled if they make restitution by either returning stolen goods or performing some service in lieu of actual restoration of damaged or stolen property

restitution center: an institution like those found in Georgia, Iowa and Minnesota, where criminals pay for their crimes by working and paying back their victims

restraints: ankle cuffs; belly chains; belt restraints; leg irons; straitjackets

RESTTA: Restitution Education, Specialized Training, and Technical Assistance (program funded by the Office of Juvenile Justice and Delinquency Prevention, U.S. Department of Justice)

resurrectionist: grave robber

Revolutionary Command Council: Arab terrorists headquartered in Libya but active in all parts of the Middle East

revolutions per minute: cyclic rate of bullets and other projectiles

revolverize: to shoot someone

revolving-door: revolving-door criminal-justice system, responsible for returning dangerous defendants to their communities again and again

rf: rapid fire (type of weapon); rat fink (scab or spy); rim fire (type of ammunition)

r/f: right front

RG: Rohm Gesellschaft (German—Rohm Company) initialized corporate name of the Rohm Tool subsidiary engaged in the assembly and manufacture of handguns at its Miami, Fla. plant on Northwest 20th Street

RGC: Reception Guidance Center

RGF: Red Guerrilla Family (q.v.)

RHKP: Royal Hong Kong Police

RHL: Rape Help Line (police telephone line)

Rhode Island Training School for Girls: at Howard

rhyparography: creating so-called filthy pictures by drawing, painting or photographing and reproducing them by any printing process

riah (RIAH): radioimmunoassay of hair (for drug detection)

RIC: Royal Irish Constabulary

rice-paper edition: anything printed on rice paper so it can be chewed and swallowed if its owner is caught

Richmond: Richmond Penitentiary, Public Safety Department, St. Croix, U.S. Virgin Islands

RICO: Racketeer-Influenced and Corrupt Organizations (q.v.)

RID: Regimented Inmate Discipline (program for educating felons)

Riders of the Plains: members of the Royal Canadian Mounted Police

ride shotgun: ride next to the driver, holding a shotgun in readiness to defend the driver as well as any cargo or passengers; a security guard aboard an airplane who is charged with its protection and who is suitably armed to repulse hijackers rides shotgun

ride the wave: be under the influence of drugs

Riga: main concentration camp in Riga, Latvia during the German occupation of World War II

righteous: high-quality (drink or drug)

rightist: person sympathetic to fascist, racist or ultra-conservative causes or ideological concepts

right-on: originally a slogan of black-activist agressiveness but currently a multiracial catch phrase meaning *you're for what's right and so am I*; also means "affirmed with fervor," "exactly right," "right on course"

right to know: the authority to obtain any criminal history, criminal investigative date or intelligence report granted to any agency or individual by court or legislative mandate

right-wing: conservative or reactionary (as opposed to left-wing—liberal or radical)

rigid: intoxicated

rigor mortis: (Latin—stiffening of death) first appears in the face and jaws, before proceeding downward through the neck to the arms, chest and abdomen and finally to the legs and the feet; rigor mortis of the entire body occurs within eight to 12 hours after death, but 18 more hours may pass before the body is completely enveloped; in three or four more hours rigor mortis in the upper half of the body disappears; it is with these figures that estimates are made concerning the time of death of a homicide victim

Riker's: Adolescent Remand Shelter on Riker's Island in New York City's East River, just north of La Guardia Airport in Queens; Riker's Island Penitentiary, at the same location; Riker's Island Women's Detention Center, also at the same location

Ring: The Ring, an international smuggling operation extending from Hong Kong on the South China Sea to Dubai, the Persian Gulf port of Oman; dollars, electronic devices of all kinds ranging from computers to radios, gold, immigrants, narcotics, textiles, silver, spices and watches are smuggled by the Ring to evade customs tax collectors in China, Taiwan, the Philippines, Indonesia, the countries of Southeast Asia, Bangladesh, India, Sri Lanka (Ceylon), Pakistan, Iran, Saudi Arabia and the Trucial States, as well as other countries

Ring-Ring: Copenhagen, Denmark's penitentiary with seven rings radiating from its cell-block buildings; between the spokes are yards for the prisoners to exercise in limited seclusion and maximum security

Rio Abajo: (Spanish—Down-Under River)—Panama's red-light district close to the airport

Rio Consumnes: Rio Consumnes Correctional Facility at Elk Grove, Calif., close to Sacramento

riot: public disturbance committed by three or more persons (in some states, by only two or more persons); armed rioters are subject to serious penalties

riot-chuk: combined riot stick and nonchaku made by Research Weapons of Drayton Plains, Mich., and used by many law-enforcement officers in dispersing illegal activities

riot gun: five-shot 12-gauge pump action rapid-fire short-barrel shotgun

RIP: Riker's Island Penitentiary (in New York's East River)

rip off: cheat; defraud; overcharge; swindle; steal

rip-off artist: confidence man; crook; crooked politician; robber; thief

ripped: highly intoxicated by drugs

Risdon: Hobart, Tasmania's prison and prison hospital

River Avenue: Bronx House of Detention at 653 River Ave., Bronx, N.Y.

River House: Ohio State Penitentiary on the Scioto River in Columbus

Riverside: Riverside County Jail (California)

Riverview: Interprovincial Home for

Women (misdemeanants) at Riverview, New Brunswick

RJIS: Regional Justice Information System

RLAA: Red Light Abatement Act (q.v.)

RLDPAS: Royal London Discharged Prisoners' Aid Society

RLPAS: Royal London Prisoners' Aid Society

RM: Resident Magistrate

RMP: Radio Motor Patrol (police)

RMPA: Royal Medico-Psychological Association

rn: round-nose bullet

RNWMP: Royal Northwest Mounted Police

R/O: Reporting Officer

roach: butt of a marijuana cigarette; so called as one often resembles a wet cockroach once it has been passed about and smoked a bit

roach clip: device for holding a hashish or marijuana cigarette so it may be smoked to the very end

roach holder: roach clip (q.v.)

roach pick: roach clip (q.v.)

road gang: see **chain gang**

road hustler: card and dice hustler

road trap: dynamite or other explosive concealed in a road or under a sewer manhole lid; detonated when an automotive vehicle drives over the place where the explosives are concealed

ROARE: Reeducation of Attitudes and Repressed Emotions (q.v.)

Roaston, Toaston, and Duston: nicknames given by the Japanese-Americans interned at prison camps in the roasting, toasting, and dusty desertlands of southeastern Arizona around Poston

rob: to steal from another or others using actual violence or the threat of violence; to take away as loot

Robben Island: South African penitentiary for political prisoners at the entrance to Table Bay and north-northwest of Cape Town

robbery: holdup; stealing accomplished by actual violence or by the threat of violence; unlawful taking or attempted taking of property in the immediate possession of another by force or the threat of force (see also **armed robbery** and **strong-arm robbery**)

robrep: robbery report

Rochester: detention facilities in Rochesters in Minnesota and New York State

Rock: Alcatraz Federal Prison, which once occupied a 12-acre rock in San Francisco Bay; Riker's Island, New York City's correctional facility in the East River near La Guardia Airport; San Quentin

rock: west coast U.S. name for a cheap - but - deadly form of cocaine called "crack" on the east coast

rock crusher: prisoner assigned to hard manual labor

Rockland: Rockland State Hospital for the Criminally Insane (New York)

Rockwell City: The Women's Reformatory at Rockwell City, Iowa

Rocky Butte: jail in Portland, Ore.

rod: handgun

rodman: armed holdup man

rogues' march: military quickstep played when offenders are drummed out of the army, the marines, the navy or other military units; at public floggings and executions it was the custom to have a drummer beat out the rhythm of the rogues' march

Rohwer Arkansas: relocation center for interned Japanese-Americans close to the Mississippi River

roll: to roll (a customer) while he is drunk and take away his belongings and money; to roll a marijuana cigarette; a roll of paper money; a roll of metal foil containing drugs

roller: the police

rollie: homemade cigarette

rolling machine: device for rolling cigarettes of hashish, marijuana, tobacco or their mixtures

roll through the rye: drink while driving

roll up: arrest; capture; possess

rollup: Soviet torture wherein wet canvas, tightly wrapped around a victim, is allowed to dry; it contracts and thereby inflicts terrible pain; it is not removed until a confession has been extracted

roomie: cellmate

Roosevelt: Roosevelt Hospital (and morgue) at 58th Street and 10th Avenue in New York City

rope: hangman's rope; marijuana; vein

ror (ROR): release on recognizance

roscoe: handgun; pistol; revolver

rose: benzedrine tablet

Rostov-on-Don: Soviet state police prison, also called House 33

rotan: thin rattan lashing stick used for inflicting corporal punishment in Malaysia and Singapore, where culprits are often caned as well as fined and jailed

rotgut: rotgut liquor (inferior or poisonous alcoholic mixtures)

Roth Steyr: Austrian 8mm pistol

Round House: Fremantle, Western Australia's oldest structure built in 1830 as a jail; site of the first execution in the area

roust: arrest

Royal Canadian Mounted Police: rural constabulary originally organized to prevent Indian disorders; long famous for many daring exploits while trailing criminals to even the most remote places, as well as in crowded metropolitan centers

Royal Canadian Mounted Police Museum: open daily from June 1 through Nov. 15; free; in Regina, Saskatchewan

R/P: Reporting Person

rpm: revolutions per minute (q.v.)

r/r: right rear

RR—IM: Research Reports—Intelligence Memorandum

RSB: Revolutionary Student Brigade

RSHA: *Reichssicherheitshauptamt* (German—Reich Central Security Department)—combined Gestapo, Kripo, and SD secret police

RSL: Revolutionary Socialist League

RSPCA: Royal Society for the Prevention of Cruelty to Children

RTU: Rahway Treatment Unit (for sex offenders incarcerated in New Jersey's Rahway State Prison)

rubbed out: assassinated

rubber bullets: relatively harmless projectiles fired by the police to disperse mobs and control rioters

rubber check: check returned for lack of funds; it is said to "bounce" as if made of rubber

rubber heel: detective; policeman

rubber hose: a short length of rubber hose is often used to punish or subdue unruly mobsters or prisoners because few traces of flogging are left on the victim's body

rubber room: padded cell (usually reserved for self-destructive or violent prisoners)

rubbers: rubber bullets (used in controlling mobs and violent individuals)

rub out: assassinate; murder

Ruby: Spanish revolver manufactured by Gabilondo

RUC: Royal Ulster Constabulary

Ruger: American manufacturer of handguns and rifles

Rule G: Association of American Railroads' rule prohibiting employees from drinking or using narcotics; violaters often found it extremely difficult to get another job if they were fired for breaking Rule G

rumbag: drunkard

rumble: gang fight

rumdum: alcoholic in her or his last stages of mental and physical degeneration; an alcoholic or narcotic addict whose addiction is obvious

rum hound: alcoholic

rummy: alcoholic

rumpot: alcoholic

run: amphetamine binge

RUN: Revolutionary United Nations

runaway: juvenile leaving the custody and home of her or his parents, guardians or custodians without permission and failing to return within a reasonable length of time

runner: person carrying drugs from a vendor to buyers

rush: ecstatic moment reported by users of drugs

Russian roulette: deadly game of chance wherein each player spins the cylinder of a revolver loaded with a single shot before pointing the muzzle to his head and pulling the trigger

rustle: steal cattle

rv: recoil velocity (of a weapon)

RVPA: Rape Victims Privacy Act

rws (RWS): release with services

S

s: secret; solo

s (S): suspect (also abbreviated **susp** or susps—suspects)

SA: Salvation Army; Savage Arms; single-action (handgun); Special Agent (FBI); Springfield Armory

SA: *Sturmabteilung* (German—Storm Detachment) Hitler's Brownshirts or Stormtroopers

SAA: Singapore Aftercare Association (hostel for ex-convicts)

SAAMI: Sporting Arms and Manufacturers Institute

SABA: South African Black Alliance (q.v.)

saber: curve-blade sword for cutting, slashing and thrusting; up to the early 1900s sabers were used to lop off heads and limbs

sabot: sabotage; saboteur

sabotage: malicious destruction of property such as commodities, goods and machinery for the purpose of weakening an employer during a labor dispute or a nation in time of war

saboteur: person committing sabotage

Sabre-Six: trade name of an electric cattle prod often used to control violent behavior of people in mobs

SAC: *Sociedad de Albizu Campos* (Puerto Rican militant organization active in the New York City area)

SAC: Special Agent in Charge (FBI)

SACB: Subversive Activities Control Board

Sacco and Vanzetti: Nicola Sacco and Bartolomeo Vanzetti, Italian-American anarchist who were tried, convicted and executed in 1927 for murdering an armed guard and a shoe-factory paymaster in South Braintree, Mass. in 1920; liberals worldwide protested the sentence and the execution; during World War II, Carlo Tresca, an anarchist editor and leader, told Max Eastman "Sacco was guilty but Vanzetti was not"; later ballistic tests revealed that Sacco's gun fired the fatal bullets, whereas his comrade Vanzetti was an accessory

Sachsenhausen: main Nazi concentration camp close to Berlin

SACP: South African Communist Party

sacred mushrooms: hallucinogenic fungi used by some American and Mexican Indians in sacred tribal ceremonies; also used by others outside of religious contexts

sacrilege: defacing a church, synagogue or temple; stealing from a church, synagogue or temple; taking away the property of a religious institution; violating what religious persons hold to be sacred

SACRO: Scottish Association for the Care and Resettlement of Offenders

SADD: Students Against Drunk Driving

SAD: Social Affairs Department (q.v.)

sadism: sexual aberration wherein cruelty is inflicted to attain sexual release

sadist: person deriving pleasure, especially sexual pleasure, from inflicting pain on others

sadomasochist: person deriving pleasure from physically or psychologically hurting another or being hurt by another

SAFE: Security Against Fatal Encounter; Security Assured For Each

safe-blower: expert in blowing open doors of safes with well-placed explosives or picking their combination locks as well as peeling safe metal with special chisels

safe cracksman: burglar expert in opening safes and vaults

safe house: military jail; place where prostitutes undergo rehabilitation; un-bugged or unsuspected meeting place; shelter for battered women whose address is secret

safekeeper(s): felon(s) prevented from escaping by being put in maximum, medium, or minimum custody, depending on his record

safety cell: padded cell (for self-destructive or violent prisoners)

Safety Lock Co.: New York underworld nickname for the Police Department's Safe and Loft Squad

safety shield(s): roll bar(s) and safety shield(s) installed in police cars as a means of protecting the driver and/or arresting officer from any person(s) in the rear of the auto

Safford: Federal Prison Camp at Safford, Ariz.

Sagmalcilar Hilton: inmates' nickname for the principal prison of Istanbul

SAIC: Special Agent in Charge (FBI)

St. Albans: medium-security correctional facility at St. Albans, Vt.

St. Anthony: the State Youth Training Center at St. Anthony, Idaho

St. Augustin: headquarters of West Germany's anti-terrorist commandos near Bonn

St. Bartholomew: a massacre; a mass murder; after the St. Bartholomew's Day Massacre on Aug. 24, 1572 when more than 3,000 Protestant Huguenots were murdered on the orders of the Catholic queen Catherine de Medicis (Caterina de Medici)

St. Bridget's Well: original name of London's Bridewell prison, once a royal palace of King Edward VI

St. Catherine's: Jamaican district prison close to Kingston

St. Cloud: 26, rue Armengaud, St. Cloud (Paris), France (headquarters of the general secretariat of Interpol—the International Criminal Police Organization); Minnesota State Prison at St. Cloud, Minn.

St. Cyrille: the Maison Gomin correctional facility for women at St. Cyrille, Quebec

St. Gabriel: Louisiana Correctional Institute for Women at St. Gabriel

St. John's: Her (His) Majesty's Penitentiary at St. John's, Newfoundland

St. Martin's evil: dipsomania

Ste. Marguerite: old prison close to the coast of Cannes where the Man in the Iron Masque was imprisoned by Louis XIV from 1687 to 1698 and immortalized in the novel by Alexandre Dumas, *The Man in the Iron Masque*

Sako: popular Finnish rifle

Salaspils: Nazi concentration camp near Riga, Latvia

Salem: Oregon Women's Correctional Center at Salem; West Virginia Industrial Home for Girls at Salem

sally port: first gate to a prison

Salpetrière: Paris hospital for the criminally insane

salt and pepper: low-grade marijuana

salt-and-pepper police teams: white and black policemen teamed to work together

Saltillo: prison in Saltillo, capital city of the state of Coahuila in northeastern Mexico

Salt Lake: Salt Lake Detention Home, Salt Lake County, Utah

sam: federal law-enforcement agent on the payroll of Uncle Sam (the United States government)

Samarkand Manor: for female misdemeanants and juvenile delinquents; at Eagle Springs, N.C.

San Anto: (Mexican-American—San Antonio, Texas) jail-name and place-name nickname

San Bruno: San Francisco County Jail at San Bruno, Calif.; a relocation center for Japanese-Americans in World War II

sanctification: blackmailing to obtain political favors or secret data or evidence

sand: (prison argot) sugar

sandbag: sand-filled bag, sack or sock used as a weapon, to deliver a stunning blow

s & c: search and clear

sand club: sand-filled canvas bag or sock used as a weapon

s & m: sado-masochism

Sandstone: Federal Correctional Institution at Sandstone, Minn.

S & W: Smith & Wesson firearms

S & W bracelets: Smith and Wesson handcuffs

San Francisco bomb: mixture of cocaine, heroin and LSD

sanitize: make acceptable by removing objectionable features, ideas or words; protect participants by removal of all clues; protect the work of undercover agents

San Jo: (Mexican-Americanism—San Jose, Calif.) jail-name and place-name nickname

sanlo: low-grade opium made from the residue of smoked opium

San Luis Potosi: prison in San Luis Potosi, capital of the Mexican state of the same name, northwest of Mexico City

s-a-n man: stop-at-nothing man (desperate criminal)

San Quentin: California State Prison at San Quentin

Santa Ana: nickname of the central penitentiary of Occidente's Ejido Trujillo in Venezuela; Orange County courthouse and jail southeast of Los Angeles, California

Santa Fe: New Mexico Penitentiary at Santa Fe

Santa Marta gold: prime Colombian marijuana grown in the Santa Marta Mountains and smuggled into Canada and the United States from Barranquilla, Cartagena, Riohacha and Santa Marta

Santa Rita: Santa Rita Rehabilitation Center in California's Alameda County, near Oakland

Santé: Parisian prison at 422 rue de la Santé known as *la Santé*, meaning "health" or a toast to one's health or, in this instance, quarantine or segregation from society

SAODAP: Special Action Office for Drug Abuse Prevention (Washington, D.C.)

sap: blackjack or flexible billy, often covered with plain or woven leather

SARC: Sexual Assault Referral Centre (Australia)

sarin: chemical warfare agent of high toxicity, known by the code name of gb or GB ($C_4H_{10}FO_2P$)

SAS: Special Air Service (q.v.)

SASR: Special Air Service Regiment (q.v.)

SAT: Security Air Transport (q.v.)

Satan's Sinners: motorbike gang active on the West Coast

satch: cotton used to strain heroin solutions before injection; satch cotton is often consumed by addicts when no heroin is available

sat in the hot seat: died by electrocution

Saturday-night special: cheap handgun of the type produced in large quantities by RG Industries of Miami, Fla.

satyriasis: compulsive male sexual activity; female form is nymphomania

Sauer: German double-action 7.65mm pistol

Saughter: prison in Edinburgh, Scotland

sáu-liuh: (Cantonese Chinese—handcuffs)

'sault &: assault and battery

Savage: American manufacturer of firearms

Savage combination: model 24V combination gun chambered for the .222-caliber Remington and a 20-gauge shot shell by Savage Arms

SAVAK: Sazemane Attalat va Anmiyate Keshvar (Persian—Iranian Security and Intelligence Organization)

sawbuck: $10 bill

sawed-off: sawed-off shotgun (usually 12-gauge)

sawed-off rifle: rifle with a barrel shorter than 14 inches

sawed-off shotgun: shotgun with a barrel shorter than 18 inches from breech to muzzle or an overall length less than 26 inches

sawi: green-leaved hashish grown in India

saxitoxin: shellfish toxin that causes death within seconds

s/b: southbound

SB: Special Branch

SBIW: Sybil Brand Institute for Women, a correctional facility in Los Angeles, Calif.

sbs: sidie-by-side (double-barrel shotgun)

sbt (SBT): Screening Breath Test (given drivers who are suspected of being under the influence of alcohol)

SC: Special Constable

s/c: suspicious circumstances

scab: to cheat; a strikebreaker

scag: one of heroin's many nicknames

scagged: addicted to heroin

scag jones: heroin addiction

scam: to pilfer, rob or steal; a method of pilfering, robbing, stealing, etc.; a confidence game; the game plan of any scheme

scam: escape from jail or prison

scan.: suspected child abuse and neglect

Scanray: Scanray Corporation's scan-ray X-ray system for seeing what is inside parcels brought into jails or prisons by family and friends of inmates

Scarface: Al Capone, Chicago gangster-racketeer who was long in control of bootlegging, brothels and protection rackets

scarperer: British term for a fugitive from justice or a runaway; to scarpe is to run away without paying one's bills or providing for one's family

scattergun: machine-gun

SCC: Student Coordinating Council (formerly SNCC—Student Nonviolent Coordinating Council); Surveillance Coordination Center

SCCF: Security Clearance Case Files

scd (SCD): security coding device

scene: the scene where a crime was committed

Schlüsselburg: Leningrad prison built in czarist times

schoolboy: nickname for codeine

school of crime: epithet applied to many prisons

School on Counter-Insurgency: abbreviated SCI; conducted at Eglin Air Force Base, Florida (near Pensacola)

sci (SCI): secret confidential informant

SCI: School on Counter-Insurgency (q.v.)

SCCI: Servicio Central de Inteligencia (Spanish—Central Intelligence Service)

SCLED: South Carolina Law Enforcement Division

SCM: Society of Connoisseurs in Murder (q.v.)

scope: microscope; periscope; telescope; telescopic gunsight

score: to have sexual intercourse; to make a contact; to purchase narcotics; the proceeds of a burglary or of a con-game

SCORE: Special Covert Operations for Resale (q.v.)

scot free: entirely free

Scotland Yard: original headquarters of London's Metropolitan Police in Scotland Yard and Whitehall Court; the Scotland Yard built in 1912, described in the Sherlock Holmes tales, extending from Derby Gate to the Thames Embankment; the new New Scotland Yard, at the corner of Broadway and Victoria St., near Victoria Station

SCPAs: State Criminal-Justice Planning Agencies

scragsman: British term for a hangman

scrap iron: prison drink made of alcohol, hypochlorite solution and mothballs

scratches: marks left on the arm by injections of narcotics

scratchman: forger

screw: prison guard

screwman: (British underworld slang) key-making and safe-breaking specialist

scrip: $1 bill; paper money

script writer: prescription forger; physician sympathetic to addicts and willing to write the prescriptions they need to purchase dangerous drugs

scrubber: (Cockney English) prostitute

scupper: prostitute

sd: shit disturber (troublemaker)

SDCINTF: San Diego County Integrated Narcotic Task Force

SDCJ: San Diego County Jail

SDECE: Service de la Documentation Exterieure et du Contre-Espionnage (French—Overseas Documentation and Counter-Espionage Service) French version of the CIA

SDPD: San Diego Police Department

SDPOA: San Diego Police Officers Association

SDRs: Special Drawing Rights

Seagoville: Federal Correctional Institution at Seagoville, Texas

sea lawyer: sailor who seems to know all the laws affecting seamen and may also have a talent for provoking arguments about many, many subjects

SEARCH: System for Electronic Analysis and Retrieval of Criminal Histories

search warrant: document issued by a judicial officer directing a law-enforcement officer to conduct a search for specified property or persons at a specific location, to seize the property or persons, if found, and to account for the result of the search to the judicial officer

Seat of Government: Washington, D.C. headquarters of the FBI

Seavy's Island: the U.S. Naval Prison at Portsmouth, N.H. is on this island and is sometimes called by its name

SEC: Securities and Exchange Commission (q.v.)

seccy: seconal

seclusion: solitary confinement

seconal: quick-effect barbiturate used as a sedative

second-degree murder: killing committed during the course of a quarrel and in the heat of passion

second-generation money: checks

secret agent: operative of a secret service; person secretly collecting information; spy

Secret Service: law-enforcement division of the U.S. Treasury Department; established in 1865 to investigate and prevent counterfeiting; since the assassination of Pres. McKinley in 1901, it has also been charged with protecting the president as well as his immediate family, the vice president, the president- and vice president-elect, former presidents and their wives, widows of former presidents (unless they remarry) and visiting heads of state; also investigates check and bond forgeries

Section 8: person discharged from the miliitary for psychological reasons; section of the military code providing for discharge on psychological grounds

secure telephone: telephone whose location cannot be detected even by checking with the telephone company; conversations on such telephones cannot be intercepted

Securicor: British security company whose guards and guard services are often hired by the Home Office for duty at such places as Heathrow Airport

Securities and Exchange Commission: U.S. government agency charged with protecting investors in connection with the public issuance and sale of corporate securities

security: freedom from anxiety, attack or danger; freedom from espionage, crime, escape and sabotage; security office(r)

Security Air Transport: California airline specializing in transporting prisoners from one facility to another; passengers include bad-check writers, murderers, rapists, thieves and all types of men and women in trouble with the law

security and privacy standards: principles and procedures developed to safeguard the confidentiality and security of criminal or juvenile record information

Security Express: Britisih security guard service used by the Foreign Office along with Securicor and Group 4

security housing: section of a prison where hardened and hard-to-handle prisoners are segregated

Security Islands: Iles du Salut off the coast of French Guiana; three rocky islets—Ile du Diable (Devil's Island), Ile Royale, and Ile Saint Joseph—surrounded by shark-infested waters; until the 1950s political prisoners were isolated here along with incorrigibles

security superintendent: house detective; superintendent of security forces

Sedgewick Sisters: New York gang of violence-prone girls who seem to destroy just for the sake of destruction

SEE: Society of Explosives Engineers

seed: marijuana cigarette butt; morning-glory seed (*Rivea corymbosa*) often chewed to produce hallucinogenic effects; some users report it also produces diarrhea, dizziness and vomiting

seg: segregate; segregated; segregation(ist)

seggy: seconal

segregation: isolation of criminals from other members of society; racial segregation; solitary confinement

SEIA: Security Equipment Industry Association

selective enforcement: discretionary power of district attorneys and other public prosecutors to choose which persons to prosecute and which to let go

self-protection products: ammunition, arms and chemical gases used in self-defense

sell a bill of goods: defraud by selling something difficult to use or resell

sell down the river: betray or desert, like slaveowners who would sell their slaves and break up slave families if it proved profitable

semi-synthetic narcotics: diprenorphine, etorphine, heroin, hydromorphone and oxycodone

Semper Fi House: subversive group working at the naval base in Iwakuni, Japan; part of the GI Project Alliance (GIPA), involved with revolutionary subversion in the U.S. Navy

Send: detention center in Surrey, England

send up: sentence to imprisonment; *they'll send him up for 19 years*

sensitive payment: bribe given by some American corporations to foreign governments in return for their facilitating sales orders and/or payments

sensor personnel intrusion device: apparatus for detecting illegal aliens crossing a border or any intruders attempting to enter a protected area

sentence: penalty imposed by a court upon a convicted person or the court's decision to suspend execution of the penalty (see also **mandatory sentence** and **suspended sentence**)

Sepa: maximum-security prison in the remote jungles of Peru where escape can be worse than incarceration and segregation

serious headache: euphemism for a gunshot wound in the head

serve a sentence: spend time in jail

serve time: spend time in jail or prison

SETAF: Southern European Task Force (confinement facility in Italy)

Settlement Island: former penal colony within Macquarie Harbour on the Indian Ocean coast of Tasmania

setup: a police trap

s-e 22: silencer-equipped 22-caliber revolver (favored by Mafia assassins and others)

seven deadly sins: defined in popular criminology as assault, burglary (illegal entry into homes and places of business), motor-vehicle theft, rape, robbery (holdups), violent crimes against persons and willful homocide

seven-percent solution: seven-percent solution of cocaine injected by the fictional Sherlock Holmes

Seven-Step Foundation: halfway house for released convicts

sewer: vein used by addicts, who inject drugs into it as if it were a sewer

sewing machine: (motorcycle-gang slang) Japanese motorcycle

sexual harassment: making sexual acquiescence a condition of employment or promotion

sexual psychopath(s): person(s) exhibiting bizarre or compulsive sexual behavior

SFCJ: San Francisco County Jail

SFH: Semper Fi House (q.v.)

SFPD: San Francisco Police Department

SFPs: Sinn Fein Provisionals (Provos)

sfs: strictly for suckers

SFSAFBI: Society of Former Special Agents of the FBI

Sgt: Sergeant

SGUs: Special Guerrilla Units (q.v.)

sh (SH): sexual harassment

shade: receiver of stolen goods

shades: heavily-tinted glasses; sunglasses

shadow: detective (the term originated in mid-19th century London)

shady: verging on the illegal (*he's an expert in promoting shady deals*)

shakedown: payoff made to a corrupt official or racketeer; gangster activity, harassment or the threat of some sort of exposure or of physical harm is usually enough to insure that payoffs will be made by those who are vulnerable

Shaker Road: Albany County Penitentiary on Shaker Road in the Colonie section of Albany, N.Y.

Shakopee: Minnesota Correctional Institution for Women at Shakopee

sham: policeman; law-enforcement officer

shampoo: champagne; sparkling wine

shamus: detective or policeman, especially one of Irish origin; believed to be derived from Seamus, which means James in Gaelic Irish

shanghai: abduct; kidnap; put someone aboard a ship by means of drugs such as alcohol; term comes from the practice of doing the last for Orient-bound ships of evil reputation

shank: handmade knife or other pointed weapon; double-edge dagger (often made by prisoners from eating utensils or bits of scrap metal); knife-inflicted wound

sharp: hypodermic needle

sharpshooter: expert marksman; lawyer adept at aiming at legal loopholes facilitating the release or exoneration of his client

sheet: police blotter; police record; restraining sheet designed to confine a person to bed should he or she become violent

sheet artist: agent for the numbers racket

shell company: a corporation without assets (these are often established and used by white-collar criminals in bond swindles, money-laundering operations and mutual-fund schemes)

shellfish toxin: deadly poison effective within ten seconds; the victim dies of painless paralysis

shelter: confinement facility for the care of juveniles held pending adjudication

Shelton: Washington State Corrections Center at Shelton, close to Olympia and west of Tacoma; Women's Correctional Facility, also at Shelton, Wash.

Shelton Abbey: old Irish prison near Arklow on the east coast of Ireland south of Dublin

Sheridan: the Wyoming Girls School at Sheridan

sheriff: appointed or elected chief officer of a county law enforcement within the county and for the operation of the county jail

sheriff's department: county law-enforcement agency, directed by a sheriff

Sherlock: a police computer recording and releasing information about criminal activities; nickname for any good detective; both are named in honor of the great

detective created by novelist Sir Arthur Conan Doyle—Sherlock Holmes

Sherm: Sherman (q.v.)

Sherman: a cigarette, especially a marijuana cigarette, dipped in pcp (PCP) solution; named for their resemblance to the Sherman brand of cigarettes

shesha: hashish plant grown in Israel by Arabs, who smoke it and sell it both local and to overseas customers

shield: detective's or policeman's badge

shifter: handler of stolen goods

Shih: Jewish intelligence service active in Israel

shillelagh: Irish cudgel or walking stick; also known as a blackthorn

Shin Bet: Israel's internal security department

shine: moonshine

shine one on: tell lies to another

shiner: black eye

shiruken: Chinese throwing star used as a weapon and generally outlawed

shit: heroin (*she sniffs shit*); worthless or untrue material or statement (*that's a lot of shit*); unworthy person (*he's just a shit*)

shit on a raft: (naval and prison slang) creamed beef or chicken on toast

shit on a shingle: (military and prison slang) creamed beef or chicken on toast

shiv: knife made in prison; switchblade knife

shiv artist: person adept at knifing and razor slashing

shizos: Soviet solitary-confinement cells

shoebox money: unaccounted and hence untaxed money such as that collected from bribes, under-the-table deals, etc.

shoofly: internal investigative officer within a law-enforcement agency who is charged with detecting and reporting any corrupt practices such as bribe-taking by members of the agency

shoot: to inject a drug; to shoot a bullet

shoot-'em-up: Western-type movie featuring gunplay

shooting gallery: alleyway, hallway, toilet or other quiet place where drugs are injected

shooting iron: gun

shootout: gunfight between criminals and law-enforcement officers

shoot the main line: inject drugs into the large vein in the arm at the crook of the elbow

shoot up: inject drugs

shoplift: steal from shops, stores or supermarkets

Shore Patrol Tank: nickname for a lockup in the downtown section of many large American ports frequented by the Navy, whose shore patrol assists the local police in maintaining order

shortchange: cheat; giving a customer less than the full amount of change

short count: less than the usual quantity

short eyes: child molester

short ringup: ringing up sales on a cash register for less than the full amount of a purchase and thereafter pocketing the difference; for example, the cash sale of a $10 shirt is rung up on the cash register as a $1 sale to cover the subsequent dip into the cash drawer for $9

short stretch: short prison sentence

short-term adult penal institutions of the U.S. Bureau of Prisons: these are located in Allenwood, Pa.; Eglin Air Force Base, Florida; El Paso, Texas; Florence, Ariz.; Montgomery, Ala.; and Safford, Ariz.

shot: a drink; an injection

shot down: under the influence of drugs

shot in the arm: injection in the arm; injection of approval or funding designed to raise morale; *a public works program would be a big shot in the arm for the economy and the nation*

shoulder holster: easily-concealed under-the-armpit handgun holster

shovel into bed: put to bed dead drunk

shrouding: design feature of hard-to-pry-open locks, padlocks, and shackle locks

shuck: deception; fraud; sham; trick

shuteyes: sex offender

shut mouth never fills black coffin: keep quiet and you'll live longer (underworld epigram attributed to Chicago gangsters of the 1920s and still in use)

shylock: exact exhorbitant interest rates exceeding the legal maximum; engage in loan sharking

shyster: pettifogging or unscrupulous attorney

Siakhal: Iranian terrorists who surfaced in the United States when the Shah of Iran visited Pres. Carter in November 1977

SIB: Special Investigation Branch (police)

Siberian salt mines: nickname for the many forced-labor camps and prisons scattered throughout Siberia and other places in the USSR

siba: long-stemmed Moroccan pipe for smoking kif

SIC: Security Intelligence Corps

SIC: Societé Internationale de Criminologie (French—International Society of Criminology)

Sicilian Vespers: a massacre; a mass murder; named after the mass murder of

the French in Sicily on Easter Sunday 1228 while the vesper bells tolled

sick: distressed for lack of drugs

sickie: mentally-sick person

SID: Security and Intelligence Department

Sidro Boys: San Diego-area gang based in San Ysidro, on the Mexican border at Tijuana, which preys on illegal aliens and others

SIFA: Seguridad e Inteligencia de las Fuerzas Armadas (Spanish—Security and Intelligence of the Armed Forces) Venezuelan agency

SIG: Swiss industrial company that manufactures firearms

sigint: signal intelligence

Sigmund Fraud: nickname for anyone practicing psychiatry without a license

Sig Saus: Sig Sauer (pistols)

silence bell: evening bell rung to advise prison inmates they must cease all talking and noisemaking

silencer: attachment for a gun that reduces the amount of sound it produces when fired

silent system: method of imprisonment characterized by enforced silence at all times and by night confinement in small solitary cells; inmates are allowed to congregate with other prisoners during meals and while at work; also known as the Auburn System

silver-plated Gillette: razor blade employed by cocaine users for cutting lumpy powder so it may be inhaled more effectively; also worn as a neck charm

sim: self-inflicted mutilation

SIM: Servicio Inteligencia Militar (Spanish)—Military Intelligence Service; Servizio Informazioni Militari (Italian)—Military Information Service

SIME: Security Intelligence Middle East (British)

sim excu: simulated execution

sim sui: simulated suicide

simple assult: unlawfully and intentionally threatening, attempting to inflict or inflicting less than serious bodily injury in the absence of a deadly weapon

Simsbury: early American prison built within an abandoned copper mine on the Farmington River 10 miles (16 kilometers) northwest of Hartford, Connecticut, where it was in use from 1773 to 1827; like so many penal institutions it was named for the place where it was located, the old town of Simsbury settled in 1660

sin: any offense against ethical standards or moral laws

sing: inform; tell something about another

singbird: informer; prisoner giving useful information to law-enforcement officers

Sing Sing: New York State Penitentiary at Ossining, N.Y.—*"up where the (jail)birds warble twice"*; known as the Ossining Correctional Facility

sin tax: tax imposed on cigarettes, gambling, liquor, racing, state-approved prostitution, etc.

SIO: Special Intelligence Office(r)

Sioux Falls: South Dakota Penitentiary at Sioux Falls

SIS: Secret Intelligence Service (British organization formerly called MI—Military Intelligence)

sister: female cooperating in sexual entrapment for purposes of blackmail or forcing the seduced male to reveal secrets to an enemy

sit in: mass action in which a group sits on the floor of an executive's office or a public area until their demands are met or they are arrested and evicted

sit in the hot seat: die by electrocution

sitter: part-time prostitute

sitting for company: prostitute's way of saying she is waiting for a client

SIU: Special Investigating Unit (New York Police Bureau of Narcotics)

siw: self-inflicted wound(s)

six bits: 75 cents

six gun: handgun holding six rounds of ammunition

Six plus One: Spanish prison sentence of six years plus one day for anyone found in possession of or using narcotics or psychedelic drugs; many young Americans are serving or have served the *seis y uno* sentence imposed in Spain

six shooter: revolver holding six rounds of ammunition

SIZ: Security Identification Zone

sizzle: die in the electric chair

sizzle seat: electric chair

sizzling: wanted by the police

sjambok: rhinoceros-hide whip popular in some parts of South Africa; sjamboks are also made from hippopotamus hide

SKA: Switchblade Knife Act

skachet: all-purpose utility tool combining the functions of a skinning knife, hammer, hatchet and hunting knife

skagtown: drug-addicted community

skee: opium

skel: skeleton; skeleton key (passkey)

skene: broad-bladed two-edged pointed knife used by ancient Irish warriors

skibby: Japanese prostitute

skid: heroin

skid row: rundown section of a city inhabited by drunkards living on the street

Skid Row Court: Branch 28 of Chicago's Municipal Court

skim: conceal income to avoid taxes; secretly divert unreported profits

skin: cigarette rolling paper used for making marijuana cigarettes

skin complaint: bullet hole; bullet wound

skin game: dishonest scheme; fraudulent practice

skinner: skinning knife

skinning: skin popping (q.v.)

skip out: abandon; desert; run off

Skowhegan: Women's Correctional Center at Skowhegan, Maine

skunk: a potent variety of marijuana surreptitiously cultivated in California state parks and adjacent rural areas

skyjack: seize control of an airplane by threatening its crew and passengers

sky marshal: armed guard, usually in plain clothes, assigned to prevent skyjacking

SLA: Symbionese Liberation Army (q.v.)

SLAB: Students for Labelling Alcoholic Beverages

slam: jail; prison

slammed: jailed

slammer: jail or lockup

slander: spoken defamation, as opposed to libel—written defamation

slasher: garment-district thief adept at slashing the canvas covers of dress racks and stealing as many dresses as he can carry off without being caught

SLATS: Safe, Loft, and Truck Squad (of a police department)

slave: drug addict

sleeper: potential espionage agent; sleeping pill

sleeping pill: sleep-inducing barbiturate or similar drug

sleep off: sleep until the major effects of alcohol or other drugs pass

sleepwalker: heroin addict

Sleepy Hollow: Trenton Prison in New Jersey

sleigh ride: effects induced by cocaine

sleuth: detective; investigator

slewfoot: law-enforcement officer

SLIC: Sober Live-In Center (for drug-troubled teenagers)

slingshot: a hand-held Y-shaped stick provided with an elastic strip connecting the prongs; used for shooting small missiles such as ball bearings, marbles and stones; sometimes called slugshot or slungshot; sometimes made of heavy-duty plastic or steel

slither: counterfeit coin

slot machine: gambling device popularly known as a one-armed bandit

slow time: the seemingly-slow time spent by prison inmates

SLP: San Luis Potosi (Mexican state); Socialist Labor Party

s-l stil: spring-loaded stiletto

slug: bullet; drink; blow with a fist

slum: (prison argot) stew—also called slum gullion

slumlord: slum landlord

slurb: sleazy suburban dweller; sleazy suburb; suburban slum

slush: bribe

slush fund: money set aside for bribing venal politicians and others whose influence is believed valuable

slush money: bribes

SMA: Safe Manufacturers Association

smack: (Yiddish) heroin

smacker: dollar; loud kiss

small arms: firearms designed for hand-held use by one person

SMART: Silent Majority Against Revolutionary Tactics

SMART: Stop Marketing Alcohol on Radio and Televison

smart money: funds invested or money wagered by those in the know, such as top financiers

smash-and-grab man: person adept at smashing showcases or store windows and grabbing their most attractive contents

smashed: intoxicated

smears: lsd (LSD)

smell a rat: suspect something is not honest; suspect there is treachery

smell of cordite: gunpowder odor

SMERSH: *Smert Shpionam* (Russian—Death to Spies) Soviet organization for murdering political enemies

SMF: South Moluccan Force (q.v.)

smg: submachine gun

SMILE: Something Meaningful in Local Effort (q.v.)

SMNA: Safe Manufacturers National Association

smogged: executed in a gas chamber

smoke: nickname for antifreezes, lacquer thinners, paint removers and solvents drunkards and vagrants drink when alcohol is unavailable; many of these substances are toxic and often deadly; also slang term for cheap alcoholic beverages

smoke a bowl: smoke a bowl of hashish or of opium

smoke out: bring into the open; make visible

smokescreen: camouflage; cover-up

smoky: nickname for a highway patrolman or patrolwoman or a highway patrol car

smoky bear: national park police; traffic police

smuggle: illegally export or import goods or persons to evade paying customs duties or meeting customs or immigration requirements

Smuggler's Gap: getaway and hideaway used by many outlaws operating in the Big Bend country of Texas near the Rio Grande and the Mexican border

S/N: Serial Number; Service Number

SN: Surete Nationale (French—National Security) law-enforcement agency

Snake Oil Sam: nickname for a fraud, a racketeer, a schemer or a swindler

snakesman: (British slang) small person adept at entering a locked room through a door transom or other narrow window; many a snakesman was a chimney sweep trained for this criminal specialty

snapblade: spring-loaded stiletto

snatch: kidnap

SNCC: Student Non-Violent Coordinating Committee

sneaky: easily hidden device for recording conversations or taking pictures

sneeze: arrest

sneeze gas: mob-control poison gas irritating the nose and throat; tear gas (chloroacetophenone) plus diphenylamine chloroarsine produces sneeze gas

SNIE: Special National Intelligence Estimate

sniff: inhale powdered cocaine or heroin

sniffer: device preventing automobile drivers from driving if any alcoholic scent is detected; its legal requirement on all automotive vehicles would probably decrease the accident rate and save thousands of lives

snitch: informant; person cooperating with law-enforcement officers by giving information about the activities of criminals

snoot full: intoxicated

snop: marijuana, especially a marijuana cigarette

snort: to inhale a powdered drug such as cocaine; a small drink

snow: cocaine crystals; heroin

snowbird: cocaine addict

snowcaine: cocaine

snowshoe: detective

snub out: extinguish (as a cigarette); kill; snuff out

- snuff spoon: tobacco snuff spoon, used also

as a cocaine sniffing spoon; also called a coke spoon

snug: small handgun

S/O: Station Officer

soaked: intoxicated

soaper: methaqualone capsule

Sobibor: extermination camp close to the main concentration camp of Lublin in Poland during the German occupation of World War II

Social Affairs Department: communist China's espionage agency

social associate: in the underworld this refers to anyone who interacts on a voluntary basis with a member of an organized crime group

social escort: euphemism for a prostitute

social evil: excusatory term for prostitution (also called a necessary evil)

social killing: imposition of the death penalty

social-political organized crime: a continuing course of criminal activity whose goal is to destroy, modify or weaken an existing political and/or socioeconomic structure

Society for Alleviating the Miseries of Public Prisons: Quaker group that planned the Eastern State Penitentiary in North Philadelphia, Pennsylvania, which operated for more than a century; prisoners were kept in individual cells and each cell had an adjacent exercise yard; prisoners were supposed to become reformed by reading the Bible and reflecting on their crimes

Society for the Prevention of Crime: founded in 1877; awards Charles Parkhurst Scholarship for studies in crime prevention

Society of Connoisseurs in Murder: a 60-member organization made up mostly of doctors, lawyers and writers who meet to discuss such arcane matters as murders committed in or near trucks or murders involving clergymen

sociology: science or study of the development, history and organization of human society

sociopath: person who is hostile to society and without conscience, remorse or any sense of right and wrong

sociopathic personality: antisocial character disorder marked by moral deviation and often total involvement in crime

sock it to me: tell me the simple, unvarnished truth; report it exactly as it happened or as it was

sod.: sodomite; sodomy

SOD: Special Operations Division (CIA)

Sodom and Gomorrah: biblical places near the Dead Sea noted for their depravity and vice; hence, any depraved and vicious place

sodomy: oral or (especially) anal intercourse with a person or an animal

SOE: Special Operations Executive (q.v.)

soft drug: psychologically but not physically addictive drug such as hashish, marijuana and related hemp plants and products

soft money: easily-made or illegally-made money; paper money, especially inflated currency with little or no backing

soft stuff: see **soft drug**

SOG: Seat of Government (q.v.)

sol: solitary confinement

Soledad: Correctional Training Facility of the State of California at Soledad (a Spanish word meaning "solitude")

solidified alcohol: see **Sterno**

solitary system: method of imprisonment designed to provide inmates with isolation from other criminals and prolonged opportunity for reflection and self-reform; many subjected to this system went insane; also known as the Pennsylvania System

Solothurn: Swiss-made submachine gun

Somers: Connecticut Correctional Institution at Somers, close to the Massachusetts border and north-northwest of Hartford

Something Meaningful In Local Effort: an Orange County, Calif. computer program aiding law enforcement

Sonderbehandlung: (German—Special Treatment)—coverup term meaning killing at Nazi concentration camps before or during World War II

Sonderkommando Umsiedlungslager: (German—Special Unit Resettlement Camp)—Hitlerian euphemism for a quick-extermination concentration camp such as Sobibor

songbird: informer

Sonkom: Sonderkommando (German—Special Commando)—Hitler organization working at concentration camp crematoria and gas chambers where some of the younger and stonger inmates were forced to assist their armed guards in killing weaker prisoners and removing their remains; a few set up underground resistance groups resolved to fight their Nazi oppressors; only a very few escaped and survived

Sons of Southern Lebanon: Arab terrorist group that claimed credit for a shootout at Orly Airport near Paris

sop.: sleeping-out pass

sope: methaqualone capsule

soporific: sleep-producing drug or hypnotic effect

Soria: Madrid, Spain's great prison

soup: nitroglycerine (used in blowing open safes and vaults or manufacturing explosive devices such as bombs)

SOUP: Students Opposed to Unfair Practices

souse: drunken person

soused: intoxicated (also "soused to the gills")

South Bay Regional Center: euphemistic name for San Diego, California's new jail, opened in Chula Vista in late 1981 to relieve overcrowding in the downtown jail

South Carolina School for Girls: at Columbia

South Eastern Region Correction Institute: Juneau, Alaska's facility for felons, misdemeanants and juvenile delinquents of both sexes

Southern Michigan: Southern Michigan Prison at Jackson

Southern Steel: San Antonio, Texas firm engaged exclusively in the manufacture of detention equipment

South Lansing: the South Lansing School for Girls at South Lansing, N.Y.

South Moluccan Force: anti-Indonesian underground terrorist organization active in the Netherlands, where they have some sympathizers

southpaw shot: left-handed shot

Southwark: London borough on the south bank of the Thames infamous for its Clink Prison reserved for heretics; the prison is gone but the expression—*in the clink*—remains

Soviet Kolyma: deadliest penal colony in the Soviet Union and part of what Solzhenitsyn called the *Gulag Archipelago*

sow.: (bystanders or others) sent on (their) way

sozzled: intoxicated

SP: Shore Patrol; Shore Police; Socialist Party

sp: soft-point bullet

spaced out: mentally disorganized, especially by drugs

Spandau: Berlin's great prison in the Tiergarten section of the metropolis; many political prisoners have been detained here since the time of the kaisers as well as the Nazis; for years Rudolph Hess has been its only prisoner

Spanish windlass: straitjacket

Spassk: Soviet prison camp in Kazakhstan

SPB: Special Branch Policeman (British term for a detective)

SPC: Service Processing Centers (these were formerly called Immigration and Naturalization Detention Centers); Society for the Prevention of Crime (organized in 1877); Suicide Prevention Center; Suicide Prevention Clinic

SPCA: Society for the Prevention of Cruelty to Animals

SPCC: Society for the Prevention of Cruelty to Children

SPCW: Society for the Prevention of Cruelty to Women

speakeasy: clandestine saloon of the sort popular during the Prohibition era in the United States (from 1919 until 1933)

Special Air Service: British anti-terrorist commando unit, reputed to be the world's toughest

Special Air Service Regiment: Britain's anti-terrorist commando force, capable of combating guerrillas and rescuing hostages held by terrorists

Special Branch: Ireland's secret service

Special Covert Operations for Resale: St. Louis police unit organized to pose as a fence for stolen goods and to arrest all who are involved in attempting to dispose of stolen goods in this fashion as well as to recover the stolen property

Special Guerrilla Units: anti-communist Indochinese underground forces sustained by the CIA, and formerly by the French, who called them *BG—Bataillons Guerriers*

Special Operations Executive: British espionage, sabotage and subversive organization active during World War II

special ops: special operations (assassinations and sabotage)

special psychiatric hospitals: Soviet name for prisons where dissenters are kept

Special Tactics Against Robberies: criminal arrest program using plainclothes and uniformed officers, afoot and in patrol cars, in target areas identified by the computerized integrated criminal apprehension program (ICAP); successful in reducing the robbery rate when assisted by citizens who report suspicious persons and circumstances to the police

Special Weapons and Tactics: team of law-enforcement officers trained to combat guerrillas and terrorists

specs: specifications

speed: (nickname for dexedrine sulfate) an amphetamine that stimulates the central nervous system and produces anxiety, irritability, rapid heartbeat and restlessness

speedalyzer: automatic radar-controlled automotive-vehicle speed analyzer (for detecting speeders)

speedball: cocaine-and-heroin injection

speed freak: amphetamine addict

speed link: device for holding and rapidly loading bullets into a revolver

SPI: Society of Professional Investigators; Southern Police Institute (Louisville, Ky.)

spid: sensor personnel intrusion device (q.v.)

spieler: (Cockney slang) gambling place

spike: hypodermic needle

spill: spill the beans—inform; report

spill one's guts: confess; tell all

Spitz: Spitzer pointed bullet

spiv: British term for a black marketeer, petty thief, pimp or racetrack tout

splash: amphetamine drug

splashover effect: upsurge in assault and robbery created in neighborhoods given over to pornography and prostitution, as in midtown Manhattan in New York City and in similar metropolitan centers

SPLC: Southern Poverty Law Center (see also **Team Defense)**

spliff: hashish or marijuana cigarette

splim: marijuana

split bit: prison sentence providing for both a maximum and a minimum sentence (see also **flat bit)**

splits: tranquilizers

splivins: amphetamine powder

sponging house: jail where debtors were kept for a day to give them a chance to settle their debts before being imprisoned or transported overseas

spook: undercover investigator

spoon: one-sixteenth ounce of heroin, measured out in a tiny spoon

spouse abuse: sociological jargon for wife-beating

SPP: Suicide Prevention Program

spring: to release from a jail or prison

Springfield: Medical Center for Federal Prisoners at Springfield, Mo.; Springfield rifle (45-caliber breech-loading single-shot rifle used in the U.S. Army from 1867 to 1893; also a 30-caliber bolt-action rifle used by the United States during World War I)

spring gun: booby-trapped weapon designed to fire at an intruder, such as a burglar or a rapist

spring-loaded stiletto: popular knife made in Spain and imitated in Japan

SPRS: State Police Radio System

sprung: released from jail on bail

SPSC: Scottish Prison Service College

SPT: Shore Patrol Tank (q.v.)

spy in the sky: police-manned helicopter

SQP: San Quentin Prison (California)

square(s): non-user(s) of drugs

square groupers: drug traffickers' nickname for oblong or square bales of marijuana; named for the big-bodied groupers (fish) characteristic of Caribbean countries where marijuana is produced (Colombia, Cuba, Haiti, Jamaica, etc.); the bales are shipped aboard freighters and tossed into the sea at remote places along the coasts of the United States, where they are retrieved by smaller craft or by shore gangs

square up: to start a new life along conventional law-abiding lines

squat: to be electrocuted

squawk box: citizens-band radio

squeal: to inform; to tell the police

squirrel cage: hospital for the criminally insane

squirrels: lsd (LSD)

SRC: Strict-Regime Camp (q.v.)

SRD: Society for the Right to Die

SRW: State Reformatory for Women (Dwight, Ill.)

SS: Schutzstaffel (German—Security Staff) Hitler's elite corps of black-shirted troops

SS: Secret Service; sharpshooter; Social Security; Steamship; Surveillance Station; sworn statement

ss: suspended sentence

SSA: Society for the Study of Addiction (to alcohol and other dangerous drugs)

SSCA: Southern States Correctional Association

SSCI: Social Sciences Citation Index (published by the Institute for Scientific Information)

SSD: Staatssicherheitsdienst (German—State Security Service) East German political police

SSDC: Social Science Documentation Center (UNESCO)

SSF: Seven-Step Foundation (halfway house for released convicts)

SSI: Social Sciences Index

SSS: Special Social Services (in New York City)

SSV: Society for the Suppression of Vice

stack: large amount of money

stacked deck: deck of cards arranged so that when they are dealt the dealer will have an unfair advantage over other players

stagger juice: rum

stake-out: disguised observation of an illegal activity such as transporting and selling contraband; law-enforcement officers frequently engaged in stake-outs so they can arrest criminals in the act of committing a crime

Stalin: Josef Vissarionovich, whose party name was Stalin (Russian—steel) and who, from the death of Lenin in 1924 to his own in 1953, was the personification of the ruthless dictator; he was responsible for the forced labor, torture and death of millions of people

standup: defiance to authority such as a policeman's or even a teacher's

Stanley: Hong Kong's maximum-security prison where many Europeans were interned during World War II

Stapleton: Staten Island Detention Pens at 67 Targee St. in the Stapleton section of Staten Island, N.Y.

Star: trade name of the Spanish firm of Echeverria, specializing in the manufacture of pistols, shotguns and submachine guns

STAR: Special Tactics and Response (police unit); Special Tactics Against Robberies (q.v.)

star-class: star-class prisoners (English penal classification) long-term prisoners who are first offenders

star dust: slang for cocaine

Starke: Florida State Penitentiary at Starke, between Gainesville and Jacksonville

star prisoner: inmate believed susceptible to rehabilitation and even some special treatment

START: Special Treatment and Rehabilitation Training (program for criminals)

stash: to conceal drugs, liquor or loot

state bear: state trooper

state chemist: euphemism for an executioner who is charged with poisoning convicts in a gas chamber

state electrician: euphemism for an executioner who is charged with electrocuting convicts in an electric chair

State Farm Spur: Illinois penal institution near Vandalia

state highway patrol: law-enforcement agency charged with the detection, investigation and prevention of motor vehicle offenses as well as the apprehension of traffic offenders

state police: state law-enforcement agency often charged with maintaining statewide police communications, aiding local police in criminal investigation, police training, guarding state property and highway patrol tasks

state prostitution: state-controlled prostitution, involving licensed brothels and frequent medical inspection of all prostitutes plus free clinics for the control and cure of venereal diseases among the general public

State Road: Philadelphia address of the Detention Center opened as Moyamensing Prison in 1835 but replaced in 1963 and also the House of Correction begun in 1874, reconstructed in 1928

state's evidence: evidence given for the state by an accused person testifying against alleged accomplices; under British law this is termed king's evidence or queen's evidence, depending on who is on the throne

Statesville: prison at Joliet, Ill. where Jeremy Bentham's unique panopticon design permits guards in a central tower to watch over every cell (see also **panopticon**)

State Youth Training Center: at St. Anthony, Idaho

station chief: intelligence officer heading espionage efforts conducted from an embassy

station worker: narcotic user who injects drugs into his or her arms or legs

status offender: juvenile delinquent possessing and using alcoholic beverages or other drugs, running away from home, violating curfew, leading an immoral life or proving incorrigible and in need of supervision

status offense: misdeed committed by a juvenile

statutory offense: euphemism or legalism for fornication with an underage female (in many states this means under 18)

statutory rape: sexual intercourse with a female who has consented in fact but is deemed, because of age, to be legally incapable of consent because she is underage

STB: Sandatahang Tanod ng Bayan (Filipino—People's Home Defense Guard) guerrilla group led by the Huks

std: sexually-transmitted disease

stealers: fingers

Sten: Sten gun, a British submachine gun popular during World War II; copied since then by gun makers in Argentina, Belgium, China, Germany and Indonesia

Stench: nickname for the British Sten gun

STEP: Short-Term Elective Program

sterile arms: death-dealing devices whose origin cannot be traced

sterile telephone: device whose location cannot be detected even by checking with the telephone company

Sterno: brand name of a solidified alcohol used for heating foods cooked over portable stoves; sometimes taken internally by alcoholic addicts, often with fatal consequences

Stevenson House: Milford, Delaware's facility for children from ages 8 to 18 held for court

Stevens School: at Hallowell, La., for female juvenile delinquents from 11 to 17

stew builder: jail or prison cook

stewbum: drunken bum

stewed to the gills: completely intoxicated

stick: marijuana cigarette

stick of gage: marijuana cigarette

stickup: armed robbery; robbery at the point of a gun

stickyfinger: shoplifter

stiff: corpse, especially a stiffened corpse; intoxicated person

stiff hunter: body-snatcher employed provide medical schools with fresh corpses needed for anatomical studies and dissections

stiffs: stiff shackles connected by a solid metal bar, making hand movements almost impossible

Stillwater: Minnesota State Prison at Stillwater, east-northeast of St. Paul

stimulant drugs: amphetamines such as biphetamine, dexamyl, dexedrine, dephetamine, preludin endurets and tenuate dospan

sting: swindle

stinking: stinking drunk; under the influence of alcohol or other drugs

stinko: drunk

stir: jail; prison

stir bug: insane prisoner whose insanity seems to be linked to long confinement or the thought of long confinement

stir crazy: driven insane by long confinement

S-341: code name of a deadly drug used to cause death by blocking nerve impulses, including those of the heart and lungs

STJ: Special Trial Judge

Stockholm syndrome: misplaced compassion expressed by victims of terrorists, who may tend to identify with their abductors, as in the case of a group that was held within a bank vault in Stockholm

stocks: obsolete device for punishing lawbreakers by locking their hands and feet within a wooden framework designed to make them the object of public ridicule, as stocks were usually placed in a public square for all to behold

Stoeger: midtown New York importer of handguns

stone blind: intoxicated

stoned: intoxicated; under the influence of alcohol or drugs (especially marijuana)

stone dump: prison

stoner: teenage gang member engaged in throwing stones to destroy property or injure others; person who is under the influence of alcohol or other drugs

stonewall: impede an investigation by beclouding issues and supplying misleading testimony

stool: inform

stoolie: informer; stool pigeon

stool pigeon: informer

stoppers: barbiturates

Stop the Robberies, Enjoy Safe Streets: program of the Detroit Police Department

storefront: empty storefront rented by a police department in high crime areas so that an officer assigned there can assist law-abiding citizens in crime prevention and the organization of neighborhood watch groups

Storyville: restricted area for prostitutes operating in a 38-block section of New Orleans adjacent to Canal Street and the French Quarter

stowaway: person who conceals herself or himself aboard an airplane or a ship and then remains aboard after it has taken off or left port in order to avoid paying for transportation

STP: a dangerous hallucinogenic drug whose initials also stand for an additive (scientifically-treated petroleum) used in automobiles

straight: not involved in crime or in such illicit activities as drug taking

straight jacket: alternate spelling for straitjacket

straitjacket: restraining jacket used to control violent or unruly persons

straight masseuse: girl or woman performing massages unaccompanied by sexual activity of any sort

strapped: strapped to the electric chair; penniless

Stratford: Stratford, Ontario's jail

streaking: full-speed or reckless driving; running about nude in public places

street dealer: middleman in the long chain of intermediaries between the importer(s) and the juggler(s) or pusher(s) of dangerous drugs such as heroin

Street Haven: Toronto, Ontario's center for the social rehabilitation of prostitutes and wayward girls

street man: undercover agent specializing in recruiting and training spies and running so-called dark-alley operations

street value: price of drugs charged by on-the-street pushers (sellers) to buyers

streetwalker: prostitute soliciting business on the streets

street whore: term usually applied to a poor alcoholic or narcotic addict engaged in prostitution

STRESS: Stop the Robberies, Enjoy Safe Streets (q.v.)

stretch: prison sentence

stretch hemp: execute by hanging

Strict-Regime Camp: one of 35 or more Soviet imprisonment centers in the Urals and other far-flung areas of the USSR

stripes: vertically-striped prison clothes of the type worn in many places as recently as the first half of the 20th century when expressions such as *you'll look good in stripes* was a grim reminder to behave or be imprisoned

Stromboli: one of the Lipari Islands off the north coast of Sicily in the Tyrrhenian Sea used since Roman times as a place to exile convicts and political prisoners

strong-arm: use psychological persuasion or physical force

strong-arm robbery: mugging, strangling, yoking; unlawful taking or attempted use of force without the use of a weapon

strung out: high on drugs

strych injec: strychnine injection (death brought about by an injection of strychnine)

strychnia: strichnine

strychnine: effective chemical agent in rat poison; causes convulsions followed by failure of the central nervous system, resulting in death; often used by humans as a murder weapon

stuff: hashish, marijuana and other drugs, such as cocaine and heroin

stun gun: barb-firing high-voltage gun used to subdue victims by electric shocks, which disrupt their nerves so they slump to the ground and jerk spasmodically; also called **Taser**

stunned: intoxicated

Sturm, Ruger: American manufacturer of handguns sold under the name of Ruger

Stutthof: main Nazi concentration camp in the north of Poland on the Bay of Gdansk called Sztutowo by the Poles

subcutaneous injection: injection made under the skin

submarine: plastic bag used to cover a prisoner's head to induce choking or fainting

subpoena: written order issued by a judicial officer requiring a specified person to appear in court at a specified time and to serve as a witness or bring material to a court for use as evidence

subs: substantial violations (FBI abbreviation)

sucked into: sucked into the crowd (arrest-avoidance technique used by many criminals and suspects who lose themselves in a crowd of people just as they are about to be detained by the police or other law-enforcement officers)

sucker: dupe; victim of a scheme

sucker clipper: confidence man; swindler

sucker pocket: hip pocket, which is easily picked by pickpockets

sucker slop: high-priced alcoholic drinks

Sugamo: Tokyo prison where Japanese war criminals were executed by occupying Allied forces at the end of World War II; prison site now occupied by a 60-story building

sugar cube: LSD-impregnated cube of sugar

sugaring: dropping lumps of sugar into the gasoline tank of an automotive vehicle (an act of sabotage that makes an overhaul of the disabled engine necessary)

suicide: self-destruction

suicide pact: agreement between two or more persons to commit suicide together or to kill the other(s) and then commit suicide

suicide season: Christmas-New Year holidays, when many lonesome persons feel alienated and take their own lives

suicide shrine: any place favored by suicides, such as a high bridge or the top floors of high buildings; the Golden Gate Bridge in San Francisco is one of many suicide shrines

suicidology: study of suicide and its prevention

sui rep: suicide report

suitcasing: handling bribes or so-called slush money on such a large scale that the money must be transported in suitcases

Sukhanovka: czarist monastery converted into a prison near Gorki, one of the most terrible according to Solzhenitsyn

Sullivan Law: New York State's gun-control statute, which has served as a model for many other states

suma: *Cannabis* plant grown and used in the Congo; also called "dacha"

summons: written order issued by a judicial officer requiring a person accused of a criminal charge to appear in court and answer the charge(s)

supreme penalty: death

surrept: surreptitious(ly)

surreptitious entry: breaking and entering with a court order, given to aid in the collection of evidence

surrogate warfare: conflict carried on by world-wide underground groups such as those claiming credit for many bombings, kidnappings, and other forms of terror

survivor syndrome: many victims of criminal attacks who live to tell the tale describe such aftereffects as chronic anxiety, depression, flattened emotions, guilt and recurring nightmares

sus: suspect(ed); suspected person

susp: suspect; person suspected

suspect: person thought by a criminal-justice agency to be the one who may have committed a criminal offense but who may or may not have been arrested or charged

suspended sentence: court decision not to impose a sentence that has been pronounced upon a convicted person

suspicion: belief that a person has committed a criminal offense based on facts and circumstances that are insufficient to constitute probable cause

sv: security violator

sv: sotto voce (Italian—in an undertone; in a whisper)

s.v.m.: spiritus vini methylatus (Latin—methyl alcohol) commercial paint solvent, usually deadly to those who drink it after mistaking it for ethyl alcohol

S & W bracelets: Smith and Wesson handcuffs

swag: stolen goods

swallows: see **vamps**

SWAT: Special Weapons and Tactics (q.v.)

swazzled: intoxicated

swbld: switchblade (knife or stiletto)

sweat: hard labor

Sweeney: The Sweeney—Cockney nickname for the flying squad of the London Metropolitan Police, honoring its founder, an Irishman named John Sweeney

sweet lucy: marijuana

sweet morpheus: morphone

Swift Trail: Swift Trail Federal Prison Camp at the foot of Mount Graham in the Pinaleno Mountains near Safford, Ariz., northeast of Tucson

swindle: to cheat or defraud another person or persons or obtain property by false pretenses

swindle sheet: expense account

swing: die by hanging

swing club: two-handed policeman's club, sometimes nicknamed a prosecutor

swinger: narcotics dealer who sells unadulterated drugs

swingman: drug pusher

swipe: shoplift; steal

Swiss bank account: account whose number is known only by the bank and the depositor; often used as a hideaway for funds collected illicitly or for income tax-evasion purposes

switch: massage wherein the masseuse massages the customer and then in turn is massaged by the customer; switchblade knife

switchblade: spring-release pocketknife whose long single blade springs out of its handle the moment its release button or catch is depressed; many deadly knifings involve the use of switchblades

switchman: hijacker who drives his truck through a business or shipping district and, when finding a driver away from another truck, quickly transfers the cargo to his truck and gets away before the loss is discovered

swivels: swivel non-locking handcuffs

SWP: Socialist Workers Party (Trotskyite activists)

Sybil: Sybil Brand Institute (Los Angeles county jail for women)

Sykes-Fairbairn: commando's killing knife designed by E.A. Sykes and W.E. Fairbairn of British commando and Shanghai police fame, respectively

SYLP: Support Your Local Police (acronymic message displayed on bumper stickers supplied by law-and-order groups)

Symbionese Liberation Army: underground revolutionary cult whose membership included Patricia (Patty) Hearst, alias Tania

syndicate: a combination of gangsters such as the Mafia; in France, Italy, Latin America, Portugal and Spain the term "syndicate" also refers to a radical labor organization

synesthesia: subjective sensation of another sense than the one being stimulated—sensation of being able to hear colors, see music or smell words, e.g.

synthetic narcotics or opiates: Demerol (meperidine), Dolophine (methadone), Emperin compound with codeine, Fiorinal with codeine, Leritine (anileridine), Meperidine (penthidine) and Percodan are some

synthetics: synthetic narcotics

systemic analgesics: pain killers affecting the central nervous system; (see also **narcotic antagonist** and **synthetic narcotics or opiates**)

T

t (T): tea (marijuana)

T-4: *Tiergarten 4* (German—Zoological Park 4)—Berlin address of medical facility imposed by the Nazis, who used this cover address for the facility and its director—Doctor Josef Mengele

tab: bill; tabulation; drug-filled capsule or tablet

TAB: Totalizator Agency Board (q.v.)

Tac: Tactical Patrol Force officer

taco bender: (slang) Mexican-American; Mexican

TACT: Truth About Civil Turmoil

tactical grenade: riot-control grenade

tactical intelligence: intelligence immediately useful to the enforcement forces of any agency

tactical police: special unit equipped and trained to control crowds, demonstrations, rioting mobs and violent individuals engaged in attempted getaways or shootouts

tactical vandalism: damage done to advance some end other than the acquisition of money or property; tactical vandals may, for example, commit destructive acts so their superiors will discharge them from military duty or work

tactical vest: bullet-proof vest

TADARF: Toronto Alcoholism and Drug Addiction Research Foundation (Canada)

Tafuna: Territorial Correctional Facility at Tafuna, near Pago Pago on the island of Tutuila in American Samoa

tag: license, especially a motor vehicle license plate

tagawi: try and get away with it

take: the proceeds of a burglary, a con game, a sale of worthless bonds or stocks, etc.; bribes, favors, gifts, etc., exchanged for favors, inside information, votes, etc.

take a main: inject into a vein

take a powder: take a drug in powdered form; take leave suddenly; *if the police come we'll have to take a powder*

take French leave: depart secretly

taken off: robbed

take off: become intoxicated by drugs; inject drugs; mug

takeoff artist: drug addict who sustains her or his habit by stealing from other addicts

take the cure: stop drinking alcoholic beverages; stop smoking cigarettes; stop taking drugs

take the electric cure: die by electrocution

take the pipe: commit suicide

take the rap: accept punishment for a crime even if it was committed by someone else

take the stand: sit in the witness box and be subjected to interrogation

take the weight: refuse to inform; take the blame

take to the tall timbers: go into hiding

take to the (tall) tules: evade arrest; hide out, as in the bamboo-like tall tule grass that borders waterways in the American Southwest

talcum powder: hghly adulterated narcotic; simulated narcotic

Talladega: Federal Correctional Institution in Talladega, Ala., east of Birmingham

Tallahassee: Federal Correctional Institution at Tallahassee, Fla.

Tampico: prison in Tampico, a Mexican seaport on the Gulf of Mexico

tank: prison cell

tanked: intoxicated

tank up: get drunk

tap code: code created by prisoners who are not allowed to talk to one another but manage to communicate by tapping messages or signals on cell bars or plumbing pipes

tapioca'd: (gambling slang) busted; ruined

tar: gum opium

target study: background study made of any potential secret agent or suspect

Tartu: university city in east-central Estonia where Nazis killed more than 12,000 men, women, and children in a concentration camp they built here; Dorpat was the original name of Tartu

TASC: Treatment Alternatives to Street Crime (committed by alcoholics and drug addicts)

Taser: trade name of an electronically-activated stunning device used by law-enforcement officers in subduing violent offenders; acronym for "Thomas A. Swift Electric Rifle," after Tom Swift of fictional fame

Task Force on Alcoholism: sponsored by the Federation of Jewish Philanthropies in New York

taste: small quantity of a drug such as heroin

tattoo: tattoo with a number; this practice was used by the Nazis to identify their victims, and also by Latin American criminal syndicates to identify prostitutes in their service

tax evasion: illegal attempt by taxpayers to escape paying taxes

taxi steerer: taxicab driver who will guide patrons to prostitutes

tax stamp: for $500 a year bookmakers, embezzlers, heroin dealers, madams, pimps and other lawbreakers can buy a tax stamp from the Internal Revenue Service that assures confidentiality regarding their names and occupations; the oft-quoted rationale of the IRS, *it doesn't pay to start making moral judgments*, sounds like "get the money, no matter how"; many law-abiding taxpayers wonder if hindering law-enforcement agencies and making moral judgments are truly compatible

Taycheedah: the Wisconsin Home for Women at Taycheedah

TBI: Tennessee Bureau of Investigation

T-bowl: toilet bowl; *they flushed the evidence down the T-bowl*

tcc: topical cocaine compound

TCJC: Texas Criminal Justice Council

TDC: Texas Department of Corrections

TDS: Tennessee Department of Safety

tea: marijuana

tea'd up: under the influence of marijuana

tea head: habitual user of marijuana

Team Defense: Atlanta-based group of attorneys, sponsored by the Southern Poverty Law Center, who are dedicated to the elimination of the death penalty; techniques include appealing to logic rather than compassion, prolonging trials so jurors become better acquainted with the defendants, making many legal motions so that later an appeal may be used as another delaying tactic and using social scientists to assist in evaluating the composition of jury pools and challenging prospective jurors

Teapot Dome: scandal exposed by a Senate investigating committee in 1922 and 1923, when it was discovered that U.S. naval oil reserves had been leased to private interests that had bribed two of Pres. Harding's cabinet members; a Supreme Court decision was required to restore the oil reserves to the U.S. Navy

tear gas: chloroacetophenone, an irritant gas; used to quell riots, as it causes temporary blindness and severe irritation of the mucous membranes and the skin

tear-gas baton: combined billy club and tear-gas cartridge

tear-gas billy: 20-gauge blast-type combined hand billy and tear-gas gun

tear-gas gun: 1 1/2-inch (37mm) single-shell firearm, sometimes loaded with a parachute-suspended 30,000-candlepower flare; also called a riot gun

tecata: heroin

technical services: specialized law-enforcement agency or police department functions such as communication, identification, laboratory activities, record-keeping, temporary detention, etc.

tecpert: technical expert; some criminals as well as sleuths define this as a person skilled in opening letters and microfilming their contents, picking locks, tapping telephones and planning clandestine or criminal operations such as break-ins and burglaries

TECS: Treasury Enforcement Communications System (q.v.)

Tecumseh: Girls' Town correctional facility for misdemeanants at Tecumseh, Okla.

teddy boy: male juvenile delinquent in the British Isles, especially England

teddy girl: female juvenile delinquent often found with gangs of teddy boys

teed up: intoxicated

teenyhooker: pubescent prostitute

teeto: teetotaler

teetotaler: person who abstains totally from alcoholic drinks of any kind

Tehachapi: California Correctional Institution at Tehachapi in the Tehachapi Mountains, close to the western edge of the Mojave Desert

telephone boiler room: bank of telephones used by swindlers adept at talking people out of their money in return for worthless bonds, real estate or stock; also known as a bucket shop

telephone-pole design: seen from above this type of prison design, first introduced at Lewisburg, Pennsylvania in 1932, resembles a telephone pole with its crossarms; cellblocks and workshops are at right angles to a central corridor; this design provides flexibility in layout and coordination of elements for control and supervision of the inmates; the long connecting corridor (the telephone pole) extends from the administrative building past dining rooms and shops, and is bisected by cellblocks

telephone transceiver: illegal device, also called a black box or a blue box, for bypassing the telephone company's switching system so that calls can be made without the knowledge of the telephone company

Temposil: see **Antabuse**

ten: 10-milligram tablet of amphetamine

ten-cent pistol: poison-filled bag of heroin

tenner: $10

10-point man: lawyer specializing in settling personal-injury suits by bribing insurance-claim adjusters; such lawyers usually get paid 10 percent of the total settlement, giving half to the claim adjuster and retaining half for themselves

10-spot: $10 bill

Tepic: prison in Tepic, capital of the Mexican state of Nayarit, on the Pacific coast south of Mazatlan

Tepito: open-air black market in the middle of Mexico City often described as a smuggler's supermarket, dealing in everything from perfume to tape recorders, from TV sets to imported watches; local police officers crack down on vendors who fail to bribe them to look the other way during routine inspections

Terlingua: jail in Terlingua, a Mexican mining town close to the Rio Grande across the border from the Big Bend section of Texas

termcert: terminal certificate (death certificate)

terminal communication: death certificate; death notice; death order of execution; death warrant

Terminal Island: Federal Correctional Institution, an all-male, medium-security facility, at Terminal Island, Calif.

terminate with extreme prejudice: assassinate; kill

terpin hydrate: cough syrup containing codeine

terr: terrorist

Terre Haute: U.S. Penitentiary at Terre Haute, Ind.

Territorial: Territorial Prison

terrorism: violence or intimidation involving the threat of violence, used against the public or any section of the public and designed to further political or sectarian ends

terrorist hot line: see **red telephone**

Terrorist International: movement of Arabic, Japanese, Latin American, West German and other terrorists, including the IRA, to insure coordinated action and

funding and the spread of terrorist technology

terrorize: coerce through intimidation, including cruelty, threats and acts of violence

tetrahydrocannabinol: psychotoxic substance found in hashish and marijuana as well as all plants of the genus *Cannabis*

Texarkana: Federal Correctional Institution at Texarkana, Texas

Texas Rangers: originally a mounted fighting force, organized in 1835 during the Texas Revolution; later charged with defending the frontier as well as maintaining law and order in their vast territory; merged with the state highway patrol in 1935

Texas tea: Texas-grown marijuana

TF: Travail Forcé (French—penal servitude)

TFA: Task Force on Alcoholism (q.v.)

tfis: theft from an interstate shipment

Thai-sticks: hashish cigarettes made in Thailand; many times more potent than marijuana

thanatomania: mad urge to kill or to commit suicide

thanatophobia: abnormal fear of death

thc (THC): tetrahydrocannabinol (q.v.), the active constituent of marijuana

theater of terror: any public execution or punishment such as flogging

theft: burglary, extortion, hijacking, robbery and other offenses sharing the element of larceny

theft of opportunity: easy-to-steal-and-carry item; examples are cameras and lenses, clothing, jewelry, pet dogs and cats, portable radio and TV sets, silverware, small objects of art, etc.

The Pas: Correctional Institution for Women at The Pas, Manitoba

therapeutic correctional community: prison

therapeutic effect: amount of a drug and/or treatment needed to heal someone

The Walls: Huntsville Unit in Texas state prison at Huntsville

thief-taker: English term originally used to describe a receiver of stolen goods (a person who would buy things delivered by thieves); later used to describe a person empowered to track down and arrest thieves and fugitives from justice; i.e., a detective

Thieves' Palace: nickname for the Surrey Prison

third arm of the Kremlin: Soviet secret police (OGPU, GPU, MVD, KGB, etc.)

third degree: use of intensive questioning

by the police to extract a confession; in past times torture was used as well as cross-examination

third-generation money: electronically controlled funds

Third Street: New Jersey State Prison in Trenton on Third St. between Cass and Federal—square block of red stone walls studded with guard towers

13-m: marijuana (as "m" is the 13th letter of the alphabet)

Thomastown: Maine State Prison at Thomastown

Thompson: a submachine gun, also called a tommy gun, named for its inventor—Col. John Taliaferro Thompson, U.S. Army

Thorn: Nazi concentration camp in Poland, where it was known as Torun, on the east bank of the Vistula River

thou: thousand: *"put me down for a thou,"* he muttered when he heard his pal was in jail and needed bail

threat dog: dog trained to bark and snarl at intruders

three Cs: Central Criminal Court

Three Cs: U.S. federal prison system logotype standing for "Care, Custody, and Correction"

three deuces jammed: three concurrent two-year sentences

three deuces running wild: three consecutive two-year sentences

three sheets to the wind: intoxicated and reeling, like a sailing vessel with three loose sails

three-time loser: person returning to prison for the third time

throttle: to choke or strangle

throw a brick: commit a crime

throw a brody: pretend to be sick so a doctor will prescribe some drug the malingerer can use or sell to an addict

throw a game: purposely lose in order to win bets made on the outcome of a game

throw a race: purposely lose a race so bets placed on its outcome will prove profitable

throw a show at: to kick

throw a walleyed fit: get excited; simulate madness and raving

throwaway: juvenile delinquent or young adult criminal living in the same city or place as his or her parents but out of their care or control

throw a wingding: feign withdrawal symptoms so as to convince a doctor to prescribe some narcotic

throw rocks: commit a crime

throw the book at: exact the maximum penalty

throw the hooks: throw the hooks into a person; cheat

thruster: amphetamine tablet

thug: criminal or vicious mischief-maker; after the Thugs, an ancient Indian religious sect of robbers and murderers, also known as Phansigers (muggers or stranglers); between 1829 and 1848 the British suppressed them by means of mass arrests and speedy executions; Thugs went about in bands, disguised as merchants or religious mendicants

thumb: large marijuana cigarette

thumbprint: individual's distinctive mark; *he left his thumbprint on just about everything he ever did—he was an original*

thumbs: thumbcuffs, a device for controlling and holding unruly prisoners while being transported from the place of arrest to the jail; a smaller version of handcuffs

thump: to fight

TI: Terrorist International (q.v.)

TI: Terminal Island (Federal Correctional Institution at Terminal Island, California in Los Angeles harbor)

ticker: heart; ticker-tape machine giving news and stock-market quotations

ticket-of-leave: permit allowing a convict to leave prison before the expiration of his or her sentence and to work under certain restrictions; parole certificate

ticket-of-leave man: parolee

ticket-of-leaver: parolee

tickle: (British underworld term) steal

tie: belt, elastic band or tourniquet used to make a vein stand out so that drugs can be injected into it; sometimes addicts actually use a necktie; hence the origin of this term

tie on a bag: get drunk; go on a spree

tie one on: get drunk; *let's tie one on*

tiger cage: underground prison cell

tiger piss: homemade, low-grade, strong-smelling whiskey

tiger sweat: cheap hard liquor, such as low-grade gin, rum or whiskey

tight: close; intoxicated

tight money: money that is hard to beg, borrow or steal; *tight money is almost like no money*

Tijuana: Mexico's most notorious jail, on downtown Tijuana's Avenue of the Constitution

Tijuana Hilton: nickname of San Diego's multistory Metropolitan Correctional Center, tall enough to afford its many inmates a restricted view of across-the-border Tijuana in Mexico and luxurious enough to remind them of the great Hilton chain of high-class hotels

Tijuana 12s: cigarettes containing marijuana and regular smoking tobacco

till tapping: stealing from the cash register or till

time off: time off for good behavior (while imprisoned)

time out: time out of sight (in a solitary-confinement cell)

timer: safe or vault with a time lock

time served: total time spent in confinement before and after sentencing

Times Square: center of New York City's entertainment industry, spilling over into many side streets off Broadway above 42nd St.; the area is replete with adults-only bookstores and pornographic movie houses

tinhorn: a dubious character, not to be trusted

tin throne: metallic toilet; prison-cell toilet; slop bucket

tiny terr: tiny terrorist (child used by terrorists to run errands or spot enemies)

tip: to leave (jail); essential information provided by a tipster or tipsters concerning the identity of persons to be killed or mugged, the location of anything to be stolen or the outcome of any sporting event

TIP: Terrorist Information Project (of OC-5—q.v.)

tippler: alcoholic

Tipton: State Correctional Center for Women at Tipton, Mo.

tire burner: rapid pursuit of one vehicle by another; usually involves the pursuit of an escaping criminal or criminals by law-enforcement forces

ti-slash: tire slashing (see also **icepick**)

TLA: Trial Lawyers' Association

Tlaxcala: prison in Tlaxcala, capital of the Mexican state of the same name, just east of Mexico City

TM: *Therapia Magna* (Latin—Great Therapy)—unofficial euphemism invented by Nazi doctors in concentration camps where they participated in mass killings

T-man: special agent of the U.S. Treasury Department or the Internal Revenue Service (IRS)

t-n-t: trans-national terrorism; transnational terrorist

tnt (TNT): trinitrotoluene (q.v.)

toadstabber: dagger or knife

toil factory: prison workshop

Tokarev: 7.62mm Soviet automatic pistol named for its designer, who used the American Browning as his model; it will accept 7.63mm cartridges made for the Mauser

toke: to puff, or a puff on, a hashish or marijuana cigarette

toke pipe: short-stemmed pipe used by marijuana smokers

Toledo: high-grade dagger, knife or sword of the type originally made in Toledo, Spain

tolerance: immunity to a drug built up by the body; increasing amounts must consequently be taken to produce the same effect

Toluca: prison in Toluca, capital of the Mexican state of Mexico, southwest of Mexico City

Tom: $2 bill bearing Thomas Jefferson's portrait; often used by short-change artists as a substitute for a $20 bill

tomahawk: stone hatchet or weapon of American Indian design; still used in some remote places

Tombs: old New York City prison in downtown Manhattan adjacent to the Criminal Court Building on the Lower East Side

tommy gun: submachine gun (see **Thompson**)

tonk: honky tonk; illegal alien; Mexican alien

Toodyay: an old jail in Western Australia that is now an historical museum

tool man: safe-cracking specialist

tools: drug-injecting equipment

Topaz: relocation center for Japanese-Americans interned in central Utah following the attack on Pearl Harbor

Tootsie Roll: see **black tar**

TOPCOPS: The Ottawa Police Computerized On-line Processing System

Topenish: abandoned Japanese-American relocation center near Yakima, Washington, where an investigation made by the American Friends Service Committee forced the government to abandon the place even though nearly $50,000 had been spent on its rehabilitation; its buildings were reported to have been even worse than the horse stalls at Santa Anita or Tanforan or the pigpens at Puyallup, where other so-called suspicious enemy aliens of Japanese-American ancestry had been interned

topi: peyote

toponym: place-name; usually convicts use toponyms when telling where they have been incarcerated—e.g., "Atlanta" for the federal penitentiary in Atlanta, Ga., etc.

Top 10: the FBI's list of the 10 most-wanted fugitives from justice

torch: an arsonist; a firebug; a handgun; to burn; to set afire

torchman: arsonist; expert in setting fires

torch off: set fire to a building, a field, a person or a vehicle

torn up: intoxicated by drugs

torpedo: professional murderer

Tortilla Curtain: nickname for the poorly fenced Mexican Border extending from El Paso, Texas and San Diego, California; sometimes extended from Brownsville to El Paso along the Rio Grande between Texas and Mexico

torture chamber: jail or prison where drugs are not to be had at any price

TOSCA: Toxic Substances Control Act

toss: search for concealed weapons, drugs or stolen property

Totalizator Agency Board: Australian betting system designed to channel money away from off-track bookmakers and grafters such as venal policemen and politicians

total segregation: solitary confinement

Tower of London: originally a fortified palace, then a prison, and today an arsenal museum housing the British crown jewels as well as ancient armor and many weapons; also called the Bloody Tower, as many were executed within its walls

tox: toxemia; toxic; toxicant; toxicologist; toxicology

toxemia: blood poisoning

toxic: poisonous

toxic dosage: amount of a drug needed to produce symptoms of poisoning (see also **abusive dosage, lethal dosage, maximal dosage** and **minimal dosage**)

toxicologist: scientist dealing with poisons and their effects

toxicology: science and study of poisons and their effects as well as their antidotes and their detection

toxicomania: drug dependency

toxicophobia: abnormal dread of being poisoned

toxin: poison

toye: small tin of opium

TPBA: Transit Patrolmen's Benevolent Association

TPF: Tactical Patrol Force (police)

tr: tracer (bullet)

TRACIS: Traffic Records and Criminal Justice Information System (q.v.)

track: injection-needle scar

tracked up: covered with hypodermic-needle scars

trade: the trade—customers of prostitutes and of sex-related businesses

tradecraft: espionage and undercover techniques

traffic in damnation: drug peddling

traffic in drugs: buy or sell drugs

traffic in flesh: buy or sell the services of prostitutes; buy and/or sell slaves (still done in some Arab countries)

Traffic Records and Criminal Justice Information System: Iowa's computerized file kept by its law-enforcement people

tragic magic: heroin

train arrived: (prisoners' jargon) means that drugs have just arrived in the prison

training school: juvenile correctional institution

Training School for Girls: Trenton, New Jersey's correctional facility for female juvenile delinquents from eight to 17 years of age

Traitors' Gate: Thames River waterside gateway to the Tower of London, where prisoners were rowed in before being executed or serving long prison terms

tramp: a vagrant who rarely works

tramp college: old nickname for an American county jail

Trani: Italian prison near Bari on the Adriatic and the scene of some deadly prison breaks

trank: tranquilizer

tranquilizer: psychotropic drug used to counteract high blood pressure as well as emotional anxiety and tension; sometimes taken by drug addicts at the onset of withdrawal symptoms; popular brands obtained by a physician's prescription include Atarax, Compazine, Harmonyl, Librium, Mellaril, Serpasil (reserpine), Sparine, Stelazine, Thorazine (chlorpromazine) and Valium

tranquilizing fluid: wine (technically a source of energy as well as a tranquilizing agent when used in moderation)

transceiver: see **black box, blue box** and **telephone transceiver**

transnational terrorism: movement of Arabic, Japanese, Latin American, West German and other terrorist factions, united to insure coordinated action, funding and the spread of terrorist technology needed to defeat nations hostile and unsympathetic to these terrorists; transnational terrorists are not associated with any government, although they may be supported by sympathetic countries

transportation: movement of prisoners to an overseas penal colony, as was the

French custom until the 1950s; today the practice is on the decline except in a few countries such as Brazil, Cuba, Ecuador, Italy, Mexico and the USSR; most of these use nearby islands as penal settlements

tranx: tranquilizer(s)

trap: entrapment of criminals; entrapment of clients by prostitutes; hiding place for contraband, stolen goods or weapons; jail or prison

trap gun: loaded firearm connected to a string or wire; when the string or wire is tripped, the gun discharges

trapper: expert at extracting important letters from sealed envelopes and replacing them without leaving a trace

trash: vandalize; *they trashed all the cars in the parking lot*

trauma: emotional shock resulting from mental stress or physical injury; a blow; an injury

trauma room: hospital emergency ward

Trautenau: forced-labor subcamp in western Czechoslovakia where it served the Nazis during World War II

travel agent: drug pusher

treason: the crime of aiding and comforting an enemy of one's country, or attempting to overthrow the government to which one owes allegiance, or revealing restricted information to the enemies of one's government or nation or injuring or killing one or more of its executives

Treasure Island: first brig for women sailors, opened in February 1981 at the U.S. Navy base at Treasure Island in San Francisco Bay, under the Oakland Bridge

Treasury Enforcement Communications System: criminal data system of the U.S. Treasury Department's law-enforcement offices

Treblinka: Nazi gas-chamber-equipped concentration camp in Poland where during World War II the Jews revolted; 600 escaped but only 40 survived to tell the tale of some 700,000 other victims

trembler: prisoner who is afraid of other prisoners

trench knife: knife used in World War I in hand-to-hand combat

Trenton: New Jersey State Prison outside Trenton; Training School for (delinquent) Girls at Trenton, N.J.

trey: $3 bag of heroin

trial: examination of issues of fact and law in a case or controversy

trial court: trial without a jury wherein the judicial officer determines all issues of fact and law

trick room: room used for prostitution

trig: trigger; triggerman

trig: trigamist; trigamy

trigger: plan a criminal action such as a hold up or a murder; triggerman

trigger happy: ready to shoot without warning

triggerman: assassin; killer

trill: prostitute

trinitrotoluene: a dangerous and powerful explosive

trip: drug-induced emotional experience

Triple A: Apostolic Anti-Communist Alliance (Spanish ultra-rightist terrorists)

tripping out: high on psychedelics

TROA: The Retired Officers Association

trouble: person likely to cause trouble

Trostyanets: site of a Nazi concentration camp near Minsk in Byelorussia where thousands of victims of Hitler's onslaught are buried in mass graves

trouble: person likely to cause trouble

Trubetskoi: bastion of the Peter and Paul Fortress, used as a prison in Leningrad

truck drivers: amphetamines

true crimes: aggravated assault, burglary, murder, rape, robbery and grand theft, according to some penologists who insist they should be the main targets of any law-and-order program

Truk: prison camp erected by the Japanese during World War II in the Caroline Islands of the western Pacific Ocean

trull: low-class prostitute

trunch: truncheon

truncheon: policeman's club or watchman's nightstick

Truro: the Nova Scotia School for Girls at Truro

trusty: trustworthy convict who is allowed special privileges

truth serum: hyoscine, scopolamine and other drugs (now usually sodium amytal) administered hypodermically; the subject becomes mildly delirious and responds truthfully to questions; its use has broght about self-incrimination and the implication of others connected with crimes

TRY: Teens for Retarded Youth (juvenile correctional program)

TSD: Technical Services Division (CIA)

TTSU: Taxi-Truck Surveillance Unit (New York City Police Department)

tub-a-puke: tub of vomit (overweight alcoholic)

Tucker: Arkansas Intermediate Reformatory at Tucker

Tudeh: Iran's communist party

TUG: The Urban Guerrilla (publication of

the New World Liberation Front, active on the West Coast)

Tule Lake: waterless relocation and segregation center near the Oregon border of northern California where many Japanese-Americans were interned after Pearl Harbor

Tullahoma: Tennessee State Vocational School for Girls at Tullahoma

tunnel: to hide; a hiding place

Tuol Sleng: Cambodian interrogation center where more than 20,000 were executed by the Khmer Rouge

Tupamaros: Uruguayan terrorists also known as the MLN (*Movimiento de Liberacion Nacional*, or National Liberation Movement); named for Tupac Amaru, an Inca chief who was beheaded by the Spaniards and known as the Last of the Incas until a descendant, known as Jose Gabriel Condorcanqui, took his name while leading Peruvian revolutionaries in the late 1700s; Condorcanqui was also captured and killed by the Spaniards

turf: territory; *the Young Lords fought five other gangs to extend their turf*

Turk dope: Turkish-produced heroin made from Turkish-grown opium

turkey: drug substitute; imitation drug sold by pushers to unsophisticated users; no drugs or narcotics present; Japanese neon sign in the shape of a turkey indicating that a Turkish bath, complete with initimate sexual massage, is available; simple-minded or stupid person

turkey gun: combined .222-caliber rifle and 12-gauge shotgun made in Finland by Tikkakoski and sold in the United States by Ithaca

turkey trots: hypodermic needle marks and scars

turkish massage: brothel specialty and nickname of Tokyo's Yoshiwara district

Turk lab: Turkish laboratory producing heroin

turn: sell narcotics

turn a new leaf: reform, start anew

turnback: procedure whereby Mexican drug smugglers apprehended at the U.S. border are given a choice by American narcotics agents of becoming informants or of being turned back to authorities in Mexico, who often torture them while seeking information about other smugglers

turned on: taking drugs; very aware; very responsive

turn a trick: engage in an act of prostitution

turnkey: anyone entrusted with the keys to a prison (usually a correction officer, jailer or warden; sometimes a trusty)

turn on: to introduce someone to drugs; to give someone heroin

turn tail: run away

Turrell: Turrell Residential Group Center at Farmingdale, N.J.

turtle: armored car or truck of the type used to transport money from place to place

Tuxtla Gutierrez: prison in Tuxtla Gutierrez, capital city of Chiapas, Mexico, near the border with Guatemala

TVPA: Thames Valley Police Authority

TV rental: TV rental parlor (law-evasion device used by massage-parlor operators dodging California's Red Light Abatement Act)

tweak: (motorcycle-gang slang) inject heroin

Tweed Ring: New York grafters led by Boss (William Marcy) Tweed, who in the 1860s and early 1870s allegedly robbed city and state treasuries of more than $200 million; their downfall was initiated by a series of cartoons by Thomas Nast, printed in *Harper's Weekly* from 1869 through 1871

Twin Maples Farm: British Columbia's facility for treating women inmates with alcoholic problems

twist: marijuana

twisted: under the influence of alcohol or drugs; suffering a hangover or withdrawal symptoms

twister: key

twist out: cooperate with law-enforcement officers in detecting crime and apprehending criminals

two-faced: deceitful; disloyal

two-O: $20

two-spot: $2 bill

two-thumbed shuffle: dexterous shuffle of playing cards

two-time: secretly commit adultery while married

two-time loser: person going to prison for the second time

two-worlder: person with connections both above ground and underground; person who is legitimately employed but spends much leisure time in the crime-connected underworld

typewriter: machine gun; submachine gun

typewriter party: machine-gun killing

typist: machine gunner

U

U: : U-boat (q.v.); you (as in IOU)

U-boat: gangster who is disloyal to his chief and ready to torpedo him

uc: undercover agent

u-c man: undercover narcotics agent

UCPP: Urban Crime Prevention Program

UCRs: Uniform Crime Reports (compiled by the FBI)

UDPS: Utah Department of Public Safety

UF: Uniformed Force (of a police department)

ufac: unlawful flight to avoid confinement

ufap: unlawful flight to avoid prosecution

uffi: morphine

UFIRS: Uniform Fire-Incident Reporting System

UFPO: Underground Facilities Protective Organization

ugly customer: dangerously quarrelsome person

UHF: United Holyland Fund (q.v.)

UHU: Unhappy Hookers United (q.v.)

UISP: *Union Internationale des Syndicats de Police* (French—International Union of Police Trade Unions)

UKA: United Klans of America (q.v.)

UKKKK: United Kingdom Ku Klux Klan

u/l: upper left

Ulster Volunteer Force: Protestant organization in Northern Ireland

ultimate crime: murder

ultimate drug: cocaine (so named because of its euphoric high, high cost and non-addictive nature)

ultimate penalty: death; life imprisonment without parole

ultrafiche: microfiche of printed matter reduced as much as 100 times to facilitate secrecy, security and storage

ultras: militant extremist Italian gangs

Ulysses: $50 bill, bearing the portrait of Ulysses S. Grant

UMC: Union Metallic Cartridge Company

UN: United Nations

un-American: contrary to the American way of life; contrary to democratic tradition and constitutional government, guaranteeing, among other benefits, trial by jury and equal opportunity regardless of color, creed, national origin or political affiliation

UNARCO: United Nations Narcotics Commission

unauthorized departure: prison parlance for an escape

UNCCP: United Nations Commission on Crime Prevention

UNCIWC: United Nations Commission for the Investigation of War Crimes

uncle: pawnbroker

Uncle Sam: federal law-enforcement agent(s); the United States of America

Uncle Sugar: the FBI (Federal Bureau of Investigation)

Uncle Whiskers: (underworld slang—Uncle Sam) the government of the United States

unconscious person: (police-dispatcher euphemism) dead person

uncut: undiluted (as a drug)

undeco: underground economy (q.v.)

undercover narc: undercover narcotics agent

underground: conspiratorial organization created to disrupt or resist an established government, whether elected or imposed by a dictator or by an invasion of foreign forces; an underground movement may be made up of libertarians, subversives or totalitarians

underground economy: composed of persons who report less income than they earn, including all who engage in bartering or who work for cash only as well as those who file no income tax returns; the drug traffic and organized crime are major segments of the underground economy

underground kite: secret message circulated throughout a prison or from one prisoner to another

underground press: clandestine publishing ventures usually representing minority ethnic or political groups suppressed by dictators; often solely responsible for letting the outside world know what is going on in a totalitarian country

underground railroad: escape route for slaves running from the South to Canada, where many Negro runaways sought refuge before the Civil War; also describes route of deserters and draft dodgers who went to Canada from the United States during the Vietnam War

underground tunnel: secret system for introducing contraband such as drugs, tools and weapons into prisons

underkill: lacking the force needed to defeat or eliminate the enemy

under the counter: secret exchange of money, especially a bribe

under the gun: under observation or surveillance by the police or other law-enforcement officers

under the influence: under the influence of alcohol or drugs

under-the-influencer: alcoholic or narcotic addict

under the table: done illegally and secretly, as a bribe passed under the table; extremely intoxicated

under the tongue: method of passing narcotics into prisoners' mouths used by their girlfriends and wives, who are allowed to visit and kiss them

underworld: the criminal elements of society; the world of organized crime

underworld elite: con men who hold themselves aloof from the rest of the underworld and generally are accorded elite status by other underworldlings

undoc: undocumented alien

undocumented alien: illegal alien

undocumented worker: another term for illegal alien

undergrnd: underground

underwrld: underworld

unethical: contrary to the rules or standards for correct conduct and legitimate practice

UNFDAC: United Nations Fund for Drug Abuse Control

unfit to plead: mentally incompetent

Unhappy Hookers United: San Francisco prostitutes' group

unhook: unfasten the handcuffs

UNICOR: trade name of the Federal Prison Industries corporation maintaining 89 industrial operations in 39 penal institutions

Unisex: Los Angeles Police Department's program to train recruits on a sexually equal basis regardless of physical limitations

Unit 731: Japanese biological warfare complex at the Harbin Military Hospital in Manchuria where during World War II American, Australian, British, Chinese, Korean, and Russian prisoners of war were used in deadly experiments

United Holyland Fund: Chicago-based

fund-raising organization for financing Arab terrorists

United Klans of America: post-1976 version of the Klu Klux Klan; espouses the same racist program under a new name

United Prisoners Union: revolutionary underground organization of hard-core convicts incarcerated in prisons such as San Quentin and Soledad

United Red Army: Japanese terrorist group

United States Coast Guard: responsible for controlling the smuggling of aliens and of dangerous drugs as well as promoting safety at sea

United States Police Canine Association: conducts seminars in canine coordination and training; publishes *Canine Couriers* bimonthly

universal staircase: nickname for the treadmill once operated by felons

unkie: morphine

unlawful assembly: planned meeting of three or more persons to carry out some form of demonstration with force and violence; such assembly may be determined unlawful on the grounds that it may grow in numbers and take on the proportions of a riot

UNSDRI: United Nations Social Defence Research Institute

unsus-look(ing): unsuspicious-look(ing)

Unterlüss: Nazi subcamp close to Bergen-Belsen near Hannover, Germany

UNWCC: United Nations War Crimes Commission

UOC: Uniform Offense Classification

up: stimulant drug; under the influence of alcohol or a drug

up above: in New York City police parlance this refers to any place north of 42nd St. on Manhattan, whereas *down below* refers to any place south of 42nd St.

Up Changi Road: Singapore's Prison Headquarters at Kilometer 17 outside the city and nicknamed for the road on which it is located

up in arms: angry and ready to fight

upl: unauthorized practice of law

UPOA: Ulster Police Officers Association

upper: stimulant drug

upperworld criminals: white-collar criminals, who are often protected by their political or social position from many of the hazards feared by their underworld counterparts

uppie: amphetamine pill

UPS: Underground Press Syndicate (original name of the Alternative Press

Syndicate, or APS); Underground Publications Society

up the river: Sing Sing prison, up the Hudson River from New York City in the town of Ossining

up tight: unable to purchase drugs

up to the gills: completely intoxicated

UPU: United Prisoners Union (q.v.)

u/r: upper right

urban blight: decay observed in metropolitan core areas, where crime often flourishes

urban guerrilla: city-based terrorist

urban terrorism: metropolitan-style guerrilla warfare, such as evidenced in Beirut and Belfast

URP: United Revolutionary Party

USA: United States Army; United States Attorney

USA: Unser Shtickel Arbeit (Yiddish—Our Bit of Work; Our Piece of Work) rifle grenade produced in Palestine by David Leibowitz for use against Arab guerrillas

USACIC: United States Army Criminal Investigation Command

USBC: United States Bureau of the Census; United States Bureau of Customs

USBP: United States Board of Parole; United States Border Patrol; United States Bureau of Prisons

U.S. Bureau of Prisons institutions for juvenile and youth offenders: these are located in Ashland, Ky.; Englewood, Colo.; and Morgantown, W. Va.

USCG: United States Coast Guard (q.v.)

USCP: U.S. Capitol Police (Washington, D.C.)

USCS: United States Customs Service

USDB: United States Disciplinary Barracks

USDC: United States District Court

USDEA: United States Drug Enforcement Administration

USDJ: U.S. Department of Justice (see entry)

used up: informer unable to purchase narcotics

USEP: United States Escapee Program

user: one who uses dangerous drugs; one who has handguns (armed policemen are so named in the British Isles)

USIB: United States Intelligence Board (CIA)

using the needle: addicted to narcotics

USLP: U.S. Labor Party

U.S. Marshals Service: maintains custody of federal prisoners from the time of their arrest to their commitment or release and transports federal prisoners pursuant to lawful writs and direction from the U.S. Bureau of Prisons

USMS: United States Marshals Service

USNCC: U.S. Naval Correction Center

USNDRC: U.S. Navy Drug Rehabilitation Center

USNIAAA: United States National Institute on Alcohol Abuse and Alcoholism (part of the National Institutes of Mental Health)

USNIS: United States Naval Investigative Service

USP: U.S. Penitentiary (these are located in Atlanta, Ga.; Leavenworth, Kan.; Lewisburg, Pa.; Marion, Ill.; McNeil Island, Wash.; and Terre Haute, Ind.)

USPB: United States Parole Board (see **USPC**)

USPC: United States Parole Commission (formerly the United States Parole Board)

USPCA: United States Police Canine Association (q.v.)

USPD: U.S. Parole Division of the Department of Justice

USPHS: United States Public Health Service

USPIS: United States Postal Inspection Service

USPP: U.S. Probation and Parole

U.S. Pros: United States Prostitutes collective

USSC: United States Supreme Court

USSIC: United States Sex Information Council

USSS: United States Secret Service

usury: excessive interest charged for the loan of money

utter counterfeit coin: (old British phrase) pass counterfeit money

u-v camera: ultraviolet evidence camera

UVF: Ulster Volunteer Force (q.v.)

uxb: unexploded bomb

uxoricide: husband- or wife-killer; killing one's husband or wife

Uzi: Israeli 9mm submachine gun named for its developer, Maj. Uziel Gal

V

V: vice (squad)

VA: Volunteers of America

VAC: Voluntary Action Center (q.v.)

Vacaresti: Romanian prison, formerly a monastery, on the outskirts of Bucharest

vacation near Chappaqua: do time in Sing Sing

Vacaville: psychiatrically oriented prison at Vacaville, Calif., about midway between Sacramento and San Francisco

VACRP: Victorian Association for the Care and Resettlement of Prisoners

vag: vagabond or vagrant—a person wandering from place to place without lawful or visible means of support, who may be involved in crimes ranging from arson to shoplifting; vagrancy

vag charge: vagrancy charge

Valhalla: Westchester County Penitentiary at Valhalla, N.Y.

valium: a mild tranquilizer used by many people; used continuously, it becomes addictive; withdrawal produces symptoms such as abdominal cramps, convulsions, sweating and tremors

vamoose: decamp; leave huriedly (derived from *vamos*—Spanish for "let's go")

vampire: extortionist

vamps: vampires (sexually-attractive enemy agents, also called swallows, capable of compromising diplomatic and military personnel

vandal: person, usually juvenile, who ignorantly, maliciously or willfully defaces, destroys or mutilates private or public property; name derived from the Vandals, a fifth-century Germanic tribe of Aryan-Christian Huns who ravaged much of France, Spain and North Africa before sacking Rome in 455 A.D.

vandalism: defacement, destruction or mutilation of private and public property; littering; out-of-season hunting; willful destruction of artistic or literary treasures

vandal-mark remover: see **zep erase**

Van Dieman's Land: former name of Tasmania and generic name for the great Australian penal settlement begun in the early 1800s and lasting up to 1853, when the last shipment of convicts arrived and Tasmania became its official name

v & mm: vandalism and malicious mischief

Vanier: Vanier Centre for Women at Brampton, Ontario

VAP: Victim's Advocate Program (q.v.)

varnish remover: cheap or low grade liquor

vault: safe-deposit vault; treasure vault

VC: *Vehicle Code*

VC: Vigilante Corps (q.v.)

VCB: Victim Compensation Board (New York State)

VCIS: Vermont Crime Information System

VDC: Venereal Disease Clinic

Vega Alta: Industrial School for Women at Vega Alta, Puerto Rico, for felons, misdemeanants and women awaiting trial

veg'ed out: reduced by the action of alcohol or drugs to a vegetable-like state

vehic manslgtr: vehicular manslaughter

vehicular manslaughter: causing the death of another by grossly negligent operation of a motor vehicle

vehicular weapon: automotive vehicle such as an automobile, motorcycle or truck used as an offensive weapon by its driver in assaulting another

velvet: mad money; *he's got plenty of velvet saved for his vacation*

vendetta: (Italian—vengeance) attempt to gain revenge for a wrong done to a friend, a fellow gangster or a relative

venireman: juror or prospective juror

ventilated rib: device for air-cooling shotgun barrels

Ventura Reception Center and Clinic: at Camarillo, Calif.

venue: jurisdiction wherein a trial will be held; defendants asking for a change of venue do so because they believe the community or the judge will be hostile and unfair; hence they wish to be tried somewhere else

verdict: decision made by a judicial officer or a jury that the defendant is guilty or not guilty of the offense(s) with which he or she is charged

Vergennes: the Weeks School for delinquent and unmanageable males and females at Vergennes, Vt.

Vernichtungslager: (German—extermination camp)—extermination-type concentration camp of the type many built and operated by German Nazis in Poland during World War II

VES: Voluntary Euthanasia Society

vest-pocket gun: the easily concealed .22 automatic or the somewhat larger but more effective .38 double Deringer, which fits solidly into the hand and cocks readily to fire two loads in quick succession

vet: examine whether legally or physically; inspect

vfr's: visiting friends and relatives

vic: convict; victim

vice: a word meaning different things to different people in different times and places; vice has been variously defined as depravity, evil conduct, immorality, indulgence in degrading appetites, moral corruption, etc.; the vice—nickname for a vice squad or one of its members

vice area: neighborhood largely given over to alcoholics and narcotic addicts, pimps and prostitutes and porno shops and theaters

vice ladies: female auxiliary of vice lords (q.v.), and like them engaged in such criminal acts as extortion, gambling, mugging, prostitution and selling drugs

vice lords: ghetto street fighters, often assisted by vice ladies (q.v.)

vice squad: plainclothes policemen charged with the detection of vice

Vickers: Vickers-Maxim automatic machine gun, made in England at the Vickers factory in Sheffield and the Maxim factories in Birmingham and elsewhere

victim: person who has endured mental or physical suffering, loss of property or death resulting from an actual or attempted criminal offense committed by another

victimal: being or involving a victim (the opposite of "criminal")

victimity: quality or state of being victimal (the opposite of "criminality")

victimization: state of being victimized

victimol: victimological(ly); victimologist; victimology

victimological: pertaining to the study of the criminal-victim relationship

victimologist: expert in or student of victimology

victimology: study of criminal-victim relationships and hence the reverse of criminology; study of the victimization of society by criminals

victimous: victimal

Victim's Advocate Program: program of therapy for elderly victims of crime in Fort Lauderdale, Fla.

Victims of Violent Crimes Program: initiated in California in 1965 to compensate crime victims or their surviving relatives for funeral expenses, lost wages and medical costs; the first such program in the United States

Victim/Witness Project: program in San Diego, Calif. to help victims of crime on a 24-hour basis

vig: vigilante; vigorish

vigilance committee: group of citizens who take law enforcement and the execution of justice into their own hands when they feel the courts and the police are not capable of maintaining law and order

vigilante: (Spanish—vigilant guard; watchman) member of a self-appointed law-enforcement group that is intent on enforcing order, even if it means taking the law into the group's hands

Vigilante Corps: police aides recruited from among responsible teenagers in Singapore

vigilantism: order enforced by vigilante groups that have taken the law into their own hands

vigorish: portion of a bet withheld by a bookmaker

VIJ: Vera Institute of Justice (New York, N.Y.)

Villahermosa: prison in Villahermosa, capital of the Mexican state of Tabasco, whose shores are washed by the Bay of Campeche in the Gulf of Mexico

vin (VIN): vehicle identification number

Vincennes: French prison just east of Paris notorious for its many famous inmates dating from the 14th century, when it was a castle and dungeon

vindictive vandalism: destroying or stealing property as a form of revenge

vino: wine-consuming alcoholic

Violence Commission: National Commission on the Causes and Prevention of Violence

violent crime: the most notable examples are aggravated assault, rape, murder, non-negligent manslaughter and robbery

vip (VIP): Volunteers in Probation

vipe: to smoke hashish or marijuana; a dealer in drugs; a marijuana smoker

viper's weed: one of marijuana's many nicknames

visible crime: crime that is committed and reported

vision-inducing drug: psychedelic drug

Vista: San Diego County jail in Vista, Calif.

vituperation: verbal abuse

vivisepulture: bury someone alive

voice check: radio check

voiceprint: spectographic sound representation of a person's voice; voiceprints are used for identification much like fingerprints, palmprints and footprints

volar: volunteer army (sometimes assembled to repel invaders or resolve law-and-order problems beyond the power of the police)

volatile solvents: easily-vaporized fluids such as airplane glue, brandy, lighter fluid and even some perfumes; capable of producing a kind of intoxication when their fumes are inhaled

Voluntary Action Center: facility developed by some community welfare agencies, courts and probation departments to employ the skills of persons convicted of minor crimes in lieu of costly imprisonment; VACs have been successful in the Los Angeles area

voluntary manslaughter: intentionally causing the death of another with reasonable provocation

voluntary return: voluntary deportation of illegal aliens

volunteer: drug addict who volunteers to commit herself or himself for treatment

Volunteers in Probation: publishes *VIP Examiner* quarterly, as well as books about probation

vongony: *Cannabis* plant grown and smoked on the island of Madagascar in the Indian Ocean

VORP: Victim Offender Reconciliation Program

voyager: person under the influence of a hallucinogenic drug; many such persons imagine they are taking a trip or a voyage

VPCP: Volunteer Probation Counseling Program

VPR: Vanguarda Popular Revolucionaria (Portuguese—Popular Revolutionary Vanguard) Brazilian terrorist organization

vr: ventilated rib (q.v.)

vr (VR): voluntary return (of illegal aliens)

v-r'd: voluntarily returned (deported)—*109 Mexicans were v-r'd*

vs: vein shot (intravenous injection)

V-spot: $5 bill

VTLs: Vehicular Traffic Laws

VU: Vice Unit (of a police department)

Vucetich: Juan Vucetich of the Buenos Aires police, who in 1893 published his book *Sistema de Filacion* (System of Recognition) showing how far superior dactyloscopy or fingerprinting is to the Bertillon System of anthropometric measurements for the identification of criminals and others

vulcanized: very intoxicated

VU—PD: Vice Unit—Police Department

VVCC: Val Verde County Clink—nickname for the county jail in Del Rio, Texas

VVCP: Victims of Violent Crimes Program (q.v.)

VWP: Victim/Witness Project (q.v.)

W

W: wife

WAD: World Association of Detectives (q.v.)

wad cutter: bullet capable of cutting a clean hole in its target

Wah Ching: gang active in San Francisco's Chinatown, responsible for several murders

wail: police siren sound of prolonged duration (see also **yelp**)

Wakefield: jails in Wakefields in Massachusetts, Michigan and Rhode Island

waker-upper: drug addict's first injection of the day, taken shortly after awakening

wake-up: waker-upper (q.v.)

walk: to be acquitted; to walk out of prison

walkie-t: walkie-talkie (q.v.)

walkie-talkie: portable two-way radio (for person-to-person communication)

walk off with: steal

walk out on: abandon; desert

wall: firing wall (place of execution by a firing squad)

Walla Walla: Washington State Penitentiary at Walla Walla

wallbanger: intoxicated person

Wallen: Walletjes (Dutch diminutive—walls)—this euphemism for Amsterdam's redlight district goes back to bygone times when the district was at the city's walls; now it is more centrally located and is abutted by its oldest church

wallet gun: easy-to-conceal wallet-shaped handgun

wall-eyed: extremely upset; deeply inebriated

Wallkill: experimental medium-security prison in Ulster County, N.Y.

wall-to-wall bears: occupied by many police

Wall-Wall: prison in Walla Walla, Wash.

Walnut Street: Philadelphia's oldest jail, dating from 1790; its inmates were originally subjected to solitary confinement, designed to prevent any association with other criminals and to promote reflection and self-reform

Walpole: Massachusetts Correctional Institution at Walpole, southwest of Boston

Walther: German semi-automatic pocket pistol

wAm: white American male

W & I: Welfare and Institutions (Code)

wangula: southern African name for hashish, hemp or marijuana

wanted: wanted by the police or other law-enforcement officers

WAR: Women Against Rape

war crimes: crimes against humanity, violating the established customs and laws of war; at the end of World War II many trials held in Nuremberg, Germany resulted in the conviction of a number of civil and military war criminals who had ordered devastation, mistreatment of prisoners of war and mass murders not justified by military necessity

warden: prison administrator

wardress: female warden

warex: we have a warrant and will extradite (appears as WAREX on police teletype)

warrant: legal document issued by a judicial officer authorizing a law-enforcement officer to arrest an individual, search a premise or perform any act specified by the warrant

washing machine: process created to cleanse funds earned illegally by putting them through banks, brokerage firms and lawyer's offices willing to channel them into legitimate businesses; nickname given certain banks in such places as the Bahamas, the Cayman Islands and Switzerland where depositors place funds for so-called cleansing, for tax evasion or for both cleasing and tax evasion

waste: to kill

watchhouse: police station; police station lockup

Watergate: synonym for a national scandal first detected at the Watergate hotel office complex on the Potomac River waterfront of Washington, D.C., where the Democratic Party headquarters was invaded by underground agents of Pres. Nixon in 1972; an exposé of this and related actions led to their imrisonment and to the resignation of Pres. Nixon

watering hole: cocktail bar; saloon; tavern

water pipe: tobacco water pipe—name given bhang or hookah pipes touted for their smoke-conserving abilities and used by many hashish, marijuana and opium smokers

Watts: predominantly black section of Los Angeles where large-scale arson and rioting occurred in August 1965, costing 35 lives and more than $200 million in property damage

WAVAW: Women Against Violence Against Women

Wayne: Wayne County Jail (serving the Detroit area)

w/b: westbound

WBSI: Western Behavioral Sciences Institute (q.v.)

wc: wad cutter (q.v.)

WCA: Washingtonian Center for Addiction; Women's Correctional Association

WCAC: Women's Crusade Against Crime (St. Louis)

WCC: Western Cartridge Company

WCC: War Crimes Commission

WCS: Wisconsin Correctional Service Center (q.v.)

WCTU: Women's Christian Temperance Union (q.v.)—or according to some of its opponents, "Wild Cats and Tigers United"

WDC: Women's Detention Center

Weatherby: American rifle manufacturer providing a full line of special cartridges

Weaver: Weaverscope (rifle telescope)

WEBA: Women Exploited by Abortion

WEBDBC: W.E.B. Du Bois Club(s)—communist-front organization(s) named for the expatriate American communist

Webley: Britain's most popular revolver from 1898 through the end of World War II; many of these .455-caliber handguns are still found in former British territories as well as in the British Commonwealth

WE CAN: Walking Enforcement Campaign Against Narcotics (on-foot police officers appointed to detect and arrest drug peddlers)

weed: marijuana

weedhead: hashish or marijuana user

Weeks School: for delinquent and unmanageable males and females; at Vergennes, Vt.

weight: bulk quantity of hashish, heroin, LSD, marijuana or any other drug

weight dealer: dangerous-drug middleman

Weisswasser: forced-labor subcamp operated by the Nazis during their occupation of Czechoslovakia

welcher: person who fails to repay money he or she owes

welfare king: make criminal adept at using aliases to steal goods and money from various welfare programs

welfare queen: female criminal adept at using aliases to steal goods and money from various welfare programs; a Chicago welfare queen used 31 different addresses, three Social Security numbers and the records of eight deceased husbands before she was finally arrested

Welfare Security Program: guarantees the safety of prisoners who provide useful information to authorities

well-oiled: intoxicated

wen-chee: gum opium

We Never Sleep: trademark message of Pinkerton's National Detective Agency (printed beneath a picture of a wide-open eye)

Westerbork: see **Lager Westerbork**

Western Behavioral Sciences Institute: La Jolla, California institution where a robbery-prevention program was devised for a large chain of food stores; the program leads many to believe that the serious development and application of crime-prevention techniques could reduce crime rates substantially

Western Guard: racist Canadian group notorious for its attacks on Asian and West Indian black immigrants (see also **East Indian Defense Committee**)

Western Penitentiary: old prison located at Pittsburgh, Pa.

Westfield Farm: the New York Reformatory for Women

West Street: Federal Detention Headquarters on West Street in New York City

West Virginia Industrial Home for Girls: in Salem, W. Va.

wet affairs: Soviet euphemism for assassinations

Wethersfield: Connecticut State Prison at Wethersfield

WeTip: We Turn in Pushers (of narcotics)—a toll-free telephone number, 800-472-7785, is operative Monday through Friday from noon to 6 p.m. for collecting information about drug pushers; a citizens' nonprofit organization protecting informants and cooperating with law-enforcement agencies

WFO: Washington (D.C.) Field Office (FBI)

whammy: hate-filled eyes or face

WHD: Women's House of Detention (New York City)

wheat: marijuana

wheeler-dealer: person involved in financial deals, often made deliberately complex to conceal their illegality

wheelman: skilled driver, usually part of a gang and adept at providing a fast getaway from the scene of the crime

wheels: automobile(s); motorcycle(s); vehicle(s) used in transporting drugs

where it's at: where drugs are for sale; where prostitutes are available

whippet: racing dog; shotgun with two-thirds of the barrel and two-thirds of the stock sawed off to facilitate concealment and firing at very close range

whipping post: vertical post set in the ground before a courthouse; prisoners were chained or lashed to the post and beaten before the public

whips and jingles: withdrawal symptoms suffered by addicts to alcohol or narcotics

whirlee: humiliating torture in which the victim's head is shoved into a toilet, which is then flushed; sometimes used by students during hazing ceremonies as well as by terrorists

whistle blower: informant

white: white stuff (whitish heroin of French manufacture)

White Brigade: Mexico's anti-terrorist paramilitary force—*La Brigada Blanca*

white Christmas bash: cocaine party

white-collar crime: violations of criminal law by upper-class and upper-middle-class members of society and by businesses and corporations; expense-account padding, price-fixing, product adulterations and misrepresentation and stealing office supplies and equipment are but a very few examples of white-collar crime

white flag: white flag of peace; white flag of truce

White Flags: Burmese terrorist organization

white girl: cocaine

white goods: colorless high-alcohol-content drinks (aguardiente, akavit, gin, rum, schnapps, vodka)

white intelligence: information that can be obtained from books, official reports and periodical literature available to any reader

white junk: heroin

white lady: heroin

white lightning: ethyl (grain) alcohol; homemade liquor such as corn whiskey or hard cider; lsd (LSD)

white merchandise: morphine

white nurse: morphine

White People's Socialist Party: San Diego-based racist group

whites: amphetamine-sulfate tablets; gonorrhea; leukorrheal discharge

white slave: girl or woman forced into prostitution; they are often sold by one white slaver to another or even shipped overseas

white slavery: organized prostitution, with girls and women being forced to work as prostitutes

White Slave Traffic Act: federal law forbidding the transportation of girls or women from state to state for immoral purposes; also called the Mann Act

White Street: Manhattan House of Detention for Men at 125 White St. in New York City

white stuff: cocaine; heroin; morphine

whitewash: concealment of crime by cover-up

white whiskey: peyote cactus berries chewed by some American and Mexican Indians, who evidence a mild intoxication from this practice

Whiteman: Marjorie Millace Whiteman's 15-volume *Digest of International Law*

whiz bang: cocaine-and-heroin or cocaine-and-morphine mixture

WHODAP: White House Office of Drug Abuse Prevention

whodunit: who-done-it? (detective story; murder mystery)

Who Killed Kennedy Committee: made up of leading British statesmen and writers such as J.B. Priestley, Hugh Trevor-Roper and Bertrand Russell, who demanded to know more about the assassination of John F. Kennedy, as it seemed the United States government was hiding the facts about the murder of the president by conducting its inquiries in the strictest secrecy; this, they felt, endangered the security of the United States and the world

whore: prostitute

whoremaster: man who spends time with whores as a client or as their manager

whoreson: Middle English term meaning exactly what it says—the son of a whore; used in more modern times as a synonym for "bastard" or "scoundrel"

whoretel: hotel or motel frequented by whores

wide-open town: any place where vice is uninhibited by police interference or surveillance

wig: to overdose

willful homicide: intentionally causing

another's death, with or without legal justification

willie weaver: drunk driver

Wilmas: (Mexican-Americanism—Wilmington, Calif.) nickname for the penitentiary on nearby Terminal Island

Wilmington: Correctional Institution for Women at Wilmington, Del.

Wilmington 10: nine black men and one white woman convicted of firebombing a grocery store in Wilmington, N.C. during a racial disturbance in 1971

Winchester: rifle, especially a repeating rifle; after Winchester, an American manufacturer of ammunition and firearms, including the famed repeating rifle named for its creator, Oliver Fisher Winchester; also refers to jails in Winchester in Connecticut, Virginia and 16 other states

Winchester Gun Museum: free exhibit open daily except on national holidays; firearms from all over the world are displayed from 9:00 a.m. to 4:00 p.m. at 275 Winchester Ave. in New Haven, Conn.

windowpane acid: high-quality LSD, also called clear light by pushers and users, who get it in gelatin tablets

window tappery: whorehouse wherein women tap at the winndows to attract men passing by; one part of the main street of Cleveland was once noted for the noise made by its window tappers

wingding: orgy; spree; wild party

wings: floating on wings or flying with wings—effect experienced by some people taking their first main-line injection of any powerful narcotic

wino: wine addict

Winslow: American rifle manufacturer

wiped out: intoxicated

wipe out: assassinate; kill; murder

wire: communication; information; message; piece of thin wire used to clean out a hypodermic needle; short length of wire used by muggers and others to choke their victims

wired: addicted; electrocuted

wired on whites: addicted to benzedrine

wiretap: use an electronic eavesdropping device, with or without a court order or warrant

Wisconsin Home for Women: at Taycheeddah, Wis.

Wisconsin School for Girls: at Oregon, Wis.

wit.: witness

withdraw: stop indulging in an addictive habit

withdrawal symptoms: persons withdrawing from drugs report all sorts of horrible mental and physical ailments, including convulsions, delirium, nausea and painful vomiting

WKKC: Who Killed Kennedy Committee (q.v.)

WOAR: Women Organized Against Rape

Wobblies: members of the IWW (International Workers of the World)—so named because when some Chinese-American members were asked what they were, they replied: *I Wobbly Wobbly*

Wolfenden: Sir John Wolfenden, C.B.E., chairman of the Department Committee On Homosexual Offenses and Prostitution, was appointed in 1954 to consider what changes should be made in British laws governing homosexuals and prostitutes; recommendations made, liberal in character, were incorporated into the Sexual Offenses Act of 1956; in general, homosexual behavior between consenting adults in private is no longer a criminal offense in Britain (the age of adulthood is fixed at 21); laws concerning prostitution now aim at medical and social control of prostitutes and the elimination of brothels and pimps, madams and whoremasters

wolf pack: roving gang of teenagers of the sort that has preyed on the elderly and the helpless in South Philadelphia, West Philadelphia and similar metropolitan areas

wolf packing: gang activity, especially mugging

wolfsbane: popular name of a deadly poison, aconitine nitrate

woman in the business: woman in the business of prostitution

woman of the town: old-fashioned euphemism for a prostitute

Women's Christian Temperance Union: organization most active at the turn of the century; strongly committed to the elimination of prostitution, to temperance in drinking and to universal peace

Women's Prison Association: New York City service agency for prisoners; publisher of *A Study in Neglect*—a report on women prisoners

Women's Ward: Oklahoma State Penitentiary at McAlester

Women's Unit: organization providing group training for female prison inmates in British Columbia

wooden kimono: casket; coffin

Woods Haven-Kruse School for Girls: at Claymont, Del.

Woolworth: nickname for the inexpensive but effective Sten submachine gun

woozy: slightly drunk

wop: without official (immigration) papers (pejorative term sometimes applied to Italians or Italian-Americans)

workhouse: old American term for a prison; British word for a poorhouse, where the indigent got shelter in return for doing such work as picking oakum or sewing mail sacks

working chick: prostitute

work over: assault; beat; punch

work release program: rehabilitation plan whereby convicts are allowed to work outside of prison during the last part of their terms and receive the same pay as other workers

works: the works—apparatus for injecting heroin and other dangerous drugs

World Association of Detectives: formerly World Secret Service Association; promotes highest ethical practices and seeks to elimnate incompetent, irresponsible and unreliable members of the profession

World Correctional Service Center: Chicago-based information clearinghouse

world's oldest profession: prostitution, according to students of ancient history

wormwood: *Artemisia absinthium*, a European plant whose dark-green oil and bitter taste impart the color and flavor to the liqueur called absinthe; its abuse can lead to blindness as well as deterioration of the nerve centers; this condition is called absinthism

Wormwood Scrubs: English prison in the West London Stadium area for young male offenders

WPA: Women's Prison Association (q.v.)

WPA & H: Women's Prison Association and Home

WPP: Witness Protection Program

WPSP: White People's Socialist Party (q.v.)

WRA: Winchester Repeating Arms Company

wrapper: inconspicuous-looking brown-paper bag containing marijuana or other drugs

wrecked: drug-addicted; under the influence of alcohol and/or drugs

wrecker: criminal who lived by plundering the cargoes of vessels in distress or of vessels they lured to shore by means of false beacon lights; wreckers often facilitated their work by killing the crews and passengers of the ships they wrecked

W.R. Knottman: (abbreviated signature—we are not man and wife) appears on the pages of many hotel and motel registers

WSP: Witness Security Program (program protecting informants in criminal cases)

WSSA: World Secret Service Association (see **World Association of Detectives**)

WSTA: White Slave Traffic Act (q.v.)

w/t: walkie-talkie (q.v.)

WVSP: West Virginia State Police

W-W: Winchester-Western

Wyantskill: Wyantskill Center for Girls at Wyantskill, N.Y.

Wyoming Girls School: at Sheridan, Wyo.

X

X: gang territorial marker or place where one gang will fight another; the signature of the illiterate (her or his mark); ten; $10 bill; symbol for a kiss or for a motion picture not suitable for viewing by minors; the spot where the body was found or the crime was committed (X marks the spot)

x-con(s): ex-convicts(s)

x'd: executed; wiped out

X division: branch of society consisting of swindlers and thieves

x'd out: eliminated; killed; wiped out

xenophobia: fear or hatred of foreigners, foreign ideas and foreign things

X marks the spot: X marks the spot where the body was found; X marks the spot where the crime occurred; X marks the spot where the treasure was buried

x out: erase; cross out; get rid of; kill

xplo: explosion

xplos: explosive

X-rated: X-rated district (area where gambling joints, porno shops and whorehouse-type massage parlors operate without serious restrictions); X-rated moving picture (for adults only)

X-ray: apparatus used to detect letter bombs, parcel bombs, weapons concealed in luggage, etc.

X-17: mortality table

XX: double-cross; double strength; twenty; $20 bill

Xylocaine: trade name of lidocaine, used as a local anesthetic by dentists and doctors

XYY syndrome: a male who possesses an extra Y chromosome, and is often unusually aggressive, is afflicted with this syndrome

Y

Y: Yard (The Yard—Scotland Yard); you

y: yellow (cowardly); yen

YA: Yasser Arafat—leader of the Palestinian terrorist group Al Fatah

YACA: Youth and Correctional Agency (q.v.)

YAD: Youth Aid Division (New York City Police Department)

yaffle: steal

yahoo: vicious person—in *Gulliver's Travels* the yahoos were described by Jonathan Swift as a race of brutes resembling man and having all his vices

yakenal: nembutal

Yakima: Yakima County Jail in Yakima, Wash.

Y and CA: Youth and Correctional Agency (q.v.)

yard: prison yard

Yard: Scotland Yard

yardarm: either end of a yard in a merchant or naval sailing vessel; offenders were traditionally hanged from one of the ship's many yardarms and left suspended until they were dead (and sometimes even longer, as a warning to mutineers)

yardbird: convict; ex-convict; jailbird; recidivist

yard bull: prison guard; railroad detective; railroad-yard policeman

yataghan: Middle Eastern saber characterized by the double curve of its long blade

yb: yard bird (one confined to a military camp)

YCA: Youth Correction Act

YCC: Youth Correctional Center

YCI: Youth Correctional Institution (Bordentown, N.J.)

YCL: Young Communist League (section of the Moscow-based-and-directed Komsomol, q.v.)

YCW: Young Christian Workers

YDI: Youth Development Inc. (q.v.)

yeaster: beer-drinking alcoholic

yegg: burglar who wanders about from city to city and place to place

yellow: cowardly; also a nickname for nembutal

yellow jackets: barbiturates; nembutal capsules

yellow-tooth burglar alarm: dog trained to bark at strangers; any dog can discourage burglars and prowlers by persistent barking

yelp: police siren sound of short duration (see also **wail**)

yelper: person skilled at imitating the voices of others; ventriloquist

yen: desire for drugs; sexual desire for another person

yenhok: needle-like device used for shaping opium pills; opium addict(ion)

yenning: undergoing withdrawal symptoms

yenpok: cooked opium pill

yenshee: opium residue found within the bowls of opium pipes; yenshee is often mixed with opium gum to produce more pills

yenshee baby: a bowel movement so difficult and so painful as a result of drug-induced constipation that it seems a baby is trying to emerge

yenshee boy: opium addict

yenshee gow: opium-bowl scraper

yenshee quoi: opium smoker

yenshee suey: opium

yen sleep: drowsy but restless state often experienced during withdrawal from dangerous drugs

yerba: marijuana

yesca: marijuana

YGC: Youth Guidance Center (San Francisco)

yike: (Australian slang—brawl; fight)

YIP: Youth International Party (whose members were called "Yippies")

yoke: to mug by attacking from behind and then seeming to stick a knife into the victim's throat

York: State Reformatory for Women at York, Neb.

yot (YOT): youthful offender treatment (q.v.)

young-adult penal institutions of the U.S. Bureau of Prisons: these are located in El Reno, Okla.; Lompoc, Calif.; Milan, Mich.; Oxford, Wis.; Petersburg, Va.;

Seagoville, Texas; and Tallahassee, Fla.

young horse: (prison argot) roast beef

young stir: boys' reformatory (nickname created by a punning youngster)

Young Workers Liberation League: Marxist-Leninist youth organization active in the United States

Youth and Correctional Agency: organization combining California's Board of Prison Terms, California Youth Authority, Correctional Industries Commission, Department of Corrections, Institutional Review Board, Narcotic Addict Evaluation Authority and Youthful Offender Control Board; abbreviated YACA and Y and CA

youth and juvenile penal institutions of the U.S. Bureau of Prisons: these are located in Ashland, Ky.; Englewood, Colo.; and Morgantown, W. Va.

Youth Development Inc.: juvenile education and rehabilitation program

youthful offender: person adjudicated in criminal court who may or may not be legally a juvenile but who is younger than the specified upper age limit for offenders for whom record-sealing and special correctional treatment are available

youthful offender treatment: court trial that is neither publicized nor a matter of record

youthploitation: youth exploitation (commercial exploitation of gullible youngsters with ads for fads in clothing, hair styling, etc.)

Youth Studies Center: Philidelphia's juvenile correctional facility

YSB: Youth Service Bureau

YSC: Youth Studies Center (q.v.)

YSD: Youth Services Division

YTS: Youth Training School

yum-yums: drug available to teenagers, who often take them from the family medicine cabinet

YWLL: Young Workers Liberation League (q.v.)

Z

z: an ounce of a narcotic (truncation of "oz."—abbreviation for "ounce"); zoo (jail or prison)

Zacatecas: prison in Zacatecas, capital of the Mexican state of the same name, northwest of San Luis Potosi

Zacatecas purple: potent and purplish marijuana grown in the Mexican state of Zacatecas, between Durango and San Luis Potosi

Zahal: Israeli Defense Force (which was responsible for the capture of war criminal Adolf Eichmann)

zamal: name for hashish on the islands of Madagascar and Reunion in the Indian Ocean

zap: destroy with a sudden burst of gunfire; kill quickly, as with a machine gun or tommy gun

Zapp: microdot technique developed by one Professor Zapp during World War II and used by many espionage organizations

Z-car: (British slang) police car

zebras: black and white couple(s)

zelda: straitlaced girl or woman

zen: one of many nicknames for LSD

Zen-Ai-Kaigi: All-Japan Patriotic Foundation (ultra-nationalist organization whose gangster-infested 10,000-man paramilitary force, ostensibly set up to combat communism, combines underground and underworld activities)

Zero: Japanese gang whose graffitic zeros deface many public parks and places in large seaport cities of Japan; right-wing underground organization of Cuban exiles claiming credit for bombings and killings here and overseas

zero in on: attack, especially suddenly; come to grips with; confront

zex: warning—be careful, someone's coming

Z-gas: Zyklon-B gas (deadly gas used by Nazis in exterminating concentration-camp prisoners)

zip gun: muzzle-loading weapon consisting of a metal pipe filled with broken glass, nails or stones, which are propelled by the explosion of broken matchheads; gun made by prison inmates

zip up your fly: shut up

zombie: (Cockney slang) policewoman

zonked (out): under the influence of alcohol or other drugs

zonker: alcoholic

zonk oneself: commit suicide; kill oneself

zoo: police station

zook: prostitute

zoom: first effects of hallucinogens and opiates

Z-table: mortality table

zuch: an informer; to inform

ZUF: Zapata Urban Front (Mexican terrorist group)

Zurich account: deposits held by a bank in Zurich, Switzerland, where such accounts are identified only by a secret number, not by the depositor's name

Zwodau: forced-labor subcamp operated by the Germans during their occupation of Czechoslovakia during World War II

FOREIGN TERMS

This section includes a selection of terms and phrases relating to crime from various foreign languages. (Please note that certain foreign words or phrases whose use in English is very frequent are included in the main section of this book.)

aap: (Afrikaans—dagga) another name for marijuana

aap trein: (Afrikaans—smoking dagga) smoking marijuana

abadessa: (Spanish—abbess) madam in charge of a whorehouse

abrigo de triply: (Mexican-American criminal slang—three-ply plywood overcoat) a wooden coffin of the type promised to those who fail to obey gangsters

abse. re.: *absente reo* (Latin—defendant absent)

abuja: (Calo or Mexican-American— needle, whether for narcotic injections or for sewing) corrupted form of the Spanish *aguja*, which also means "needle"

abusador: (Spanish—bully) abusive male

abusadora: (Spanish—bully) abusive female

Accion Cubana: (Spanish—Cuban Action) anti-Castro terrorist group of specially trained commandos moving out of Madrid, Mexico City and Miami to attack Cuban government property in Canada, Chile, Mexico, Peru and elsewhere

acido: (Spanish—acid) nickname for LSD

actus reus: (Latin—defendant's act) legalism meaning that an act must have been overt and must have resulted in harm to be considered criminal

adicta: (Spanish—addict) female addict

adicto: (Spanish—addict) male addict

adormidera: (Spanish—opium poppy)

adulterio: (Portuguese—adultery)

adulterio: (Spanish—adultery; fraud)

Afyon: *Afyonkarahisar* (Turkish—Black Castle of Opium)—in west-central Turkey where much of the world's opium is grown; Afyon is the nickname of its prison

agent de police: (French—policeman)

agente de policia: (Portuguese or Spanish— policeman)

agente de policia feminina: (Portuguese— policewoman)

agente femenino de policia: (Spanish— policewoman)

agente investigativo: (Italian—investigative agent) detective

agent provocateur: (French—provoking agent) secret agent who joins an underground or underworld group for the purpose of provoking its members to commit criminal acts so they can be arrested

age-ya: (Japanese—houses of assignation) places where prostitutes are exposed to their clientele

aikuchi: (Japanese—dagger)

aislamiento penal: (Spanish—penal isolation) solitary confinement

ajusticiamiento: (Spanish—execution of a criminal) political assassinations are often rationalized by using this term

alambre: (Spanish—wire) chain-link fence erected along the Mexican border to keep Mexican citizens and others from coming into the United States illegally

alambrista: (Calo or Mexican-American Spanish—wire person) anyone who has come into the United States illegally, as by crawling under the wire fence separating the United States and Mexico

alcahueta: (Spanish—madam; female procurer)

alcahuete: (Spanish—pimp; male procurer)

alcahuetear: (Spanish—to ponder; to procure women for immoral purposes)

alcahueteria: (Spanish—brothel)

alcoviteira: (Portuguese—madam; female procurer)

alcoviteiro: (Portuguese—pimp; male procurer)

algemas: (Portuguese—handcuffs)

alguacil: (Spanish—constable) local law-enforcement officer

Alianza: *La Alianza Federal de las Mercedes* (Spanish—Federal Alliance of Mercedes) New Mexican group organized by Reies Lopez Tijerina to reclaim all the land that was once Mexican and has been acquired by the United States

allumer: (French—to excite sexually)

allumeuse: (French—call girl; whore)

a l'ombre: (French—in the shadow) in jail

amant de coeur: (French—boyfriend; lover) a call-girl's male friend who shares her bed after her paying customers have left

amarilla: (Spanish—the yellow one) Colombian slang for marijuana

Amerika: (German—America) word appearing in many underground handbills, pamphlets and signs used to discredit the United States by suggesting that it is on a par with Hitler's Germany

ametralladora: (Spanish—machine gun)

amicus curiae: (Latin—friend of the court) disinterested but knowledgeable advisor who provides expert advice before or during a trial

anarquia: (Spanish—anarchy)

andar locote: (Calo or Mexican-American Spanish—walk crazily) be high on drugs

antecedentes criminales: (Spanish—criminal record)

anti-gang: (Franglais—police)

apache: (French—Apache; French hooligan)

apartheid: (Afrikaans—apartness) program of racial segregation and white supremacy practiced in the Republic of South Africa

apuñalar: (Spanish—to stab)

Araisa: (Calo or Mexican-American nickname—Arizona) slang term used by many illegal Mexican aliens to disguise where they crossed into the United States

Arbeitsdorf: (German—work village)—included in the name of one of many concentration camps built by the Nazis

arbrisseau de coca: (Spanish—coca bush) coca leaves yield cocaine

arguimenda: (Sicilian-Italian slang—argument) Mafia policy-making meeting

arg. ad bac.: argumentum ad baculum (Latin—argument of the club)—appeal to force

arg. ad hom.: argumentum ad hominem (Latin—personal attack argument)

arg. ad ignor.: argumentum ad ignorantum (Latin—argument from ignorance)

arg. ad miser.: argumentum ad misericordiam (Latin—argument appealing for pity)

arg. ad veri.: argumentum ad vericundiam (Latin—argument based on misuse of authority)

arma: (Spanish—firearm; weapon)

arreador: (Spanish—cattle herder) drug pusher

arruaceiro: (Portuguese—hoodlum; hooligan; street fighter)

asesinato: (Spanish—murder)

asesino: (Spanish—murderer)

assassina: (Italian or Portuguese—female murderer)

assassinat: (French—murder)

assassinio: (Italian or Portuguese—murder)

assassino: (Italian or Portuguese—murderer)

assommoir: (French—blackjack; bludgeon; dive; gin mill)

Ausbruch aus dem Gefangnis: (German—prison break)

ausgevished: (Yiddish—killed at Auschwitz)

auto-du-fe: (Portuguese—act of the faith) burning or execution of a heretic following the trial by the court of the Inquisition; in Spain the same treatment of heretics and unbelievers was called *auto-de-fe*; the plural forms are, respectively, *autos-da-fe* and *autos-de-fe*

autonomi: (Italian—autonomous groups) militant gangs and groups active in the underground

autoriduttori: (Italian—self-appointed price cutters) young radicals who practice sabotage in public to express the extreme but often popular views about the high cost of living

avisador: (Spanish—signalman) person adept at transmitting warnings; many *avisadores* are found along the Mexican border

avocat au criminel: (French—criminal lawyer)

azul: (Spanish—blue) blue-uniformed police or police in general

babbeljas: (Afrikaans—bubble ass) a hangover

bador: (Aztec—infants; small children) hallucinogenic morning-glory seeds

bagne: (French—convict prison; hulk)

bajur: (Romany—confidence game) a gypsy swindle, also known as *xoxano baro*

baksheesh: (Persian—bribe; gratuity; tip) in many Middle Eastern countries it is often impossible to do business without paying some baksheesh

bakuchi: (Japanese—gambling)

bakudan: (Japanese—bomb)

bala: (Portuguese or Spanish—bullet)

balacera: (Mexican Spanish—shootout)

balai polis: (Malay—police station)

bala projetil: (Portuguese—bullet)

balle: (French—bullet)

bambalache: (Puerto Rican Spanish—marijuana)

banasto: (Spanish—basket) slang term for a cell or prison

bandeira branca: (Portuguese—white flag) flag of surrender or truce

bandeira de pirata: (Portuguese—pirate flag) flag of death or piracy

bandera blanca: (Spanish—white flag) flag of peace or of truce

bandera negra: (Spanish—black flag) flag of anarchy or of piracy

bandera roja: (Spanish—red flag) flag of communism or of revolution

Bandera Roja: (Spanish—Red Flag) Venezuelan terrorist organization

bandida: (Spanish—female bandit)

bandido: (Spanish—male bandit)

bandoleira: (Portuguese—bandolier)

bandoleirismo: (Portuguese—banditry)

bandoleiro: (Portuguese—bandit)

bandolera: (Spanish—bandolier; female bandit)

bandolerismo: (Spanish—banditry)

bandolero: (Spanish—bully; male bandit)

barrio: (Spanish—district; quarter; slum) *barrio chino* is the redlight district, whereas *barrio* by itself means the district or the slum

bastille: (French—small fortress) *La Bastille* was the infamous Paris prison destroyed by French revolutionaries on July 14, 1789, a day celebrated by Frenchmen ever since as Bastille Day; *bastille* has long been a synonym for "prison," especially one holding political prisoners

batedor de carteiras: (Brazilian slang—wallet hunter) pickpocket

batida policial: (Portuguese—raid; round-up)

bato: (Mexican Spanish—gangster; tough guy)

bato loco: (Mexican Spanish—crazy gangster; daredevil)

bato marijuano: (Mexican Spanish—gangster who is a frequent user of marijuana)

bato narco: (Mexican Spanish—narcotic-addicted gangster)

bebedeira: (Portuguese—binge; drinking bout)

bei yahn gat-sei: (Cantonese Chinese—stabbed to death)

bhang: (Hindustani—intoxicating hemp) Indian hemp known in other parts of the world as hashish or marijuana; also a water pipe used for smoking marijuana

bimbo: (Italian contraction of *bambino*) baby; prostitute

bint: (Arabic—whore)

biu-sam: (Cantonese Chinese—to kidnap and hold for ransom)

blancas: (Spanish—whites) benzedrine tablets

blanche: (French—white) cocaine

blanco: (Spanish—white) Mexican slang for heroin

blousons noirs: (French—black wind-breakers) juvenile delinquents

boko suru: (Japanese—rape; violate)

bolsa: (Spanish—bag) small packet of narcotics

bom: (Dutch—bomb)

bomb: (Dano-Norwegian or Swedish—bomb)

bomba: (Italian, Portuguese, Russian or Spanish—bomb)

bombe: (French—bomb)

Bombe: die Bombe (German—bomb)

bombita: (Spanisih—small bomb) amphetamine capsule; any drug in solution used for injection, such as liquid cocaine

bomme: (French-Canadian—bum; tramp; vagrant)

boncha: (Mexican Spanish—bunch; gang members)

bonche: (Spanish-American slang—bunch) group of marijuana smokers

boob: (Australian slang—jail; prison)

bordeel: (Dutch—brothel)

Bordeel: das Bordeel (German—the brothel)

bordeelhouder: (Dutch—brothelkeeper)

bordel: (French or Portuguese—brothel)

bordello: (Italian—brothel)

bori-jaya: (Japanese—low-class teahouse) combined bordello and teahouse

borsaiuolo: (Italian—pickpocket)

bote: (Spanish-American slang—jail or prison)

bouh-duhng: (Cantonese Chinese—riot)

brandbom: (Dutch—fire bomb)

brandgranaat: (Dutch—fire grenade)

brandstichting: (Dutch—arson)

Brandstiftung: (German—arson)

Brandstifungstrieb: (German—pyromania)

Brigada Blanca: (Spanish—White Brigade) Mexico's anti-terrorist paramilitary force

brigade des moeurs: (French—morals brigade; vice squad)

Brigade de Sureté: (French—Security Brigade) original name of the first detective force in Paris, organized by a former criminal named Vidocq

brigade mondaine: (French—worldy brigade) the vice squad

Brigatas Rossa: (Italian—Red Brigades) Italy's terrorist organization active in Italy

brigatisti: (Italian—brigadiers) members of terrorist organizations such as the Red

Brigades

brott: (Swedish—crime)

bruja: (Calo or Mexican-American—prostitute) the same word in Spanish means "witch" and is often applied to an ugly old woman

bulto: (Spanish—bale) bale of marijuana

bunteny: (Hungarian—crime)

burdeel: (Dutch—brothel)

burdel: (Spanish—brothel; whorehouse)

caballo: (Calo or Mexican-American Spanish—horse) person who carries drugs into jails and prisons; also a nickname for heroin

cabo general: (Spanish—chief corporal) head inmate or trusty in a prison

cabronazo: (Spanish-American slang—vicious blow)

cabronismo: (Spanish—prostitution of a wife by her husband) a fairly common practice in many Latin American port cities, where prostitution is tolerated as a female profession

caca: (Spanish—excrement) nickname for counterfeit heroin

cache-sexe: (French—hide sex) G-string-type covering worn by some exotic dancers; minimum clothing allowed by law

cachot: (French—underground prison cell)

cadeia: (Portuguese—jail; prison)

cadela: (Portuguese—jail)

cafard: (French—cockroach; squealer) favorite underworld epithet

caiman: (Spanish-American—alligator-like or cunning person; racketeer; schemer)

caimanera: (Spanish-American—habitat of the caiman, an alligator-like species) hangout of racketeers

caimaneria: (Spanish-American—racketeering)

cala: calabozo (Spanish—cell; dungeon; jail)

calabouco: (Portuguese; jail)

calabozo: (Spanish—dungeon; jail)

Califas: (Calo or Mexican-American slang—California) term widely used by illegal Mexican aliens crossing into the United States

camison de madera: (Mexican Spanish—wooden nightshirt) coffin

camorra: (Spanish—fight; hassle; struggle)

campamento para presos: (Spanish—prison camp)

camp de prisonniers: (French—prison camp)

Campo Numero 1: (Spanish—Camp Number 1) maximum-security military prison near Mexico City that holds many hardened convicts as well as political prisoners

canaille: (French—mob; rabble)

cañon automatico: (Spanish—automatic cannon) machine gun

can xa: (Vietnamese—hashish; hemp; marijuana)

cao policial: (Portuguese—police dog)

Capo: (Italian—Chief) Mafia leader

capo di tutti capi: (Italian—boss of all bosses) top leader of the Mafia

capo regime: (Italian—head of government) Mafia lieutenant assisting a *sotto capo* (second in command), who himself is beneath the chief or *capo*

captivus: (Latin—captive; prisoner)

carabina: (Portuguese or Spanish—carbine)

carabinieri: (Italian—carbineers) paramilitary police usually seen in two-man squads

carcel: (Spanish—jail; prison)

carceleras: (Spanish—prisoner songs)—a flamenco song form allegedly developed by prisoners incarcerated in Ronda and celebrated in a zarzuela—*Las Hijas del Zebedeo*, The Daughters of Zebedee

carcelero: (Spanish—jailer; warden)

carcer: (Latin—jail; prison)

carcerario: (Italian—prison)

carcere: (Italian, Portuguese—jail)

carcereiro: (Portuguese—jailer)

carceriere: (Italian—jailer)

caricatore: (Italian—round of ammunition)

carne: (Calo or Mexican-American Spanish—meat) slang term for heroin

cartucho: (Portuguese or Spanish—cartridge)

casa de correccion: (Spanish—house of correction) reformatory

casa de prostitucao: (Portuguese—whorehouse)

casa de putas: (Spanish—whorehouse)

casa de sita: (Spanish—assigned house) house of assignation; whorehouse

casa de tolerancia: (Spanish—house of correction) reformatory

casa di correzione: (Italian—house of harlots) whorehouse

casanieres: (French—house girls) girls who work in a whorehouse

casa publica: (Spanish—public house) brothel

cassino: (Portuguese—casino; gambling house)

catin: (French—whore)

cavale: (French slang—prison escape)

cave: (Latin—beware)

caveat actor: (Latin—let the doer beware)

caveat emptor: (Latin—let the buyer beware) a warning meaning that the seller is not responsible for his goods after the sale has been completed

caveat viator: (Latin—let the traveler beware) a warning meaning a carrier (airline, bus company, railroad, steamship line, etc.) is not responsible after the trip is completed

cayenne: (French slang—prison ship)

cela: (Portuguese—cell) prison cell

celda: (Spanish—cell) prison cell

cella: (Italian—cell) prison cell

cert: certiorari (Latin—to certify; to be informed)—an order from a superior court to a lower court to produce papers needed for a review of a case

ceza evi: (Turkish—house of punishment)— prison

chaai-gun: (Hong-Kongese Chinese— police station)

chaai-yahn: (Hong-Kongese Chinese— police)

chabouk: (Hindi—whip) rawhide whip used to punish offenders or rioters

chak: (Cantonese Chinese—burglar)

chandu: (Malay—opium)

charas: (Hindi—narcotic drug) usually made of hashish resin, fat and oxblood for use in hookah pipes and narcotic candies

chauki: (Hindustani—jail) apparently this term was derived from the British *choky*, meaning the same thing, as another Hindustani word for jail is *thana*

chaya: (Japanese—teahouse) euphemism for a whorehouse

chequard: (French—check taker) usually a venal politician whose influence, inside information or vote is for sale

cherchez la femme: (French—look for the woman) there must be a woman at the bottom of it

cheung: (Cantonese Chinese—loot; plunder)

chicaneria: (Spanish-American slang— cheating; chicanery; counterfeiting; deceiving; defrauding; swindling)

chicharra: (Puerto Rican slang—marijuana cigarette)

chingadazo: (Spanish-American slang— foul blow; serious wound)

chirona: (Spanish slang—jail; prison)

chiva: (Calo or Mexican-American Spanish—heroin)

chivera: (Mexican Spanish slang— smuggler)

chota: (Puerto Rican slang—informer; Spanish-American—the police)

Chuco: (Calo or Mexican-American nickname—El Paso, Texas) term widely

used by illegal Mexican aliens who use the nickname to disguise their place of entry into the United States

cinayet: (Turkish—crime)

cinedo: (Italian—catamite, male whore)

citi: (Mexico-American slang—citizen) usually refers to a U.S. citizen

clandes: (French—clandestine brothels) many are disguised as hotels

clavo: (Mexican-Spanish slang—cache; hiding place; stash)

cleptomanear: (Spanish—to steal)

clochard: (French—drunken vagrant; hobo; tramp)

cocaina: (Italian, Portuguese or Spanish— cocaine)

cocaine: (Dutch or French—cocaine)

cocaismo: (Spanish—cocaine addiction)

coche celular: (Spanish—prison van)

cochineria: (Spanish—dirty tricks; filthy business; meanness)

cochino: (Spanish—pig) anything dirty is called *cochino* or *muy cochino*—very dirty

coco: (French—cocaine) slang term also referring to a guy or a nutty guy

codigo penal: (Portuguese—criminal code)

codo: (Mexican-Spanish slang—having drugs; being stingy)

cola: (Spanish—tail) flowering tops of the marijuana plant are called *colas* in many Latin American countries

colorado: (Spanish—having color; verging on red) seconal

comisaria de policia: (Spanish—police station)

commissione: (Sicilian-Italian slang—commissioners) elderly members of the Mafia called upon to meet from time to time to approve of decisions and policies

conciergerie: (French—porter's lodge; prison)

condamnation: (French—conviction)

condamné: (French—condemned; sentenced)

condanna: (Italian—conviction)

condannato: (Italian—convict)

condao: (Mexican-American Spanish— county jail) corruption of the Spanish word for county, *condado*

condena: (Spanish—conviction)

condenacao: (Portuguese—conviction)

condenado: (Portuguese or Spanish—convict)

condominio: (Spanish—condominium) euphemism for jail or prison

congal: (Mexican Spanish—with girl) actually means a whorehouse, as *congal* is *cuarto con gal* (room with girl) contracted

congalero: (Mexican-Spanish slang—man

who hangs around whorehouses)

congolera: (Mexican-Spanish slang—whore)

contrabande: (Dutch—contraband)

contrabandear: (Portuguese or Spanish—smuggle)

contrabandista: (Portuguese or Spanish—smuggler)

contrabando: (Portuguese or Spanish—contraband)

contrabbandare: (Italian—smuggle)

contrabbandiere: (Italian—contrabandist) smuggler

contrabbando: (Italian—contraband)

contreband: (French—contraband; smuggled goods)

contrebandier: (French—smuggler)

corpus delicti: (Latin—the body of the crime) the fact of death caused by a criminal and not the body of the murdered man, as popularly translated

corralon: (Mexican Spanish—corral) detention camp where illegal entrants await deportation

corre: (Calo or Mexican-Americanism—correctional institution; penitentiary) truncation of the Spanish *correccional*

cortar: (Spanish—to cut) among many in the Mexican aHd Puerto Rican underworld, *cortar means "to adulterate" (a drug)*

Cosa Nostra: (Italian—Our Thing) criminal society or syndicate, often called the Mafia

cosca: (Sicilian Italian—clique) local group of Mafia members; Mafiosi

cosca nostra: (Italian—our family) criminal organization more frequently but less correctly called **Cosa Nostra**

coup: (French—round) round of ammunition

coup de grace: (French—compassionate bullet fired to relieve a person dying in extreme agony or compassionate blow or sword thrust made to aid the dying)

coup de poignard: (French—stab)

coup mortel: (French—fatal stabbing)

courtisane: (French—courtesan) nice word for a prostitute, dating back to royal France and court life

coyote: (Calo or Mexican-Americanism—dealer in illegal Mexican aliens; criminal who intercepts illegal entrants crossing the Mexican border, using the cover of night to rob them of their clothes and any contraband such as drugs they may be carrying as well as their money and other possessions)

crima: (Romanian—crime)

crime: (French or Portuguese—crime)

crime d'état: (French—crime against the state) treason

crime d'incendie volontaire: (French—crime of voluntary incendiarism) arson

crime mala prohibita: (Latin—offenses not necessarily causing abhorrence or calling for punishment) adultery, blasphemy, gambling, incest, intoxication, profanity, etc.

crimen: (Latin or Spanish—crime) usually a grave crime such as homicide

crimen continuum: (Latin—continuous crime)

crimen extraordinaria: (Latin—extraordinary crime) an offense undefined and not given a fixed punishment under Roman law but punishable according to the demands of public policy

crimen falsi: (Latin—crime of falsification) crimes involving deceit, falsification, forgery or fraud as well as perjury

crimen furti: (Latin—larceny; theft)

crimen laesae majestatis: (Latin—the crime of high treason)

crimenlese: (Italian—lese majesty) treason

crime passionnel: (French—crime of passion) murder incited by the infidelity of a lover or a mate

crimepie: (Afrikaans—crime)

crimes mala en se: (Latin—crimes bad in themselves) arson, burglary, larceny, rape, murder, etc.

crimes mala prohibita: (Latin—bad crimes prohibited by statute) crimes infringing on the rights of others

crimina: (Latin—crimes)

crimina extraordinaria: (Latin—extraordinary crimes) such crimes as those which were not specifically defined under Roman law but were punishable as demanded by public policy

criminal: (Portuguese or Spanish—criminal)

criminale: (Italian—criminal)

criminalidad: (Spanish—criminality) the quality of being criminal

criminaliser: (French—to transfer from civil to criminal proceedings)

criminalista: (Italian or Spanish—criminal lawyer; criminologist)

criminaliste: (French—criminalist; criminal jurist; criminologist)

criminalisti: (Italian—criminal lawyers)

criminalita: (Italian—criminality)

criminaliste: (French—criminality)

criminaliteit: (Dutch—criminality)

criminalmente: (Italian, Portuguese, Spanish—criminally)

criminare: (Italian—to charge with a crime)

crimineel: (Dutch—criminal)

criminel(le): (French—criminal; guilty of

crime)

criminellement: (French—according to criminal law; criminally)

criminologia: (Italian, Portuguese or Spanish—criminology)

criminologie: (French—criminology)

criminologista: (Portuguese or Spanish—criminologist)

criminologiste: (French—criminologist)

criminologo: (Spanish—criminologist)

criminosita: (Italian—criminality)

criminoso: (Italian or Portuguese—criminal; heinous)

cuchara: (Mexican-Americanism—heroin measure) corruption of the Spanish word for spoon

cuete: (Mexican-Americanism—drunk; firearm; pistol)

cui bono?: (Latin—who benefits?)

cura: (Spanish—cure) heroin shot

curara: (Romany—killers; people of the knife; stabbers) killer Gypsies

curi: (Romany—knife) Gypsy dagger or stiletto

dacoits: (Hindi—professional robbers and murderers) noted throughout Burma and India for their ruthless efficiency

dactiloscopia: (Spanish or Portuguese—fingerprinting) also called *datiloscopia* in Portuguese

dactyloscopie: (French—fingerprinting)

damasu: (Japanese—swindle)

datiloscopia: (Portuguese—fingerprinting) also called *dactiloscopia*

dedo: (Calo or Mexican-Americanism—informer) derived from the Spanish word for finger, *dedo*

degradacao: (Portuguese—degradation) prostitution

deih-hah-jou-jik: (Cantonese Chinese—underground group)

delito: (Spanish—delinquency; less serious crime) misdemeanor

delitto: (Italian—crime)

demi-castor: (French—high class prostitute)

demimondaine: (French—prostitute; woman of the underworld)

demimonde: (French—underworld)

de novo: (Latin—afresh; anew) as if there had been no earlier decision

derecho penal: (Spanish—criminal law)

dessous de table: (French—under the table) bribe

Detektiv: der Detektiv (German—detective)

detenu: (French—prisoner)

detenuta: (Italian—detainee; prisoner)

DGSE: Directorat Général de Securité External (French—General Directorate of External Security)

diambista: (Central American or Cuban Spanish—marijuana)

direito penal: (Portuguese—criminal law)

dite: (Mexican-Americanism—detention hall) place where illegal aliens must wait while being investigated

doku: (Japanese—poison)

Dolch: der Dolch (German—dagger or dirk)

doli capax: (Latin—capable of committing a crime)

doli incapax: (Latin—incapable of committing a crime)

dolk: (Dano-Norwegian, Dutch, Swedish—dagger)

droga: (Spanish—drug)

drogado: (Spanish—drugged)

drogue: (French—drug; drug addict) term covers anything from hashish to heroin, from marijuana to morphine

droit criminel: (French—criminal law)

dr pén: droit pénal (French—penal law)

dr rom: droit romain (French—Roman law)

dr trav: droit du travail (French—labor law)

duhk: (Cantonese Chinese—poison)

Durchgangslager: (German—Transit Camp)—established in German-occupied countries for the transport of Jews and others to concentration camps

dyun-gim: (Cantonese Chinese—dagger)

ella: (Spanish—she) Colombian nickname for marijuana

el mundo del hampa: (Spanish—the world of vagabonds) the underworld

embalao: (Puerto Rican Spanish—addicted and debilitated)

emeute: (French—insurrection; riot; violent outbreak)

en cache: (French—cached; hidden; secreted)

encuesta: (Spanish—inquest)

Endlösung: (German—Final Solution)—Hitlerian euphemism for the annihilation of all Jews under Nazi authority before and during World War II

engañador: (Spanish—swindler; trickster)

en ganchos: (Spanish—hooked) addicted to drugs

engañifa: (Spanish—slang—fraud, swindle, trick)

engaño: (Spanish—fraud, swindle, trick)

en' glima: (Modern Greek—crime)

enlever: (French—to rape)

enormia: (Latin—crimes; illegal acts)

enquete: (French—inquest)

entraineuse: (French—call girl)

entremetteur: (French—pimp)

eroina: (Italian—heroin)

escopeta: (Spanish—shotgun)

escroquer: (French—swindle)

escupe: (Calo or Mexican-American Spanish—homemade gun)

esposas: (Spanish—wives) handcuffs

Esquadrao da Morte: (Portuguese—Death Squad) Brazilian vigilantes pledged to avenge the death of law-enforcement officers by killing criminals; also called the White Hand—*Mano Blanco*

esrar: (Turkish—secret concoction) hashish-tobacco mixture smoked to cover up the odor of hashish, as it has been outlawed since the 19th century in this opium-producing nation

estilete: (Portuguese or Spanish—stiletto)

estileto: (Italian—stiletto) switchblade used for stabbing

estocada: (Portuguese or Spanish—stab)

estofa: (Puerto Rican jargon—stuff) drugs

estraperlista: (Spanish—black marketeer)

estraperlo: (Spanish—black market; black market price; racket; ripoff)

estupefaciente: (Spanish—narcotic)

evade: (French—escapee; fugitive) escaped prisoner

evade de prison: (French—prison breaker)

evaso dal carcere: (Italian—prison breaker)

ex curia: (Latin—out of court) settled by arbitration or without litigation

ex post facto: (Latin—after the fact) retroactive

Fabrica de Hombres Nuevos: (Spanish—Factory of New Men) Mexico City's hotel-style prison, designed for overnight visits made by the wives of its prisoners

facon: (Argentine Spanish—large knife) gaucho knife

falsi crimen: (Latin—crime of falsification) counterfeiting; forgery

falsitas: (Latin—deceit; falsity; treachery)

falta: (Spanish—fault; minor crime)

fange: (Dano-Norwegian—prisoner)

fascinus: (Latin—crime; misdeed)

faderales: (Mexican Spanish—federal law-enforcement officers)

fei-jai: (Cantonese Chinese—young hoodlum) juvenile delinquent

femme-agent: (French—policewoman)

fengsel: (Dano-Norwegian—prison)

ferbrechen: (Yiddish—crime)

Fianna Eireann: (Irish—Young Ireland) IRA youth organization engaged in many militant actions

ficha: (Mexican-Americanism—money); (Spanish—chip; counter; police record; token)

fiebre carcelaria: (Spanish—prison fever) fear of imprisonment

fierro: (Calo or Mexican-Americanism borrowed from archaic Spanish for *hierro*—homemade gun) also a steel blade such as a dagger, knife, machete or switchblade

fila: (Spanish—file) knife made from a file

fileraso: (Calo or Mexican-American Spanish—heroin fix; knife wound; needle stab)

filero: (Mexican-Americanism—knife; stiletto)

fille: (French—daughter) often used to describe a prostitute

fille de joie: (French—maid of joy) courtesan or prostitute

fille du regiment: (French—daughter of the regiment) camp follower; soldiers' prostitute; when initially capitalized (*Fille du Regiment*) it is the title of an opera by Donizetti, whose heroine is a good girl

Fingerabdruck: (German—fingerprint)

fingeravtrykk: (Dano-Norwegian—fingerprint)

fiscales: (Mexican Spanish—treasury law-enforcement officers) roughly equivalent to the U.S. Customs Service; engaged in apprehending smugglers who may be bringing firearms or other contraband into Mexico

flic: (French—policeman)

foco: (Spanish—center of action; focus; touch hole of a cannon) small revolutionary group active in guerrilla warfare

fong-fo: (Cantonese Chinese—arson)

forbrydelse: (Dano-Norwegian—crime)

forbryter: (Dano-Norwegian—criminal)

forcat: (French—convict) prisoner

fornicateur: (French—fornicator; whoremonger)

fort-à-bras: (French—strong-arm) bully of the type found in every gang and in every prison

fraudem: (Latin—fraud)

frauder: (French—smuggle)

fudotoku: (Japanese—vice)

fuete: (Cuban Spanish—whip) narcotic needle

fuggitivo: (Italian—escaped prisoner; fugitive from justice)

fugitivo: (Portuguese or Spanish—escaped prisoner; fugitive from justice)

fumo d'Angola: (Portuguese—Angola smoke) hemp smoke produced by users of cannabis who, as slaves, brought it across the Atlantic from Angola to Brazil

furyo: (Japanese—prisoner of war)

fusilimiento: (Spanish—execution by firing squad or musketry)

gaam-faan: (Cantonese Chinese—prisoner)

gaam-fohng: (Cantonese Chinese—prison cell)

gaam-yuhk: (Cantonese Chinese—prison)

gaba(cho): (Calo or Mexican-American Spanish—white Anglo-American) term of derision equivalent to *gringo*

gageur: (French—bettor; gambler)

ganea: (Latin—brothel)

ganga: (Calo or Mexican-American Spanish—gang); (Hindi—hashish) *Cannabis indica*

Garda Siochana: (Gaelic—National Police) Ireland's main defense against terrorists and crime

garde du corps: (French—bodyguard)

garjma: (Arabic—crime)

Gefangene: (German—prisoner)

Gefangenenwagen: der Gefangenenwagen (German—prison van)

Gefangnis: das Gefangnis (German—prison)

gei-gwaan-cheung: (Cantonese Chinese—machine gun)

geih-neuih: (Cantonese Chinese—prostitute)

Geisel: (German—hostage)

gelap: (Malay—contraband)

gendarme: (French—military policeman; policeman)

gendarmerie: (French—corps of gendarmes; military police; police force)

gens de loi: (French—lawyers; men of the law)

geole: (French—jail)

geolier: (French—jailer)

Geschoss: (German—bullet)

gevangene: (Dutch—prisoner)

gevangenis: (Dutch—prison)

Gew: Gewehr (German—rifle)

gift: (Dano-Norwegian—poison)

Gift: (German—poison)

gijzelaar: (Dutch—hostage)

ging-chaat: (Cantonese Chinese—police)

ging-chaat-guk: (Cantonese Chinese—police station)

ging-hyun: (Cantonese Chinese—police dog)

giuocare d'azzardo: (Italian—gamble; play for risks)

giuocatore: (Italian—gambler; player)

goewerments-hond: (Afrikaans—government hound) policeman

golpe final: (Portuguese or Spanish—final blow) death blow

gouvernante: (French—manageress) whorehouse madam

granada: (Portuguese or Spanish—grenade)

granata a mano: (Italian—hand grenade)

grenade: (French—grenade)

gringa: (Mexican-American or Mexican Spanish—white Anglo-Saxon female) term of derision

gringo: (Mexican-American or Mexican Spanish—white Anglo-Saxon male) term of derision believed to have originated when invading American troops marched into Mexico singing *That's Where the Green Grass Grows*; the last three words sounded to the Mexicans like *gringos*

grisette: (French—peasant prostitute)

guarda costa: (Italian, Portuguese, Spanish—coast guard)

guardia: (Spanish—guard; police)

guerrilheiro: (Portuguese—guerrilla; partisan) a member of the militant underground is sometimes called *adepto* or *sectario*

guerrillero: (Spanish—guerrilla; partisan)

guillotineur: (French—guillotiner)—executioner using the guillotine

gumi: (Japanese—criminal groups)

gunja: (Sanskrit—hashish; hemp; marijuana)

gwaii-daai: (Cantonese Chinese—to kidnap a child)

gwaai-ji-lou: (Cantonese Chinese—kidnapper)

gwo-leuhng: (Cantonese Chinese—overdose)

habitué: (French—habitual [visitor]) person who usually hangs around the same neighborhood, nightclub, redlight district, etc.

habitué de la maison: (French—habitual male visitor to the house) a steady customer

habituée: (French—habitual female visitor)

hah-lauh-seh-wui: (Cantonese Chinese—underworld)

Hakendreuz: (German—crooked cross) Hitler's swastika symbol, used by the Nazis and their followers

halbstarken: (German—half-starched) juvenile delinquents

hale pa'ahao: (Hawaiian—prison)

hampa: (Spanish—criminal class; lowlifers; underworld)

hampo: (Spanish—criminal, delinquent, gangster, mobster, underworldling)

hampon: (Spanish—gangster; tough guy; thug; underworld character)

hamponeria: (Spanish—racketeering)

handboei: (Dutch—handcuff)

Handfesseln: (German—handcuffs)

Handgranata: (German—hand grenade)

handjern: (Dano-Norwegian—handcuffs)

hannin: (Japanese—criminal)

hanzai: (Japanese—crime)

hara-kiri: (Japanese—belly cut; knife-in-the-gut suicide) once a popular form of

self-destruction; now practiced but rarely
hareng: (French—herring) pimp
Haschisch: das Haschisch (German—hashish)
hascisc: (Italian—hashish)
hashhashin: (Arabic—assassins) the name of an Arabic terrorist group called Black September as well as Al Fatah
haxixe: (Portuguese—hashish)
Heroin: das Heroin (German—heroin)
heroina: (Portuguese or Spanish—heroin)
heroine: (French—heroin)
hierros: (Spanish—irons) handcuffs
hiki-te-jaya: (Japanese—introducing tea-houses) places where men seeking sexual excitement are introduced to whores
himitsu no: (Japanese—secret; underground)
hin-bing: (Cantonese Chinese—military police)
hirondelle de nuit: (French—night swallow) euphemism for a prostitute
hitogoroshi: (Japanese—murder)
hoja: (Spanish—leaf) Colombian slang for the larger, lower leaf of the marijuana plant
homicida: (Latin—homicide) murder
homicide infortunium: (Latin—accidental killing) justifiable homicide
homicide se defendendo: (Latin—self-defense homicide) justifiable killing
homicidio: (Spanish, Portuguese—homicide; murder)
horizontale: (French—horizontalist) euphemism for a prostitute
horosha: (Japanese—vagrant)
huda: (Mexican-American—policeman)
huellos digitales: (Spanish—fingerprints)
huis: (Chinese-Hawaiian—syndicates) many huis make their profits from organized prostitution in the Hawaiian islands
hung-bou: (Cantonese Chinese—terror)
hung-bou-fahn: (Cantonese Chinese—terrorist)
hung-sau: (Cantonese Chinese—murderer)
Hure: die Hure (German—the whore)
huren: (German—to fornicate; to whore)
ignorantia iuris non excusat: (Latin—ignorance of the law is no excuse)
ignorantia legis neminem excusat: (Latin—ignorance of the law excuses no man)
ilegal: (Mexican-American—illegal alien)
impronta digitale: (Italian—fingerprint)
imprudencia temeraria: (Spanish—criminal negligence; criminal temerity)
imputata: (Italian—female juvenile offender)
in camera: (Latin—in chambers) hearings,

investigations and trials held *in camera* are held in secret
incendiare: (French—incendiarist) arsonist; pyromaniac
incendiario: (Italian, Portuguese or Spanish—incendiarist; pyromaniac)
incendio doloso: (Italian—fraudulent fire) arson
incendio malicioso: (Spanish—arson)
incendio premeditado: (Portuguese or Spanish—premeditated incendiarism) arson
incendium: (Latin—arson)
inchiesta: (Italian—inquest)
incriminare: (Italian—charge with a crime; incriminate)
incurcion: (Spanish—incursion; rade; roundup)
indic: indicateur (French—informer)
in flagrante delicto: (Latin—while the crime was blazing) (caught) in the act
informatore: (Italian—informant)
injaga: (Kingarawanda—hashish, hemp, marijuana) popular name for cannabis in Rwanda
in propria persona: (Latin—in one's own behalf) acting as one's own defense attorney
inquerito: (Portuguese—inquest)
inu: (Japanese—dog; informer)
irhaab: (Arabic—terrorism)
irhaabi: (Arabic—terrorist)
j'accuse: (French—I accuse) famous first words of an open letter written by Emile Zola exposing the anti-Semitic persecutors of Capt. Dreyfus, who was sent to Devil's Island for crimes committed by others
jadaan: (Cantonese Chinese—bomb)
jaga: (Malay—guard; watchman)
jahm-sei: (Cantonese Chinese—kill by drowning)
jaula: (Spanish—cage) slang term for jail
jenayah: (Malay—crime)
jettard: (French—jail)
jeuih: (Cantonese Chinese—crime)
jeuih-faan: (Cantonese Chinese—criminal)
fihad: (Arabic—holy war) often a coverup for armed insurrection in Moslem lands
jih-saat: (Cantonese Chinese—suicide)
jing-sei: (Cantonese Chinese—put to death)
jisatsu: (Japanese—suicide)
jogador: (Portuguese—gambler; player) feminine form is *jogadora*
jogar: (Portuguese—gamble; play)
jo-leun: (Cantonese Chinese—revolver)
jolope: (Puerto Rican jargon—holdup)
joro: (Japanese—prostitute)
jotu no yuju: (Japanese—first-class prostitute)

jouer: (French—gamble)

joueur: (French—gambler)

judas: (Spanish—warden's peephole in a prison-cell door)

judex damnatur cum nocens absolvitur: (Latin—the judge is condemned when the guilty go free)

judicium capitale: (Latin—capital punishment)

jugador: (Spanish—gambler; player) feminine form is *jugadora*

junsa: (Japanese—police)

juquearse: (Puerto Rican jargon—to inject oneself with a hard drug)

jura: (Mexican-American slang—police; policeman) corruption of the Spanish *jura*, meaning an oath

jus: (Latin—law)

jus publicum: (Latin—penal law; public law)

kancha: (Thai—hashish; hemp; marijuana)

kanhcha: (Cambodian—hashish; hemp; marijuana)

kannabis: (Greek—hemp) source of hashish and marijuana; English generic (*cannabis*) name derived from *kannabis*

kan xa: (Lao—hashish; hemp; marijuana)

kapidiye: (Turkish—hardened criminals)—the most feared in prisons where they bribe the guards and rule the other inmates

Kapitalverbrechen: (German—capital crime)

kashi-zashi: (Japanese—brothels)

katorga: (Russian—hard penal servitude)

Katzenjammer: (German—cat's whining; hangover; misery) morning-after-the-night-before symptoms of overeating and/or overdrinking; word also applied to the sound of an orchestra tuning up

kedjahatan: (Bahasa Indonesian—crime)

kef: (Arabic—hashish) *Cannabis indica*

keimusho: (Japanese—prison)

keisatsu: (Japanese—police station)

kempeitai: (Japanese—military police)

kenju: (Japanese—revolver)

keris: (Malay—dagger; kris)

keuhng-gaan: (Cantonese Chinese—rape; ravishment)

kidnappeur: (French—kidnapper)

kif: (Arabic—peace; tranquility) North African hashish, also called *kef*

kikear: (Calo or Mexican-American—to kick; to kick the drug habit)

Kinderraub: (German—kidnapping)

kinzhal: (Russian—dagger)

klein crimepies: (Afrikaans—small crimes)

klepto: kleptomane (French—kleptomaniac) compulsive thief

kodomo-ya: (Japanese—children's houses)

houses of male prostitution

kogel: (Dutch—bullet)

Kokain: das Kokain (German—cocaine)

Konterbande: die Konterbande (German—contraband)

Konzentrationslager: (German—concentration camp)

korosu: (Japanese—kill)

kosho: (Japanese—licensed prostitute) an unlicensed prostitute is called *shisho*

kraal: (Afrikaans—prison; stockade; stockaded village)

kraym: (Russian—crime)

krestypeek: (Russian—criminal)

Kriminal: (German—criminal)

kriminal: (Malay—criminal)

Kriminalist: der Kriminalist (German—criminologist)

Kriminalistik: die Kriminalistik (German—criminology)

Kriminalstrafkunde: die Kriminalstrafkunde (German—penology)

kriminell: (Swedish—criminal)

krimo: (Esperanto—crime)

ku-gai: (Japanese—painful world) term describing the life of a whore

kulan: (Russian—wild ass) nickname applied to any headstrong juvenile delinquent

Kupplers: (German—pimps)

kuroi kiri: (Japanese—black mist) bribery; corruption; under-the-table payoff(s)

kurveh: (Yiddish—prostitute)

kyofu seijii: (Japanese—terrorism)

kyofu seijika: (Japanese—terrorist)

kyushu: (Japanese—raid)

La Causa: (Spanish—The Cause) the Chicano cause; the Puerto Rican cause; the Spanish cause

ladron: (Spanish—robber; thief)

La Linea: (Spanish—The Line) the border, especially the Mexican-American border

La Nuestra Familia: (Spanish-American jail jargon—Our Family) prison racketeers who deal with homosexual prostitution, loan sharking, murder contracting and narcotics; a Mexican-American Mafia

La Raza: (Hispanic-American Spanish—The Race) synonym for Hispanic power

leno: (Latin—pimp)

lenon: (Spanish—pimp)

lenoncinio: (Spanish—pandering; pimping)

lese-majeste: (French—high treason)

lestrikos polemos: (Greek—little war) guerrilla war or insurgency

lex: (Latin—law)

lex non scripta: (Latin—unwritten law) law derived from custom and often used as the justification for vengance

lex scripta: (Latin—statute law; written law)

lex talionis: (Latin—law of retaliation) "an eye for an eye and a tooth for a tooth"; under this Roman law a man who cut off another man's hand was liable to lose his own hand, e.g.

ley de fuga: (Spanish—law of flight) legal privilege of law-enforcement officers who may kill anyone attempting to escape; it is not uncommon for prisoners to be encouraged to escape so they may be killed legally while escaping

libéré: (French—liberated convict) free from prison confinement but not free to leave a penal settlement, as in French Guiana, where many *libérés* died of tropical diseases worsened by hunger

likvidatsiya: (Russian—liquidation) Soviet synonym for execution

lista negra: (Portuguese, Romanian, Spanish—blacklist) device used by employers as well as racists wishing to deny work to, or impose annihilation or imprisonment upon, those who are blacklisted

lista negro: (Italian—blacklist)

lobato: (Mexican Spanish—wolf cub) nickname given to a Mexican child or juvenile who comes north across the U.S. border to engage in automobile theft, mugging, robbery, prostitution or shoplifting

loco: (Spanish—crazy)

locus criminis: (Latin—scene of the crime)

locus penitentiae: (Latin—place of repentance) penitentiary

loquera: (Spanish—female warden in an insane asylum; insane asylum; madness)

lorette: (French—prostitute) named for a gang of courtesans who lived in Paris close to the Church of Notre Dame de Lorette

losbandig: (Dutch—lawless)

louh-geui: (Cantonese Chinese slang—prostitute)

lubang buaya: (Indonesian—crocodile hole) Djakarta water hole infested with crocodiles and used as a place to dispose of people at odds with the current administration, as during the abortive communist coup of 1965

Luftpiraterie: (German—air piracy) aircraft hijacking

lupanar: (French, Latin, Portuguese—brothel) name derived from the Roman god of fertility, Lupercus, in whose honor fertility rites were celebrated yearly

lupanare: (Spanish—lupanar) whorehouse

lupara: (Sicilian Italian—sawed-off shotgun)

Lusthaus: (German—lust house) brothel

Lustmord: *der Lustmord* (German—rape and murder)

maak it: (Afrikaans—make it) make a dagga cigarette

macana: (Mexican-Ameriicanism—blackjack; penis; policeman's club)

machetazo: (Spanish—cutlass stroke made with a machete) a machetazo usually results in the loss of an arm, a hand, a leg or even a head

machete: (Spanish—cane knife; corn knife; cutlass) this agricultural tool has long been the standard weapon of many country people, as well as underground forces lacking firearms or ammunition

machinegeweer: (Dutch—machine gun)

machi no shirami: (Japanese—lice of the town) hoodlums; underworldings

ma-da: (Malayan Chinese—police)

madat: (Malay—opium)

Madeleine: (French—Magdalen) name for a reformed prostitute like the original Mary Magdalene, whereas *madeleine* means a pear or a sponge cake

Mafia Mexicana: (Spanish—Mexican Mafia) south-of-the-border offshoot of the international Mafia; rivals to *La Nuestra Familia* (q.v.)

mah-da-liuh: (Malayan Chinese—police station)

mah-fe: (Cantonese Chinese—morphine)

mah-jeui-ban: (Cantonese Chinese—narcotic)

nah-jeui-yeeuhk: (Cantonese Chinese—narcotic)

mah-ji: (Cantonese Chinese—bullet)

maison: (French—house)—also a jail or lockup (*maison d'arret*) or a borstal or reform school (*maison de correction*)

maison close: (French—enclosed house) a brothel

maison d'abattage: (French—slaughterhouse) low-grade whorehouse

maison d'arret: (French—prison)

maison de correction: (French—house of correction) penitentiary

maison de force: (French—workhouse) prison where only those who work eat

maison de passe: (French—temporary house) whorehouse

maison de rendezvous: (French—meeting house) small hotel in which men meet their mistresses

maison de sante: (French—insane asylum)

maison de societe: (French—house of society) another euphemism for a brothel

maison de tolerance: (French—house of tolerance) state-controlled brothel

maison de verre: (French—glass house)

brothel where nothing is secret

maison d'illusions: (French—house of illusions) brothel

maison joie: (French—house of joy) brothel, where joy is believed to reside

maison tolerée: (French—tolerated house) state-controlled brothel

maitre de plaisir: (French—master of pleasure) an arranger of sexual pleasures for others—a pimp or procurer

mala in se: (Latin—bad in itself) legal term referring to an act that is considered criminal on the assumption that natural law makes it bad in and of itself

malandro: (Brazilian-Portuguese—combine confidence man, murderer, pimp and thief preying on prostitutes)

mala praxis: (Latin—malpractice) professional carelessness and misconduct (which is on the increase, according to the insurance companies that act as a financial buffer between some doctors and their patients)

mala prohibita: (Latin—prohibited evil) legal term meaning that an act is a crime because it is prohibited by law

mala vita: (Italian—bad life) the underworld

malheureuse: (French—unfortunate female) prostitute

malocchio: (Italian—the evil eye) belief held by some Sicilians and others that they may be harmed by someone casting an evil eye upon them or their doings

malum in se: (Latin—intrinsically evil) crimes such as arson, murder, rape, etc.

malum prohibitum: (Latin—evil prohibited) driving under the influence of alcohol or other drugs, practicing medicine without a license, etc.

malum quia prohibitum: (Latin—evil because prohibited) carrying concealed weapons, parking on the wrong side of the street, racing after ambulances or fire engines, etc.

mama-san: (Japanese—boss mother) madam of a brothel

mancebia: (Spanish—brothel)

mandanta: (Spanish—female prison trusty)

mandanto: (Spanish—male prison trusty)

manette: (Italian—handcuffs)

mani in alto: (Italian—hands up)

mano: hermano (Hispanic contraction—brother); *la mano* (Spanish—the hand)

mano a mano: (Spanish—hand to hand) person-to-person delivery of drugs

Mano Negra: (Italian or Spanish—Black Hand)

manos arriba: (Spanish—hands up)

maquereau: (French—mackerel) a pimp

maranguango: (Afro-Brazilian—intoxicated) also a nickname for marijuana

mariguana: (Mexican Spanish—marijuana)

marijuano: (Mexican Spanish—dealer in marijuana)

marimbero: (Spanish-American—marijuana dealer)

marquise: (French—marchioness) madam in charge of a whorehouse

Maschinengewehr: (German—machine gun)

Maschinenpistole: (German—submachine gun)

mash Allah: (Arabic—gift of God) euphemism for opium

massa: (Dutch—mob; rabble)

matador: (Spanish—bullfighter; killer; murderer)

matadora: (Spanish—female bullfighter; female killer)

matanca: (Portuguese—killing)

matanza: (Spanish—killing; slaughtering)

matar: (Portuguese or Spanish—to kill)

mate suegra: (Spanish—mother-in-law killer) spiked ball-and-chain mace

mazmorra: (Spanish—dungeon; underground cell)

medir su aceite: (Spanish—measure his oil) stab; thrust a stiletto into someone

memisir: (Turkish—prison trusty)

menottes: (French—handcuffs)

Menschenraub: (German—kidnapping)

meretrice: (Italian—meretricious woman) prostitute

meretrix: (Latin—meretricious woman) prostitute

meretriz: (Portuguese—female mercenary) woman whose sexual favors are for hire

metralhadora: (Portuguese—machine gun)

meurtrier: (French—murderer)

meurtrière: (French—female murderer)

mezzano: (Italian—pimp)

micheton: (French—boyfriend) man who keeps a call girl, pays her and often imagines he is in love with her

migra: inmigracion (Mexican-Spanish slang—the U.S. Border Patrol of the Immigration and Naturalization Service)

Mikrop: Mikropunkt (German—microdot) microfilm marvel of World War II whereby a page of top-secret information could be reduced to a dot no larger than the dot over a letter "i," then enlarged when needed

militza: (Russian—militia) local police of most Soviet cities and towns

Min Beirut: (Arabic—From Beirut) Lebanon-based anti-capitalist, anti-

Semitic Arab terrorists supporting the Red Army Faction and responsible for the kidnapping and the killing of West German industrialist Hanns-Martin Schleyer in 1977

minet: (French—darling) pretty boy often kept by an older man or an older woman

misdaad: (Dutch—crime; misdeed)

misdadig: (Dutch—criminal)

misdadiger: (Dutch—criminal)

mitragliatrice: (Italian—machine gun)

mitrailleuse: (French—machine gun)

mitsuyunyu: (Japanese—smuggle)

m'jun-i akbar: (Arabic—goblet of jam) North African confection made of hashish and used for its hallucinogenic effect

mobb: (Danish-Norwegian—mob; rabble)

mobile vulgus: (Latin—disorderly group of people)

mo-fe: (Cantonese Chinese—morphine)

mojado: (Mexican Spanish—wetback) illegal entrant into the United States who is forced to swim or wade the Rio Grande along the Texas border

mona: (Spanish—female monkey) Colombian slang for marijuana

Monsieur de Paris: (French—Mr. Paris) the guillotine operator

montonero: (Spanish—bushwhacker; guerrilla) in Argentina the montoneros are a Marxist-oriented Peronist group, frequently terrorizing the back country as well as urban areas

moord: (Dutch—murder)

moorddadig: (Dutch—murderous)

moordenaar: (Dutch—murderer)

mord: (Dano-Norwegian or Swedish—murder)

Mord: der Mord (German—murder)

mordare: (Swedish—murderer)

mordelon: (Mexican-Spanish—corrupt policeman) grafter

morder: (Dano-Norwegian—murderer)

Morder: der Morder (German—murderer)

Morderin: die Morderin (German—female murderer)

mordida: (Spanish—diminished, lessened, wasted away) Mexicanism for *la mordida*, the bite of the grafter, whether a policeman or a high-placed politician, taking a bite of everything in sight; long considered the mainstay of venal politicians in Mexico

mota: (Mexican slang—marijuana)

motard: (French slang—motorcycle policeman)

mouchard: (French—informer)

mouton: (French—sheep)—an *agent provocateur* (provoking agent) planted by police in a prison or an underground or underworld organization

mozhno: (Russian—swallow) woman who will seduce a man so that he may be entrapped by blackmail and force to reveal secret information

mueren pigs: (Chicano graffitic inscription common in many Mexican border cities and towns—kill the cops)

mula: (Spanish—mule) Mexican-Americanism for a carrier of drugs, a prison guard or a stubborn person

mulher da rua: (Portuguese—woman of the world) prostitute

mundo do crime: (Portuguese—world of crime) the underworld

municao: (Portuguese—ammunition)

municion: (Spanish—ammunition)

musume: (Japanese—girl) often a euphemism for a prostitute

mutuus consensus: (Latin—mutual consent)

myohrtvee: (Russian—dead)

Nacht und Nebel: (German—Night and Fog) Nazi decree used during Hitler's era to annihilate prisoners without benefit of trial or condemnation

nacional: (Mexican Spanish—citizen of Mexico; Mexican national)

nafka: (Aramaic or Yiddish—prostitute; streetwalker) the antiquity of this term is evident

naigaika: (Russian—steel-tipped whip)

nalga de angel: (Spanish—angel's ass) marijuana

narcomaniaco: (Portuguese—narcotic addict)

narcotica: (Italian or Spanish—female narcotic addict)

narcotico: (Italian, Portuguese or Spanish—male narcotic addict)

narcoticum: (Dutch—narcotic)

narcotique: (French—narcotic)

narcotisch: (Dutch—narcotic)

narcotraf(ica)(ntes): (Spanish—narcotics traffic or narcotics traffickers)

nargile: (Turkish—water pipe) used for smoking tobacco, a mixture of tobacco and hashish or plain hashish

narkoman: (Swedish—narcotic addict)

narkomani: (Swedish—narcotic addiction)

narkotikos: (Greek—benumbing) ''narcotic'' and ''narcotics'' are derived from *narkotikos*

narkotisch: (German—narcotic)

navaja: (Spanish—knife) long razor-sharp blade

navaja de mue: (Spanish—silk knife; switchblade)

navaja de resorte: (Spanish—springblade

knife; switchblade knife)

nefarius: (Latin—criminal)

negligencia criminal: (Spanish—criminal negligence)

neige: (French—snow) cocaine

nervi: (French—gunman; tough guy)

ngaam-saat: (Cantonese Chinese—police whistle)

nga-pin: (Cantonese Chinese—opium)

nga-pun-yin: (Cantonese Chinese—opium)

nolo contendere: (Latin—I do not wish to contend it) defendant's formal answer in court to charges in a complaint or indictment whereby he or she states that the charges will not be contested; while not an admission of guilt, this subjects the defendant to the same legal consequences as a guilty plea; it does not, however, preclude the denial of guilt in a collateral proceeding

non compos mentis: (Latin—not in possession of her or his mental faculties; mentally incompetent)

Notzucht: (German—indecent assault; rape; violation)

nozem: (Dutch—juvenile delinquents)

nu delittu ci grida vindetta: (Sicilian Italian—a crime crying out for vengeance) Mafia term

Nuestra Familia: (Spanish—Our Family) prison-based Mexican-American underground organization engaged in jail breaks as well as narcotic trafficking

nullum crimen (nulla poena) sine lege: (Latin—no crime [no punishment] without [preexisting] law) an old Roman maxim meaning that an act cannot be considered criminal unless it has been defined as such by law

nymphe du pavé: (French—pavement nymph) girl of the streets; whore

obasan: (Japanese—auntie) madam in charge of a whorehouse

obesstvoh: (Russian—murder)

okane: (Japanese—money)

olive: (French slang—bullet; slug)

omerta: (Italian—connivance) attitude enforcing underground rules, which forbids members to call the police to settle a dispute and insists that personal offenses be settled by dueling or by one's family or friends; noble silence imposed on members of Mafia-type organizations as well as their families and friends and enforced by threats of physical violence or death to anyone who talks

omicidio: (Italian—homicide; murder)

omicidio premeditato: (Italian—premeditated murder)

ondergronds: (Dutch—resistance movement; underground)

onderwereld: (Dutch—underworld)

ontvoeren: (Dutch—kidnap)

opio: (Portuguese or Spanish—opium)

opiomania: (Spanish—addiction to opium)

opion: (Greek—sap) hence the ripe poppy sap known as opium

opium: (Dutch or French—opium)

Opium: das Opium (German—opium)

opiumkit: (Dutch—opium den)

opiumpijp: (Dutch—opium pipe)

opiumschuiven: (Dutch—opium smoke)

opiumschuiver: (Dutch—opium smoker)

O por O: Ojo por Ojo (Spanish—Eye for an Eye) Guatemalan right-wing terrorists

oppio: (Italian—opium)

Ordine Nero: (Italian—Black Order) fascistic terrorists active in Italy, where their posters appear in many cities

Organi: (Russian—Organs) Soviet slang term for the secret police

ostaggio: (Italian—hostage)

ostrog: (Russian—jail)

ostrogoth: (French slang—brute; lout; tough)

otage: (French—hostage)

otrava: (Russian—poison)

overfall: (Dano-Norwegian—raid)

oyabun: (Japanese—boss) gangster leader

oyez, oyez, oyez: (French—hear ye, hear ye, hear ye) thrice-repeated cry of the court clerk, who uses it to obtain silence before it is announced that the court is in session

paca: (Spanish—bundle; pack) tightly compressed brick of marijuana

pachuco: (Mexican Spanish—juvenile gangster)

pactum illicitum: (Latin—illicit pact) illegal contract or partnership; unlawful agreement

padrino: (Spanish—godfather; protector) nickname for an adult criminal who lives along the Mexican border and trains young Mexicans to mug, prostitute, push drugs, rob, shoplift, or steal anything from a camera or a purse to an automobile; padrinos also operate in other Latin American countries, such as Colombia and Panama

padrone: (Italian—boss; employer; patron)

padrote: (Spanish—proprietor of a brothel) whoremaster

pahleetseeyah: (Russian—police)

pah-sau: (Cantonese Chinese—pickpocket)

pakalolo: (Hawaiian—marijuana)

palacio blanco: (Spanish—white palace)— nickname of Mexico City's most modern prison for men and women; it has cement-floored steel-lined cells plus baths, a hospital, and a library

Palacio Negro: (Spaish—Black Palace) prisoners' nickname for Mexico's Lecumberri prison

palla: (Italian—bullet)

pallida mors: (Latin—pale death) death pallor

pangas: (Swahili—cane knives; corn knives; machetes) favorite weapon of many who have no firearms or ammunition; roving gangs in downtown Nairobi, Kenya are often armed with pangas

panier à salade: (French—paddy wagon; police van for transporting criminals)

pan-pan: (Polynesian—street prostitute) South Seas term introduced into Japan by the armed forces

Papaver somniferum: (Latin—soporific poppy) common source of codeine, heroin, morphine and opium, the primary product from which the others are derived

particeps criminis: (Latin—partner in crime)

Partisanenkrieg: (German—guerrilla fight; partisan fight)

patron: el patron (Spanish—boss; patron; proprietor of a whorehouse)

patrona: la patrona (Spanish—female boss; female proprietor of a whorehouse)

patrulla: (Spanish—patrol) Border Patrol

patrulla policial para combatir el vicio: (Spanish—police patrol to combat vice; the vice squad)

patrullero: (Spanish—patrolman)

pavot somnifere: (French—opium poppy)

pembunoh: (Malay—assassin)

pembunohan: (Malay—assassination)

penal: (Spanish—prison)

penalista: (Portuguese—penologist)

penalistica: (Portuguese—penology)

penalogia: (Italian or Portuguese—penologist)

pendejo: (Spanish slang—coward; idiot; stupid person)

peni: penitenciaria (Spanish—pertaining to prison; prison confessor)

penitenziario: (Italian—penitentiary)

penjara: (Malay—prison)

penologia: (Spanish—penology)

penologista: (Portuguese or Spanish—penologist)

penologo: (Spanish—penologist)

peripateticienne: (French—streetwalker)

perro guardian: (Spanish—guard dog; police dog)

perro policial: (Spanish—police dog)

persona non grata: (Latin—nonacceptable person) political or social outcast

pescha: (Hebrew—crime)

pestol: (Malay—pistol; revolver)

petit cadeau: (French—little payment) what a client pays a call girl; usually the sum is not little

petroleur: (French—petrol user) an arsonist using gasoline to set fires

pezzo grosso: (Italian—big shot)

pimpo: (Mexican or Puerto Rican Spanish—pimp)

piromaniaco: (Portuguese—pyromaniac)

piromano: (Spanish—pyromaniac)

piruja: (Mexican Spanish—prostitute)

pistola: (Italian, Portuguese or Spanish—pistol)

pistola ametralladora: (Spanish—submachine gun)

pistola-metralhadora: (Portuguese—submachine gun)

Pistole: (German—pistol)

pistoleiro: (Portuguese—gunman)

pistolero: (Spanish—armed gangster)

pistolet: (French—pistol)

pistolet-mitrailleur: (French—submachine gun)

pistolyet: (Russian—pistol)

pistool: (Dutch—pistol)

pizhdah: (Russian—pistol)

pizhdah hooey: (Russian—wet cunt) term of contempt applied to member of either sex; spoken explosively to indicate extreme disdain

pizzu: (Sicilian-Italian—enforced tribute; payoff)

planta de felicidade: (Portuguese—plant of happiness) marijuana

plastico: (Italian, Portuguese or Spanish—plastic) explosive base of nitrocellulose and nitroglycerine; explosive bomb of the type that can be mailed in an envelope or package

plastiek bom: (Dutch—plastic bomb)

plastique: (French—plastic) plastic bomb

plastische Bombe: (German—plastic bomb)

pleito: (Spanish—fist fight)

Pobel: (German—mob; rabble)

pocho: (Mexican Spanish—American-born Mexican) term of contempt

poena: (Latin—punishment)

pogrom: (Russian—destruction; devastation; riot) organized massacre of Jews by Christian fanatics in Poland, Rumania and Russia in the late 1800s and early 1900s; many Jews who survived such attacks fled to Canada and the United States to escape being beaten, pillaged, raped and killed while police and soldiers looked on

poignard: (French—dagger; dirk; stiletto)

poison: (French—poison)

police: (French—police)

Police des Moeurs: (French—Morals Police) vice squad

policia: (Portuguese, Spanish—police)

polis: (Malay—police)

politi: (Dano-Norwegian—police)

politica: (Italian, Portuguese, Spanish—female political prisoner) in recent years Portugal has had many *politicas*; in Spain, one of Franco's outstanding *politicas* was the Duchess of Medina Sidonia, a descendant of the admiral who commanded the Spanish Armada; she was imprisoned for protesting the accidental dropping of a hydrogen bomb on the village of Palomares on the Spanish coast by a U.S. Air Force jet plane in 1966

politico: (Italian, Portuguese, Spanish—male political prisoner)

politie: (Dutch—police)

politiehond: (Dutch—police dog)

politiewagen: (Dutch—police van)

politikonstabel: (Dano-Norwegian—policeman)

Polizei: die Polizei (German—police)

polizia: (Italian—police)

polizza: (Italian—lottery ticket) an important source of profit for mobsters and other unapprehended criminals, including venal politicians

pollero: (Mexican Spanish—chicken thief; poultryman) criminal who guides illegal entrants and other smugglers across the U.S. border, often turning them over to a *coyote*, who robs them of their clothes, money and other possessions

pollo: (Spanish—chicken) Mexican-American slang for an illegal alien in the United States

polytsiya: (Russian—police)

ponton: (Spanish—prison ship)

poolya: (Russian—bullet)

popolaccio: (Italian—mob; rabble)

populacho: (Portuguese or Spanish—mob; rabble)

porqueria: (Spanish—piggery) disgusting behavior or practices; filthiness

poruno: (Japanese—pornography)

posse comitatus: (Latin—power of the county) body of citizens empowered by the county sheriff to assist in the preservation of law and order

poste de police: (French—police station)

posto di polizia: (Italian—police station)

posto policial: (Portuguese—police station)

postribolo: (Italian—brothel)

poule: (French—hen) bar girl; call girl; prostitute; (slang) the police

poule de luxe: (French—high-class hen) high-class whore

presa: (Portuguese, Spanish—female prisoner)

presidio: (Spanish—military prison) may also refer to a citadel, convicts, hard labor, imprisonment or a penitentiary or prison; in the American Southwest many *presidios* were built during the days of Spanish and Mexican rule

presidio modelo: (Spanish—model penitentiary)

preso: (Portuguese, Spanish—male prisoner)

prestuplyeniye: (Russian—crime)

prigione: (Italian—prison)

prigioniera: (Italian—female prisoner)

prigioniero: (Italian—male prisoner)

prisao: (Portuguese—prison)

prision: (Spanish—prison)

prisioneira: (Portuguese—female prisoner)

prisioneiro: (Portuguese—male prisoner)

prisionera: (Spanish—female prisoner)

prisionero: (Spanish—male prisoner)

prison: (French—jail; prison)

prisonnier: (French—prisoner)

prisonnier de guerre: (French—life imprisonment)

prisonniere: (French—female prisoner)

prison perpetuelle: (French—life imprisonment)

prohibitum quia malum: (Latin—prohibited because evil) abuse of alcohol and narcotics, e.g.

pro se: (Latin—for oneself) acting as one's own defense attorney

prostibulo: (Portuguese—brothel; house of prostitution)

prostitucion: (Spanish—prostitution)

prostituee: (Dutch or French—prostitute)

prostitueren: (Dutch—to prostitute oneself)

prostituert: (Norwegian—prostitute)

prostitui: (Esperanto—prostitute)

prostituicao: (Portuguese—prostitution)

prostituidora: (Portuguese—prostitute)

prostituir: (Portuguese or Spanish—to prostitute)

prostituta: (Italian, Portuguese, Spanish—prostitute)

prostitutie: (Dutch—prostitution)

prostitution: (Dutch or French—prostitution)

Prostitution: die Prostitution (German—prostitution) a word the Germans owe to their French neighbors

prostituzione: (Italian—prostitution)

proxeneta: (Portuguese—pimp)

puella publica: (Latin—public girl) prostitute

pugnalata: (Italian—stab)

punaise: (French—bedbug) dirty prostitute
puñal: (Spanish—dagger; stiletto)
puñalada: (Spanish—stab; stab wound)
puñalejo: (Spanish—small dagger)
puñalero: (Spanish—dagger maker; knife maker; knife vendor)
punhal: (Portuguese—dagger or dirk)
puta: prostituta (Spanish contraction—prostitute)
putain: (French—prostitute)
putaismo: (Spanish—harlotry; whoredom)
putañear: (Spanish—to whore)
putañero: (Spanish—whoremonger)
putanismo: (Spanish—harlotry; whoredom)
putarron: (Spanish—low-class homo-sexual)
putarrona: (Spanish—low-class prostitute)
putassier: (French—whoremonger)
puteria: (Spanish—whoring; whore's work)
puterio: (Spanish—whorehouse)
putero: (Spanish—whoremonger)
Putsch: (German—armed uprising; riot) to push or shove; underground groups frequently indulge in putschist tactics in the hope that during the resulting confusion they may take over the government or at least eliminate some of their enemies
puttana: (Italian—whore)
puttaneria: (Italian—harlotry; whoredom)
puttaniere: (Italian—whoremonger)
putteneggiare: (Italian—to whore)
putz: (Yiddish slang—penis) also means an easy mark, a fool, a jerk
pyromane: (French—pyromaniac)
quart: (French—quarter) police station
quart d'oeil: (French—quarter eye) police commissioner
quartier chaud: (French—hot spot) red-light district
quartier tolere: (French—tolerance quarter) red-light district, where brothels are tolerated
questore: (Italian—chief constable)
questura: (Italian—police station)
quiller: (French slang—to cheat; to trick)
quimper: (French—to arrest)
qui s'excuse s'accuse: (French—he who excuses himself accuses himself)
racketteur: (French slang—racketeer)
raclette: (French slang—police squad car)
racolage: (French—pimping; soliciting)
rahzboynik: (Russian—robber)
rameira: (Portuguese—prostitute)
ramera: (Spanish—prostitute)
rapiña: (Spanish—rape)
rapire: (Italian—to abduct; to kidnap; to rape)
rapitore: (Italian—kidnapper)
raptar: (Portuguese or Spanish—to abduct; to kidnap; to rape)
rapto: (Portuguese or Spanish—rape)
raptor: (Portuguese or Spanish—rapist)
raptus: (Latin—rape)
rasoir nationale: (French—national razor) nickname for the guillotine
ratero: (Spanish—pickpocket; sneak thief)
raton: (Mexican-Americanism—thief) the Spanish word for a big rat
razzia: (Dutch, French, Italian—raid; roundup)
Razzia: die Razzia (German—raid; roundup)
rechbank: (Dutch—law court)
reclusao: (Portuguese—reclusion) solitary confinement
reclusion: (French—reclusion; seclusion) solitary confinement
reclusionnaire: (French—prisoner in solitary confinement
reconcentrados: (Spanish—concentration camps)—established by the Spaniards in Cuba in 1896 but abolished by 1898 after many protests made in England, Spain and the United States regarding the condition of these camps and their political prisoners
refem: (Portuguese—hostage)
rehen: (Spanish—hostage)
reide: (Portuguese—raid)
relegue: (French—isolated; relegated) convict condemned to banishment in a penal colony offshore or overseas
renegado: (Spanish—renegade)
respectueuse: (French—respectful) nickname for a prostitute
respirette: (French—respirator) cocaine
revelateur: (French—male detective)
revelatrice: (French—female detective)
revere: (Turkish—prison hospital)
revolver: (Dano-Norwegian, Dutch, Esperanto, French, Italian, Russian, Portuguese, Spanish, Swedish—revolver)
revolverbanditt: (Dano-Norwegian—gunman)
rezident: (Russian—resident) resident secret agent heading intelligence operations conducted from a consulate or embassy
rikos: (Finnish—crime)
rodeo criminal: (Spanish—criminal roundup; raid)
ronddolend: (Dutch—vagrant)
rover(ij): (Dutch—robber[y])
ruffianeggiare: (Italian—pandering; pimping)
rufian: (Spanish—hoodlum; hooligan; ruffian)
rurales: (Spanish—rural police)
saat-sei: (Cantonese Chinese—murder)
sakapared: (Spanish—wall jumper) second-story thief

samizdat: *samizdatel'stvo* (Russian—self-published and self-distributed) clandestine literature suppressed by the Soviet government

sans tain: (French—without silvering) a one-way mirror, often used by blackmailers and extortionists

sao: (Vietnamese—dishonest or ugly person)

satsujin: (Japanese—murder)

satyagraha: (Hindi—truth grasping) Gandhi's program of passive resistance to British rule

Saufer: (German—drunkard)

sau-liuh: (Cantonese Chinese—handcuffs)

scappare di prigione: (Italian—escape from prison)

scelerat: (French—criminal)

Schandmauer: die Schandmauer (German—Wall of Shame) West German name for the 864-mile-long network of electrified fencing, replete with armed border guards, attack dogs, ditches, land mines and tank traps as well as self-firing machine guns, that is also known as the Berlin Wall

shlockhouse: (Yiddish—gyp joint)

schmack: (Yiddish—heroin)

schmeck: (Yiddish—to sniff) sniff heroin

schmecker: (Yiddish—heroin addict)

schmecking: (Yiddish—sniffing) sniffing drugs

schmeer: (Yiddish—bribe; smear)

Schmiere: (German—bribe; grease)

Schmuggel: (German—smuggle)

schwedische Gardinen: (German—Swedish blinds) prison bars made of Swedish steel

Schwerpunktkriminaletat: (German—Heavy-Duty Criminal Establishment) West German police force dealing with drug smugglers and terrorists

Schwindel: (German—swindle)

scortum: (Latin—prostitute)

Securité: France's security service, headquartered in Paris, where it also serves as the National Central Bureau of Interpol

segregazione cellulare: (Italian—cellular confinement; close confinement) solitary confinement

Selbstmord: der Selbstmord (German—self-murder) suicide

selvmorder: (Dano-Norwegian—self-murder) suicide

sensemilla: (Spanish—without seed) high-potency marijuana produced by growing female plants in the absence of male plants and thereby creating seedless plants

seppuku: (Japanese—self-destruction or suicide) term more widely used than *hara-kiri*

serraglio: (Italian—lockup)

seui-seuhng-ging-chaat: (Cantonese Chinese—harbor patrol; marine police)

sharashka: (Russian slang—enterprise based on bluff or deceit)

shimon: (Japanese—fingerprint)

shinzo: (Japanese—young woman) euphemism for an old-hag servant in a whorehouse

shisho: (Japanese—unlicensed prostitute) a licensed prostitute is called a *kosho*

shujin: (Japanese—prisoner) criminal prisoner, as opposed to a prisoner of war (*furyo*)

sifo: (Cantonese Chinese—smuggled goods)

sigurmi: (Allbanian—security forces) secret police

sih-gaan: (Cantonese Chinese—killer; murderer)

sindacato: (Italian—syndicate) during Mussolini's regime the term referred to an organization of employers and employees as well as to a Mafia-type group of gangsters or to a radical union, as in other parts of Europe

sindicato: (Portuguese or Spanish—syndicate)

sinsemillas: (Spanish—seedless; without seeds) very potent seedless hybrid marijuana cultivated in California, where the billion-dollar annual crop attracts gangsters, poachers and law-enforcement officers; also called *sensemilla*

Sipo: Sicherheitspolizei (German—Security Police) Hitler's secret police, consisting of the Gestapo and the Kripo

skamas: (Yiddish—narcotics)

slaapwekkend: (Dutch—narcotic; opiate)

slakte: (Dano-Norwegian—kill; slay)

smitchka: (Russian—cleansing; purging) Stalin's *smitchka*, one of many culminating in the Moscow Trials, eliminated the top leaders of his armed forces and his party who would have opposed his pact with Hitler, whereby Russia gave Germany the green light to start World War II

smokkelen: (Dutch—smuggle)

smuggelin: (Low German—smuggling)

smugler: (Dano-Norwegian—smuggler)

smuglergods: (Dano-Norwegian—contraband) smuggled goods

soborno: (Spanish—bribe) perjured or suborned testimony

sobrenombre: (Spanish—alias; nickname)

soldati: (Italian—soldiers) the button men who are the lowest level of Mafia-type underworld operators, reporting to a *caporegime* or chief of an operating unit concerned with bookmaking, loan sharking, prostitution, vending machine operations and similar activities

soleta: (Mexican-Americanism—solitary confinement)

somaten: (Spanish—civilian militia; vigilantes)

sotterraneo: (Italian—underground)

sotto capo: (Italian—sub-chief) second in command in a Mafia organization

sous la table: (French—under the table) dead drunk; a deal made in which money passes unseen under the table

souteneur: (French—pimp)

souterrain: (French—cache; secret hiding place; underground cavern)

Spieler: (German—gambler; player)

spiller: (Dano-Norwegian—gambler)

Spinhaus: (German—workhouse)—old term for a house of correction

spinhuiz: (Dutch—workhouse—old term for a house of correction

Stalag: (German—prisoner-of-war camp)

Stecher: (German—sticker; stiletto)

stilett: der Stilett (German—stiletto)

Stilett: (Swedish—stiletto)

stilettata: (Italian—stab)

stiletto: (Italian—dagger; springblade; switchblade)

stiliagyi: (Russian—juvenile delinquents; young vagrants)

Stoppaglieri: (Italian—Pluggers) Sicilian underworld organization and former rival of the Mafia, later absorbed into the Mafia

Strafanstalt: die Strafanstalt (German—the prison)—also called *das Gefangnis*

Strafrecht: das Strafrecht (German—criminal law)

Strafrechtler: der Strafrechtler (German—penologist)

Strassen Dirne: die Strassen Dirne (German—street girl) streetwalker

stupefiant: (French—narcotic)

stylet: (French—stiletto)

suborno: (Portuguese—bribe) perjured or suborned testimony

sub rosa: (Latin—in secret) confidentially

subterraneo: (Spanish or Portuguese—underground)

suicidio: (Italian, Portuguese, Spanish—suicide)

suri: (Japanese—pickpocket)

sur le pave: (French—on the street) the black-market price of drugs, etc.

sus. per col.: suspensio per collum (Latin—hanging by the neck)

syfilis: (Dutch—syphilis)

syfilitisch: (Dutch—syphilitic)

syndicat: (French—syndicate) crime gang, labor union or group of investors

Syndikus: (German—syndicate) cartel; Mafia-type organization; radical labor union

tae kwan do: (Korean—art of self-defense)

tai los: (Chinese—dope bosses) some of the world's most lethal criminals, if their activities are measured by the number of victims of narcotic addiction

taksiri: (Swahili—crime)

talio: (Latin—revenge)

tante: (French—aunt) male homosexual

tantei: (Japanese—detective)

tapineuse: (French—female drummer) streetwalker; prostitute

Taschendieb: (German—pickpocket)

tata: (French—auntie) male homosexual

tau-wahn: (Cantonese Chinese—burglary)

tenancier de maison close: (French—female manager of a brothel) madam

tenant-maison: (French—brothel owner)

teriac: (Persian—antidote; cure-all) opium

terrorisme: (Dutch or French—terrorism)

terrorismo: (Italian, Portuguese, Spanish—terrorism)

Terrorismus: der Terrorismus (German—terrorism)

terrorist: (Dutch—terrorist)

Terrorist: der Terrorist (German—terrorist)

terrorista: (Italian, Portuguese, Spanish—terrorist)

terroriste: (French—terrorist)

Terroristen: (German—terrorists)

thana: (Hindustani—jail)

ticao: (Portuguese—firebug; pyromaniac)

tintureiro: (Portuguese—dry cleaner) Brazilian slang term for prison van

tirador: (Spanish—sharpshooter)

tiro: (Spanish—round) round of ammunition

tofete: (Puerto Rican jargon—tough)

tombas: (Spanish—tombs) solitary confinement cells

Tonton Macoutes: (Haitian-Creole French—Commando Uncles) dreaded terrorist secret police in Haiti, who are expert in torturing and killing while under the protection of the dictator and the sunglasses they wear

torchon: (French—dishrag) slut

toten: (German—kill)

traficante de mujeres publicas: (Spanish—trafficker in public women) pimp

trafic des stupéfiants: (French—drug traffic)

trainée: (French—trainee) euphemism for a whore

traite de blanches: (French—trade in whites)

so-called white slavery, although sexual
slavery exists almost worldwide and is no
respecter of color or racial origin

trampear: (Spanish—swindle)

transgressao: (Portuguese—crime; trans-
gression)

trapaca: (Portuguese—swindle)

traques: (Mexican-Americanism—tracks)
scars made by injecting heroin

Tres Marias: (Spanish—Three Marys)
Mexican penal settlement in the Pacific
Ocean off Nyarit; prisoners are kept on
Maria Madre Island

Trinker: der Trinker (German—drunkard)

Tripper: der Tripper (German—clap;
gonorrhea)

truffare: (Italian—swindle)

tsumi: (Japanese—crime)

tuchthuiz: (Dutch—house of correction;
workhouse)

tuer: (French—to kill)

tueur: (French—killer)

turist kogus: (Turkish—tourist cell
block—prison section reserved for
foreigners

turpitudo: (Latin—turpitude; vice)

typesse: (French—broad; dame; tart) easy-
going girl

tyurma: (Russian—jail)

ubat bius: (Malay—cocaine; narcotics)

ubat pemabop drp ganja: (Malay—hashish)

ubriaco: (Italian—drunk) the American
comedian Jimmy Durante used to mystify
some members of his audience by calling
them *ubriaco* with some vehemence

ubriacona: (Italian—female drunkard) also
shortened to *beona*

ubriacone: (Italian—male drunkard) also
shortened to *beone*

uccidere: (Italian—to kill)

uccisore: (Italian—killer)

Umoja: (Swahili—Unity) House of Umoja
in Philadelphia, designed to help black
youth involved in gang warfare

ungere la mano: (Italian—lubricate the
palm) bribe

Unione Corse: (Italian—Corsican Union)
rapidly growing underworld organization
active in Corsica, where it originated, as
well as in France, French-speaking
Canada, the Middle East, North Africa
and Indochina; active in narcotic traffic

Unione Siciliana: (Italian—Sicilian Union)
underworld organization better known by
such names as Black Hand, Cosa Nostra
and Mafia

Untergrund: (German—underground)

Untergrundbewegung: (German—underground movement)

Untermenschen: (German—gangsters,
thugs, underworlders) term also used by
Hitler and the Nazis to describe Gypsies,
Jews and all others considered inferior

Untersuchen: (German—inquest; inspection)

Unterwelt: die Unterwelt (German—the underworld)

vagabond: (French—vagrant)

vagabondo: (Italian—vagabond; vagrant)

Vagabund: (German—vagabond; vagrant)

vagabundo: (Portuguese or Spanish—
vagabond; vagrant)

vago: (Spanish—vagrant)

vagonzak: vagon zaklyuchennykh
(Russian—railroad prisoner car)

valdtakt: (Swedish—rape; violate)

valuta: (Italian—money)

vato loco: (Mexican-American slang—crazy
guy) person so stimulated by alcohol or
drugs as to act insanely or rage violently

vecindad: (Spanish-American slang—
tenement-filled slum)

veleno: (Italian—poison)

vendedor: (Spanish—seller) drug pusher

veneno: (Portuguese or Spanish—poison);
(Mexican-American and Puerto Rican expression—heroin)

venenum: (Latin—poison)

Verbrechen: das Verbrechen (German—
crime)

vergift: (Dutch—poison)

verkrachten: (Dutch—rape)

vermoorden: (Dutch—to murder)

verslaafde: (Dutch—addict)

versuchen: (German—stab)

Vesterfangsel: (Danish—Western Jail)—
Copenhagen prison

vettura cellulare: (Italian—celled vehicle)
prison van

vice: (French—vice)

vicio: (Spanish or Portuguese—vice)

vincula: (Latin—prisoners)

vinculum: (Latin—bonds; fetter; prison)

vingerafdruk: (Dutch—fingerprint)

vingt-et-un: (French—twenty-one) card
game popular at many gambling casinos

violador: (Spanish—rapist)

violar: (Spanish—to rape)

violare carnalmente: (Italian—violate
carnally) to rape

violazione: (Italian—rape)

violentador: (Portuguese—rapist)

violentia: (Latin—violence)

violer: (French—violate) rape

vita meretricia: (Latin—life of shame)
prostitution

vitelloni: (Italian—calves) juvenile delinquents

viuva-alegre: (Brazilian Portuguese—merry widow) prison van

vizio: (Italian—vice)

voiture cellulaaire: (French—celled vehicle) prison van

voldtekt: (Dano-Norwegian—rape; violate)

vor: (Russian—thief)

voyou: (French—gutter talk; hoodlum; hooligan)

vrai de vrai: (French—true, true) a pimp

vrouwelijkepolitie: (Dutch—policewoman)

vzyatka: (Russian—bribe)

wahine ho'okamakama: (Hawaiian—female prostitute)

wairo: (Japanese—bribe)

wiss Publizist: German—university-trained public-relations expert in legal science and police activities

xadrez: (Brazilian-Portuguese—jail)

xoxano baro: (Romany—big lie) Gypsy swindle or confidence game, also called *bajur*

yajiuma: (Japanese—mob; rabble)

Yakuza: (Japanese—good-for-nothings) Japan's gangsters and mobsters who control such rackets as extortion, gambling and prostitution; the anti-communist and strongly nationalist opinions expressed by the group's leaders and rank and file make it attractive to many not engaged in its illegal activities

yam-jeui: (Cantonese Chinese—drunk)

yaro: (Japanese—low fellow) male prostitute

yerba del diablo: (Spanish—devil's herb) jimson weed

yesco: (Mexican-Americanism—marijuana user)

yin-si: (Cantonese Chinese—opium)

yopparai: (Japanese—drunkard)

yukai suru: (Japanese—kidnap)

zacate: (Mexican-Americanism—marijuana) in Central America, Mexico and the Philippines, *zacate* means hay

zak: zaklyuchenny (Russian—prisoner) the contraction *zak* (pronounced *zek*) is used conversationally and in prison parlance and records

zakkenroller: (Dutch—pickpocket)

zbrodnia: (Polish—crime)

zek(s): [Soviet-Russian slang—prisoner(s)]

zelfmoord: (Dutch—self-murder; suicide)

zenkamono: (Japanese—jailbirds; tramps) the most despised elements of Japanese society; usually segregated into run-down sections of cities, such as the Sanya area of Tokyo

zigouiller: (French slang—to kill)

ziguoince: (French slang—prostitute)

zlocin: (Czechoslovakian or Serbo-Croatian—crime)

zonard: (French slang—denizen of the zone of prostitution)

zorra: (Spanish—female fox; vixen) prostitute

Zuchthaus: das Zuchthaus (German—penitentiary; prison)

Zuchthaus arbeit: (German—convict labor; prison labor)

Zuchthausler: (German—convict)

Zuchthausstrafe: (German—penal servitude)

zurribanda: (Spanish slang—beating; brawling; flogging; scuffling; thrashing)

zurriburri: (Spanish slang—confusion; cur; mob; rogue; ruffian; uproar)

zwendel: (Dutch—swindle)

PLACE-NAME NICKNAMES

Place-name nicknames are included in this book because of their widespread use in the underworld and in the upperworld. In some instances they conceal the identity of places, while in others they reveal the facility of the speaker in adding color to language. (Please note that the place-name nicknames of prisons are to be found in the main section of the book.)

Aber: Aberdeen, Scotland
Adee: Adelaide, Australia
Albuturkey: Albuquerque, N.M.
Alex: Alexandria, Egypt
Alice: The Alice (Alice Springs, Northern Territory, Australia)
Alligator Alley: the Everglades Parkway linking Florida's east coast (Fort Lauderdale) and its west coast (Naples); the Tamiami Trail linking Tampa and Miami, Fla.
Aloha State: Hawaii
Ambon: Amboina, Indonesia
America's Devil's Island: post-Civil-War nickname of the military prison at Fort Jefferson on the Dry Tortugas, 65 miles west of Key West in the Gulf of Mexico
Am Sam: American Samoa
'Aña: Agaña, Guam
Anco: Ancohuma, Bolivia
Ando: Andorra
Angkor: Angkor Thom, Kampuchea
Anto: Antofagasta, Chile
Apple Isle: Tasmania, Australia
Arkie: Arkansas
Augie: Augusta, Ga.
Auk: Auckland, New Zealand
Aussieland: Australia
BA: Buenos Aires, Argentina
Bag Town: San Diego Calif. (where many marines and sailors can be seen toting sea bags)
Balti: Baltimore, Md.
'Bama: Alabama
Banana City: Brisbane, Queensland, Australia
Bananaland: Queensland, Australia
Bank Robbery Capital of the World: Los Angeles
Barna: Barcelona, Spain
Bat Rou: Baton Rouge, Louisiana
Bayou City: Houston, Texas
B-B: Bora Bora, French Polynesia
BC: Baja California, Mexico; British Columbia, Canada
Beantown: Boston, Mass.
Bedlam: nickname of St. Mary of Bethlehem, the celebrated lunatic asylum of old London, many of whose inmates were criminally insane
Bee Wee: British West Indies
Belmo: Belmopan, Belize
Berdoo: San Bernardino, Calif.
Berm: Bermuda
Bess: Bessemer, Ala.
Best Location in the Nation: Cleveland, Ohio
Betel Nut Island: Penang, Malaysia
Beth: Bethlehem, Pa.
Big Apple: New York City
Big D: Dallas, Texas
Big Ditch: Panama Canal
Big Four: Cleveland, Cincinnati, Chicago and St. Louis
Biggest Little City: Reno, Nev.
Big Heart of Texas: Austin
Big Island: Hawaii (largest of the Hawaiian Islands)
Big Orange: Los Angeles
Big Smoke: Sydney, Australia
Big Windy: Chicago, Ill.
Bikini State: Florida
Black Heart: Black Heart of Montana (Butte)
Blighty: England
Bluegrass Capital: Lexington, Ky.
Bogland: Ireland
Bom: Bombay, India
Boy's Town: Omaha, Neb.
Brass: Butte, Mont.
Bread Basket: Fargo, N.D.
Brissie: Brisbane, Queensland, Australia
Brix: Brixham, England
Brookolino: (Italian-American slang) Brooklyn, N.Y.
Buda: Budapest, Hungary
Cabbage Patch: Victoria, Australia
Calc: Calcutta, India

Caliente: Agua Caliente (border racetrack town adjoining Tijuana, Mexico)

Capirucha: (Mexican-Americanism) Mexico City

Capital of Black America: Harlem (section of New York City's Manhattan Island)

Capital of Mudland: Georgetown, Guyana (surrounded by marshes and swamps)

Capital of Polynesia: Auckland, New Zealand

Carat City: diamond-mining Kimberley, South Africa

Celery City: Kalamazoo, Mich.

Cereal City: Battle Creek, Mich.

'Change: Royal Stock Exchange in London

Chappiequack: Chappaqua, N. Y.

Chi(c): Chicago, Ill.

Chimbo: Chimborazo, Ecuador; Chimbote, Peru

Chi-Pitts: the Chicago-Pittsburgh industrial area, including Akron, Cleveland, Detroit, Fort Wayne, Gary, Toledo, Youngstown, et al.

Cholera Capital: Calcutta, India

Christmas Cove: South Bristol, Maine

Chuco: (Mexican-Americanism) El Paso, Texas

Cigar Capital: Key West, Fla.

Cigar City: Tampa, Fla.

Cincy: Cincinnati, Ohio

Cinty: Cincinnati, Ohio

City: The City (London's financial district)

City by the Rivers: Kansas City in Kansas and Missouri at the mouth of the Kansas River flowing into the Missouri; Minneapolis-St. Paul in Minnesota and on the Minnesota and Mississippi; Philadelphia, Pennsylvania on the Delaware and Schuylkill; Pittsburgh, Pennsylvania at the confluence of the Allegheny and the Monogahela; Portland, Oregon where the Columbia is joined by the Willamette; St. Louis, Missouri where the Mississippi meets the Missouri, etc.

City of Blazing Lights: Hong Kong or Shanghai

City of Brotherly Love: Philadelphia, Pa.

City of Champions: Pittsburgh's official nickname

City of Coral: coral reefs offshore the Virgin Islands

City of Death: Kipling's name for Lahore, India

City of Dreadful Night: Calcutta, India, according to Kipling

City of Southern Charm: Savannah, Ga.

City of Spies: Beirut, Berlin, Copenhagen, Hong Kong, London, New York, Paris Singapore, Stockholm, Vienna and Zurich share this place-name nickname with some other cities that are equally important as centers of espionage activity

City of Surprises: Amsterdam, the Netherlands

City of Temples: Benares in India and Katmandu in Nepal share this nickname

City of Witches: Salem, Mass.

City That Care Forgot: New Orleans, La.

City That Knows How: San Francisco, Calif.

Clam Town: Norwalk, Conn.

Cleve: Cleveland, Ohio

Coast: The Coast (the Pacific coast of Canada or the United States)

Cockpit of Europe: Belgium

Coffs: Coffs Harbour, Australia

Como: Comodoro Rivadavia, Argentina

Conchtown: Key West, Fla.

Coon Dog Capital: Vienna (pronounced *Vienna*), Ill.

Copen: Copenhagen, Denmark

Corncob Capital: Washington, Mo.

Coto: Cotopaxi, Ecuador

Cottonwood City: Leavenworth, Kan.

Cowboy Capital: Dodge City, Kan.

Cow Capital: Wichita, Kan.

Cowtown: Fort Worth, Texas and Omaha, Neb. share this place-name nickname

Coz: Cozumel Island, Mexico

Crabtown: Annapolis, Md.

Crescent City: New Orleans, La.

Croix: St. Croix, American Virgin Islands

Cross: King's Cross (nightlife center of Sydney, Australia; also called The Cross)

Crossroads of the Pacific: Honolulu, Hawaii

Crown Jewel of the Adriatic: Venice

Crystal Meth Capital: San Diego, California

Cultured Pearl Archipelago: Japan

Cunt Town: (naval argot) Norfolk, Va. (see also **Shitport**)

Cux: Cuxhaven, West Germany

Dago: San Diego, Calif.

Damnable Place: George Bernard Shaw's nickname for Hong Kong

Dam on the Amstel: Amsterdam, the Netherlands

Day: Dayton, Ohio

Diamond Continent: Africa

Diamond Street: nickname of New York City's W. 47th St. between Fifth Ave. and the Avenue of the Americas (Sixth Ave.), where many diamond merchants maintain offices

Diego: (Mexican-American truncation—San Diego)

Diggerland: Australia

Divorce Capital of America: Reno, Nev.

Djib: Djibouti

D'Lo: The Lord, Mississippi

Dope Capital of Canada: Vancouver, British Columbia, Canada

Down Yonder: coastal North Carolina

Dream Factory of the Western World: Hollywood, Calif.

Drug Capital of America: southeastern Florida where coastal marshes and inland swamps offer opportunities for smuggling cocaine and marijuana by air and by sea for distribution throughout the United States and Canada

Dude Ranch Capital: Wickenburg, Ariz.

Dupont Town: Wilmington, Del.

East Los: East Los Angeles, Calif.

Energy City: Houston, Texas

Fag Key: Faggot Key (Key West, Fla.)

Filthydelphia: Philadelphia, Pa.

Fiordland: South Island, New Zealand's southwestern coast

Fjordland: Norway

Flabussce: (Italian-American slang) Flatbush section of Brooklyn, N.Y.

Fort Liquordale: Fort Lauderdale, Fla. (when college students make their Easter vacation visit)

Fort Savage: alleged nickname of the East Harlem police precinct in New York City

Fountain of Youth: St. Augustine, Fla.

Four-C City: El Paso, Texas (where cattle, climate, copper and cotton lure settlers and visitors as well as those wishing to cross the border into Ciudad Juarez, Mexico)

Fragrant Harbor: Hong Kong

Frisco: San Francisco, Calif.

Frostbite: Fairbanks, Alaska

Fun City: New York City

Fungus Corners: rainy Bremerton, Wash.

Gabba: Wollongabba (suburb of Syndey, Australia)

Galvy: Galveston, Texas

Gambling Capital of the Far East: Macao, Portuguese China (near Hong Kong)

Gambling Capital of the Far West: Las Vegas, Nev.

Gangland: Chicago, Ill.

Garbage Dump: the Great Meadow Correctional Facility at Comstock, N.Y.; California's San Quentin Prison, which holds felons from 12 other prisons that have sent their most hardened and troublesome inmates there

Garden Island: Kauai, Hawaii

Gas House of the Nation: Washington, D.C.

Gates of Hell: old nickname for the entrance to Macquarie Harbour on the Indian Ocean coast of Tasmania when it was a penal settlement in Van Diemen's Land

Gateway to the Gulag: Soviet port of Magadan on the Sea of Okhotsk where in the time of Stalin political prisoners were landed en route to forced-labor camps in the Gulag

Gib: Gibraltar

Gitmo: Guantanamo Bay, Cuba

'Glades: Florida Everglades

GO City: Greater Omaha, Neb.

Gold Coast: Australian beach resort area from Coolanfatta to Southport, below Brisbane; Chicago's bohemian section behind the once-elegant lake front; Florida resort area from Key West to Palm Beach; Gulf Coast of the U.S. from Key West to Texas; Ghana

Golden Gate: entrance to San Francisco Bay

Golden Prison of Paris: the Louvre (the great art museum was formerly a fortress whose subterranean vaults held hunting dogs and political prisoners)

Golden Triangle: opium-producing fields of Burma, Laos and Thailand along the border of China's Yunnan Province

Goo: Goole, England

Granite Center: Barre, Vt.

Graveyard of the Atlantic: Cape Hatteras, N.C. or Sable Island, Nova Scotia

Great Street: State Street in Chicago

Great White Strip: brilliantly illuminated main street of Las Vegas, Nev.

Great White Way: New York City's Broadway in the Times Square area

Groperland: Western Australia

'Guana: Iguana Island, British Virgin Islands

Guaya: Guayaquil, Ecuador

Guy: Guyana (formerly British Guiana)

Gypsum City: Fort Dodge, Iowa

Hamb: Hamburg, West Germany

Hamm: Hammerfest, Norway

Hangtown: place-name nickname of El Dorado or Placerville, Calif., where many bandits were hanged during the Gold Rush

Hardware City: New Britain, Conn.

Heart of Darkness: Zaire (formerly called the Congo)

Heart of It All State: Ohio

Heart of Midlothian: Tolbooth Prison in Edinburgh, Scotland

Hellhole of the Pacific: Kororareka, New Zealand

Hell in the Hills: Pittsburgh, Pa. by night when its blast furnaces illuminate its hills

Hell of Macquarie Harbour Station: nickname of an old penal colony on the Indian Ocean coast of Tasmania

Hell on Wheels: Cheyenne, Wyo.
Hell's Gates: Macquarie Harbour; Tasmania's first convict settlement
Hell's Kitchen: New York City's mid-West Side
Heroin Capital of America: New York City's Harlem
Hill: The Hill (Capitol Hill, Washington, D.C.)
Hill City: Portland, Maine
HK: Hong Kong
Hob: Hobart, Tasmania or Hoboken, N.J.
Hobo: Hoboken, N.J.
Hog Butcher for the World: poet Carl Sandburg's name for Chicago
Home of Jesse James: St. Joseph, Mo.
Home of the Bean and the Cod: Boston, Mass.
Hoosier Capital: Indianapolis, Ind.
Hotlana: Atlanta, Ga.
Hottest Town: Quartzite, Ariz. (where noon temperatures of 108° F are not uncommon)
Hous: Houston, Texas
Hub: The Hub (Boston, Mass.)
Hub City of Texas: Alice
Hub of the Caribbean: Jamaica
Huggermugger Metropolis of Cloak-and-Dagger Conspirators: Mexico City, where every foreign intelligence service tries to penetrate every other's organization, even if this requires criminal acts
Hustletown on the Canal: Houston, Texas
Indy: Indianapolis, Ind.
Insurance Capital: Hartford, Conn. or Omaha, Neb. as each contains more than 30 insurance companies
Inv: Inverness, Scotland
Ips: Ipswich, England
Irish Channel: rough-and-tumble riverfront area of New Orleans, La.
Island of Death: Kahoolawe, Hawaii (uninhabited island used for target practice)
Island of Enchantment: Puerto Rico
Island of Hell: Norfolk Island in the South Pacific, when it was the most dreaded of all Australian prison stations
Island of Venus: Tahiti
Isles of Devils: old nickname for the reef-studded Bermudas
Jam: Jamaica
Jap: Japan (the country and its people find this nickname degrading; therefore it is used less and less by foreigners)
Jax: Jacksonville, Fla.
Jeff City: Jefferson City, Mo.
Jet Town: Seattle, Wash.
Jewel: The Jewel (La Jolla, Calif.)
Jimtown: Jamestown, California or

Jamestown, North Dakota
Joburg: Johannesburg, South Africa
John: St. John, American Virgin Islands; St. John, New Brunswick, Canada
John Bull's Other Island: Ireland, before its independence was declared in 1919
John's: St. John's, Newfoundland, Canada
Juariles: (Mexican-Americanism) Ciudad Juarez, Mexico, opposite El Paso, Texas
Kat: Katmandu (capital of Nepal, close to the northern border of India)
KC: Kansas City (twin cities of Kansas and Missouri)
Kentuck: Kentucky
Kild: Kildare, Ireland
Kili: Kilimanjaro, Tanzania
Kilk: Kilkenny, Ireland
KL: Key Largo, Fla.; Kuala Lumpur, Malaysia
Kodak City: Rochester, N.Y.
Krak: Krakatoa, Indonesia
LA: Los Angeles, Calif.
Lab: Labrador, Canada
Lafe: Lafayette (in most of the 21 states where this place-name honors Gen. Gilbert de Lafayette)
Lake City: Madison, Wis.
Land Beyond the Mountains: Tennessee
'Lando: Orlando, Fla.
Land of a Million Elephants: Laos
Land of Death and Chains: Maxim Gorki's nickname for Siberia
Land of Instant Women: Thailand
Land of Peace: Thailand, formerly called Siam
Land of Political Exiles: Yakutia (northeastern Siberia in the USSR)
Land of the Boomerang: Australia
Land of the Golden Fleeced: Las Vegas, Nev.
Land of the Hummingbird: Trinidad
Land of Song: Italy
Land Time Forgot: Australia
'Lanta: Atlanta, Ga.
Last Frontier: Alaska
Last, Loneliest, Loveliest (city): Auckland, New Zealand, according to Kipling
Las Vegas East: Atlantic City, N.J.
Last Place on Earth: Antarctica
Laun: Launceston, Tasmania
Lesbos, Long Island: Fire Island, N.Y.
Leso: Lesotho
Lex: Lexington (place-name of 20 American places)
Lilac City: Spokane and Tacoma both claim this name
Lim: Limerick, Ireland
Lions Gate: entrance to the port of

Vancouver, British Columbia, Canada

Little Denmark: Solvang, Calif.

Little Egypt: the Delta country of southern Illinois

Little Havana: Cuban refugee area of Miami, Fla.

Little Lunnon: Colorado Springs, Colo.,

Little New York: Miami Beach, Florida's South Beach

Little Rhody: Rhode Island

Live Free or Die State: New Hampshire

Longos: (Mexican-Americanism) Long Beach, Calif.

Loop: The Loop (center-city Chicago)

Los: Mexican-American truncation for Los Angeles

Los Ang: Los Angeles, Calif.

Lost Wages: nickname for Las Vegas, Nevada's gambling resort

Louie: St. Louis, Mo.

Lucy: St. Lucia, British West Indies

Lutia: St. Lucia, British West Indies

Luxem: Luxembourg

Ma-Bo: Marianas-Bonin (islands)

Madhouse on the Potomac: the Capitol; the Pentagon; the White House; or Washington, D.C. in general

Mad I: Madeira Islands

Manor: The Manor—English underworld slang for London

Mardi Gras Metropolis: New Orleans, La.

Marmalade Capital: Dundee, Scotland

Martin: St. Martin or Sint Maarten in the Leeward Islands

Metroland: portion of London that is served by its underground (subway) system, the Metro

Metropolis of the World: London

Mich: Michigan; Michoacan

Mile-High City: Denver, Colo. (located a mile above sea level)

Minnie: Minneapolis, Minn.

Missie: Mississippi

Mob: Mobile, Ala.

Mo' Bay: Mobile Bay, Ala.; Montego Bay, Jamaica

Mobtown: old nickname of Baltimore, Md.

Mo City: Motor City (Detroit, Mich.)

Modern Gomorrah: nickname applied to the nightclub district of any city where much nocturnal entertainment is controlled by criminals; New York, Paris and Tijuana have been so nicknamed, as well as other places

Monte: Monte Carlo

Monte Carlo of the East: Macao, Portuguese China

Monty: Montgomery, Alabama

Monumental City: Baltimore, Md.

Mormon City: Salt Lake City, Utah

Mosquito State: New Jersey's unenviable epithet, engendered by its mosquito-infested marshes and swamps

Mother of Cities: Bombay, India, according to Kipling

Mother of Russian Cities: Kiev

Motown: Motor Town (Detroit, Mich.)

Mountain City: Chattanooga, Tenn.

Movieland: Hollywood, Calif.

Mozam: Mozambique

Murder Capital of America: Detroit, Mich., where for every crime reported three go unreported, according to *The Manchester Guardian Weekly*

Music Capital of America: Los Angeles or New York

Nail City: Wheeling, W. Va.

Nam: Vietnam

Namib: Namibia (South-West Africa)

Nanga: Nanga Parbat, India

Nau: Nauru Island in the western Pacific, just below the Equator

Nervve Center of Alaska: Anchorage

Newc: Newcastle-upon-Tyne, England

Newfie: Newfoundland, Canada

New Lon: New London, Conn.

New Mex: New Mexico

Nicolaas: Sint Nicolaas, Aruba

Nicos: Nicosia, Cyprus

Nip: Nippon (Japan)

NO: New Orleans, La.

Nogal: Nogales, Sonora, Mexico

Norf: Norfolk (in Canada, England, the United States and the South Pacific)

North Cuba: Miami, Florida

NY: New York

Nyas: Nyasaland (former name of Malawi)

NZ: New Zealand

Oak: popular truncation for any Oakland, Oak Park, Oak Ridge, etc.

Oakie City: Oklahoma City, Oklahoma

Oax: Oaxaca, Mexico

OB: Ocean Beach (seaside suburb of San Diego, Calif.)

Oil City: Bartlesville or Tulsa, Okla.

Okie: Oklahoma

Okie City: Oklahoma City, Okla.

Okin: Okinawa

Old Dorp: Schenectady, N.Y., whose nickname recalls the days of the Dutch

Old Gib: Gibralter

Old Point: Old Point Comfort, Va.

Oleander City: Galveston, Texas

Oma: Omaha, Neb.

Ooty: Ootacamund, India

Opium Kingdom: nickname applied to any country such as Bolivia, Burma, Colombia, Ecuador, Laos, Mexico or Peru where the opium poppy, the source of heroin is cultivated and processed

Opiumland: poppyfields of the Golden Triangle of northeastern Burma, northern Laos and northern Thailand; 70 percent of the world's illicit supply of raw opium is harvested here

Opo: Oporto, Portugal

Ouga: Ougadougou, Upper Volta

Owlsville: any place after midnight; originally London's post-midnight nickname

Pachuco: (Mexican-Americanism) El Paso, Texas (also called Pachucolandia)

Paddo: Paddington, Australia

Paki: Pakistan

Palmetto City: Charleston, S.C.

Pango: Pago Pago, American Samoa

Paradise Lost: New Orleans, La.

Pasca: Pascagoula, Mississippi

P-burg: Pittsburgh, Pa.

Pearl: Pearl Harbor, Hawaii

Pearl of the Adriatic: Dubrovnik (Yugoslavia's seaside resort)

Pearl of the Antilles: Cuba

Pedro: San Pedro, Calif.

Penn: Pennsylvania

Pennsy: Pennsylvania

Pensy: Pensacola, Fla.

Peory: Peoria, Ill.

Pepper Coast: Liberia

Pete: St. Petersburg, Fla.

Philly: Philadelphia, Pa.

Phx: Phoenix, Ariz.

Piccy: Piccadilly, London

Pirate City: an old nickname for Tampa, Fla., dating from when the pirate chief Gasparilla made it his headquarters

Pirate Coast: Trucial Coast of Arabia including Abu Dhabi, Ajam, Dubai, Furairah, Ras el Khaimah, Sharjah and Umm al Quwain, which comprise the United Arab Emirates

Pitts: Pittsburgh, Pa.

Pocaloo: Pocatello, Idaho

Pool: The Pool (Thames River below London Bridge)

Popa: Popayan, Colombia

Popo: Popocatepetl, Mexico

Potash City: Saskatoon, Saskatchewan, Canada

Pot Smugglers' Paradise: Florida's inlet-indented 1,200-mile coastline, whose beaches and waterways prove ideal for all who smuggle drugs into the United States

Poz: Poznan, Poland

PQ: Province of Quebec

Pretzel City: Reading, Pa.

Prison at the Bottom of the World: Ushusia, Argentina on Beagle Channel close to Cape Horn in southernmost South America

Prison of Gold: The Louvre (the great Parisian art museum and its treasures, acquired by conquest and by purchase)

Profit Center of the Southwest: Phoenix, Ariz.

Prostitution Capital of the South: old nickname for New Orleans, La.

'Pulco: Acapulco, Mexico

Punkie Town: Punxsutawney, Pa.

Punks' Paradise: nickname given Nevada by Jack Lait and Lee Mortimer, authors of *U.S.A. Confidential*

Punxey: Punxsutawney, Pa.

QC(ity): Quezon City, Philippines

Q Roo: Quintana Roo, Mexico

Quail Haven: Cedar Vale, Kan.

Quaintest City in the U.S.: Santa Fe, New Mexico

Quaker City: Philadelphia, Pa.

Quaker State: Pennsylvania

Queen Cities of the Austro-Hungarian Empire: Budapest, Prague, Vienna

Queen City: Lahore (in the Punjab of Pakistan)

Queen City of Canada: Toronto

Queen City of the Hanseatic League: Lübeck

Queen City of the Hudson: Yonkers, New York

Queen City of India: Bombay

Queen City of the Lakes: Buffalo, N.Y.; Toronto, Ontario, Canada

Queen City of the Lehigh Valley: Allentown, Pa.

Queen City of the Merrimack: Manchester, New Hampshire

Queen City of the Mississippi: St. Louis, Missouri

Queen City of the Mountains: Knoxville, Tennessee

Queen City of New Zealand: Auckland

Queen City of the North: Edinburgh

Queen City of the Pacific: San Francisco and Seattle battle for this title

Queen City of the Plains: Denver

Queen City of the Rio Grande: Del Rio, Texas

Queen City of the Sea: Charleston, South Carolina, where loyal Charlestonians agree the Ashley and the Cooper rivers join to form the Atlantic Ocean

Queen City of the Sound: Seattle, Washington on Puget Sound

Queen Maud Land: Norwegian Antarctica

Queen City of the South: Atlanta, Georgia and Sydney, Australia

Queen City of the Southern Tier: Elmira, New York

Queen of the Adriatic: Venice

Queen of the Antilles: Cuba

Queen of the Arabian Sea: Cochin, China

Queen of the Belgian Beaches: Ostend

Queen of the Caribbes: Nevis

Queen of the Comstock Lode: Virginia City, Nevada

Queen of the Danube: Budapest

Queen of the French Riviera: Nice

Queen of the Sea Islands: Beaufort, South Carolina

Queen of the Seas: Glasgow and Venice compete for this place-name nickname title

Queen of the South: New Orleans

Queen of the Spas: Saratoga, New York

Quilmas: San Quilmas (Mexican-Americanism for San Antonio, Texas)

Quoddy: Passamaquoddy Bay (between Maine and New Brunswick)

Rab: Rabat, Morocco; Rabaul, New Britain

Radio Capital: Camden, N.J.

Rand: Witwatersrand (South Africa's diamond-mining reef)

Rest and Reverie: Terminal Island, Calif.

Rifle City: Springfield, Mass.

Ring: The Ring (downtown Vienna, Austria)

Ring of Fire: volcanic zone extending from Alaska to Chile and from Siberia to New Zealand via Indonesia

Rio: Rio de Janeiro, Brazil

Rock: The Rock of Gibraltar

Rock City: Nashville, Tenn.

Rocket City: Huntsville, Ala.

Rogues' Island: Rhode Island's nickname given by Puritans of the Massachusetts Bay Colony who exiled Roger Williams, Anne Hutchinson, and many others who demanded the strict separation of church and the state they established in Rhode Island under royal charter

RoK: Republic of Korea

Rose City: Portland, Ore.

Rubber City: Akron, Ohio

Sacto: Sacramento, Calif.

Said: Port Said, Egypt

St. Barts: St. Barthelemy in the French West Indies

St. Joe: St. Joseph, Mo.

St. Kitts: St. Christopher in the British West Indies

St. Lou: St. Louis, Mo.

St. Lucy: St. Lucia, British West Indies

St. P: St. Pancras (London railway terminal); St. Paul, Minn.

St. Pete: St. Petersburg, Fla.

St. Vince: St. Vincent in the British West Indies

Salt City: Syracuse, N.Y.

Saltz: Salzburg, Austria

Sam: Samoa

San Anto: San Antonio, Texas (Mexican-American place-name nickname)

San Antone: San Antonio, Texas

San Berdoo: San Bernardino, Calif.

San Jack: San Jacinto, Texas

San Jo: San Jose, Calif. (Mexican-American place-name nickname)

San Pedro Sucio: San Pedro Sula's nickname borne by the second largest city in Honduras

San Quilmas: (Mexican-Americanism of unknown origin) San Antonio, Texas

Saudi: Saudi Arabia

Sav: Savannah, Ga.

S-bahn: *Stadtschnellbahn* (German—State Express Road) electric railway serving Berlin

Scandinavian Fun Capital: Copenhagen, Denmark

Scrapple City: Allentown, Pa.

Seafood Center: Biloxi, Miss.

Sea-Tac: Seattle-Tacoma

Separationist State: Rhode Island

Seventh Continent: Antarctica

Sex Isle: Mykonos in the Greek Island, close to Piraeus, the port of Athens

Sexyola: Sixaola, Costa Rica

Sheff: Sheffield, England

Shets: Shetland Islands off Scotland

Shining Star of the Caribbean: Puerto Rico

Shitport: (naval argot) Norfolk, Va.

Siberia: generic term meaning a remote place of exile or imprisonment; originally a Russian area given over to the exile and imprisonment of political prisoners

Siberia de las Américas: (Spanish—Siberia of the Americas)—political prisoner's nickname for the Castro-controlled prisons on the Isle of Pines (*Isla de Pinos*), renamed *Isla de Juventud* (Isle of Youth)—in the Caribbean off the southwest coast of Cuba

Siberian salt mines: nickname for the many forced-labor camps and prisons scattered throughout Siberia as well as the rest of the USSR

Silk City: Paterson, New Jersey

Silver City: Broken Hills, New South Wales, Australia

Silver Gate: entrance to San Diego Bay in California

Simons: Simonstown, South Africa

Sin Angeles: (Spanish—Without Angeles) Los Angeles, especially the barrios of East

Los Angeles

Sin Capital: Singapore's nickname, despite protests by its decent citizens

Sin City: Las Vegas, Nev.

Sing(a): Singapore

Sink of New England: Rhode Island's uncomplimentary nickname given it by Puritans in Massachusetts appalled by the separation of church and state guaranteed Rhode Island in its royal charter

Sin Strip: San Francisco's North Beach area

Six-Shooter Junction: old name of Harlingen, Texas (near Brownsville on the Rio Grande)

Sixth Continent: Australia

SJIs: San Juan Islands, between British Columbia and Washington

Skag: Skagway, Alaska

Ski Capital: Aspen, Colo.

Skid Row on the Sound: Seattle, Wash. (site of the original Skid Row)

Skunk's Misery: Scranton, Pennsylvania's old nickname and once its place-name

Slot: The Slot (Mission Street off Market in downtown San Francisco)

Smog City: any air-polluted city on the globe

Smoky City: any smoke-filled city, such as Pittsburgh or St. Louis before air-pollution cleanup was begun

Snow-Covered Continent: Antarctica

Society Capital: Newport, R.I.

Somnolent City of the Sahara: Tomboucton, Mali

Soo: Sault Sainte Marie (Michigan or Ontario) the canal or the twin city

Soton: Southhampton, England

Sou: Southhampton, England

Spirit of Freedom State: Massachusetts

Spoke: Spokane, Wash.

Spud Island: Prince Edward Island, noted for its potatoes

Square Mile of Vice: London's Soho and West End

Sri: Sri Lanka (Ceylon); Srinagar, India

Stagville: nickname for Santa Monica Blvd. in West Hollywood, Calif., where massage parlors and pornographic shops seem to outnumber all other enterprises

State of Excitement: Western Australia

States: The States (United States of America)

Statia: Sint Eustatius in the Netherlands Antilles

Stav: Stavanger, Norway

Steak Center: Kansas City, Mo.

Stirville: Ossining, N.Y. (site of Sing Sing)

Stream of Pleasure: the Thames above London

Street: The Street (New York City's Wall Street)

Street of Sorrows: New York City's Wall Street; old-fashioned nickname for any thoroughfare frequented by streetwalkers

Strip: The Strip—the main street of Las Vegas, Nev.; also called the Great White Strip

Submarine Capital: Groton, Conn.

Suds City: Milwaukee, Wis.

Sun Belt: the sun-drenched southern United States, specifically the southernmost tier of states, extending from Florida to California

Sunshine Capital: St. Petersburg, Fla. and Yuma, Ariz. compete for this place-name nickname

Swan City: Perth, Australia

Swaz: Swaziland

Swe: Sweden

Switz: Switzerland

Syd: Sydney, Australia; Sydney, Nova Scotia, Canada

TA: Tel Aviv, Israel

Tac: Tacoma, Wash.

Tai: Taipei; Taiwan

Taju: Tajumulco, Guatemala

Talco: Talcahuano, Chile

Tamiami: Tampa-Miami Trail, linking Tampa and Miami in Florida

Tamp: Tampa, Fla.; Tampico, Mexico

Tar Heel State: North Carolina

Tassie: Tasmania, Australia

Texas Cow Town: Fort Worth

Thiefrow: nickname for London's Heathrow Airport, where security has sometimes been lax and thievery prevalent

Thim: Thimbu, Bhutan

Thomas: St. Thomas, American Virgin Islands

Tinseltown: Hollywood, California

Tj: Tijuana, Mexico

TO: Toledo, Ohio

Toco: Tocopilla, Chile

'Tona: Daytona Beach, Fla.

Topo: Topolobambo, Mexico

Tortilla Curtain: nickname for the Mexican border between El Paso, Texas and San Diego, Calif.

Touquet: Le Touquet, France (on the Channel)

Town Too Tough To Die: Tombstone, Ariz.

Transv: Transvaal, South Africa

Trench Town: West Kingston Jamaica's ghetto

Tri-Lingual Land: Switzerland, whose people often speak French, German and Italian as well as Romansh and English

Tropez: St. Tropez, France (on the Riviera)

T-town: Tijuana, Mexico

Tutu: Tutuila (principal island of American Samoa)

Twilight Zone: the Mexican border

Twin Cities: Minneapolis and St. Paul, Minn.

U: Underground (London's subway system)

U-bahn: Untergrundbahn (German—Underground Road) Berlin's subway system

UD: London's Underground subway system

UK: United Kingdom (abbreviation and nickname)

UN: United Nations (abbreviation and nickname)

Unsainted Anthony: San Antonio, Texas

up the river: Sing Sing prison, up the Hudson River from New York City at Ossining

U.S.: United States (abbreviation and nickname)

U.S. Capital of Cocaine: Jackson Heights, Queens, New York, where many Colombian cocaine pushers reside

USSR: Union of Soviet Socialist Republics (abbreviation and nickname)

Valley Isle: Maui, Hawaii

Valpo: Valparaiso, Chile

Vancoo: Vancouver, British Columbia, Canada

Vapor City: Hot Springs, Ark.

Vegas: Las Vegas, Nev.

Vehicle City: Flint, Mich.

Vermilionville: Lafayette, Louisiana's nickname and former name

Vieux Carre: (French—Old Square) French Quarter of New Orleans

Vince: St. Vincent in the British West Indies

VIs: Virgin Islands in the Caribbean

Wallows: Walla Walla, Wash.

Washington State Funnypark: Washington State Prison near Walla Walla

Watergate Hilton: prisoners' nickname for the Washington, D.C. jail, near the Robert F. Kennedy Stadium

West Sam: Western Samoa

Where America's Day Begins: Guam in the Western Pacific; the largest and southernmost of the Marianas

Where the Surf Meets the Turf: Del Mar, Calif.

Whorehouse Row: nickname given South Akard Street in Dallas, Texas by its taxicab drivers

Wilmas: (Mexican-Americanism) Wilmington, Calif.

Window to Europe: Peter the Great's nickname for the capital city he began in 1703; called Saint Petersburg in czarist times, known as Petrograd from 1914 to 1924, when it was renamed Leningrad

Windy City: Chicago, Ill.

Wyo: Wyoming

Xochi: Xochimilco (outside Mexico City)

Yankee Athens: New Haven, Conn.

Yard: Scotland Yard, London

Yoko: Yokohama, Japan

Yokuska: Yokosuka (naval base and seaport below Yokohama, Japan)

Youngs: Youngstown, Ohio

Yps: Ypsilanti, Mich.

Yuca: Yucatan, Mexico

Yuk: Yukon, Canada

Zag: Zagreb, Yugoslavia

Zambo: Zamboanga, Philippines

Zanzi: Zanzibar, Tanzania

Zenith City of the Unsalted Seas: Duluth, Minn.

Zimb: Zimbabwe (Rhodesia)

Zoc: Zocalo (Mexico City's great plaza)

SELECTED SOURCES

This listing—including fiction and nonfiction, in print and in other media—describes and evaluates a broad range of works relating to crime. Entries appear here in the same format as elsewhere in this book: They are arranged alphabetically, by title, so that this section serves as an extension of, rather than an addendum to, the book.

Alcatraz Island Prison: Warden James E. Johnston's illuminating account of the maximum-security prison

American Legal Almanac: summary and update of law in all states; by Joan Robinson; Oceana Publications, Dobbs Ferry, N.Y., published in 1978

Analyzing the Criminal Justice System: J. W. LaPatra applies systems-analysis techniques to improve the criminal-justice system; published in 1978 by Lexington Books of Lexington, Mass.

Angel Death: 1969 television documentary exposing the dangers of PCP (angel dust)

Animal Factory: novel by Edward Bunker who spent most of his adult life in prison; at San Quentin he found forced homosexuality plus continuous warfare between black, Chicano and white inmates; nothing was done to deter inmates from a life of crime or to rehabilitate them in any way; published in 1977 by Viking Press, New York

Animal Farm: George Orwell's amusing allegory exposing communism and the crimes committed in the name of creating a utopia; it was described by the *New Yorker* as "A stinging, allegorical satire directed against communism and its ramifications"

Arrest by Police Computer—The Controversy over Bail and Extradition: John J. Murphy's useful guide published in 1975 by Lexington Books, in Lexington, Mass.

Arson: a handbook of detection and investigation by Brendan P. Battle and Paul B. Weston; published by Arco, New York, in 1960

Asphalt Jungle: W.R. Burnett's classic story about American newspapermen and policemen cooperating to stem the crime wave of the 1940s; published by Knopf in 1944

Assassination in America: James McKinley's readable account of political assassinations from Lincoln to Kennedy and attempted assassinations from Jackson to Ford; published in 1977 by Harper & Row, New York

Assassination of John F. Kennedy—An Annotated Bibliography: Leon G. Hunt describes methods of estimating the extent and the nature of psychotropic drug abuse in local neighborhoods; published in 1977 by Lexington Books in Lexington, Mass.

Behind Bars: illustrated and informative book about American prisons; edited by Richard Kwartler and published by Vintage Books in New York in 1977

Bibliography of Police Administration, Public Safety, and Criminology: edited by William H. Hewitt; published in 1967 by C.C. Thomas

Big-City Police: Robert M. Fogelson's history of the police in the U.S. during the past century; published in 1977 by the Harvard University Press in Cambridge, Mass.

Blacks and Criminal Justice: provocative essays compiled and edited by Charles E. Owens and Jimmy Bell; published in 1977 by Lexington Books in Lexington, Mass.

Black Watch: weekly publication of the Afro-American Patrolmen's League

Book of Numbers: contains up-to-date statistics, presented in popular form, covering many items as well as crime, drug addiction, murder, police, prisoners and venereal disease; published by Heron House, New York in 1978

Border Guard: Don Whitehead's story of the U.S. Customs Service and its war against dope and smugglers; published by McGraw-Hill, New York in 1963

Brothers in Blood: Ovid Demaris' book about the international terrorist network; published by Scribner's in New York

Bureaucratic Insurgency—The Case of Police Unions: Margaret Levi presents a historical and theoretical perspective for understanding government-worker militance; published in 1977 by Lexington Books, Lexington, Mass.

Burglar-Proofing Your Home: a how-to book published by Audel in 1975 with some illustrations

Buy and Bust—The Effective Regulation of an Illicit Market in Heroin: Mark H. Moore's valuable analysis useful to many law-enforcement officers and others; published in 1977 by Lexington Books, Lexington, Mass.

Buyers Beware: District Attorney Information Service brochure issued by the District Attorney of San Diego County—Edwin L. Miller, Jr.

Bystander: The Bystander—a book by Leon S. Sheleff, who examines the legal rights and duties of the bystander; published in 1978 by Lexington Books in Lexington, Mass.

Canadian Criminal Justice System: the only complete summary of this system, by Alice Parizeau and Denis Szabo; published in 1977 by Lexington Books, Lexington, Mass.

Canine Couriers: bimonthly publication of the United States Police Canine Association

Cannabis and Culture: essays about hashish, marijuana and related drugs; edited by Vera Rubin; published by Mouton in 1975

Can You Trust Your Bank?: financial scandals exposed by Robert Heller and Norris Willatt in a book published by Scribner's in 1977

Capital Punishment Dilemma: 1950-1977 subject bibliography by Charles W. Triche III; published by Whitson of Troy, N.Y. in 1979

Career of the Dangerous Criminal: a 25-year study made by Stuart A. Miller, Simon Dinitz and John P. Conrad; published in 1979 by Lexington Books in Lexington, Mass.

Carlos—Portrait of a Terrorist: Colin Smith's book about a Venezuelan-born Palestinian terrorist named Ilich Ramirez Sanchez whose underground name is Carlos Martinez

Catalog of Crime: annotated bibliography compiled by Jacques Barzul and Wendell H. Taylor; published in New York in 1974 by Harper & Row

Century of the Detective: Jurgen Thorwald's book about the scientific investigation of crime in the second half of the 19th and the first half of the 20th centuries; published in English in 1965 by Harcourt, Brace, Jovanovich

Check Forgers: John F. Klein and Arthur Montague examine the career of the check forger; published in 1977 by Lexington Books, Lexington, Mass.

Clearing the Record: an 18-page manual produced by two experts at a Camden, N.J. legal clinic for the poor; explains how a criminal record can be wiped clean with the proviso it does not provide for those guilty of serious crimes such as rape or robbery; relates to the New Jersey expungement law passed in 1979

Cocaine: 308-page book by Lester Grinspoon and James B. Bakalar, who examine not only the history of this drug but also its place in the disease-crime syndrome afflicting modern society

Community-Based Alternatives to Correctional Settings: a book by Yitzhak Bakal describing programs designed to replace the present system of corrections; published in 1979 by Lexington Books in Lexington, Mass.

Computer Crime: August Bequai's valuable vade mecum discussing the vulnerability of computers to crime as well as explaining problems dealing with investigation and prosecution; published in 1978 by Lexington Books, Lexington, Mass.

Concept of Cruel and Unusual Punishment: Larry C. Berkson's splendid study published in 1975 by Lexington Books, Lexington, Mass.

Condemned to Devil's Island: account by Blair Niles about the horrors of the penal camps of French Guiana; published by Jonathan Cape in 1928

Confidence Man—His Masquerade: book by Herman Melville published in 1857 and filled with accounts of slick schemes practiced aboard many Mississippi River steamers before the Civil War

Conjugal Visits in Prison: Jules Quentin Burstein's book about the psychological and social consequences of such visits on inmates and on our society; published in 1977 by Lexington Books in Lexington, Mass.

Correctional Facilities Planning: a book examining the various aspects of correctional-facilities planning; edited by M. Robert Montilla and Nora Harlow; published in 1978 by Lexington Books in Lexington, Mass.

Correctional Institutions for Women in the United States: by Katherine G. Strickland; published in 1979 by Lexington Books in Lexington, Mass.

Correctional Intervention and Research: a book by Ted Palmer of the California Youth Authority, who examines current issues and future prospects; published by Lexington Books in Lexington, Mass. in 1978

Correctional Memo: quarterly publication of the Association of State Correctional Administrators

Corrections Magazine: illustrated monthly periodical covering America's changing prison system and comparing it to foreign systems

The Corrections Officer: newsletter published by the American Association of Correctional Facility Officers (AACFO)

Corrections Today: periodical publication of the American Correctional Association

Corruption in American Politics and Life: book by Robert C. Brooks; published in 1974 by Arno

Corruption in Business: book edited by Lester A. Sobel and published in 1977 by Facts On File in New York

Counsel for the Poor—Criminal Defense in Urban America: a splendid reference prepared by Robert Herman, Eric Single and John Boston; published in 1977 by Lexington Books, Lexington, Mass.

Counterpoint: published bimonthly by the National Juvenile Detention Association

Counter-Spy: official bulletin of the Committee for Action/Research on the Intelligence Community

The Courts, the Constitution, and Capital Punishment: scholar Hugo Adam Bedau's unique record of the legal, political, and historical reflections on the death penalty from the early 1960s to the mid-1970s; published by Lexington Books, Lexington, Mass. in 1977

Crime and Capital Punishment: Robert H. Loeb Jr.'s book on both sides of the argument concerning the death penalty; published by Franklin Watts in New York in 1978

Crime and Criminals: David L. Bender's and Gary E. McCuen's anthology of opposing viewpoints on: the causes of crime, dealing with criminals, dealing with juvenile offenders, dealing with white-collar crime, gun control and crime; published in 1977 by the Greenhaven Press in Anoka, Minn.

Crime & Delinquency: monthly publication

of the National Council on Crime and Delinquency

Crime and Justice: three-volume set of scholarly essays about the criminal in society, the criminal in the arms of the law and the criminal under restraint; edited by Sir Leon Radznowics and Marvin E. Wolfgang; published in 1971 by Basic Books in New York and reissued in 1977

Crime and Punishment: Fyodor Dostoevski's classic tale about the premeditated murder of an old woman by a young student; its message is contemporary although it was first published in Russian in 1866

Crime Control in Japan: William Clifford of the Australian Institute of Criminology made this important study published in 1976 by Lexington Books, Lexington, Mass.

Crime in America: a book of essays on criminal and delinquent behavior; edited by Bruce J. Cohen and published by F. E. Peacock in 1977

Crime—International Agenda: Benedict S. Alper and Jerry F. Boren assess international investigation into crime prevention and correctional institutions; published in 1972 by Lexington Books, Lexington, Mass.

Crime in the U.S.: massive compilation of crime statistics produced annually by the FBI

Crime Pays: Thomas Plate's book about the theory and practice of professional crime in the United States

Crimes and Rights: Of Crimes and Rights—The Penal Code Viewed as a Bill of Rights; title of Judge Macklin Fleming's contribution to the administrative concept of justice—improved efficiency of court action; published by W. W. Norton in 1978

Crime Victim's Book: by Morton Bard and Dawn Sanguey; published in New York in 1979 by Basic Books

Crime Without Punishment: David A. Jones exposes plea bargaining and explains how the vast majority of crimes committed by relatively sophisticated offenders go unpunished; published in 1979 by Lexington Books, Lexington, Mass.

The Criminal Court—How It Works: Roberta Rovner-Pieczenik presents theoretical models explaining the operation of urban criminal courts; published in 1978 by Lexington Books, Lexington, Mass.

Criminal Defense Magazine: quarterly publication of the National Association of Criminal Defense Lawyers

Criminal Interrogation: Aubry and Caputo's well-known guide published by Thomas in 1975 (2nd ed.)

Criminal Investigation and Identification: V.A. Leonard's illustrated book published by Thomas in 1971—used by many law-enforcement officers

Criminal Investigation Process: Peter W. Greenwood, Jan M. Chaiken, Joan Petersilla and four other contributors discuss current practices; published in 1977 by Lexington Books, Lexington, Mass.

Criminal Justice in America: compiled by Peter C. Kratcoski and Donald B. Walker; published in 1978 by Scott, Foresman of Glenview, Ill.

Criminal Law and Its Processes: standard reference by Sanford H. Kadish and Monrad G. Paulsen; third edition published by Little, Brown in 1975

Criminal Violence, Criminal Justice: title of a book by Charles E. Silberman, whose studies were backed by a half-million-dollar Ford Foundation grant; published in 1978 by Random House in New York

Criminological Theory—Foundations and Perceptions: essays compiled and edited by Stephen Schafer and Richard D. Knudten; published in 1977 by Lexington Books, Lexington, Mass.

Criminology: quarterly publication of the American Society of Criminology

Criminology: title of the outstanding textbook by Edwin H. Sutherland and Donald R. Cressey; ninth edition published by Lippincott in 1974

Criminology Index: Wolfgang, Figlio and Thornberry's two-volume criminology citation index covering crime types, offenders, etiology, deterrence, gangs, statistics, etc.; published by Elsevier in 1975

Criminology in Perspective—Essays in Honor of Israel Drapkin: edited by Simha F. Landau and Leslie Sebba; published in 1978 by Lexington Books, Lexington, Mass.

Critical History of Police Reform—the Emergence of Professionalism: Samuel Walker's excellent history of U.S. policing; published in 1977 by Lexington Books in Lexington, Mass.

Critical Issues in Juvenile Delinquency: edited by David Shichor and Delos H. Kelly; published in 1979 by Lexington Books in Lexington, Mass.

The Dangerous and the Endangered: John P. Conrad's book on the findings of the Dangerous Offender Project and the social trends producing violence; published in 1979 by Lexington Books in Lexington, Mass.

Darkness at Noon: Arthur Koestler's novel explaining the Moscow Trials in terms of the degradation and imprisonment of an Old Bolshevik forced to confess to crimes he never committed; published by Macmillan in 1941

Demystifying Parole: policies and procedures of the U.S. Board of Parole are explained by Janet Schmidt; published in 1977 by Lexington Books in Lexington, Mass.

The Detective: journal of Army Criminal Investigation published by the Criminal Investigation Command of the U.S. Army

The Detectives—Crime and Detection in Fact and Fiction: by Frank Smyth and Myles Ludwig, who combine their reportorial and research talents in this attractively-illustrated quarto published by Lippincott in 1978 but reminiscent of the *Police Gazette* magazine once popular in nearly every barbershop and billiard hall in America

Diagnosis and Criminal Justice Systems: edited by Marvin E. Wolfgang and Franco Ferracuti; points to the need for re-evaluation and the development of new conceptual and practical methods; published by Lexington Books in 1979

Dictionary of Criminal Justice Data Terminology: first edition issued in 1976 by the U.S. Department of Justice Law Enforcement Assistance Administration's National Criminal Justice Information and Statistics Service

Dictionary of the Underworld: Eric Partridge's out-of-print classic with many terms used in the American and British underworld; appeared with new addenda in 1961

Directory of Juvenile Detention Homes: published by the National Juvenile Detention Association

Directory of Prisoners Aid Agencies: published by the International Prisoners Aid Association

Directory of Residential Treatment Centers: published by the IHHA

Discipline and Punish: title of Michel Foucault's book about the birth of the prison; published in 1978 by Pantheon in New York

Diversion, Delinquency, and Labels: six

authors (Tellmann, Klein, Lincoln, Labin, Landry and Maxon) deal with issues surrounding juvenile-justice programs; published in 1979 by Lexington Books in Lexington, Mass.

Doing Justice—By the Community: a welcome work on the side of the victim; by Benedict S. Alper and Lawrence T. Nichols; published in 1979 by Lexington Books in Lexington, Mass.

Dragon: bi-monthly publication dealing with the underground in the United States; published in Berkeley, Calif., by the Bay Area Research Collective (BARC)

Dreamers, Dynamiters, and Demagogues: Max Nomad's extensive account published in 1964 by University Place

Dream Sellers: book by R. H. Blum and associates, who provide insight and perspectives on drug dealers; published in 1972 by Jossey-Bass of San Francisco

Drugs: multimedia sourcebook for young adults; compiled by Sharon Ashenbrenner Charles and Sari Feldman; published in 1979 by ABC-Clio in Santa Barbara, Calif.

Drugs of Abuse: free Drug Enforcement Administration (DEA) publication

Dry Guillotine: Rene Belbenoit's factual account of prison conditions in the tropical hellhole of French Guiana, known popularly as Devil's Island; published by Dutton in 1938

Education for Crime Prevention and Control: R. J. McLean's illustrated study published in 1975 by Thomas

Elsevier's Dictionary of Criminal Science: eight languages are covered in this compilation made by Johann Anton Adler and published by Elsevier in 1960; long out of print despite its polyglot utility

Encyclopedia of American Crime: compilation assembled by Carl Sifakis and published in 1981 by Facts On File in New York

Encyclopedia of Mystery and Detection: published by McGraw-Hill in 1976

Enforcement Journal: published quarterly by the National Police Officers Association of America

Escape from Justice—Nazi War Criminals in America: documentary television broadcast made over ABC stations in early 1980

Evaluative Research in Correctional Drug Abuse Treatment: a guide for professionals in criminal justice and the behavioral sciences edited by Jerome J. Platt, Christina Labate and Robert J.

Wicks; published in 1977 by Lexington Books in Lexington, Mass.

The Executioner's Song: Norman Mailer's Pulitzer Prize-winning book about the dilemma of capital punishment as indicated by the life and death of Gary Gilmore

Eye of Dawn: biography about the rise and fall of the Dutch-born German spy Mata Hari, who, in World War I, used seductive arts to gain her ends until executed by a French firing squad

Eye Opener: inmate publication of the Oklahoma State Penitentiary

Eye-Witness Identification in Criminal Cases: Patrick M. Wall's useful reference, published by Thomas in 1975

Falcon and the Snowman: Robert Lindsey's non-fiction account of the drug trade and espionage in California in the late 1970s; published by Simon & Schuster in New York

Fall River Legend: endless relation of the Fall River, Mass. murder supposedly committed by one Lizzie Borden in August 1892, when she was charged with killing her father and her mother with a hatchet but was released after a jury acquitted her

Felons in Court: a book by Winifred Lyday and Simon Dinitz examining the effects of plea bargaining in felony dispositions; published in 1979 by Lexington Books in Lexington, Mass.

Fingerprinting: Eugene B. Block's book published in 1969 by McKay and bearing the subtitle *Magic Weapon Against Crime*

Fire and Arson Investigator: bimonthly publication of the International Association of Arson Investigators

The Fire Next Door: Bill Moyer's award-winning television documentary exposing the arson, poverty, vandalism and violence afflicting New York City's South Bronx and other depressed metropolitan areas everywhere in the 1980s

Flag on Devil's Island: first-hand illustrated account of prison life in French Guiana by a prisoner named Francis (Flag) Lagrange, whose book and pictures were published in 1961 by Doubleday

The Forbidden Game: title of a social history of drugs by Brian Inglis; published in 1975 by Scribner's

For Capital Punishment: crime and the morality of the death penalty ably presented by Walter Berns and published by Basic Books in 1979

Forecasting Crime Data: an empirical analysis by James Alan Fox of the trends in crime data; published in 1978 by Lexington Books, Lexington, Mass.

Fountain Pen Conspiracy: Jonathan Kwitny's book explaining how a half dozen professional swindlers fleece hundreds of millions of dollars from banks, businesses and private investors, published by Knopf in 1973

French Connection: Robin Moore's book, subtitled *The World's Most Crucial Narcotics Investigation*; published in 1969 by Little, Brown and reissued as a Bantam paperback in 1971

Fundamentals of Criminal Investigation: Charles E. O'Hara's illustrated work, now in its third edition; published by Thomas in 1974

Fundamentals of Criminal Justice Research: Robert S. Clark's valuable reference, published in 1977 by Lexington Books, Lexington, Mass.

Future of Violence: Gerald Priestland's book, published in London and New York by Hamish Hamilton in 1974

Gambling and Organized Crime: Rufus King's book, published by the Public Affairs Press

The Godfather: Mario Puzo's novel revealing the gang wars and the violence-infested society of the Mafia; a former member declares Puzo's portrait of the Syndicate is most accurate

The Godfather Saga: by Mario Puzo; televised novel revealing the criminal pattern of contemporary mobsters ranging from pre-Castro Havana to Lake Tahoe, Las Vegas and the New York City area

The Grapevine: bimonthly publication of the American Association of Wardens and Superintendents

Gulag Archipelago: Aleksandr I. Solzhenitsyn's title for the thousands of prisons in the USSR from the Bering Strait to borders near the Bosporus and for his classic book about the system; Gulag stands for the Chief Administration of Corrective Labor Camps, Prisons and Special Settlements of the Soviet Secret Police, who held him prisoner for unspecified crimes against the state; published by Harper & Row in 1975

Hacks, Blacks, and Cons: race relations in a maximum-security prison are the main thrust of this study by Leo Carroll; published in 1974 by Lexington Books, Lexington, Mass.

Handbook on Hanging: Charles Duff's book published in 1929 by the Boston firm of Hale, Cushman, and Flint; nothing is left to the imagination of the hangman or the reader

Hashish in Marseilles: Walter Benjamin's vivid description of the effects of this drug appear in a collection of his essays, *Reflections*; published by Harcourt Brace Jovanovich in 1978

Hell Beyond the Seas: Aage Krarup-Nielsen's book about his stay in the convict colony of French Guiana; published by Dutton in 1940

Hell on Trial: ex-prisoner Rene Belbenoit's exposé and indictment of the penal system he encountered in French Guiana, where he also wrote **Dry Guillotine**

Heroin Use in the Barrio: Bruce Bullington's book discussing criminal-justice agencies and the effects on addiction in the Chicano culture; published in 1977 by Lexington Books, Lexington, Mass.

Holdups, Muggings, and Pursesnatches—Robbery in America: Floyd Feeney studies robbery from the point of view of everyone concerned and involved; published in 1979 by Lexington Books in Lexington, Mass.

Homicide and Suicide: edited by Stuart Palmer and published by Lieber-Atherton

Hostage Cop: The New York City Police Hostage Negotiating Team and the Man Who Leads It: by Capt. Frank Bolz and Edward Hershey; published in 1979 by Rawson, Wade in New York

Housewife's ABC of Home-Made Explosives: handbook produced by Col. Colin Gubbins and printed on rice paper in 1939, when a British guerrilla army was being organized to resist a Nazi invasion of the British Isles; it is still used by underground groups

Illustrated Story of Crime: Edgar Lustgarden's pictorial book, published by Follett in Chicago in 1976

Indicators of Justice: a guide for measuring the performance of prosecution, defense and court agencies involved in felony proceedings; by Sorrel Wildhorn, Marvin Lavin and Anthony Pascal; published in 1977 by Lexington Books, Lexington, Mass.

Insanity Defense—A Blueprint for Legislative Reform: ready reference prepared by Grant H. Morris; published in 1976 by Lexington Books in Lexington, Mass.

Inside the World's Toughest Prison: Warden Joseph E. Ragen's book about Joliet; its co-author was Charles Finston

Interpol: Peter G. Lee's accurate and interesting description of the international police organization, so successful in the apprehension of criminals; published by Stein and Day in 1976

Intersearch: biweekly newsletter published by the International Terrorist Research Center in El Paso, Texas

In the Penal Colony: Franz Kafka's chilling description of a tropical penal settlement and the operation of its guillotine entails a philosophical and psychological examination of man's inhumanity to man

Intimate Victims: a study of violence among friends and relatives; free copy can be obtained by writing the National Criminal Justice Reference Service, Box 6000, Rockville, MD 20850

Introduction to Clinical Criminology: Israel Drapkin's book dealing with the origin and evolution of the basic concepts of clinical criminology; published in 1979 by Lexington Books, Lexington, Mass.

Introduction to Criminology: Stephen Schafer's up-to-date text, published in 1976 by the Reston Publishing Co.

Investigator: monthly publication of the National Jail Association

Jail Management: problems, programs and perspectives of jail management, with emphasis on tested measures for improving conditions and attaining major goals; a book by E. Eugene Miller, published by Lexington Books in Lexington, Mass. in 1978

Jails—The Ultimate Ghetto: Ronald Goldfarb's book about the brutality and injustice rampant in American jails; published in 1975 by Anchor Press in New York

J. Edgar Hoover: Ralph De Toledano's account of the man who was chief of the FBI and its principal organizer; published in 1973 by Arlington House

Jefftown Journal: prisoner's periodical published at Jefferson City, Mo.

Journal of Correctional Education: quarterly publication of the Correctional Education Association

Journal of Criminal Justice: publication of the Academy of Criminal Justice

Journal of Criminal Justice and Behavior: published by the American Association of Correctional Psychologists

Journal of Police Science and Administration: quarterly publication of the International Association of Chiefs of Police

Jury Verdicts: Michael J. Saks gives psychological insights into the role of group size and social decision rule in this book, published in 1977 by Lexington

Books in Lexington, Mass.

Justice and Older Americans: provocative essays about the social victimization of the elderly in America; edited by Marlene A. Young Rifai and published in 1977 by Lexington Books in Lexington, Mass.

Justice for Our Children: Dennis A. Romig's book examining juvenile delinquent rehabilitation programs; published in 1977 by Lexington Books in Lexington, Mass.

Just Measure of Pain: the penitentiary in the industrial revolution—1750 to 1850—by Michael Ignatieff; published by Pantheon in New York in 1978

Killer: a journal of murder by Thomas E. Gaddis and James O. Long; based on the autobiography and confession of Carl Panzram, who called himself "the world's worst murderer"; published in 1970 by Macmillan

Kind and Unusual Punishment—The Prison Business: Jessica Mitford's scathing critique of the penal system; published in 1973 by Knopf

Law and Order: an independent magazine of the police profession published in New York, N.Y.

Law and Order Reconsidered: title of the report of the Task Force on Law and Law Enforcement to the National Commission on the Causes and Prevention of Violence; an in-depth analysis of the status of our current legal, social and political institutions; published in 1970 as a Bantam Book

The Law and the Dangerous Criminal: statutory attempts at definition and control—a book by Linda Sleffel, published in 1977 by Lexington Books in Lexington, Mass.

Law Officer: bimonthly publication of the International Conference of Police Associations

Legal Aspects of International Terrorism: articles and essays compiled and edited by Alona E. Evans and John F. Murphy of the American Society of International Law; published in 1978 by Lexington Books in Lexington, Mass.

Legal Rights of Prisoners—An Analysis of Legal Aid: Geoffrey P. Alpert develops a strong case calling for the rapid expansion of legal-aid programs for prisoners; published in 1978 by Lexington Books in Lexington, Mass.

Lethal Aspects of Urban Violence: essays edited by Harold Rose and published in 1978 by Lexington Books in Lexington,

Mass.

Life and Death in Sing Sing: Lewis Edward Lawes' account of his eight-year tenure as warden of Sing Sing

Locking Up Children: Spencer Millham, Roger Bullock and Kenneth Hosie collaborated in writing this book analyzing high-security units for youthful offenders; published in 1978 by Lexington Books in Lexington, Mass.

M: Morder (German—murderer): title of director Fritz Lang's film classic in which Peter Lorre made his motion picture debut in the role of a compulsive child murderer; he is brought to justice by the cunning organization of the Berlin underworld, whose reputation for essential decency was at stake

Madchen in Uniform: (German—Women in Uniform): 1931 film classic showing what goes on in a female prison

Mail Fraud Laws—Protecting Consumers, Investors, Businessmen, Patients, Students: 28-page pamphlet issued by the U.S. Postal Service and sold by the U.S. Government Printing Office

Making of a Spy: Raymond Palmer's contribution in book form to The Library of Espionage and Secret Warfare, titled *Undercover*, published in 1976 by the Crescent Books Division of Crown Publishers

Managing Criminal Investigations: eight experts tell how to achieve improvements in the number of arrests and convictions as well as overall operating efficiency; published in 1979 by Lexington Books in Lexington, Mass.

Managing Patrol Operations: four experts (Cawley, Miron, MacFarlane and Richard) describe how the techniques of organizational management are applied to the solution of police patrol management; published in 1979 by Lexington Books in Lexington, Mass.

Marijuana—Deceptive Weed: this in-depth study by Dr. Gabriel G. Nahas makes clear that all available evidence indicates regular *Cannabis* consumption is associated with multiple drug use, including the use of opiate derivatives whenever handy; published by Raven Press in 1975

Menard Time: prisoner's publication issued by the Menard branch of the Illinois State Penitentiary

Minimanual of the Urban Guerrilla: Brazilian terrorist Carlo Marighella's handbook, banned in many Latin American lands

Mob—The Story of Organized Crime in America: by Leslie Walker; published by Delacorte in 1973

Mobs and the Mafia—The Illustrated History of Organized Crime: by Hank Messick and Bert Goldblatt; published by Ballantine in 1973

Model Penal Code: modern codification of basic criminal law, published by the American Law Institute in 1962

Modern Theories of Criminality: C. Barnaldo De Quiros' study, still quite modern although published in 1911 by Agathon Press in New York

Modern Transportation and International Crime: impact of aviation and containerization on crime; by Gordon Fraser; published by Thomas in 1970

The Mugging: Morton Hunt's dramatic narrative of America's most feared crime and an in-depth portrait of American justice today; published by Atheneum in 1972

Murder and Madness: Donald T. Lunde's study, published in 1975 by the Stanford Alumni Association at Stanford, Calif., highlights the very strong relationship of alcohol and drug abuse to murder

Murder Ink: an argument-settler reference book by Dilys Winn; published in 1977 by Workman Publishing, it contains entries on crime writers and their critics as well as ex-spies and others

National Black Police Association News: quarterly publication of the Afro-American Patrolmen's League

National Police and Fire Journal: published by the National Police and Fire Fighters Association

National Sheriff: bimonthly publication of the National Sheriffs Association

Neither Cruel Nor Unusual: Frank C. Carrington's presentation of the case for capital punishment; published by Arlington House, New Rochelle, N.Y. in 1979

New Era: prisoner's newspaper published at Leavenworth, Kansas

New Horizons in Criminology: historian Harry Elmer Barnes and penologist Negley K. Teeters are the authors of this text in which they indicate a trend away from words such as convict and criminal

New Paths in Criminology: essays concerning interdisciplinary and intercultural explorations; edited by Sarnoff A. Mednick and S. Giora Shoham; published in 1978 by Lexington Books in Lexington, Mass.

The Night Watch: David Atlee Phillips,

formerly of the CIA, tells almost all you think you need to know about his espionage activities; published in 1977 by Atheneum in New York

Of Crimes and Rights: Macklin Fleming's book, published in 1978 by W.W. Norton

Offender Restitution in Theory and Action: edited by Burt Galaway and Joe Hudson; victimology and victim-service programs are discussed; published in 1978 by Lexington Books in Lexington, Mass.

Offenders in the Community: Edwin M. Lemert's and Forrest Dill's study of the California probation subsidy, designed to reduce prison and juvenile commitments by providing more effective correctional services; published in 1978 by Lexington Books in Lexington, Mass.

"—officer down, code three.": title of a book by Pierce R. Brooks, who relates 20 cases of police killings and explains the 10 deadly errors or fatal mistakes the men made; published in 1975 by Motorola Teleprograms in Schiller Park, Ill.

Organizational Politics of Criminal Justice: Virginia Gray and Bruce Williams explore policy in context; published in 1979 by Lexington Books in Lexington, Mass.

Organized Crime: August Bequai's compendium of case histories of organized crime; published in 1979 by Lexington Books in Lexington, Mass.

Organized Crime in America—A Book of Readings: edited by Gus Tyler and published in 1962 by the University of Michigan Press

Organizing the Non-System—Government Structuring of Criminal-Justice Services: revealing title of Daniel L. Skolar's book, published in 1977 by Lexington Books in Lexington, Mass.

Outlaw: bimonthly publication of the Prisoner's Union

Out of Circulation: the dangerous offender in prison is examined by Robert Freeman, John P. Conrad, Simon Dinitz and Israel Barak of the Academy for Contemporary Problems; published by Lexington Books of Lexington, Mass. in 1979

Papillon: (French—Butterfly) nickname of ex-convict Henri Charriere and the title of his book about prison life in French Guiana, as well as the adventures of an escaped convict in such countries as Trinidad, Venezuela and Colombia

Passage to Marseille: melodramatic moving-picture commentary on the old French penal colony in Guiana and its inmates, played by Humphrey Bogart, Peter Lorre and others, along with its wardens, symbolized by Sydney Greenstreet at his meanest; produced in 1944

The Penalty of Death—The Canadian Experiment: by C.H.S. Jayewardene; published in 1977 by Lexington Books in Lexington, Mass.

Periscope: newsletter published by the Association of Former Intelligence Officers

Picture History of Crime: profusely illustrated book edited by Sandy Lesberg and first published in New York in 1976 by Peebles Press

Plea Bargaining or Trial?—The Process of Criminal Case Disposition: by Lynn M. Mather; published in 1979 by Lexington Books in Lexington, Mass.

Plot to Kill the President: exploitation of the mob-did-it theory explaining who assassinated Pres. Kennedy; by C. Robert Blakey and Richard N. Billings; published by Times Books, New York in 1981

Police Accountability—Performance Measures and Unionism: volume II of a four-volume series published by Lexington Books under the general title of *Innovative Resource Planning in Urban Public Safety Systems*

Police Chief: monthly publication of the International Association of Chiefs of Police

Police Computer Technology—Implementation and Impact: volume III of a four-volume series published by Lexington Books under the general title of *Innnovative Resource Planning in Urban Public Safety Systems*

Police, Crime, and Society: illustrated work edited by Clarence H. Patrick and published by Thomas in 1972

Police Deployement—New Tools for Planners: volume I of a four-volume series published by Lexington Books under the general title of *Innovative Resource Planning in Urban Public Safety Systems*

The Police Family—From Station House to Ranch House: Arthur and Elaine Niederhoffer focus on the interaction of the policeman's occupation and his family; published in 1978 by Lexington Books, Lexington, Mass.

Police Magazine: published monthly by Criminal Justice Publications in New York City

Police Plaintiff: national quarterly magazine reviewing court actions and providing valuable tips to law-enforcement officers who are defamed or harassed

Police Revitalization: Gerald E. Calden's book discussing efforts to update the police in the United States since 1965; published in 1977 by Lexington Books of Lexington, Mass.

Police—Streetcorner Politicians: William Ker Muir's easy-to-read study, published by the University of Chicago in 1977

Police Times: published monthly by the American Law Enforcement Officers Association

• *Police Times Magazine:* published monthly by the American Federation of Police

Political Corruption in America: George C. S. Benson, Steven A. Maaranen and Alan Heslop examine the reasons why America has the worst rate of corruption in any modern democracy; published in 1978 by Lexington Books of Lexington, Mass.

Political Terrorism—The Threat and The Response: Francis M. Watson's book, published in 1976 by Robert B. Luce of New York

Political Violence and Civil Disobedience: title of an informative an scholarly book by Ernest van den Haag, published in 1972 as a Harper Torchbook

Polygraph Handbook for Attorneys: Stanley Abrams prepared this easy-to-read and informative reference published in 1977 by Lexington Books in Lexington, Mass.

Poso del Mundo: (Spanish—Cesspool of the World): exposé of crime along the Mexican border from Tijuana to Matamoros; by Ovid Demaris; published by Little, Brown in 1970

The Possessed: Dostoyevski's searing satire of underground groups psychologically possessed of the delusion that assassination, conspiracy, revolt and violence will produce utopia

Predicting Dangerousness: Stephen J. Pfohl's book about the social construction of psychiatric reality and the concept of dangerousness; published in 1978 by Lexington Books in Lexington, Mass.

Presidio: prisoner's publication issued bimonthly by the Iowa State Penitentiary at Fort Madison

Prisoners' Self-Help Litigation Manual: James L. Potts and Alvin J. Bronstein of the National Prison Project of the American Civil Liberties Union designed this book for use by prisoners preparing legal actions; published in 1977 by Lexington Books in Lexington, Mass.

Prisoner Subcultures: a reference book by Lee H. Bowker; published in 1977 by Lexington Books in Lexington, Mass.

Prisonization, Friendship, and Leadership: John Anthony Slosar Jr.'s in-depth study of how inmates choose their friends and the effects of such choices on prison atmosphere as well as the prospects of socialization after release; published in 1978 by Lexington Books in Lexington, Mass.

Prison Medical Journal: British semi-classified periodical for prison doctors

Prisons: Leonard Orlov's book, subtitled *Houses of Darkness* and published by The Free Press in New York and London in 1975

Prostitutes and Their Parasites: J.G. Mancini's book-length report, written in 1962

Prostitution and Morality: Dr. Harry Benjamin's expose; published in 1964

Prostitution and Society: Fernando Henriques' two-volume survey, published in 1962 and 1963 in London

Punishing Criminals: Ernest van den Haag's scholarly and sensible response to such questions as whether punishment deters crime and whether poverty breeds crime; also deals with how society is to handle the criminal; published by Basic Books in 1975

Q & A: Judge Edwin Torres, of the New York County Criminal Court, wrote this novel about the New York City Police Department; its title comes from the question-and-answer session, when a suspect is first interrogated by the police; published by The Dial Press in 1977

Racketeering in Washington: an expose by Raymond Clapper; published in 1974 by Arno

Rape—How to Avoid It and What to Do about It If You Can't: by June and Joseph Csida; published in 1974 by Books for Better Living

Reaching Judgment at Nuremberg: Bradley F. Smith wrote this book about the untold story of how the Nazi war criminals were judged; published by Basic Books of New York in 1977

Readings in Criminology: annotated bibliography edited by Peter Wickman and Phillip Whitten; published in 1978 by D.C. Heath of Lexington, Mass.

Realities of Crime and Punishment: Warden Fred T. Wilkinson's book about prisoners and prisons; a fact-filled testament with many thought-provoking pages

Rebel Without a Cause: prison psychologist Dr. Robert Lindner's out-of-print book about prisoners he knew at Lewisburg

Recreational Drugs: fact-filled paperback book about everything from A (for alcohol and amphets) to Z (for zen—nickname for LSD) by Lawrence and Linda Young, Marjorie and Donald Klein, with Dorianne Beyer; published in 1977 by Berkley Books in New York

Reducing Delinquency: a book by Gregory P. Falkin, who evaluates the cost of various criminal-justice policies and simulates their effects on crime reduction; published in 1979 by Lexington Books in Lexington, Mass.

Reefer Madness: Larry Sloman's history of marijuana in America; published in 1979 by Bobbs-Merrill of Indianapolis and New York

Reforming Juvenile Corrections: alternatives and strategies presented in book form by Yitzhak Bakal and Howard W. Polsky; published in 1978 by Lexington Books in Lexington, Mass.

Restraining the Wicked: a retrospective and prospective look exploring the extent to which severe sentencing can reduce crime; published in 1979 by Lexington Books in Lexington, Mass.

Road Hustler: Robert C. Prus describes the career contingencies of professional card and dice hustlers in this fascinating study published in 1977 by Lexington Books in Lexington, Mass.

Robbery and the Criminal Justice System: by John E. Conklin; published by Lippincott in 1972

Safe Passage on City Streets: Dorothy T. Samuel's valuable study, published in 1975 by Abingdon

Sane Asylum: Charles Hampden-Turner's study of ex-criminals made inside San Francisco's Delancey Street Foundation in 1976 and published by the San Francisco Book Co.

San Quentin Story: Warden Clinton T. Duffy's revealing book about a prison he ran and the concern he felt for its inmates

Scarperer: Brendan Behan's book describing a Dublin jail and reporting the slanguage of its inmates; published by Doubleday in 1964; first appeared in *The Irish Times* in 1953, when Behan used the pen name of Emmet Street

The Search for Criminal Man: a conceptual history of the dangerous offender by Yasabel Rennie; published in 1978 by Lexington Books in Lexington, Mass.

Settling the Facts — Discretion and Negotiation in Criminal Court: Pamela J. Utz develops the case for negotiation; published by Lexington Books of Lexington, Mass. in 1978

Shooter's Bible: standard firearms reference published yearly by Stoeger in South Hackensack, N.J.; fully illustrated

Short Eyes: play about prison life written by Miguel Pinero while in Sing Sing for armed robbery

Sisters in Crime: Freda Adler's illuminating book about the rise of the new female criminal; published in 1975 by McGraw-Hill

Slavery and the Penal System: J. Torsten Sellin, author of many books on crime and delinquency, is the author of this work published by Elsevier in 1976

Smuggling Business: Timothy Green's book in the *Undercover* series titled The Library of Espionage and Secret Warfare; published in 1976 by the Crescent Books Division of Crown Publishers

Sourcebook of Criminal Statistics: published by the Law Enforcement Assistance Administration of the U.S. Department of Justice in Washington, D.C.

Spectator: prisoner's publication of the Michigan State Prison at Jackson

Spies and Spymasters: a concise history of intelligence by Jock Haswell; published by Thames and Hudson in 1977

Spring 3100: official magazine of the New York City Police Department

The Stretch: prisoner's periodical published at Lansing, Kan.

Study in Neglect: a report on women prisoners published by the Women's Prison Association in New York

Suicide—A Selected Bibliography of Over 2200 Items: compiled by Ann E. Prentice and published by Scarecrow in 1974

Techniques of Crime Scene Investigation: Arne Svensson is the author of this handbook, published by Elsevier in 1965

Televison Violence and the Adolescent Boy: William Belson of North East London Polytechnic describes techniques he developed to measure the effects of exposure to various forms of violence upon the behavior of adolescent males; published in 1979 by Lexington Books in Lexington, Mass.

Terrorism—From Robespierre to Arafat: Albert Parry's historical study, published in 1976 by Vanguard Press

Terrorism and Criminal Justice: an international perspective by Ronald D. Crelinsten, Danielle Laberge-Altmejd and Denis Szabo; published in 1978 by Lexington Books of Lexington, Mass.

Terrorism Reader: from Aristotle to the IRA and the PLO; historical anthology edited by Walter Laqueur and published by New American Library in New York, London and Scarborough, Ontario in 1978

The Terrorists: by James Davis, San Diego's National University professor of criminology

Theft of the City—Readings on Corruption in Urban America: edited by John A. Gardiner and David J. Olson; published in 1974 by Indiana University Press

Theft of the Nation—The Structure and Operations of Organized Crime in America: by Donald R. Cressey; published in 1969 by Harper & Row

Thoery of Criminal Justice: criminal jurisprudence in a democratic society is examined by Hyman Gross in this book, published in 1979 by the Oxford University Press in New York

Thief's Journal: autobiography of Jean Genet, who spent years among beggars, homosexuals, prostitutes and thieves in the jails and on the streets of Belgium, Czechoslovakia, France, Poland, Spain and Yugoslavia; published by Grove in 1964

Thinking About Crime: James Q. Wilson's argument against leniency; American Spectator, Bloomington, Ind. in 1979

Twenty Thousand Years in Sing Sing: Lewis Edward Lawes' book about the life and problems of a warden

The Ultimate Weapon—Terrorists and World Order: Jan Schreiber's book, published in 1978 by Morrow in New York, covers almost all lands from Albania to Zambia

Undercover: E. Howard Hunt's memoirs of an American secret agent discloses clandestine CIA operations such as the ill-fated Bay of Pigs invasion as well as his own role in the Watergate break-in, which resulted in the resignation of Pres. Nixon

Urban Terrorism: Anthony Burton's book about the theory, practice and response to terrorism; published by the Free Press Division of Macmillan in New York in 1975

Valachi Papers: title of a book by Peter Maas, who wrote the first inside story of Mafia life; a 1968 Bantam book

Victim Compensation: Roger E. Melners examines its economic, legal and political aspects in this useful work, published in 1978 by Lexington Books in Lexington, Mass.

Victimology: quarterly international journal edited by Emilio Viano and published in Washington, D.C.

Victims: J. L. Barkas' book presenting the case for the victims of crime; published in 1978 by Scribner's in New York City

Vidocq Dossier: biographical account of France's ex-convict-turned-detective, the organizer of the *Brigade de la Surete*; by Samuel Edwards, whose real name is Noel Bertram Gerson; published in 1977 by Houghton Mifflin in Boston

The View from Behind the Gun: an hour-long television documentary concerning young criminals and their victims, who are often very helpless or very old; produced in 1978 by ABC as a news closeup, followed by another hour of discussion by legislators and sociologists

Vigilante!: title of splendid in-depth study William E. Burrows made of American vigilantism; published in 1976 by Harcourt Brace Jovanovich

Violent Crime—Environment, Interaction, and Death: an informative book by Richard Block of the University of Chicago Law School; published in 1977 by Lexington Books in Lexington, Mass.

The Violent Few: a study of dangerous juvenile offenders arrested at least once for crimes of violence by Donna Hamparian, Richard Schuster, Simon Dinitz and John P. Conrad; published in 1978 by Lexington Books in Lexington, Mass.

Voiceprinting: Eugene B. Block's treatise, published in McKay in 1975

Wall Shadows: Frank Tannenbaum's book about prison management and psychology

Waterfront: Bud Schulberg's novel, exposing the criminal terrorists controlling the Port of New York waterfront in the 1950s; published by Random House in 1955, it is also known as a film classic entitled *On the Waterfront*

What Is A Terrorist—A Psychological Perspective: informative article written by Dr. H. H. A. Cooper in vol. 1, no. 1 of the *Legal-Medical Quarterly*, published in 1977

What Textbooks Say about Criminality: in-depth article by Ernest van den Haag in the Autumn 1980 issue of *The University Bookman*, edited by Russell Kirk

White-Collar Crime—A 20th Century Crisis: August Bequai defines white-collar crime as well as dealing with its investigation and prosecution; published in 1978 by Lexington Books in Lexington, Mass.

White-Collar Crime—Everyone's Problem, Everyone's Loss: 100-page booklet issued by the Chamber of Commerce of the United States in 1974; describes illegal schemes and tells how to spot them

Who Rules the Joint?: Gabrielle Tyranauer and Charles Stastny's study of the ever changing political culture of America's maximum-security prisons' published in 1979 by Lexington Books in Lexington, Mass.

Wife Beating—The Silent Crisis: Roger Langley and Richard C. Levy's study of the problem; Dutton published the book in New York in 1977

Women, Crime, and the Criminal Justice System: by Lee H. Bowker, with contributions by Meda Chesney Lind and Joy Pollock; a book covering the frequency of crime, the types of crime, comparative international crime rates and the victimization of females by criminals; published in 1978 by Lexington Books in Lexington, Mass.

Women in Law Enforcement: brochure issued by the International Association of Women Police

Women of the Streets: C.H. Rolph's sociological study, undertaken for the British Social Biology Council in 1955

World Without Prisons: a book by Calvert R. Dodge detailing alternatives to incarceration in Canada, the United States and Western Europe; published in 1979 by Lexington Books in Lexington, Mass.

Writing Police Reports: 100-page paperback by Alec Ross and David Plant; published in 1977 by Motorola Teleprograms of Schiller Park, Ill.

"... the imagination of man's heart is evil from his youth."
Genesis 8:21